# Global warming and energy demand

## Edited by Terry Barker, Paul Ekins and Nick Johnstone

Foreword by Sir John Houghton

Global Environmental Change Programme

London and New York

First published 1995
by Routledge
11 New Fetter Lane, London EC4P 4EE

Simultaneously published in the USA and Canada
by Routledge
29 West 35th Street, New York, NY 10001

© 1995 Terry Barker, Paul Ekins and Nick Johnstone

Typeset in Times by Solidus (Bristol) Limited
Printed and bound in Great Britain by
Biddles Ltd, Guildford and King's Lynn

*British Library Cataloguing in Publication Data*
A catalogue record for this book is available from the British Library

*Library of Congress Cataloging in Publication Data*
A catalogue record for this book has been requested

ISBN 0–415–10980–9
ISBN 0–415–11601–5 (pbk)

# Contents

# Figures

# Tables

# Contributors

| | |
|---|---|
| Jago Atkinson | Formerly a research student in the Department of Economics, University College of Swansea. Currently an economist at the Welsh Development Agency, Cardiff. |
| Terry Barker | Senior Research Officer in the Department of Applied Economics, University of Cambridge and Chairman of Cambridge Econometrics. With Paul Ekins he is directing an ESRC-funded project, 'Greenhouse gas abatement through fiscal policy'. |
| Laurence Boone | Postgraduate student at the Centre for Economic Forecasting, London Business School. |
| Paul Ekins | Research Fellow at Department of Economics, Birkbeck College, University of London, UK. With Terry Barker, he is directing an ESRC-funded project, 'Greenhouse gas abatement through fiscal reform'. |
| Mikael Franzén | Postgraduate student at the University of Gothenburg, Sweden. |
| Michael Grubb | Head, Energy and Environment Programme, The Royal Institute of International Affairs. |
| Stephen Hall | Director of Research at the Centre for Economic Forecasting, London Business School. |
| Derek Hodgson | Senior Economic Adviser in the Economics and Statistics division of the DTI. |
| Alan Ingham | Lecturer in Economics at the University of Southhampton. He has been a visitor at the Catholic University of Louvain and the University of British Columbia, Canada. |
| Tim Jackson | Stockholm Environment Institute. |
| Nick Johnstone | Junior Research Officer at the Department of Applied Economics, University of Cambridge, UK. |
| David Kemball-Cook | Lecturer in Economics, Southwark College, London. |

Neil Manning            Lecturer in Economics, University of Wales at
                        Swansea.
Keith Miller            Economic Adviser in the Economics and Statistics
                        Division of the DTI.
M. Hashem Pesaran       Professor of Economics at the University of
                        Cambridge and University of California at Los
                        Angeles.
Stefan P. Schleicher    Professor of Economics at the University of Graz,
                        Austria.
Clare Smith             Research Fellow at the Centre for Economic
                        Forecasting, London Business School.
Ron Smith               Professor of Applied Economics at Birkbeck College,
                        University of London.
Thomas Sterner          Associate Professor of Environmental Economics at
                        the University of Gothenburg, Sweden.
Lakis Vouyoukas         Head, Economic Analysis Division, International
                        Energy Agency.

# Foreword

*Sir John Houghton*

In June 1992 at Rio de Janeiro in Brazil, about 25,000 people gathered for the world's largest conference ever. Often known as the Earth Summit because of the large number of world leaders and heads of government who attended, and held under United Nations' auspices, it was concerned with environment and development. How can the right balance be struck between our need to develop and to improve human quality of life and the important imperative to preserve the environment? In other words how can the goal of sustainable development be achieved?

One of the main outcomes of the Earth Summit was the Framework Convention on Climate Change. The Convention recognizes that climate is changing as a result of the increase in greenhouse gases arising from the burning of fossil fuels and that action needs to be taken to limit these anthropogenic emissions (in particular those of carbon dioxide). The Objective of the Convention, which is to achieve stabilization of the concentration of greenhouse gases in the atmosphere, puts this action in the context of sustainable development. Action taken must allow 'economic development to proceed in a sustainable manner'.

Since a large proportion of carbon dioxide emissions is associated with the provision of energy in its various forms, a vital input to the proper consideration of the Convention's Objective concerns the economics of the energy industry. How can carbon dioxide emissions from energy production be reduced, how much will these reductions cost and how can that cost be minimized are three of the key questions.

International action in response to the requirements of the Climate Convention demands that the very best particular expertise be brought to bear from the disciplines of technology, economics, risk analysis and human behaviour. In the chapters in this book some of this expertise is brought to bear on particular economic analyses; they form a valuable contribution to the lively debate concerning how the Convention's Objective can be realized.

# Preface

Energy use is central to many economic and environmental problems, particularly global warming. The responsiveness of energy use to changes in prices, taxes and incomes is critical in assessing the feasibility of a massive reduction in greenhouse gas (GG) emissions, deemed necessary by the climatologists to reduce the rise in atmospheric GG concentrations.

This book originated in a two-day workshop 'Estimating long-run energy elasticities' held at Robinson College, Cambridge, 29–30 September 1992. The workshop was organized as part of a two-year project on 'Policy options for sustainable energy use in a general model of the UK economy' in the Department of Applied Economics, University of Cambridge, which was being funded under Phase 1 of the ESRC's Global Environmental Change Programme. This project has been succeeded by another 'Greenhouse gas abatement through fiscal policy' under Phase 3 of the Programme, also involving the editors of this book. The workshop was seen as covering one important intellectual foundation for research into policy options for reducing fossil fuel use: What do we know about responses of the energy markets to increases in prices? Are these responses applicable in projections of the economy in which policies are designed to minimize costs of adjustment?

The book is not the proceedings of the workshop. The original papers have been revised, some extensively, and new chapters have been specially written to address these questions. The book is a contribution to the ESRC's Programme in that it reviews and extends the literature on energy elasticities in relation to the long-term problem of reducing GG emissions.

# Chapter 1

# Introduction

*Terry Barker, Paul Ekins and Nick Johnstone*

## THE OBJECTIVES OF THE BOOK

In the light of the Climate Change Convention agreed upon at the Earth Summit in Rio de Janeiro in 1992, it is inevitable that many governments will be addressing the problem of global warming. Moreover, recent discussions in both the United States and the European Union concerning the introduction of carbon and/or energy taxes indicate that significant changes in fiscal policy are likely to result as a consequence. Given the percentage reductions estimated by the Intergovernmental Panel on Climate Change (IPCC) as being necessary to stabilize carbon dioxide ($CO_2$) concentrations, the rates of such a tax will have to be of considerable magnitude.

The purpose of this book is to explore the estimation of the likely responses of energy demand to measures designed to abate greenhouse gas (GG) emissions, particularly fiscal measures to abate $CO_2$ involving changes in energy taxes and thus prices. More particularly, the book is about the problems of estimating energy *demand* elasticities, the treatment of energy and fuel demand in macroeconomic models, the implications for GG abatement policy and the limitations of the approach: How can energy modelling techniques and results, usually arising from research with a different purpose in mind, be applied to the long-term problem of GG abatement through a carbon or energy tax? How should the published results be interpreted for this purpose? What are their limitations and strengths?

Apart from this introductory chapter, the book is divided into two parts. Part I is concerned with the methods of estimating energy demand elasticities, the resulting estimates, and the modelling of energy–economy interactions by the International Energy Agency (IEA) and the UK Department of Trade and Industry (DTI) for the purpose of informing government policy. Part II links this approach to the problem of abating GG emissions by means of taxation and other government policies: models are developed to assess the response of nine OECD economies and the UK economy to carbon/energy taxes; the limitations of relying on the price mechanism and constant elasticities alone are explored; the literature on the economic costs of global warming is reviewed; and the possibility that the price responses are asymmetric is discussed. The book concludes with an assessment of the elasticities approach and suggests new directions in the treatment of long-term energy demand for the analysis of GG abatement.

This chapter first provides a brief introduction to forecasts of global warming and discusses some of the views of the economic and associated costs. This is preparatory to an explanation of the role of energy markets in contributing to GG emissions from economic activities. The concepts of energy elasticities are introduced and their limitations with respect to analyses of global warming are explored. The chapter also considers wider issues including the treatment of technological change in energy demand modelling, the question of international migration of carbon-intensive activities and, briefly, implications for global energy supply.

## 1.1 THE FORECASTS OF GLOBAL WARMING

The greenhouse effect is a universally accepted phenomenon whereby certain gases in the earth's atmosphere (most importantly water vapour and $CO_2$) are more transparent to the short-wave radiation from the sun than to the long-wave re-radiation from the earth's surface. Thus the atmosphere traps solar radiation in a manner similar to a greenhouse. It has been estimated that without the greenhouse effect the earth's average surface temperature would be $-18\ °C$ rather than $+15\ °C$ (Cline 1992: 15).

Human (anthropogenic) activities, especially economic activities, are adding significantly to the atmosphere's greenhouse gases, most importantly through the emission of $CO_2$ from the burning of fossil fuels and deforestation, but also from emissions of chlorofluorocarbons (CFCs), methane and nitrous oxide as well as the formation of low-level ozone. This has led to scientific speculation about an anthropogenic greenhouse effect which could lead to further warming of the earth's average surface temperature, and which may well have already done so. Indeed, $CO_2$ levels in the atmosphere have risen about 25 per cent since pre-industrial times owing to human activities; and the concentration of methane has more than doubled from pre-industrial levels. The different warming potentials of different gases are commonly converted to '$CO_2$ equivalents', and a benchmark for the assessment of anthropogenic global warming is often taken as the doubling of these $CO_2$ equivalents over pre-industrial levels. On current trends this is expected to be reached by 2025. The 1992 supplementary report of the IPCC (1992) re-affirmed the 1990 estimate that a doubling of $CO_2$ equivalents would lead to a warming of the earth's average surface temperature in the order of 1.5–4.5 $°C$ (with a best guess value of 2.5 $°C$), perhaps after a considerable period due to the thermal lag of the oceans. While this assessment does not command total scientific consensus, it does represent a clear majority view among the world's climate scientists. Yet, as Cline emphasizes, without significant policy changes, the atmospheric concentration of greenhouse gases is likely to rise several times beyond a doubling of $CO_2$ equivalent with a concomitant commitment to global warming. Indeed, it is most unlikely, given the political difficulty of abating $CO_2$ emissions, that this first doubling can now be prevented, so that the earth appears already committed to a likely warming of 2.5 °C. Cline has calculated, using the IPCC climate parameters, that business-as-usual projections of greenhouse emissions to 2275 would result in global warming of 6–18 °C, with a central value of 10 °C (Cline 1992: 57).

Such estimates are not universally accepted, however. Indeed, Solow's (1991) review of the scientific evidence of climate change casts doubt on the reliability of current climate models' prediction of future warming since they are unable to explain the warming that has taken place over the past century. While the average magnitude of such warming is broadly as predicted, the models do not explain its time profile or spatial distribution. Moreover, the warming that has occurred could be explained as a natural recovery from the last pulse of the 'Little Ice Age' in the late eighteenth century. However, notwithstanding these doubts, Solow concludes: 'Based on a balanced reading of the scientific literature, it is virtually certain that global warming will occur in response to ongoing changes in atmospheric composition' (Solow 1991: 25).

## 1.2 ECONOMIC AND ASSOCIATED EFFECTS OF GLOBAL WARMING

The effects of global warming are far more uncertain than the warming itself. On the one hand, as Schelling says: 'We will be moving into a climate regime that has never been experienced in the inter-glacial period' (Schelling 1992: 3). On the other, as Schelling also notes, the absolute temperature differences seem quite small and rather less than migrants in previous ages, and travellers today, have been and are able to adjust to quite comfortably.

However, a relatively modest average warming of the earth's surface is likely to include larger individual variations at local level which have important effects on the environment and humanity. Three economists who have made a detailed study of the consequences of the greenhouse effect have come to the following conclusions. Schelling says: 'Natural ecosystems will be destroyed; plant and animal species will become extinct; places of natural beauty will be degraded. Valuable chemistries of plant and animal life will be lost before we learn their genetic secrets' (Schelling 1992: 7–8). Cline's assessment of the economic impacts, although stated less dramatically, is no less disturbing:

Global warming could cause agricultural losses in many regions. The level of the seas would rise, imposing costs of barrier protection of coastal cities and the loss of land area (including valuable wetlands). There would be increased electricity needs for air conditioning, potentially serious declines in the availability of water to agriculture and cities, increased urban pollution, increased intensity and frequency of hurricanes, increased mortality from heat waves, and losses in leisure activities associated with winter sports.

(Cline 1992: 30–1)

Like Schelling, Broome also accepts that 'the strains on natural ecologies are likely to be very great' (Broome 1992: 13) and, like Cline, identifies substantial costs associated with global warming:

Without increased sea defences low-lying areas will become more susceptible to flooding. The danger will be amplified if storms become more frequent or more severe. . . . Regions threatened by flooding include densely populated areas. Eight to ten million people live within one metre of high tide in each of the unprotected river deltas of Bangladesh, Egypt and Vietnam. A flood in Bangladesh, caused by a tropical storm in 1970, killed 300,000 people. Rising sea levels, then, must be expected to kill very large numbers of people. This is an enormous and easily predictable harm that will be caused by global warming. Moreover, sea levels will continue to rise for centuries. This must cause large migrations of population and it is difficult to see where the people can move to. There seems to be inevitable harm in this too: the forced migration of many million people is inevitably a disaster. Another class of bad effects is also quite easily predictable. As the world warms, more people will become subject to tropical diseases. This, too, will shorten many people's lives.

(Broome 1992: 14)

Moreover, $CO_2$ pollution is not the only negative environmental effect of the use of fossil fuels. On the basis of UK Department of Environment data, Barker (1993: 4) has calculated that, in the UK, 99 per cent of $SO_2$ and $NO_x$, 97 per cent of CO and 91 per cent of particulate matter, as well as substantial contributions to methane (48 per cent) and volatile organic compounds (38 per cent), all come from this source. Barker found that the associated damages from these emissions are substantial.

Solow (1991: 25) points out that the estimates of damage from global warming have been moving away from 'apocalyptic scenarios'. For example, likely sea-level rise over the next hundred years is put at less than one metre now, as opposed to three metres or more predicted a few years ago. Global warming could also have some beneficial effects. An atmosphere richer in $CO_2$ may enhance photosynthesis and raise productivity in agriculture and forestry. More northerly latitudes, becoming warmer, may become more agriculturally productive. Warming may also lead to greater physical comfort in such latitudes. Warmer climates in some places may benefit industries as diverse as tourism and construction.

The analyses of Broome and Schelling, and of other major contributors in this field such as Nordhaus (1991a), focus exclusively on global warming and its likely effects over the course of the next century. However, as noted above, it is quite likely that the temperature rise will be much more significant in the ensuing years. This much larger temperature change would amplify global warming's negative effects and reduce its benefits. Cline warns:

> It is important to recognize from the outset, however, that as a general rule one would expect the economic size of damage from global warming to rise more than linearly with the magnitude of warming. The costs of 10 °C warming in the very long term could thus be far more than four times the costs of the 2.5 °C benchmark warming for a doubling of carbon dioxide equivalent.
>
> (Cline 1992: 72)

Of course, the further one projects into the future, the less reliable are the estimates generated, not least because of the likely technological changes in the meantime. Beckerman (1991: 63) considers that 'nobody can suppose that the world of the late twenty-first century will bear much resemblance to the world that we know today' and is generally optimistic that new technologies for energy supply, energy efficiency and agriculture will have rendered largely irrelevant current concerns over these issues. However, this does not appear to change the fact that, unless these new technologies act over the next century to curtail greatly the expanded use of fossil fuels that is expected, global warming will eventually be substantially greater than that associated with the doubling of $CO_2$ equivalents in the atmosphere. Furthermore, with ample world supplies of coal, it is difficult to see what incentive there will be for the development of new carbon-free supplies and energy-efficient technologies without substantial real increases in carbon/energy taxes above present levels (or the development of a global coal cartel capable of raising prices substantially and willing to do so).

This greater warming would increase the possibility of some catastrophic climate reaction to higher average temperatures. Even with the relatively low temperature increase foreseen within the hundred-year time-frame, Broome observed: 'Human-induced global warming, then, could possibly start a chain of events that could lead to the extinction of civilization or even of humanity. This is a remote possibility, but it exists' (Broome 1992: 16).

## 1.3 GREENHOUSE GAS EMISSIONS AND THE ECONOMY

Economic behaviour and the availability of fossil fuels have led to greatly increased GG emissions from human activity and the unrestrained future increase in emissions is a risk to life on earth; *but the GG emissions are not wanted for their own sake.* The conflict between environmental quality (represented by lower GG emissions in the future) and economic welfare (represented by higher economic activity and improved quality of life) is not a direct one. Indeed some greenhouse gases are poisonous (carbon monoxide), others are repugnant (methane), and GG emissions in general are associated with other by-products of combustion, such as sulphur dioxide, soot and oxides of nitrogen, which also damage health and welfare as well as the environment more generally.

However, there are economic goods which *are* wanted – such as physical comfort from warm (or cool) buildings, transport services, and all other consumer goods which generate GG emissions in production – yet which are also, at least at present, inextricably bound up with the emission of greenhouse gases. The close relationship between such economic services and emissions of greenhouse gases is due in large part to the fact that the atmosphere has been traditionally treated as common property, with no charge for its use for dumping wastes, so the emissions are only subject at most to local restrictions concerned with local air quality. Although these economic services could be provided at very low levels of emissions, or indeed in some cases with no emissions whatsoever, the alternative processes of production are perceived as being too expensive or inconvenient, or they carry with them other social or environmental costs.

From an economic policy perspective, the problem of global warming possesses a number of characteristics which affect the means by which it can be regulated. On the one hand, since there is no economic technology to absorb the primary greenhouse gas, $CO_2$, any abatement policy must focus on source reductions and not clean-up technologies. Moreover, since each of the individual fuels possess distinct, but unique, carbon contents, $CO_2$ emissions are a function of the type of fuel used. In addition, since global warming is a global common property issue the location of emission sources is irrelevant to the determination of environmental damages. For these reasons, differential taxation of fuel types will effectively tax carbon inputs, $CO_2$ emission outputs and environmental damages. (This is in contrast with the abatement of acid rain. Since different grades of coal possess widely varying sulphur content, since 'end-of-pipe' abatement technology such as flue-gas desulphurization exists, and since there is spatial differentiation in environmental effects, the relationship between fuel and environmental damage is not unique.)

Moreover, since the different primary energy carriers (coal, oil, gas) have clearly defined markets and sources of supply it is a relatively straightforward matter to apply such tax rates. And finally, given that the fuels are already taxed or subsidized extensively, the administrative and institutional costs of further taxation are relatively small (compare the administrative costs of the introduction of the EU's carbon/energy tax with those of VAT for example). For these reasons, in addition to the fact that emissions of most non-$CO_2$ greenhouse gases are closely associated with the burning of fossil fuels (the exceptions being CFCs and methane from gas leaks, animals and waste tips), most of the literature, including this book, is concerned with $CO_2$ abatement in particular rather than with GG abatement in general and with abatement via a carbon tax which is expected to change energy and fuel prices and, via price elasticities, energy demand and $CO_2$ emissions (see Poterba 1991; Pearce 1992; Barker 1993).

These characteristics illustrate the importance of fully specifying the relationship between the environmental consequences of pollution and the economic processes which generate polluting agents. In terms of $CO_2$ emissions, the relationships can be represented as in Figure 1.1. The arrows indicate the direction of flows of energy, emissions, goods or services and the ovals represent energy conversion.

Working backwards from the fundamental source of demand for energy, economic goods and services, the relationship between the economy, energy and the environment can be traced. At the first stage (top left-hand corner of Figure 1.1), a variety of economic processes (e.g. manufacturing, household heating and transportation) employ energy services (e.g. motive power and heat). The provision of such services is realized through the employment of both energy carriers and capital goods. Flows of energy carriers can be subdivided into fuels (e.g. oil products, gas, coal and coal products) and electricity. Energy-related capital can also be subdivided into generating

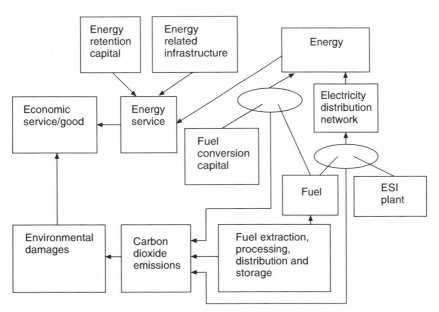

*Figure 1.1* Economy–energy–environment interactions, carbon dioxide emissions and global warming

equipment involved in fuel combustion (e.g. electricity generating plants, domestic and industrial boilers and vehicle engines), capital equipment related to energy retention (e.g. building insulation, waste energy recovery systems, and flywheels used in transport systems) and public-energy-related infrastructure (e.g. road networks, railway systems and combined heat and power systems). The first affects the flows of energy directly through combustion while the last two affect the volume of flows required to meet given energy service demands. Carbon is embodied within some fuels (fossil fuels) and is released as $CO_2$ emissions upon combustion in the electricity supply industry and in other sectors as well as in the extraction, processing and distribution processes. The $CO_2$ emissions then impact upon the environment, and thus the economy, in the manner outlined above.

## 1.4  CARBON DIOXIDE EMISSIONS AND ENERGY ELASTICITIES

The fact that there appear to be no economic prospects for end-of-pipe technology for the abatement of $CO_2$ emissions and that there is no spatial differentiation of the effects of such emissions simplifies the problem of designing an optimal environmental policy considerably since a tax on carbon as an input into economic processes will achieve the desired environmental objective. Unlike other pollutants, there is no need to adjust tax rates to reflect the characteristics and location of production processes.

Given these characteristics, the demand elasticities of the fuels which possess carbon should, in some sense, reflect the difficulty involved in achieving the desired environmental objective. However, at the same time that the environmental relations discussed above facilitate the design of an appropriate policy, the economic relations described above indicate that the estimation of such elasticities is rather problematic, and as such the interpretation of such elasticities and their application to economic models must be treated with caution. First, carbon, and indeed primary fuels, are not goods in their own right, but are instead demands derived from the demand for energy services used as inputs in economic processes. Second, both primary fuels and energy-related capital equipment are joint inputs used in the provision of such energy services. On the one hand this implies that estimates of energy elasticities are only useful to the analysis of global warming in so far as energy reflects embodied carbon. In this sense, models which incorporate the possibility of substitution between fuels with different carbon contents are of considerably more interest than those which treat energy as an aggregate. In this volume the chapters by Barker, by Hodgson and Miller and by Manning and Atkinson are of particular relevance to this question. On the other hand, it is important to distinguish between demand for the fuel which is used in the provision of energy services and the energy services themselves. The elasticities estimated are therefore a reflection not of the demand for fuel *per se* but of demand for fuel in the provision of different energy services. The latter point is closely related to the nature of energy and capital as joint producers of energy services. Reduced fuel consumption may reflect a change in the means by which the service is obtained and not reduced provision of the service. These points are made emphatically by Jackson and Schleicher in Chapters 10 and 11.

This is of some concern for short-term price and income elasticities but is, of course, of considerably more importance for long-term elasticities. Thus, attempts to address the problem of global warming must address the particular features of the demand for carbon (an input which is embodied in fuels which are themselves derived demands for the energy service) and the supply of the energy service (a joint product of the primary fuel and all energy-related capital equipment). Attempts to apply demand elasticities estimated on the basis of historical evidence of fuel consumption must recognize that demand for fuel is derived from the demand for the energy service and that all the various links in the supply network are contextual, and subject to change.

## 1.5 SHORT-TERM AND LONG-TERM ENERGY ELASTICITIES

Given the long-term nature of the environmental consequences of global warming, as well as policies designed to mitigate such warming, estimates of very-long-term energy elasticities (i.e. periods of more than twenty years) are clearly of more relevance than estimates of short-term energy elasticities. However, most empirical studies of energy demand (including those surveyed and presented in this book) have focused on elasticities estimated on data usually covering twenty- to thirty-year periods, since the objectives of the research have not usually extended to issues involving time-frames such as those required for the analysis of global warming and the data for longer periods are either unavailable or unreliable.

There are, moreover, methodological problems associated with the estimation of long-term energy elasticities. For instance, in order to estimate long-term elasticities using time-series data it is necessary to introduce sufficiently long lags to allow the economy to adjust fully to price changes. This implies that all of the energy-related capital stock (e.g. generating plants, domestic and industrial boilers, vehicles and infrastructure) has adjusted to the change in relative prices. A variety of functional forms have been posited to capture these effects, including lagged endogenous models, inverted-V lag models and polynomial distributed lag models. However, given the nature of both the demand for fuels (derived from the demand for energy services as an input in economic processes) and the supply of energy services (a joint product of fuel, capital equipment and public infrastructure) it is exceedingly difficult to estimate elasticities of sufficiently long length on the basis of such models. Thus, not surprisingly, there is wide discrepancy in both the absolute magnitude and the statistical significance of elasticities estimated using different functional forms. In their account of the modelling of UK energy demand Hodgson and Miller discuss some of the difficulties.

In this light, it believed by some (Griffin 1981b) that elasticities estimated on the basis of time-series data are inherently incapable of capturing the long-term effects of price changes due to the length and variability of the adjustment lags involved. As a consequence, in the literature it is commonly asserted that cross-section studies are better able to capture the long-term effects of price changes, since data collected from different countries reflect long-term structural characteristics (Griffin and Gregory 1976). For instance, cross-section studies would capture the structural consequences of persistently low historical energy prices in North American and East European economies relative to some West European and East Asian economies.

A number of chapters address these issues explicitly. In the survey conducted by Manning and Atkinson, results are cited from a wide variety of time-series, cross-section and pooled time-series cross-section studies. For the most part, the price elasticities derived from time-series studies tend to be significantly lower than those of other studies. Conversely, in his chapter Sterner finds that the long-term price elasticities of gasoline demand derived from lagged endogenous models range from +0.1 to −2.3, while the estimates from cross-section data yield elasticities which range from −0.8 to −1.3. Pesaran and Smith attribute some of the discrepancies in results between time-series and cross-section studies to methodological problems biasing the estimates. Using heterogeneous panel data for East Asian economies they suggest that time-series estimates should be estimated for individual groups (countries) and then averaged and these estimates should then be compared with cross-section estimates based on long-term averages.

## 1.6 STRUCTURAL BREAKS IN THE DEMAND FOR ENERGY

Closely related to the question of distinguishing between short-term and long-term elasticities is that of recognizing structural breaks in the demand for energy. Thus, it is felt that there might be instances in which the demand for energy undergoes a fundamental structural change and that this would be reflected not only in changed energy consumption patterns but also in changed elasticities. In particular the oil shocks of 1973 and 1979 are frequently cited as instances where the demand for energy changed qualitatively and not just quantitatively. This is believed to be of particular relevance to the problem of global warming since the price increases experienced were of a similar magnitude to those which would be required to stabilize energy consumption. In addition, the elasticities used in models to assess the effects of abatement policies are estimated from data in which changes in energy and fuel prices are dominated by the effects of the two oil price shocks of 1973 and 1979 and the oil price collapse of 1985.

It should be emphasized, however, that the responses to the large fluctuations in energy and fuel prices in the 1970s and 1980s may be different in a number of specific respects to those following the introduction of a carbon or energy tax to curb $CO_2$ emissions.[1]

1   *Motivation*   The global oil price changes were induced by factors which are perceived to be unstable (e.g. oil cartels); in contrast the motivation to curb emissions is more stable (e.g. government policy). In one instance the price increase may be perceived to be temporary, while in the other it may be perceived as being rather more permanent since taxes are rarely withdrawn once introduced, particularly if the motivation for the tax (GG abatement) represents a long-term objective. In addition, the oil shocks were precisely that – sudden, largely unanticipated, exogenous shocks.

2   *Speed of adjustment*   A second difference between circumstances of the oil price shocks and those of an increase in energy price due to abatement policy is in the speed at which the price will rise and consequently the time period for energy users to adjust. The 300 per cent rise in crude oil prices over the course of *six months* in 1973–4 should be contrasted with a 10 per cent a year increase in carbon contents of energy carriers over the course of *twenty years*. The long period of adjustment greatly reduces costs of adjustment (see Chapter 5) since it allows capital stock to be replaced as it comes to the end of its useful like, rather than being scrapped when energy prices rise.

3   *Expectations*   The transformation of fiscal policy so as to address the problem of global warming would be introduced gradually and with significant forewarning. Thus, economic actors will be able to anticipate, and indeed are at present anticipating, the introduction of such measures. In this light, the credibility of government policy, the amount of warning given by the government, and the means by which price expectations are reflected in anticipatory behaviour by the private sector, may be of more significance than the absolute magnitude of the price increase.

4   *Revenue recycling*   The basis for the price increases in the two cases has even more fundamental repercussions when the recipients of the revenues generated are distinguished. In one case (the oil shock) the revenue accrued to the oil-producing countries, while in the other (carbon/energy tax) the governments of the energy-consuming countries would receive the revenue. In the latter case, therefore, the recessionary effects of the price increase could be mitigated, or indeed reversed, by removing other more distortionary taxes. Alternatively, the revenue could be retained, reducing the public-sector borrowing requirement and possibly increasing long-term growth prospects.

5   *Macroeconomic effects*   The oil price shocks were associated with increases in inflation in the consuming countries, which in turn triggered tighter monetary policies and higher interest rates. If the revenues from carbon/energy taxes accrue to the domestic governments, then either they can reduce other indirect taxes and hold down inflation directly, or they

can save the revenues and reduce government borrowing. Either way, there would not be an association of higher energy prices with higher interest rates. The estimation of aggregate production functions from data in which increases in the price of energy take place at the same time as increases in the price of capital means that it is difficult to disentangle the two effects, with the risk that energy is treated (wrongly) as complementary to capital equipment rather than as a substitute for it.

## 1.7  TECHNOLOGY AND CHANGES IN ENERGY USE

The distinction between long-term elasticity estimates derived from time-series data and those derived from cross-section and pooled data raises the important question of the treatment of technological change in the characteristics of energy-using capital equipment. In effect, to a great extent difficulties associated with the estimation of long-term energy elasticities arise from difficulties associated with the treatment of changes in the characteristics of the capital stock. This problem is addressed by both Jackson and Schleicher who distinguish between bottom-up engineering-based models which attach considerable importance to the nature of capital and top-down macroeconomic models which treat capital as a homogeneous input (see also Wilson and Swisher 1993). Given the joint-product nature of demand for primary fuels and energy-related capital equipment in the provision of energy services it is asserted that it is vitally important to give an empirical content to capital. Thus, the potential for the employment of more energy-efficient production processes (energy conservation) will depend upon the prospects for technological innovation and market penetration of energy-related capital equipment. Similarly, given the limited potential for interfuel substitutability for specific pieces of capital equipment, the potential for the employment of less carbon-intensive production processes (fuel substitution) will also depend upon the prospects for changes in the characteristics of the capital equipment employed.

The most common means of attempting to incorporate the effects of changing technological characteristics of energy-related capital equipment in economic modelling is through the use of a simple time trend, which is estimated on the basis of historical evidence and then introduced as an exogenous variable over the course of the forecast. Indeed in many of the aggregate production function models which dominate the literature on the economics of global warming a simple trend increase in energy efficiency is applied over the course of forecasts as long as a hundred years. Given the discussion above this is rather unsatisfactory.

Conversely, in the chapter by Boone *et al.* the problem of technological innovation in energy-using capital equipment is addressed by means of the inclusion of an endogenous trend variable. Thus, technological innovation is determined within the model by a set of explanatory variables such as investment levels, non-fossil-fuel expansion and structural changes in the energy markets. In his chapter Ingham uses quite a different model. Based on capital vintages his analysis distinguishes between short-run responses to price changes, wherein only variable factors of production (labour, materials, energy) and output levels can adjust, and long-run responses wherein fixed factors (capital) can also adjust. However, the degree of variable factor adjustment which can take place is determined at the point of initial investment in fixed factors. Thus, expectations about future price changes become vital to the degree of flexibility incorporated into existing capital. This has profound implications for the path of technological change in the face of anticipated increases in the price of energy. Barker uses bottom-up methodology to give an empirical content to electricity-generating capital. He incorporates a full engineering-based submodel of the electricity supply industry into the macroeconomic model and using plant profiles (capacities, fuels employed, energy efficiency and working lives) he is able to make informed judgements about future fuel inputs into the electricity sector on the basis of technical requirements. And finally, in their chapter, Hodgson and Miller recognize the necessity of conducting similar analyses for industrial boilers in the manufacturing sector and are extending the existing DTI model along these lines.

## 1.8 ENERGY ELASTICITIES AND MARKET SATURATION

Much as country-specific structural characteristics should be recognized in the estimation of energy elasticities, temporal characteristics related to a given economy's position on the development curve must be recognized as well. For instance, energy use in many of the most energy-intensive sectors may eventually be constrained by market saturation, with respect either to energy-related capital goods or to the energy service itself. Thus, caution must be exercised when applying elasticities estimated on the basis of the existing economic structure to make forecasts stretching into the distant future when the economy may have matured considerably.

For instance, price elasticities may be very different when the market for various pieces of energy-using capital equipment in the domestic sector (e.g. ownership of central heating, electric appliances or vehicles) is saturated. Thus, the response of a household to a change in fuel prices would be reflected, even in the long term, more in adjustments of the variable input (the fuel) and less in changes in the fixed input (the boiler or vehicle) which would be determined by replacement demand. Similarly income elasticities may be very different once the saturation point is reached. Thus, in terms of demand for energy services themselves, increases in real income may have little effect on fuel use in domestic heating once a satisfactory level of physical comfort has been realized. Analogously, with respect to demand for energy-using capital, changes in real income may have little effect on car ownership, and thus to some extent fuel use, once the market is completely saturated. Indeed, once saturation is complete, energy elasticities in many sectors will probably be asymmetric with little potential for increased consumption but significant potential for downward adjustment, indicating relatively higher downward income elasticity and upward price elasticity. These questions are discussed explicitly in Hodgson and Miller, but are of considerable relevance to the chapters by Sterner and Franzén as well as Grubb.

It should be recognized, moreover, that in a number of important sectors the saturation rate is not a fixed parameter but is instead contextual. For example, households with a saturated demand for domestic heat may find that their demand becomes relatively more price inelastic because warmth becomes accepted as a necessity. Another example is in the transport sector where a number of models indicate that it is average commuting times and not ownership rates *per se* which represent the fundamental determinant of saturation rates for travel to work, although these averages and the distances travelled have been getting longer. This underlines the importance of distinguishing between the energy service (mobility) and the means by which it is realized (fuel and capital). It would also indicate that public investment in transport infrastructure can be better understood as a significant determinant of transport mode splits (road, rail, air, water) and not purely as a reaction to consumer demand for different modes. Given the different energy intensities of different modes this would indicate that long-term transport-related energy elasticities dcpend, implicitly or explicitly, upon government policy.

## 1.9 SECTORAL COMPOSITION, COMPETITIVE DISPLACEMENT AND GLOBAL WARMING

National attempts to address the problem of global warming have significant international repercussions, in both economic and environmental terms. As such it is vitally important to determine the sources of consequent reductions in energy consumption in the economy. Decomposing changes in energy use into those associated with changes in the level of output (activity effects), those associated with a changing sectoral composition of output (sectoral effects) and those associated with increased energy efficiency (intensity effects), it is possible to distinguish between the sources of changes in energy consumption (Schipper and Meyers 1992). Thus, it is quite possible to have decreased energy consumption in a growing economy with no increase in energy efficiency. This would arise if there was a fundamental transformation away from more energy-intensive sectors as the economy matured (Solow 1987). The input–output analysis of Proops *et al.* (1993) indicates that this has been the case for the UK between 1971 and 1982.

The environmental and economic significance of such a development path depends upon the tradeability of the affected sectors. Thus, it is important to distinguish between changing sectoral composition of output which reflects a demand response and that which reflects a supply response. Given the pure common property nature of the environmental consequences of $CO_2$ emissions such a distinction is of considerable significance. For instance, policies which reduce domestic energy consumption in the non-tradeable transport sector would certainly have benign environmental consequences; policies which result in decreased domestic energy consumption in highly tradeable manufactures may conceivably have malign environmental consequences, depending on international trade flows and production technology elsewhere.

This emphasizes not only the importance of international policy co-ordination, but also the importance of the careful interpretation of the true causes which lie behind changed energy consumption in national economies. For this reason, the causes behind changes in energy consumption in the fastest-growing economies may be of particular significance. In this light, the chapter by Pesaran and Smith on energy elasticities in East Asian economies and many of the results cited in the survey by Manning and Atkinson are of considerable interest.

## 1.10  MODELLING THE ECONOMIC EFFECTS OF $CO_2$ ABATEMENT POLICIES

All the chapters in the book are concerned ultimately with the modelling of $CO_2$ abatement policies. Chapters 2–4 are concerned with estimating long-term price and income elasticities of the demand for energy and substitution elasticities for the demand for different fuels to meet the energy demand. Chapter 5 is a detailed treatment of the response of UK manufacturing to particular energy price shocks showing how the changes in boiler stock may affect the response. Chapters 6 and 7 show how the elasticity approach is incorporated into national and international models designed to assess policy responses as well as to develop energy scenarios. Chapters 8 and 9 discuss the specification and construction of models incorporating energy demand equations which provide estimates of energy price elasticities for nine OECD countries and for the UK. The models are designed to assess GG abatement policy and Chapter 9 in particular looks at the effects of different estimated price elasticities in relation to the EU's proposed carbon/energy tax. Chapters 10 and 11 go beyond the price elasticities to consider technological aspects and the potential for energy saving. Chapter 12 reviews the published estimates of the costs of GG abatement, suggesting why in many cases these may have been overestimated. Chapter 13 is a pointer to the way modellers are dealing with the effects of technological change in economic models; it expounds the idea that price responses might be asymmetrical as a result of induced technical change. This direction of research is taken up in the conclusions in Chapter 14: modelling of long-term GG abatement is seen as requiring both an economic and an engineering component if the full range of policy options is to be addressed. Models should then be in a better position to explore policies which could yield net economic benefits if there is a move towards a low-carbon economy.

## NOTE

1    The Council of Economic Advisors' *Report to the President* in 1990 was influential in promoting the idea that the costs of abatement were unimaginably large. The *Report* quoted estimates of costs to the US economy of $3.6 trillion and suggested that US growth could be cut in half. However, the *Report* used US experience following the oil shocks as an illustration of the effects of abatement policies and relied on studies of the effects, e.g. Jorgenson and Hogan (1990), which also depended heavily on data dominated by the 1973 and 1979 oil price shocks. Moreover, the $3.6 trillion estimate does not seem quite so large if reinterpreted as a reduction in the US growth rate 1990–2010 from 2.52 per cent per annum to 2.46 per cent (Barker 1991).

# Part I

# Estimating long-term energy elasticities

# Chapter 2

# Alternative approaches to estimating long-run energy demand elasticities

## An application to Asian developing countries

*M. Hashem Pesaran and Ron Smith*

**ABSTRACT**

Long-run energy elasticities have been estimated using time series for individual countries, cross-sections over countries and pooled data for panels of countries. This chapter reviews what is known about the properties of these estimators, emphasizing the potentially misleading results that can be obtained by pooled estimators in dynamic heterogeneous panels. The issues are illustrated by an application to aggregate energy demand in ten Asian countries over the period 1973–90. Although these results can only be tentative because of the problems caused by aggregation they illustrate the methodological problems raised by the theoretical discussion.[1]

## INTRODUCTION

Long-run energy elasticities have been estimated from dynamic time-series models for individual countries, from cross-section models across countries and from pooled models on panels of data: time series for a number of countries or regions, such as US states. The estimates obtained from the various methods have tended to differ substantially. Bohi (1981) reviews and highlights the differences in the estimates of the energy demand elasticities in the early literature. A more recent review can be found in Hawdon (1992). The purpose of this paper is to review the properties of the various estimators, cross-section, time-series, pooled, used to estimate elasticities and illustrate the issues with an application to energy demand in ten Asian developing countries.

The differences between the estimates produced by the various procedures is not a new problem, and it is often argued that cross-sections provide better estimates of long-run effects than time series do. For instance, Baltagi and Griffin (1984) argue that time-series estimates of energy demand elasticities are misspecified by omitting the long distributed lags typical of energy demand, e.g. because of the time it takes consumers to adjust their capital stock – to replace cars or heating appliances etc. Thus time series will underestimate the total effect of the price change, as it works slowly through the system. They show through Monte Carlo simulations that for equations typical of estimated energy demand, where long distributed lags on price are important, the time-series estimates are biased downwards but cross-section estimates produce more sensible long-run estimates. They also give references to the large literature trying to interpret the relationship between cross-section and time-series estimates.

The issue is important, because it is now quite common to have panels in which both $N$ (the number of groups) and $T$ (the number of time periods) are quite large. With such panels it is possible to compare the properties of the various procedures employed to estimate long-run effects and that is the objective of this chapter. Quah (1990) calls such panels *fields*, to distinguish them from the small $T$ panels typical of microeconometrics. A comprehensive survey of the literature on panel data is provided by Hsiao (1986) and Matyas and Sevestre (1992).

In this chapter we consider panels in which both $N$ and $T$ are large, although some of our results have implications for small $T$ panels. We assume that the panels are heterogeneous, in the sense that parameters vary randomly across groups, and are dynamic, in the sense that each equation includes a lagged dependent variable. There are four procedures that can be applied to such panels. The data are averaged over groups and aggregate time series are estimated; they are averaged over time and cross-sections are estimated on group means; they are combined imposing common slopes but allowing for fixed or random intercepts and pooled regressions are estimated; or separate regressions are estimated for each group and the coefficients are averaged over groups. This last procedure we shall refer to as the 'mean group estimator'.

In the static case, where the regressors are strictly exogenous and the coefficients differ randomly and independently of the regressors across groups, all four procedures provide consistent (and unbiased) estimates of the coefficient means. It often seems to be assumed that a similar result holds for dynamic models, i.e. all four procedures give consistent estimators. This is not the case; in particular aggregating and pooling can produce highly misleading estimates of long-run effects in heterogeneous dynamic panels. The panel literature tends to assume homogeneity of slope coefficients, but this seems implausible for many energy applications; thus our results are of some practical importance. Griliches and Mairesse (1990) discuss heterogeneity in production function estimates.

The chapter is in two parts: first, Sections 2.1–2.5 review the theoretical issues; and second, Section 2.6 contains the empirical application. Sections 2.2–2.4 summarize the detailed technical results in Pesaran and Smith (1995), and assume that the underlying relations are correctly specified. Section 2.5 discusses the consequences of certain types of misspecification in the context of estimating short- and long-run energy demand elasticities. In the second part, Section 2.6, the theoretical issues are illustrated by an application to aggregate energy demand equations estimated for ten Asian developing economies over the period 1973–90. Given the limited econometric evidence available on energy demand in developing countries, the time-series data and the empirical results discussed in Section 2.6 may be of general interest to energy economists, although the highly aggregative nature of the analysis means that the elasticity estimates should be treated as preliminary and with due caution.

## 2.1 STATIC MODELS OF HETEROGENEOUS PANELS: A BRIEF REVIEW

Initially, we assume static relationships with coefficients that are constant over time but differ randomly across groups, and that the distribution of the coefficients is independent of the regressors. Suppose the parameters of interest are the averages over groups of the coefficients. More specifically, suppose $x_{it}$ and $\beta_i$ are $k \times 1$ vectors with

$$y_{it} = \beta_i' x_{it} + \varepsilon_{it} \qquad \begin{aligned} i &= 1, 2, \ldots, N \\ t &= 1, 2, \ldots, T \end{aligned} \qquad (2.1)$$

where the $\varepsilon_{it}$ are serially uncorrelated with zero means and constant variances. We assume that the coefficients vary according to

$$\beta_i = \beta + \eta_i \qquad (2.2)$$

where $\beta$ is fixed and the $\eta_i$ have zero means and a given covariance matrix. We also assume that $\{x_{it}\}$, $\{\varepsilon_{it}\}$ and $\{\eta_i\}$ are independently distributed. There are four procedures that could be applied to such data fields.

### 2.1.1 Cross-section estimators

The data could be averaged over time periods and a cross-section regression run on these 'time averages' defined by

$$\tilde{y}_i = \sum_{t=1}^{T} \frac{y_{it}}{T} \quad \text{and} \quad \tilde{x}_i = \sum_{t=1}^{T} \frac{x_{it}}{T}$$

The cross-section regression is given by

$$\tilde{y}_i = \beta' \tilde{x}_i + \tilde{\upsilon}_i$$

which yields the estimates

$$\hat{\beta}^c = \left( \sum_{i=1}^{N} \tilde{x}_i \tilde{x}_i' \right)^{-1} \left( \sum_{i=1}^{N} \tilde{x}_i \tilde{y}_i \right)$$

This is known as the 'between' estimator in the panel literature.

### 2.1.2  Aggregate time-series estimators

The data could be averaged over groups and an aggregate time-series regression run on the group means (aggregates for each period). This is the dominant practice in macroeconomic analysis of long-run relationships. The procedure involves forming group averages for each period

$$\bar{y}_t = \sum_{i=1}^{N} \frac{y_{it}}{N} \quad \text{and} \quad \bar{x}_t = \sum_{i=1}^{N} \frac{x_{it}}{N}$$

and running the aggregate time-series regression

$$\bar{y}_t = \beta' \bar{x}_t + \bar{v}_t \tag{2.3}$$

giving

$$\hat{\beta}^a = \left( \sum_{t=1}^{T} \bar{x}_t \bar{x}_t' \right)^{-1}$$

### 2.1.3  Pooled estimators

The data could be pooled assuming common slope parameters. Different pooled estimators are obtained depending on whether the intercepts are assumed to be the same or different across groups. In the latter case, two estimators are proposed in the literature, depending on whether the intercepts are treated as fixed unknown parameters or random. These are referred to as the 'fixed-effects' and 'random-effects' estimators. In the case of common intercepts (i.e. the simple pooled estimator) the procedure involves running the ordinary least squares (OLS) regression $y_{it} = \beta' x_{it} + v_{it}$ over $i = 1, 2, \ldots,$ $N$ and $t = 1, 2, \ldots, T$. Thus:

$$\hat{\beta}^p = \left( \sum_{i=1}^{N} \sum_{t=1}^{T} x_{it} x_{it}' \right)^{-1} \left( \sum_{i=1}^{N} \sum_{t=1}^{T} x_{it} y_{it} \right)$$

### 2.1.4  Mean group estimators

Finally the data could be used to estimate coefficients for each group separately, which is possible given that $T$ is assumed large, giving

$$\hat{\beta}_i = \left( \sum_{t=1}^{T} x_{it} x'_{it} \right)^{-1} \left( \sum_{t=1}^{T} x_{it} y_{it} \right) \qquad i = 1, 2, \ldots, N$$

The parameters of interest, the average of $\hat{\beta}_i$, can then be calculated explicitly. There are a number of ways such an average can be computed. We refer to these estimators as the 'mean group estimators'. One possibility would be to use a simple average over the coefficient estimates for each group. Alternatively, it may be of interest to use a weighted average of $\hat{\beta}_i$s, such as the generalized least squares estimator suggested by Swamy (1971). In the case of a Swamy-type estimator the weights are inversely related to the standard errors of the estimated coefficients (e.g. Hsiao 1986, 1992).

All four procedures give average estimates of $\beta_i$. The difference is that in the case of the last estimator the averaging is explicit, while in the other cases it is implicit. In applied work, the time-series and cross-section procedures are most commonly used, the pooled estimators less often, and explicit averaging over estimates for each group is rather rare. In the case where the regressors are all strictly exogenous and the parameters are assumed to be random and distributed independently of the regressors, then all four procedures give unbiased estimates of the mean of the parameters, albeit with different variances. Thus applied workers can argue that if they are primarily interested in unbiased estimates of the mean effect, it does not matter which they use. This is essentially the argument of Zellner (1969), who showed that there is no aggregation bias under these conditions.

There also seems to be an implicit assumption that the above argument can be extended to dynamic models with lagged endogenous variables, in the sense that all four estimators will be consistent rather than unbiased. However, it is not true that time-series, cross-section and pooled estimators will generally give consistent estimates in dynamic random coefficient models. We provide a different explanation from those current in the literature of why estimates based on time series and cross-sections tend to provide conflicting results. Bohi (1981) discusses the differences in the estimates of energy demand elasticities for OECD countries. The fact that the time-series and cross-section estimates commonly differ is usually taken to suggest that there is misspecification in one or both of them. Because the pattern of correlation between included and excluded variables will differ in time-series and cross-section regressions, model misspecification will have quite different effects in each (see, for example, Hsiao 1986: 212). In the models we examine in Sections 2.2, 2.3 and 2.4, we assume that there is no misspecification in the micro relations. We have thus excluded a number of possible reasons that are given for cross-sections providing different estimates of the long-run relationship than time series. Instead we have adopted an approach which is closer to that of Haavelmo (1947), who posed the issue as two problems of aggregation. We are concerned with the different effects of averaging over groups or over time periods. The properties of time-series regressions on group averages are examined in more detail by Pesaran *et al.* (1989) and Lee *et al.* (1990).

## 2.2 DYNAMIC MODELS OF HETEROGENEOUS PANELS

Consider the following simple dynamic generalization of (2.1):

$$y_{it} = \lambda_i y_{i,t-1} + \beta_i' x_{it} + \varepsilon_{it} \qquad \begin{aligned} i &= 1, 2, \ldots, N \\ t &= 1, 2, \ldots, T \end{aligned} \tag{2.4}$$

where the coefficients $\lambda_i$ and $\beta_i$ are assumed to vary randomly across groups. The argument below applies to models with lags of higher order on both $y$ and $x_{it}$. A random intercept can be allowed for in this model by including unity as an element in $x_{it}$. Dynamic models for panels where the slope coefficients are assumed to be fixed across groups are surveyed by Sevestre and Trognon (1992). The first issue is that the choice of the long-run parameters of interest and the specification of the random coefficient model is not unambiguous in dynamic heterogeneous panel models. The long-term mean effects of $x_i$ on $y$ can be defined as being equal either to a long-run estimate calculated from the means of $\beta_i$ and $\lambda_i$, namely $\bar{\beta}/(1 - \bar{\lambda})$ where $\bar{\beta} = \sum_{i=1}^{N} \beta_i/N$ and $\bar{\lambda} = \sum_{i=1}^{N} \lambda_i/N$, or to the mean of the long-run estimates, defined by $\sum_{i=1}^{N} \theta_i/N$ where $\theta_i = \beta_i/(1 - \lambda_i)$. Corresponding to these two different 'average' long-run concepts, we can model the random parameters either by

$$H_a: \qquad \lambda_i = \lambda + \eta_{1i} \qquad \beta_i = \beta + \eta_{2i} \tag{2.5}$$

or by

$$H_b: \qquad \theta_i = \theta + \xi_{1i} \qquad \mu_i = \mu + \xi_{2i} \tag{2.6}$$

where $\theta_i = \beta_i/(1 - \lambda_i)$ are the long-run individual group coefficients and $\mu_i = \lambda_i/(1 - \lambda_i)$ are the mean lags for the individual groups. If we assume, for $j = 1, 2$, that $E(\eta_{ji}) = 0$, then $E(\xi_{ji})$ cannot equal zero, and may not even exist, and vice versa.

For panels where $N$ and $T$ are large, separate regressions can be run for each group and the mean group estimators can be computed for the long-run effects from the individual group estimates. These estimates, whether obtained by simple averaging or by weighted averaging, will yield consistent estimates of $\lambda$ and $\beta$ under $H_a$, and of $\theta$ under $H_b$, for both $N$ and $T$ large.

In the case where $x_{it}$ are integrated of order 1, namely $x_{it} \sim I(1)$, and there is a *single* cointegrating relationship between $y_{it}$ and $x_{it}$, a simple regression of $y_{it}$ on $x_{it}$ will yield super-consistent estimates of $\theta_i$, the cointegrating vector.[2] These could be averaged over groups. In this case the weighted mean group estimator (obtained, for example, using the Swamy procedure) may not be appropriate since the estimated standard errors from the cointegrating regression are incorrect. Estimating the $N$ separate regressions also allows one to test the hypothesis that the coefficients are independent of the regressors, an assumption we maintain for the moment. However, in empirical applications estimating $N$ separate regressions is rare. We shall now consider the application of the other three estimation procedures discussed in Section 2.1 to the dynamic heterogeneous panel model (2.4), under the two random coefficient hypotheses $H_a$ and $H_b$, and under two assumptions about the process generating the $x_{it}$, namely when the $x_{it}$ are I(0) and when they are I(1) variables.

## 2.3  THE CROSS-SECTION ESTIMATOR

Aggregating (2.4) over time we obtain

$$\bar{y}_i = \beta'_i \bar{x}_i + \lambda_i \bar{y}_{i,-1} + \bar{\varepsilon}_i \tag{2.7}$$

or

$$\bar{y}_i = \beta'_i \bar{x}_i + \lambda_i (\bar{y}_i - \Delta_T y_i) + \bar{\varepsilon}_i \tag{2.7a}$$

where $\bar{y}_{i,-1} = \sum_{t=1}^{T} y_{i,t-1}$, the growth term $\Delta_T y_i = (y_{iT} - y_{i0})/T$ captures the end effects, and $\bar{\varepsilon}_i = \sum_{t=1}^{T} \varepsilon_{it}/T$. Consider now the properties of the cross-section estimator under $H_a$ and $H_b$ defined by (2.5) and (2.6).

### 2.3.1  Short-run coefficients random

Under $H_a$ defined by (2.5), (2.7) becomes

$$\bar{y}_i = \beta' \bar{x}_i + \lambda \bar{y}_{i,-1} + \tilde{v}_i \tag{2.8}$$

where

$$\tilde{v}_i = \eta'_{2i} \bar{x}_i + \eta_{1i} \bar{y}_{i,-1} + \bar{\varepsilon}_i \tag{2.9}$$

The regression defined by (2.8) is the 'between' regression for the dynamic model and will produce biased estimates of $\beta$ and $\lambda$ even if the intercept parameter in (2.4) is the *only* parameter that varies across groups and $N$ and $T \to \infty$. This is due to the fact that $\tilde{v}_i$ is correlated with $\bar{y}_{i,-1}$ even for large $T$. A more promising route is to rewrite (2.7a) under $H_a$ as a cross-section (rather than 'between' regression):

$$\bar{y}_i = \frac{\beta'}{1 - \lambda} \bar{x}_i - \frac{\lambda}{1 - \lambda} \Delta_T y_i + \frac{1}{1 - \lambda} \tilde{v}_i \tag{2.8a}$$

where

$$\tilde{v}_i = \eta'_{2i} \bar{x}_i + \eta_{1i} (\bar{y}_i - \Delta_T y_i) + \bar{\varepsilon}_i \tag{2.9a}$$

Thus the coefficients of the level of the explanatory variables in the cross-section regression are in fact the appropriate long-run averages. It may appear that the usual cross-sections, estimated purely from levels, are misspecified to the extent that they omit the growth terms $\Delta_T y_i$. However, asymptotically the growth terms such as $\Delta_T y_i$ (and $\Delta_T x_i$, had $x_{i,t-1}$ appeared in the regression) are uncorrelated with the levels terms, so omitting them does not affect the consistency of the average long-run effects. This also indicates that cross-section estimates of the average long-run effect will be robust to dynamic misspecification of the underlying micro model.

For a finite $T$, the familiar cross-section estimator of $\beta/(1 - \lambda)$ or $\theta$ obtained by running the least squares regression of $\tilde{y}_i$ on $\tilde{x}_i$ will not be unbiased, and the bias disappears only under $H_b$ and as $T \to \infty$. Increasing the number of groups, $N$, while holding $T$ fixed does not eliminate the bias. Pesaran and Smith (1995) give a formal proof and provide some indications of the direction and the size of the bias under certain assumptions.

### 2.3.2  Long-run coefficients random

We now turn our attention to the hypothesis $H_b$, under which the random components in the parameters are introduced through the mean lags and the long-run coefficients (see (2.6)). In this case we have

$$\tilde{y}_i = \frac{\beta'_i}{1 - \lambda_i} \tilde{x}_i - \frac{\lambda_i}{1 - \lambda_i} \Delta_T y_i + \frac{1}{1 - \lambda_i} \tilde{\varepsilon}_i$$

$$= \theta'_i \tilde{x}_i - \mu_i \Delta_T y_i + \frac{1}{1 - \lambda_i} \tilde{\varepsilon}_i$$

which under $H_b$ yields

$$\tilde{y}_i = \theta' \tilde{x}_i - \mu \Delta_T y_i + \tilde{u}_i$$

and noting that $1 + \mu_i = 1/(1 - \lambda_i)$ we have the following expression for $\tilde{u}_i$:

$$\tilde{u}_i = (1 + \mu + \xi_{2i}) \tilde{\varepsilon}_i + \xi'_{1i} \tilde{x}_i - \xi_{2i} \Delta_T y_i$$

In this case, it can also be shown that for a finite $T$ the cross-section estimator yields a biased estimator of the mean of the long-run coefficients (i.e. $\theta = E[\beta_i/(1 - \lambda_i)]$). But for stationary $x_{it}$s, the bias will be of the order of $T^{-1}$, which is of a lower order of magnitude than the bias in estimating the average long-run coefficient from the means of the short-run micro coefficients (i.e. $\beta/(1 - \lambda) = E(\beta_i)/[1 - E(\lambda_i)]$). It is therefore more reasonable to interpret the cross-section estimator of $\theta$ as an estimator of the mean of the long-run coefficients rather than the estimator of the long-run coefficients calculated from the means of the short-run micro coefficients.

In short, the above results indicate that cross-section estimates of dynamic random coefficient models will not produce unbiased estimates of the long-run parameters unless $T$, the number of time periods used to form the average, is large and the randomness in the parameters is introduced through long-run coefficients and the mean lags. This casts serious doubt on the common practice of basing the estimation of long-run coefficients on cross-sections for a single year or a handful of years.

### 2.3.3 Cross-section estimates with integrated variables

We now examine the impact of non-stationary variables on the cross-section estimates. Consider the disaggregated time series relations

$$y_{it} = \beta_i x_{it} + \varepsilon_{it}$$

where $y_{it}$ and $x_{it}$ are each I(1) and pairwise cointegrated, namely $\varepsilon_{it}$ is I(0). To allow for an intercept, we can consider $y_{it}$ and $x_{it}$ being measured as deviations from their initial values $x_{i0}$ and $y_{i0}$, treating these as fixed and assuming that $\varepsilon_{i0} = 0$. Here for simplicity of exposition we also consider the case where $x_{it}$ is a scalar variable.

Averaging the data across time periods and assuming random coefficients as in (2.5), the OLS regression from the cross-section yields

$$\hat{\beta}^c = \frac{\sum_{i=1}^{N} \tilde{y}_i \tilde{x}_i}{\sum_{i=1}^{N} \tilde{x}_i^2} = \beta + \frac{\sum_{i=1}^{N} \eta_i \tilde{x}_i^2}{\sum_{i=1}^{N} \tilde{x}_i^2} + \frac{\sum_{i=1}^{N} \tilde{\varepsilon}_i \tilde{x}_i}{\sum_{i=1}^{N} \tilde{x}_i^2}$$

On the assumption that the $x_{it}$ follow random walks with drifts, namely

$$x_{it} = x_{i,t-1} + \mu_i + u_{it},$$

then Pesaran and Smith (1995) show that, as $N \to \infty$, $\hat{\beta}^c \xrightarrow{p} \beta$, even if $T$ is finite. This result indicates that the spurious correlation problem does not arise in the case of cross-section regressions, even if the underlying variables $x_{it}$ and $y_{it}$ contain unit roots. Under the assumption that $x_{it}$ and $\varepsilon_{it}$ are independently distributed, $\hat{\beta}^c$ is also an unbiased estimator of $\beta$, though the usual standard error formulae are no longer valid.

The cross-section disturbance is

$$\tilde{v}_i = \tilde{y}_i - \beta \tilde{x}_i = \tilde{\varepsilon}_i + \eta_i \tilde{x}_i$$

with variance

$$V(\tilde{v}_i | x) = V(\tilde{\varepsilon}_i) + \omega^2 \tilde{x}_i^2$$

where $\omega^2$ is the variance of $\eta_i$. The first term is likely to be small, particularly if $T$ is large, and the cross-section variance will be dominated by parameter heterogeneity. In general, therefore, the disturbances of the cross-section equation are heteroscedastic, but consistent estimates of the conditional variances of the cross-section coefficients can be obtained using the procedure suggested, for example, by White (1980). It is important to note, however, that the above results are valid under the rather strong assumption that the $x_{it}$ are strictly exogenous, and do not hold in the standard case discussed in the time-series literature of cointegrated variables where possible dependence between $x_{it}$ and $\varepsilon_{it'}$ (for some $t$ and $t'$) is not ruled out.

The consistent estimate of the long-run effect in the cross-section is in striking contrast to the estimates from the aggregate time-series estimator. Pesaran and Smith (1995) show that, if the $x_{it}$ are serially correlated, then the error in the aggregate equation will also be serially correlated, producing inconsistent estimates if a lagged dependent variable is included; and that if the regressors are I(1) and the micro relationships cointegrate for each group, then the aggregate relationship need not be cointegrated.

## 2.4 POOLED ESTIMATORS

With the pooled estimator the same problem arises as with the aggregate time-series estimator. The imposition of a common slope across different micro relations induces serial correlation in the composite disturbances of the pooled regression if the $x_{it}$ are themselves serially correlated, producing inconsistent estimates if a lagged dependent variable is included in the regression. Robertson and Symons (1992) consider the case where the data are generated by

$$y_{it} = \beta_i x_{it} + \varepsilon_{it} \qquad \begin{aligned} i &= 1, 2, \ldots, N \\ t &= 1, 2, \ldots, T \end{aligned} \tag{2.10}$$

$$x_{it} = \rho x_{i,t-1} + u_{it} \qquad u_{it} \sim (0, \tau_i^2) \tag{2.11}$$

and the estimated model is

$$y_{it} = \gamma x_{it} + \lambda y_{i,t-1} + \upsilon_{it}. \tag{2.12}$$

They show that for $V(\varepsilon_{it}) = 1$, $N = 2$ and $|\rho| < 1$,

$$\underset{T \to \infty}{\text{plim}} (\hat{\gamma}) = \frac{\beta^*(1 - \rho^2)}{1 - h\rho^2} \tag{2.13}$$

$$\underset{T \to \infty}{\text{plim}} (\hat{\lambda}) = \frac{\rho(1 - h)}{1 - h\rho^2} \tag{2.14}$$

where

$$\beta^* = \sum_{i=1}^{N} w_i \beta_i \qquad h = \left( \sum_{i=1}^{N} w_i \beta_i \right)^2 \left( \sum_{i=1}^{N} w_i \beta_i^2 \right)^{-1} \qquad w_i = \frac{\tau_i^2}{\sum_{j=1}^{N} \tau_j^2}$$

The long-run estimator $\hat{\theta} = \hat{\gamma}/(1 - \hat{\lambda})$ has the probability limit $\beta^*(1 + \rho)/$

$(1 + \rho h)$. Furthermore, as $\rho$ approaches its upper bound ($\rho = 1$) from below, then $\text{plim}(\hat{\beta})$ and $\text{plim}(\hat{\lambda})$ tend to zero and unity respectively.

In more general models similar results are obtained even when $x_{it}$ are serially uncorrelated. Consider the following simple dynamic generalization of (2.10):

$$y_{it} = \beta_{i1}x_{it} + \beta_{i2}x_{i,t-1} + \varepsilon_{it}$$

where

$$\beta_{i1} = \beta_1 + \eta_{i1}$$

$$\beta_{i2} = \beta_2 + \eta_{i2}$$

and $\eta_{i1}$ and $\eta_{i2}$ have means zero with variances $\omega_{11}$ and $\omega_{22}$ and the covariance $\omega_{12} = \omega_{21}$. Assume further that the $x_{it}$ are generated as in (2.11) and the estimated model is

$$y_{it} = \gamma_1 x_{it} + \gamma_2 x_{i,t-1} + \lambda y_{i,t-1} + v_{it}$$

For large $T$ and $N$, Pesaran and Smith (1995) show that

$$\text{plim}(\hat{\gamma}_1) = \beta_1 \qquad\qquad (2.15)$$

$$\text{plim}(\hat{\gamma}_2) = \beta_2 - \lambda*(\beta_1 + \rho\beta_2) \qquad\qquad (2.16)$$

in which

$$\lambda* = \text{plim}(\hat{\lambda}) = \frac{\rho(\omega_{11} + \omega_{22}) + (1 + \rho^2)\omega_{12}}{\omega_{11} + \omega_{22} + 2\rho\omega_{12} + (1 - \rho^2)(\beta_2^2 + \sigma^2/\tau^2)}$$

where $\hat{\gamma}_1$, $\hat{\gamma}_2$ and $\hat{\lambda}$ are the OLS estimators of $\gamma_1$, $\gamma_2$ and $\lambda$ respectively in the pooled regression. Further, the estimator of the long-run coefficient $\hat{\theta} = (\hat{\gamma}_1 + \hat{\gamma}_2)/(1 - \hat{\lambda})$ has the following probability limit:

$$\text{plim}(\hat{\theta}) = \beta_1 + \beta_2 + \frac{\lambda*\beta_2(1 - \rho)}{1 - \lambda*} \qquad\qquad (2.17)$$

These results have a number of important features:

1   The 'average' short-run impact of $x_{it}$ on $y_{it}$ is consistently estimated by $\hat{\gamma}_1$.
2   The pooled regression will generally yield an inconsistent estimator of the 'average' long-run impact of $x_{it}$ on $y_{it}$. As with the Robertson and Symons example, the extent of the bias depends on the magnitude of $\rho$. As $\rho$ approaches unity from below ($|\rho| < 1$), $\lambda$ also tends towards unity and the long-run coefficient may become computationally unstable. Letting $\rho \rightarrow 1$, we have

$$\operatorname*{plim}_{\rho \to 1}(\hat{\theta}) = \beta_1 + \beta_2 + \frac{\beta_2(\omega_{11} + \omega_{22} + 2\omega_{12})}{\omega_{11} + \omega_{22} + 2(\beta_2^2 + \sigma^2/\tau^2)}. \tag{2.18}$$

It is important to note that this result holds only for values of $\rho$ approaching unity from below and is not valid for $\rho = 1$.

3    The inconsistency of the pooled estimator vanishes *only* under the parameter homogeneity assumption. In this case $\omega_{ij} = 0$, $i, j = 1, 2$, and $\hat{\gamma}_1$ and $\hat{\gamma}_2$ both converge to the fixed coefficients $\beta_1$ and $\beta_2$, respectively. Notice also that unlike in the Robertson and Symons example the inconsistency of the pooled estimators remains even if the $x_{it}$ are serially uncorrelated.

Hence in this model the primary source of the bias is the heterogeneity of the coefficients $\beta_{i1}$ and $\beta_{i2}$ that are ignored in the pooled regression. The serial correlation in the $x_{it}$ tends to accentuate the problem. The direction of the bias critically depends on the signs and the magnitudes of $\omega_{12}$ and $\rho$. When these are positive we have $\lambda^* > 0$ and there will be a tendency to underestimate the 'average' impact of $x_{i,t-1}$ and overestimate the 'average' long-run impact of $x_{it}$ on $y_{it}$. Remarkably, in this example the 'average' short-run impact of $x_{it}$ on $y_{it}$ is consistently estimated by the coefficient of $x_{it}$ in the pooled regression.

The Robertson and Symons result arises because when the $x_{it}$ are serially correlated the errors in the pooled regression associated with the micro relations (2.10) will also be serially correlated, and therefore mistakenly including a lagged dependent variable in the equation will result in inconsistent estimates. A similar kind of problem is present, however, even if the pooled regression is not misspecified. Suppose the micro relations are correctly specified by (2.4) explicitly including an intercept term, with random parameters defined according to $H_a$ in (2.5). The pooled regression is given by

$$y_{it} = \alpha_i + \lambda y_{i,t-1} + \beta' x_{it} + v_{it}, \tag{2.19}$$

where $\alpha_i$ is the intercept term and

$$v_{it} = \varepsilon_{it} + \eta_{1i} y_{i,t-1} + \eta_{2i} x_{it}. \tag{2.20}$$

Different group-specific fixed or random effects can be included in the pooled regressions through the intercept term $\alpha_i$. It is easily shown that $y_{i,t-1}$ and $x_{it}$ are correlated with $v_{it}$, thus rendering the pooled estimators inconsistent, and $E(y_{i,t-1} \, v_{it})$ does not vanish even if the $x_{it}$ are serially uncorrelated. Instrumental variable estimation of the pooled regression faces major difficulties. Given the structure of the composite disturbances $v_{it}$, it may not be possible to come up with variables that are uncorrelated with $v_{it}$ while at the same time having a non-zero correlation with the variables included in the pooled regression.

Integrated variables also cause difficulty for the pooled regression. Suppose each micro relationship cointegrates with different parameters. The pooled regression by imposing a common parameter on all the micro relations generates a residual which has an I(0) component, the residual from the cointegrating micro relationship, and an I(1) component, the product of the difference between the micro and imposed parameter and the I(1) regressor. Thus the pooled regression will not constitute a cointegrating regression and the parameter estimates will not be consistent.

The traditional argument for pooling is that one obtains more efficient estimates of the average effect by imposing the restriction that the coefficients are the same. What the argument of this section suggests is that pooling is likely to produce inconsistent effects of the average effect in dynamic models. Most of the literature on pooled estimation of dynamic models avoids the difficulties discussed in this section by focusing on the intercept term $\alpha_i$ as the main source of parameter heterogeneity in the model and assuming that the slope coefficients $\lambda_i$ and $\beta_i$ are the same across groups. But this is a very strong assumption which is not likely to be met in many energy applications.

## 2.5  MODEL MISSPECIFICATION AND ALTERNATIVE ESTIMATES OF LONG-RUN ELASTICITIES

In the discussion above it was assumed that the model was correctly specified, in which case the cross-section if based on relatively long time averages can provide quite reasonable point estimates of the mean of the long-run coefficients, although more efficient estimates might be obtained from a weighted average of the individual time-series estimates – what we have called mean group estimates. However, different types of misspecification of the model are likely to have different effects on the two estimators, and here we briefly discuss the consequences of four types of misspecification on these estimates. In each case, comparison of the mean group estimates and cross-section estimates may be informative about the likelihood and possible form of the misspecification. In many cases, the misspecification can be thought of as inducing a correlation between the estimated coefficients and the regressors, contrary to our maintained assumption so far that they were independent. This correlation can be investigated empirically when time-series equations are estimated for each group separately.

If the estimated equation omits relevant dynamics, the cross-section may be more robust to dynamic misspecification than the averages of the individual time series as in the case Baltagi and Griffin (1984) examined. The estimation of long-run effects using time-series estimates in situations where substantial lags exist between price and income changes, and changes in energy demand, may require very long spans of data. For example, the full impact of price changes on residential energy demand may take up to ten years for it to become complete, as it takes time to get vehicles, central heating systems and household appliances replaced.

Similar considerations also apply to interfuel substitution at the industry level. However, when considering long time periods the assumption of structural stability is less likely to be fulfilled. Despite the recent advances in the theory of cointegrated systems (e.g. Engle and Granger 1991), identification of adjustment dynamics in most time-series applications remains troublesome, and the estimates of the long-run effects can be very sensitive to the particular dynamic specification chosen.

To examine the effects of dynamic misspecification, consider the following random coefficient distributed lag model:

$$y_{it} = \alpha + \beta_{0i}x_{it} + \beta_{1i}x_{i,t-1} + \ldots + \beta_{pi}x_{i,t-p} + \varepsilon_{it} \quad i = 1, 2, \ldots, N; t = 1, 2, \ldots, T$$

where $\beta_{ji}$ are distributed independently of the $\varepsilon_{it}$ and $x_{it}$ with means $\beta_j$ and constant variances. Suppose now that the lags are omitted in error and the static time-series regressions

$$y_{it} = a_i + b_i x_{it} + \upsilon_{it}$$

are estimated. Further assume that

$$x_{it} = \mu_i + \rho x_{i,t-1} + \upsilon_{it} \quad |\rho| < 1.$$

The probability limits of the OLS estimates of $b_i$ in the above static regressions are given by[3]

$$\operatorname*{plim}_{T \to \infty} (\hat{b}_i) = \beta_{0i} + \rho\beta_{1i} + \rho^2\beta_{2i} + \ldots + \rho^p\beta_{pi}.$$

If $\rho = 0$, the time-series estimate $\hat{b}_i$ measures the short-run effect $\beta_{0i}$. If $\rho = 1$ and $y$ and $x$ are cointegrated, then

$$\operatorname*{plim}_{T \to \infty} (\hat{b}_i) = \beta_{0i} + \beta_{1i} + \beta_{2i} + \ldots + \beta_{pi},$$

which measures the long-run effect. However, for values of $\rho$ between zero and unity, $\hat{b}_i$ yields a biased estimate of both the short-run and long-run effects, and for $\rho > 0$ it lies somewhere between the two. Aggregating the distributed lag equations over time gives

$$\bar{y}_i = \alpha_i + \beta_{0i}\bar{x}_i + \beta_{1i}\bar{x}_{i,-1} + \ldots + \beta_{pi}\bar{x}_{i,-p} + \bar{\varepsilon}_i$$

where $\bar{x}_i = \sum_{t=1}^{T} x_{it}/T$ and $\bar{x}_{i,-j} = \sum_{t=-(j-1)}^{T-j} x_{it}/T$. In terms of the growth terms $\Delta_j x_i = (x_{i,-(j-1)} - x_{i,T-j})/T$, we now have

$$\bar{y}_i = \alpha_i + \phi_{0i}\bar{x}_i + \sum_{j=1}^{p} \phi_{ji} \Delta_j x_i + \bar{\varepsilon}_i$$

where

$$\phi_{ji} = \beta_{ji} + \beta_{j+1,i} + \ldots + \beta_{pi} \quad j = 0, 1, 2, \ldots, p$$

For large $T$ and assuming $|\rho| < 1$, the covariances between the terms in $\Delta_j x_i$

and $\bar{x}_i$ will tend to zero, and the OLS estimate of $\beta$, say $\hat{\beta}$, in the cross-section regression

$$\bar{y}_i = \alpha + \beta \bar{x}_i + u_i$$

will give a consistent estimate of the 'mean' long-run effect of $x_{it}$ on $y_{it}$, assuming that the micro coefficients $\beta_{1i}$ and $\varepsilon_{it}$ are independently distributed. More formally, we have

$$\underset{\substack{T \to \infty \\ N \to \infty}}{\text{plim}} \, (\hat{\beta}) = E(\phi_{0i}) = \sum_{j=0}^{p} \beta_j$$

where $\beta_j$ is the mean over the $N$ groups of the coefficients of $x_{i,t-j}$.[4]

To illustrate the problem graphically, consider an extreme case. Suppose $y_{it}$ is the logarithm of real expenditure on energy and $x_{it}$ the logarithm of the relative price of energy. Suppose further that there is a J-curve effect in the sense that in the current period an increase in prices increases expenditure on energy because consumers are locked into inflexible capital stocks. However, in the long run, after one period say, demand is elastic and they can adjust fully. Thus, assuming homogeneity of coefficients across groups, we have

$$y_{it} = \alpha_0 + \beta_0 x_{it} + \beta_1 x_{it-1} + \varepsilon_{it} \qquad \beta_0 > 0; \beta_0 + \beta_1 < 0$$

The static time-series regression for each group is

$$y_{it} = a_i + b_i x_{it} + u_{it}$$

and the cross-section regression is

$$\bar{y}_i = \alpha + \beta \bar{x}_i + u_i$$

If prices were serially uncorrrelated, i.e. $\rho = 0$, all the time-series estimates would be positive, $\text{plim}(\hat{b}_i) = \beta_0 > 0$, and the cross-section estimates would be negative, $\text{plim}(\hat{\beta}) = \beta_0 + \beta_1 < 0$, as shown in Figure 2.1.

Hsiao (1986: 7, Figure 2.3) presents the same picture but interprets it differently, as the consequence of intercept heterogeneity. The probability limits of the time-series intercepts are $\text{plim}(a_i) = \alpha_0 + \beta_1 \mu_i$, differing between groups and correlated with $\bar{x}_i$, the estimate of $\mu_i$. In this example, which admittedly is somewhat artificial, the intercept heterogeneity is induced by dynamic misspecification of the time-series model. This misspecification also induces the correlation between the time-series estimates of the intercept and the regressors, which causes the cross-section estimate to differ from the average of the time-series estimates.

Measurement error in the independent variable, which will produce a downward bias in the slope of a bivariate regression, can have similar effects. The size of the bias depends on the variance of the measurement error relative to the variance of the independent variable. In cross-section, the variance of the independent variables tends to be much larger than in time series; thus the

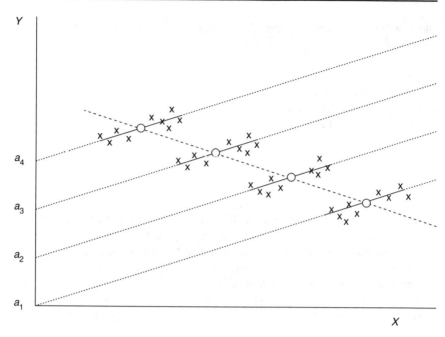

*Figure 2.1* Time-series and cross-section estimates

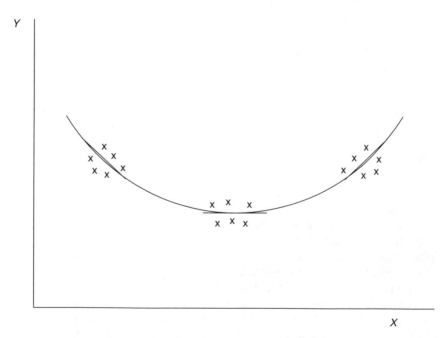

*Figure 2.2* Non-linearity and the relationship between coefficients and regressors

measurement error bias is smaller. This is the essence of Friedman's explanation of the smaller estimate of the elasticity of consumption to income in time series than in cross-section. The true explanatory variable is permanent income, but actual income includes a transitory component viewed as a measurement error.

Figure 2.2 shows how non-linearity, not obvious from time series, can induce a relationship between the coefficients and the regressors. In this case, there is a positive relationship between the slopes and the level of the explanatory variable. Time-series estimates for countries with low average levels show a negative effect; for countries with moderate levels, no effect; and for countries with high levels, a positive effect. Such non-linearities would be apparent either from the cross-sections on the means or from the association between the coefficients and the regressors. In the case of energy such non-linearities may arise in the course of development as households and producers switch between non-commercial and commercial sources of energy.

Cross-sections and time series alone are each inherently unable to identify the effect of certain types of variables. In panels, it is common to have some variables which differ substantially across groups but vary little over time. In the time series estimated for each group, such effects will be picked up by the group-specific intercept, which will then be correlated with the relevant group-varying measure. An example might be the effect of population density on demand for gasoline; it is clearly important but in any one country it changes so slowly over time that time-series estimates will not be able to reveal its impact on gasoline demand. Other variables differ substantially over time but vary little over groups. In cross-sections estimated for each time period, such effects will be picked up by the year-specific intercept, which will be correlated with the relevant time-varying measure. An example is gasoline prices for a cross-section of individuals in a particular country. Variations between individuals in the price they face tend to be quite small or correlated with other relevant variables, e.g. isolated rural communities may face higher prices because of transport costs. A heterogeneous panel model which includes both types of variables may take the form

$$y_{it} = \alpha_i + \beta_i x_{it} + \gamma z_i + \delta_i w_t + \varepsilon_t$$

where $z_i$ stands for the variable that differs across groups but not over time, and $w_t$ is the variable that varies over time but not across groups. Since $z_i$ is constant for each group, we cannot identify different group-specific coefficients of $z$. However, for each group we can estimate

$$y_{it} = a_i + \beta_i x_{it} + \delta_i w_t + \varepsilon_{it}$$

Then if we assume that $\alpha_i = \alpha + \eta_i$, where $\eta_i$ is random and distributed independently of $z_i$, we can estimate the regression

$$a_i = \alpha + \gamma z_i + \eta_i$$

using the estimated $a_i$ for each group as dependent variable. This approach is widely used in the panel literature. See, for example, Hsiao (1986: 50–2).

Because the traditional panel literature is concerned with cases where $T$ is small, it has focused on heterogeneity of the intercepts. In cases where we have data fields, i.e. large $N$ and $T$ panels, the same type of procedure can be applied to the slope coefficients $\beta_i$. In particular the assumption that the coefficients are random can be examined by regressions of the form

$$\hat{\beta}_i = a + b\,\bar{x}_i + u_i$$

Under the null hypothesis that the coefficients are random $b = 0$ and the error $u_i$ contains two components:

$$u_i = (\beta - \beta_i) + (\beta_i - \hat{\beta}_i)$$

the random differences between groups and the estimation error for a particular group. The variance of the first component is constant, but the variance of the second component differs between groups. This hetero-scedasticity can be allowed for at the inference stage by weighting the estimates $\hat{\beta}_i$ inversely by the estimate of their standard errors.

## 2.6 ALTERNATIVE LONG-RUN ELASTICITY ESTIMATES FOR ASIAN DEVELOPING ECONOMIES

Most studies of energy demand are confined to OECD countries where the required data are more readily available. The books by Pindyck (1979) and Griffin (1979) represent good examples of the early work carried out on energy demand in OECD countries. A more recent review covering some of the developments over the past two decades is given by Watkins (1991), who also focuses on energy demand in the OECD countries. In this section we use a new data set not analysed previously, and examine the empirical importance of the issues discussed above for energy demand in ten Asian developing economies over the eighteen years 1973–90. The data, taken from the Asian Development Bank (1992), are described in a data appendix and are available on request. The dependent variable is $E$, the logarithm of final commercial energy consumption in tons of oil equivalent (t.o.e.). The explanatory variables are $Y$, the logarithm of per capita GDP in 1985 prices converted into US dollars using 1985 market exchange rates, and $P$, the logarithm of the average consumer price of energy in domestic currency per t.o.e. relative to the GDP deflator (1985 = 1), converted into dollars at 1985 exchange rates. Although it is real income and the relative energy price in domestic currency that influence demand, cross-section and pooled estimates require internation-ally comparable statistics – incomes and prices in a common currency – and there is an inevitable arbitrariness in the conversion to a common currency.[5]

The empirical results reported in this section can only be regarded as illustrative of the type of methodological issues involved, because of the high level of aggregation used. Residential, industrial and transportation demands for different types of fuel will differ systematically in ways that will bias the aggregate estimates. For instance, industrial customers can substitute between fuels in response to relative price changes more rapidly than can residential customers. However, the procedures illustrated here could be readily applied to energy demand equations, disaggregated by sectors and by fuel types. There may also be a problem of identification in those countries such as India where energy prices are controlled and prices may be adjusted (through changes in energy taxes) in response to variations in energy consumption. In such cases the estimated equations would be a mixture of demand and supply responses.

We estimated two dynamic specifications of the energy demand equations for each of the ten countries. The first specification, which we denote by $M_1$, regresses $E$ on $Y$, $P$ and $E(-1)$, the lagged values of $E$. The second specification, which we denote by $M_2$, adds the lagged values of $Y$ and $P$ to model $M_1$. Table 2.1 gives the time-series estimates of $M_1$ for each of the ten countries, together with some summary and diagnostic statistics.[6] The short-term income elasticity estimates lie between 0.189 (Korea) and 1.109 (Bangladesh) and are statistically significant for seven of the ten countries. The short-term price elasticities are statistically significant in the case of five countries (Bangladesh, Indonesia, Korea, Philippines and Thailand), and have the correct negative signs except for India, Pakistan and Sri Lanka. The price elasticities for these three countries are estimated to be positive, but are not statistically significant. The estimates of the long-run elasticities together with their estimated standard errors are given in Table 2.2. The long-run income elasticities range from 0.65 (Sri Lanka) to 3.15 (Bangladesh) and the long-run price elasticities from 0.13 (Sri Lanka) to $-0.68$ (Korea). Thus there is considerable heterogeneity between these estimates, though the extreme values for Sri Lanka may reflect particular problems with data for that country. But considering the high level of aggregation and the rather doubtful quality of the underlying time-series observations at least for some of the countries, these are encouraging results and in general accord with the *a priori* theory. The individual country estimates for the long-run income elasticities are generally well determined and with a few exceptions do not differ significantly from unity. By contrast the precision of the estimates of the long-run price elasticities are rather low and are statistically significant only in the case of Indonesia, Philippines and Thailand. Given the long lags that are usually involved between price changes and changes in energy demand these results accord reasonably well with the view that time-series estimates tend to underestimate price elasticities.

Table 2.3 presents alternative mean estimates of the income and price effects for both dynamic specifications $M_1$ and $M_2$. The first two columns

Table 2.1 Individual country estimates of dynamic energy demand equations for ten Asian developing countries[a] (1974–90)

| Countries | Specification $M_1$ | | | | Summary statistics | | |
|---|---|---|---|---|---|---|---|
| | Intercept | $Y$ | $P$ | $E(-1)$ | $\bar{R}^2$ | $\hat{\sigma}$ | $\chi^2_{SC}(1)$ |
| Bangladesh | 0.349 (0.291) | 1.109 (0.479) | -0.172 (0.078) | 0.648 (0.189) | 0.911 | 0.063 | 7.06[b] |
| Hong Kong[c] | 2.690 (1.529) | 0.689 (0.256) | -0.065 (0.158) | 0.218 (0.254) | 0.936 | 0.045 | 0.28 |
| India | 3.251 (1.230) | 0.931 (0.328) | 0.019 (0.093) | 0.069 (0.350) | 0.918 | 0.043 | 3.43 |
| Indonesia | -1.318 (0.682) | 0.717 (0.234) | -0.144 (0.046) | 0.586 (0.155) | 0.982 | 0.038 | 0.89 |
| Korea | 0.59 (0.35) | 0.189 (0.107) | -0.109 (0.045) | 0.841 (0.119) | 0.992 | 0.029 | 0.20 |
| Malaysia | 0.788 (0.793) | 0.317 (0.208) | -0.108 (0.082) | 0.840 (0.167) | 0.959 | 0.039 | 0.26 |
| Pakistan | 1.963 (0.673) | 1.070 (0.341) | 0.039 (0.067) | 0.242 (0.246) | 0.983 | 0.029 | 0.01 |
| Philippines | 2.129 (0.564) | 0.594 (0.209) | -0.266 (0.056) | 0.519 (0.109) | 0.878 | 0.049 | 2.80 |
| Sri Lanka | 1.279 (1.189) | 0.358 (0.326) | 0.074 (0.123) | 0.445 (0.274) | 0.490 | 0.072 | 0.07 |
| Thailand | 2.525 (0.435) | 0.804 (0.106) | -0.204 (0.027) | 0.272 (0.124) | 0.992 | 0.021 | 0.21 |

Notes: [a]The dependent variable is $E$, the logarithm of per capita final energy consumption in t.o.e.; $P$ is the logarithm of the relative price and $Y$ is the logarithm of real per capita income. See the Data appendix for further details of the variables and the data sources. The figures in parentheses are standard errors. $R^2$ is the adjusted square of the multiple correlation coefficient, $\hat{\sigma}$ is the regression's standard error, and $\chi^2_{SC}(1)$ is the Lagrange multiplier test of residual serial correlation of order 1.
[b]Significant at the 1 per cent level.
[c]Estimated over the period 1979–90.

*Table 2.2* Individual country estimates of the long-run income and price
elasticities[a]

| | Based on the dynamic specification ($M_1$) | | Based on the cointegrating[b] relations | |
|---|---|---|---|---|
| | Income | Price | Income | Price |
| Bangladesh | 3.148 | −0.489 | − | − |
| | (0.794) | (0.305) | | |
| Hong Kong[c] | 0.881 | −0.083 | N/A | N/A |
| | (0.220) | (0.200) | | |
| India | 0.9995 | 0.020 | 1.054 | 0.124 |
| | (0.138) | (0.098) | | |
| Indonesia | 1.734 | −0.349 | 1.610 | −0.178 |
| | (0.220) | (0.167) | | |
| Korea[d] | 1.186 | −0.683 | 0.906 | −0.194 |
| | (0.271) | (0.733) | | |
| Malaysia | 1.981 | −0.673 | − | − |
| | (1.072) | (0.780) | | |
| Pakistan | 1.411 | 0.052 | − | − |
| | (0.068) | (0.088) | | |
| Philippines | 1.235 | −0.554 | 1.190 | −0.375 |
| | (0.353) | (0.120) | | |
| Sri Lanka | 0.646 | 0.133 | − | − |
| | (0.758) | (0.179) | | |
| Thailand | 1.104 | −0.280 | 1.087 | −0.252 |
| | (0.056) | (0.044) | | |

*Notes*: [a]Based on the coefficient estimates reported in Table 2.1.
[b]The cointegration relations are estimated by Johansen's approach and are reported when
the hypothesis of cointegration between $E$, $P$ and $Y$ is not rejected. Estimates of the
cointegrating vectors are only given in cases where the presence of cointegration amongst $E$,
$P$ and $Y$ could not be rejected. See Table 2.5 below.
[c]The estimates for Hong Kong are based on the sample period 1979–90.
[d]The estimates of the cointegration relation in the case of Korea are obtained assuming a
second-order vector autoregressive model for $E$, $Y$ and $P$.

present the weighted mean group estimates using the Swamy (1971) procedure.
The long-run elasticities are calculated from the means of the short-run
coefficients (see (2.5)). In this application the differences between the two ways
of calculating the long-run effects discussed in section 2.2 are not significant.
The unweighted means of the country-specific long-run income and price
elasticities reported in Table 2.1 are 1.43 and −0.29, respectively. The long-run
estimates calculated from the unweighted means of the short-run coefficients
are 1.27 and −0.18, respectively. The second two columns give the pooled OLS
estimates. These estimates graphically illustrate the theoretical points made
above about the effect of parameter heterogeneity combined with serial
correlation in the regressors on pooled estimates. The coefficient of the lagged
dependent variable (in the case of both specifications) is very close to unity. In

Table 2.3 'Average' estimates of dynamic energy demand equations for ten Asian countries, 1974–90[a]

| | Mean group[b] estimates | | Pooled OLS estimates | | Pooled fixed effect estimates | |
|---|---|---|---|---|---|---|
| | $M_1$ | $M_2$ | $M_1$ | $M_2$ | $M_1$ | $M_2$ |
| *Regressors* | | | | | | |
| Y | 0.528 | 0.438 | 0.035 | 0.3103 | 0.292 | 0.293 |
| | (0.121) | (0.181) | (0.012) | (0.111) | (0.045) | (0.111) |
| $Y(-1)$ | | 0.1350 | | -0.2895 | | -0.0706 |
| | | (0.163) | | (0.113) | | (0.118) |
| P | -0.100 | -0.1188 | -0.0745 | -0.1792 | -0.076 | -0.15 |
| | (0.040) | (0.056) | (0.013) | (0.026) | (0.018) | (0.029) |
| $P(-1)$ | | 0.0238 | | 0.126 | | 0.086 |
| | | (0.043) | | (0.025) | | (0.026) |
| $E(-1)$ | 0.594 | 0.5588 | 0.989 | 0.994 | 0.781 | 0.83 |
| | (0.096) | (0.123) | (0.011) | (0.010) | (0.043) | (0.045) |
| *Long-run elasticity estimates* | | | | | | |
| Income | 1.301 | 1.298 | 3.4354 | 3.522 | 1.336 | 1.304 |
| | (0.254) | (0.249) | (2.800) | (4.646) | (0.128) | (0.155) |
| Price | -0.247 | -0.2155 | -7.3310 | -9.106 | -0.349 | -0.37 |
| | (0.129) | (0.125) | (7.913) | (15.750) | (0.116) | (0.150) |
| Maximized log-likelihood values | 328.45 | 343.96 | 250.93 | 266.00 | 272.89 | 278.9 |
| Number of estimated parameters | 40 | 60 | 4 | 6 | 13 | 15 |

Notes: [a]The dependent variable is $E$, the logarithm of per capita final energy consumption in t.o.e.; $P$ is the logarithm of relative price and $Y$ is the logarithm of real per capita income. $P$ and $Y$ were converted to dollars using 1985 exchange rates. The figures in parentheses are the standard errors.
[b]These are the weighted Swamy (1971) estimates based on individual country coefficient estimates.

the case of $M_2$, the coefficients of current price and income variables are not very different from the mean group estimates; the same, however, cannot be said about the coefficients of lagged price and income variables. The last two columns in Table 2.3 give the pooled fixed effect estimates. Allowing for country-specific fixed effects reduces the problem somewhat, and the long-run estimates are not significantly different from the mean group estimates, but the short-run dynamics implied by the fixed effect estimator are highly misleading. The hypothesis that the slope coefficients are equal (imposed by the fixed effect estimator) is rejected for both specifications. For example, in the case of model $M_2$ the total maximized log-likelihood value for the individual time-series regressions is 344, and for the fixed effect model 279,

*Table 2.4* 'Average' estimates of long-run income and price elasticities based on static energy demand equations for ten Asian countries[a] (1974–90)

| Estimates | Long-run elasticities | | LLF |
| --- | --- | --- | --- |
| | *Income* | *Price* | *LLF* |
| 1    Mean group estimates[b] | 1.172 | −0.101 | 293.63 |
| | (0.185) | (0.052) | |
| 2    Pooled OLS estimates | 0.963 | −0.297 | −82.6 |
| | (0.035) | (0.082) | |
| 3    Pooled fixed effects estimates | 1.027 | −0.064 | 178.1 |
| | (0.038) | (0.030) | |
| 4    Aggregate time-series estimates | 1.099 | −0.083 | 43.31 |
| | (0.045) | (0.035) | |
| 5    Cross-section estimates | 1.020 | −0.549 | −3.98 |
| | (0.192) | (0.545) | |

*Notes*: [a]Based on static regressions of $E$ on $Y$ and $P$. For the variable definition and data sources see the notes to Table 2.1. LLF is the maximized log-likelihood values.
[b]Swamy's (1971) weighted estimates.

giving a log-likelihood ratio statistic of 130, which is approximately distributed as a $\chi^2$ variate with 45 degrees of freedom. This would imply the rejection of the null hypothesis of homogeneous slope coefficients even at the $\frac{1}{2}$ per cent level, critical value 72.12.

Table 2.4 gives elasticity estimates based on static regressions. Although the hypothesis that all the lagged variables are insignificant in the individual time series is rejected, the static estimates are of some interest. First, if the variables are I(1), which they seem to be (see Table 2.5), and were cointegrated, the static estimates could be interpreted as cointegrating regressions.[7] Second, were the coefficients independent of the regressors, all the procedures would provide unbiased estimators of the mean effect in a static regression. The first row of this table gives the mean group estimate of the average of the individual time series. The mean group estimates based on static coefficients are slightly lower than those based on long-run estimates from the dynamic equations, but not significantly so (1.172 in Table 2.4 compared with the estimates 1.301 or 1.298 in Table 2.3). The second and the third rows in Table 2.4 give the pooled OLS estimates (with common intercepts) and the pooled fixed effect estimates that allow for individual country intercepts. The fourth row gives the aggregate time-series estimates based on the time-series regression of the average values over the ten countries, and the last row in Table 2.4 gives the cross-section estimates.

The coefficient for income does not differ significantly (using the appropriate standard errors in the Swamy procedure) between the different methods, while the coefficient of price does, the mean group, aggregate time-series and fixed effect methods producing rather low estimates of the long-run

*Table 2.5* Tests of order of integration and cointegration[a]

| Countries | ADF(1) statistics (with trends) | | | Cointegration present? |
|---|---|---|---|---|
| | E | Y | P | |
| Bangladesh | −0.76 | −2.48 | −2.02 | No |
| Hong Kong | N/A | N/A | N/A | N/A |
| India | −0.77 | −0.95 | −2.24 | Yes |
| Indonesia | −1.82 | −1.60 | −1.38 | Yes |
| Korea | −2.44 | −1.62 | −1.64 | Yes |
| Malaysia | −2.10 | −1.89 | −1.62 | No |
| Pakistan | −2.06 | −2.87 | −2.06 | No |
| Philippines | −1.23 | −2.93 | −1.39 | Yes |
| Sri Lanka | −1.76 | −2.39 | −2.37 | Yes |
| Thailand | −0.24 | −2.19 | −0.81 | Yes |

*Note*: [a]The augmented Dickey–Fuller (ADF) statistics are computed over the period 1975–90. The ADF statistics are not reported for Hong Kong where data are available only over the period 1979–90. The 95 per cent critical value of the Dickey–Fuller statistic is −3.73. Cointegration was tested using Johansen's (1988) procedure, based on a first-order vector autoregressive model in ($E, Y, P$), with a trend. See also the notes to Table 2.1.

price elasticity, and the cross-section method a large estimate. The pooled estimates lie between the fixed effect and the cross-section estimates, as expected. The difference arises because across countries there is a correlation between coefficients in individual equations and the average values of the regressors.

Although more work is required on the interesting substantive issues raised by this data set, the results are generally in accordance with the theoretical points raised in the earlier sections of the chapter concerning the possible significance of the alternative ways of measuring average long-run effects, namely the large biases possible in dynamic pooled estimators and the significance of the assumption that coefficient variation is uncorrelated with the exogenous variables.

These results are very suggestive in that, although the data are highly aggregated and of doubtful quality, systematic patterns appear from the comparative analysis. Price and income are generally significant for these economies. The average long-run income elasticity from time-series estimates for individual countries is greater (though not significantly greater) than unity. The average long-run price elasticity is $-\frac{1}{4}$ and significantly different from zero (see Table 2.3). In cross-section, the income elasticity is almost exactly unity and the price elasticity is about a half, although it is rather poorly estimated (see Table 2.4). This higher price effect is consistent with both the folk wisdom that time-series estimates do not capture the slow adjustment to prices and our theoretical results which indicate that cross-section estimates are likely to be more robust to dynamic misspecification than the time-series estimates.

The pooled estimates showed the features our theoretical discussion predicted: coefficients of the lagged dependent variable tended towards unity; coefficients of independent variables tended towards zero if only current values were included; if lagged values were included, the coefficient of the current independent variable was close to its true value (as indicated by the average of the time-series estimates) but the coefficient of the lagged independent variable tended to become equal but opposite in sign to the coefficient of the current independent variable (see Table 2.3). In this application, OLS on the pooled regression gave ridiculous estimates of the long-run effects. When the intercepts were allowed to differ across countries the estimates were not unreasonable, though the estimates of the short-run coefficients were clearly implausible (see Table 2.3). In this example, the biases in the fixed effect estimator seem to have cancelled out, but there is no reason to assume that this will usually happen. The relatively good performance of the fixed effect long-run estimator may also reflect the similarity of the income elasticities across countries in this application.

## 2.7 CONCLUDING REMARKS

The main conclusion of this chapter is that the random coefficient argument of Zellner (1969), which seems to have been widely accepted in the literature, does not extend to dynamic models. Thus aggregating over time or pooling dynamic heterogeneous panels can produce very misleading estimates.

The lesson for applied work is that, when large $T$ panels are available, time-series regressions for individual relations should be estimated and the estimates should be averaged over groups and their standard errors calculated explicitly. With modern computational facilities this is very easy to do. The hypothesis of homogeneity, that slope coefficients are the same across group equations, can then be tested. Our experience is that the homogeneity hypothesis is regularly rejected, even when the size of the test is adjusted to take account of the large number of observations. The average of the time-series estimates for individual groups, which we have referred to as the mean group estimates, can then be compared with the cross-section estimates based on *long time averages* and the possibility of correlation between the coefficients and the regressors can be investigated.

The cross-section regression has the advantages that it can utilize the large variations that usually exist in regressors across groups; allows estimation of average long-run effects for group-specific variables which do not vary over time; and tends to be relatively robust to measurement errors and dynamic misspecifications when compared with the long-run estimates obtained from the individual group estimates. Conversely, cross-section regressions will not pick up effects that are common to countries but vary over time, and will not give estimates of the country-specific effects which differ from the average. The more coefficients differ between countries the larger is likely to be the standard error of the cross-section estimates. If the misspecification induces systematic patterns between the estimated time-series coefficients and the exogenous variables, the group mean estimates will differ from the cross-section estimates, and investigating the pattern may provide us with a clue as to how to make improvements in our specifications.

The empirical analysis of energy demand reported in the chapter could only be indicative because of the high level of aggregation and the poor quality of the data; but it did illustrate the practical importance of the methodological issues discussed. Very different estimates of the average long-run price elasticity were obtained from different procedures, with the cross-section estimate being the largest and dynamic pooled estimators showing very large biases relative to average time-series estimates. Despite the large differences between the different estimates of the long-run income and price elasticities, our results and analysis suggest a long-run income elasticity of slightly larger than unity, and a long-run price elasticity of around $-\frac{1}{4}$ for the ten Asian developing economies. Detailed and disaggregated analysis of energy demand in these economies is needed, however, before a more reliable picture can be presented.

## DATA APPENDIX

The series used were annual observations over the period 1973–90. The variables are:

GDP at 1985 prices (billion of domestic currency units)
GDP deflator (1985 = 1)
Population (million persons)
Final energy consumption (thousand tons of oil equivalent). This is the energy made available to the consumer before its final utilization or the energy consumed by the final user for all energy purposes. It excludes all energy lost in the transformation of primary to secondary energy, energy used within the transformation industries and energy lost during the transformation process. A standard ton of oil equivalent of 10 Gcal is assumed.
Consumer price of energy (in domestic currency per ton of oil equivalent)

In the regressions the dependent variable is $E$, the logarithm of final commercial energy consumption per capita in tons of oil equivalent (t.o.e.).
The explanatory variables are:

$Y$, the logarithm of per capita GDP in 1985 prices converted into US dollars using 1985 market exchange rates
$P$, the logarithm of the average consumer price of energy in domestic currency per t.o.e. relative to the GDP deflator (1985 = 1) converted into dollars at 1985 exchange rates

Mean values of real per capita income in 1985 dollars, the relative price of
energy in thousands of 1985 dollars, per capita final energy consumption in
t.o.e. and the average rate of change of these variables for each country are
given in Table 2A.

Most of the data were taken from Asian Development Bank (ADB) (1992).
In a number of cases the exchange rate, GDP and price data given in ADB did
not agree with those published in *International Financial Statistics*, in which
case the IMF data were used. There were also a number of cases where data
in the ADB summary tables did not agree with the detailed overall energy
balance tables, in which cases the latter were used.

Data for Hong Kong on energy consumption and prices were not available
for 1973–78. Except for the estimates in Table 2.1, the other parameter
estimates are based on interpolated data for these years for Hong Kong. For
the sample where the data were available, the logarithm of per capita Hong
Kong energy consumption was regressed on the logarithm of Hong Kong
output and the logarithm of average energy consumption by the other nine
countries. This equation was then used to predict Hong Kong energy
consumption for 1973–78. Similarly, the logarithm of Hong Kong dollar price
was regressed on the average dollar price for the other nine countries and this
was used to predict Hong Kong energy price for the period 1973–8. The
regression using the interpolated data was very similar to the regression
reported in Table 2.1 using actual data over the shorter period.

*Table 2A* Country mean growth rates and per capita levels[a]

| | Per capita energy use | | Per capita GDP | | Relative price of energy | |
|---|---|---|---|---|---|---|
| | Growth (% p.a.) | Level (t.o.e.) | Growth (% p.a.) | Level (1,000 1985 $) | Growth (% p.a.) | Level (1985 $ per t.o.e.) |
| Bangladesh | 4.54 | 28 | 2.03 | 0.14 | 3.62 | 161 |
| Hong Kong | 4.45 | 651 | 5.42 | 5.55 | 1.03 | 384 |
| India | 3.25 | 114 | 2.73 | 0.26 | 4.77 | 176 |
| Indonesia | 6.19 | 147 | 4.17 | 0.49 | 2.81 | 191 |
| Korea | 6.68 | 983 | 6.87 | 2.02 | 3.47 | 267 |
| Malaysia | 4.22 | 506 | 3.66 | 1.82 | 2.02 | 358 |
| Pakistan | 4.15 | 127 | 2.83 | 0.28 | 1.29 | 130 |
| Philippines | −0.78 | 169 | 0.83 | 0.62 | 6.06 | 372 |
| Sri Lanka | 0.15 | 81 | 1.68 | 0.37 | 5.81 | 324 |
| Thailand | 4.75 | 228 | 5.13 | 0.67 | 3.45 | 296 |

*Note*: [a]See the Data appendix for definitions and statistical sources.

## NOTES

1   An earlier version of this paper was presented at the Conference on Estimating Long-run Energy Elasticities, Robinson College, Cambridge, September 1992. It draws heavily on Pesaran and Smith (1992) which contains a more technical discussion. We are grateful to Victoria Saporta for helping us with the compilation of the data analysed in the paper. The first author wishes to acknowledge partial financial support from the ESRC and the Isaac Newton Trust of Trinity College, Cambridge.

2   See Engle and Granger (1991) for a discussion of integration and cointegration properties of time series and their consequences for econometric analysis.

3   The assumption that $\rho$ is the same across groups is clearly restrictive and is made here for expositional simplicity. The same results, however, follow when $\rho$ is allowed to vary across the groups.

4   Recall that by assumption $E(\beta_{ji}) = \beta_j, j = 0, 1, \ldots, p$.

5   One can also use purchasing power parity conversion factors as in Pindyck (1979), but given the illustrative nature of the present application we have not followed this route.

6   To save space the details of the estimation results for model $M_2$ are not reported here, but alternative 'average' estimates of the parameter estimates based on $M_2$ are given in Table 2.3.

7   Using Johansen's (1988) maximum likelihood procedure we were not able to reject the hypothesis that $E$, $Y$ and $P$ are cointegrated at the 10 per cent level of significance in the case of India, Indonesia, Korea, Philippines, Sri Lanka and Thailand. Because of data limitations, the test was not applied to Hong Kong. See Table 2.5. The Johansen test statistics were computed using the Microfit 3.0 package (see Pesaran and Pesaran 1991).

# Chapter 3

# A survey of international energy elasticities

*Jago Atkinson and Neil Manning*

**ABSTRACT**

This chapter considers evidence on energy elasticities gathered from a large number of studies published over the past twenty years or so. The emphasis of the survey is international and both multi-country and single-economy studies are included. The survey classifies this rather extensive literature in terms of the methodology used. The chapter also presents some estimates of long-run energy elasticities for the industrial sector in a group of fifteen countries over the period from 1960 to 1989. Estimation makes use of cointegration techniques and the resultant estimates are compared and contrasted with the results from previous studies discussed in the initial section of the chapter. The chapter further considers the reasons for differences in estimates of elasticities and considers further areas of potential study.

**INTRODUCTION**

This chapter surveys the literature on international energy elasticities, an area to which economists have paid rather less attention than one may suspect. Indeed, following the oil crisis of the early 1970s there have been numerous studies on energy elasticities at the national level but rather fewer at the international level. However, given that the direction and strength of international energy elasticities is particularly relevant to the current debate on the use of 'carbon taxes' to address the problem of global warming, evidence on international energy elasticities is of crucial interest.

As such, this review aims to summarize both the methodology employed and the results obtained in the literature on international energy elasticities. The chapter attempts to integrate those studies which are purely international in focus with some of the more influential single-country studies. The majority of the studies reviewed examine substitution possibilities between aggregate energy and both capital and labour; rather fewer consider substitution possibilities between individual fuels.

The chapter is in three sections. Section 3.1 provides some summary background on the theory of factor demands and on the econometric techniques which are commonly applied. The major part of the literature review is presented in Section 3.2 which surveys energy demand studies grouped according to methodology. Section 3.2.1 considers studies based on the translog specification, the theory of which is briefly outlined in Section 3.1.2. Sections 3.2.2 and 3.2.3 consider studies based on Cobb–Douglas and constant elasticity of substitution (CES) production functions, while Section 3.2.4 considers more *ad hoc* studies. And finally, in Section 3.3, the chapter presents the results of applying fairly standard models to an international data set from fifteen countries spanning thirty years. In particular, the time-series properties of the data are considered in Sections 3.3.1 and 3.3.2 together with evidence from the application of cointegration techniques.

## 3.1  THE THEORETICAL FRAMEWORK

### 3.1.1  Energy elasticities estimated in the empirical literature

Several concepts of elasticity are commonly used in the empirical literature on energy demand. The usual price, income and cross-price elasticities of demand, denoted $\eta$, are familiar enough and will not be discussed. In a two-factor model the elasticity of substitution is defined as

$$\sigma = -\left. \frac{d \ln(K/L)}{d \ln(P_K/P_L)} \right|_{Q=Q^0} \tag{3.1}$$

and is the elasticity of the ratio of the factors with respect to the marginal rate of substitution between them. In effect, (3.1) provides an index of the cost-minimizing factor input proportions to changes in relative factor prices (see McFadden 1978). The Allen–Uzawa elasticity of substitution (AES) is given as

$$\sigma_{ij} = CC_{ij}/C_i C_j \tag{3.2}$$

where the partial derivative $C_i = \partial C/\partial P_i$. For the translog function, the own-price AES is given as

$$\sigma_{ii} = \frac{b_{ii} + (S_i)^2 - S_i}{(S_i)^2} \tag{3.3}$$

for factor $i$ and the cross-price AES is

$$\sigma_{ij} = \frac{b_{ij} + S_i S_j}{S_i S_j} \tag{3.4}$$

where $i \neq j$. The AES holds total output and all factor prices fixed and so substitution can take place between $i$ and an input other than $j$ (see McFadden 1978). The price elasticities of demand for factor inputs in the translog model are related to the AES,

$$\eta_{ij} = S_j \sigma_{ij} \quad \text{and} \quad \eta_{ii} = S_i \sigma_{ii}, \tag{3.5}$$

and can all vary with the value of the cost shares.

The full elasticity of substitution (FES) (see Kang and Brown 1981) measures substitution between two factors when the ratio of marginal products of factor $i$ and any factor other than $j$ are held fixed. Theoretically, this implies that there is no substitution between factor $i$ and any factor other than $j$. The FES is related to the AES as follows:

$$\text{FES}_{ij} = S_j(\sigma_{ij} - \sigma_{jj}) = \eta_{ij} - \eta_{jj} \tag{3.6}$$

As noted in Section 3.1.2, various separability assumptions are employed in many of the translog-based studies. Berndt and Wood (1979) analyse engineering and econometric interpretations of energy/capital complementarity and consider utilized capital. They set up a higher stage or master production function as follows:

$$Q = F(K, L, E, M) \tag{3.7}$$

with an associated master cost function

$$C = C(Q, P_K, P_L, P_E, P_M) \tag{3.8}$$

A two-input linearly homogeneous weakly separable sub-function using capital and energy is specified as

$$K^* = f_1(K, E) \tag{3.9}$$

yielding utilized capital $K^*$. This implies that the optimal $E/K$ ratios within the sub-function (3.9) only depend upon the prices of capital ($P_K$) and energy ($P_E$). There is a similar utilized capital cost sub-function related to the master cost function. The utilized capital cost sub-function is as follows:

$$C_{K^*} = C_1(K^*, P_K, P_E) \tag{3.10}$$

where $C_{K^*} = P_K K + P_E E$. The same procedure is used on an equivalent production sub-function, $L^* = f_2(L, M)$. The master production function can therefore be written as

$$Q = F^*(K^*, L^*) \tag{3.11}$$

and the master cost function is

$$C = C^*(Y, P_{K^*}, P_{L^*}) \tag{3.12}$$

where $P_{K^*}$ and $P_{L^*}$ are unit costs obtained from the cost sub-functions $P_{K^*} = C_{K^*}/K^*$ and $P_{L^*} = C_{L^*}/L^*$.

This structure can be used to estimate gross, net and scale elasticities. Gross elasticities, which are standard price elasticities of demand when referring to a sub-function, are evaluated when sub-function output is held fixed as factor prices change. Net elasticities allow for changes in sub-function output to occur along the 'expansion path' when the unit costs $P_{K*}$ or $P_{L*}$ change and total output is assumed constant. The scale elasticity is the difference between the gross elasticity and the net elasticity. If $X_m$ is a positive, strictly quasi-concave homothetic production sub-function, the net cross-price elasticity $\eta_{ij}$ is calculated as follows:

$$\eta_{ij} = \eta^*_{ij} + S_{jm}\eta_{mm} \tag{3.13}$$

where $\eta^*_{ij}$ is the gross elasticity, $S_{jm}$ is the cost share of the $j$th input in the total cost of producing $X_m$ and $\eta_{mm}$ is the own-price elasticity of demand for $X_m$ when output at the level of the master production function is held fixed. Prywes (1986) also considers the gross and net elasticities but refers to them as engineering and economic elasticities. The AES and the gross price elasticities are estimated as usual.

Pindyck (1979a) defines partial and total elasticities for individual fuels in two-stage models with a separable (fuel) lower stage. These are related to the above net and gross elasticities. The standard own- and cross-price elasticities for fuels are 'partial' as the total quantity of energy consumed is held constant in that they only account for substitution between fuels. Total elasticities for fuels allow the total quantity of energy consumed to vary. They can be derived from the translog share equations as follows:

$$\eta^{**}_{ii} = \eta_{ii} + \eta_{EE}S_i \tag{3.14}$$

where $\eta^{**}_{ii}$ is the total own-price elasticity for fuel $i$ and $\eta_{EE}$ is the own-price elasticity of aggregate energy; $S_i$ is the share of fuel $i$ in total energy expenditure. The total cross-price elasticity for each fuel is as follows:

$$\eta^{**}_{ij} = \eta_{ij} + \eta_{EE}S_j \tag{3.15}$$

If the energy cost sub-function is homothetic, then $\eta_{iQ}^{**} = \eta_{EQ}$ where $\eta_{EQ}$ is the elasticity of energy with respect to total output.

Pindyck also calculates the elasticity of the average cost of production with respect to the price of energy ($\eta_{acE}$) and with respect to fuel prices ($\eta_{aci}$). As the energy cost function is homothetic:

$$\eta_{aci} = \eta_{acE}S_i \tag{3.16}$$

### 3.1.2  The cost functions employed in the literature

Neoclassical economists have employed production functions in empirical research for many years. The well-established Cobb–Douglas production function and constant elasticity of substitution (CES) production function are often employed, and therefore the theoretical basis of the functions will not be discussed at length. The functions, moreover, are highly restrictive and as a consequence the more flexible translogarithmic production function has been more commonly employed of late. In the translogarithmic function, which is a second-order approximation to an arbitrary production function (see Christensen *et al.* 1971) no restrictions are placed on the Allen elasticities of substitution (see the previous section). The basic function is

$$\ln Q = a_0 + \sum_i a_i \ln X_i + \sum_i \sum_j a_{ij} (\ln X_i)(\ln X_j) \tag{3.17}$$

where $Q$ is gross output, the $X_i$ are factor inputs, the $a_i$ are first-order parameters and the $a_{ij}$ are second-order parameters (see Fuss *et al.* (1978) for a survey of alternative functional forms). Given duality between cost and production and assuming exogeneity of output and factor prices, a twice-differentiable non-homothetic translog cost function, the dual to (3.17), may be written as

$$\ln C = b_0 + \sum_i b_i \ln P_i + \tfrac{1}{2} \sum_i \sum_j b_{ij} (\ln P_i)(\ln P_j)$$
$$+ b_Q \ln Q + \tfrac{1}{2} b_{QQ} (\ln Q)^2 + \sum_i b_{iQ} (\ln P_i)(\ln Q) \tag{3.18}$$

where $C$ is total cost, the $P_i$ are factor prices, the $b_i$ are first-order parameters and the $b_{ij}$ are second-order parameters. The above function is homothetic if the $b_{iQ}$ terms are zero and has constant returns to scale if $b_{QQ} = 0$ and $b_Q = 1$ (see Berndt (1991) for a summary). Additionally, the symmetry restrictions imply that $b_{ij} = b_{ji}$ for $i \neq j$. The 'traditional' static translog model (3.18) can be logarithmically differentiated to yield the estimated factor share equations via Shephard's lemma:

$$S_i = b_i + \sum_j b_{ij} \ln P_j + b_{iQ} \ln Q \qquad S_i = (P_i X_i)/(\sum_j P_j X_j) \tag{3.19}$$

where 'adding up' implies $\sum_i b_i = 1$; $\sum_i b_{ij} = \sum_j b_{ij} = 0$ since the shares, by definition, must sum to unity. The translog model provides three tests of the theory of demand. First, the assumption of homogeneity of degree one in input prices can be tested through the symmetry conditions. Second, non-negative input levels, and thus non-negative cost shares, must exist, and third, the translog function must be concave in input prices. Concavity of the cost function is satisfied if the Hessian matrix based on the parameter estimates is negative semi-definite. This is equivalent to the condition that the matrix of AES is negative semi-definite.

The basic model, with symmetry and constant returns to scale imposed, is estimated using the four factors capital ($K$), labour ($L$), energy ($E$) and materials ($M$) as set out in the influential Berndt and Wood (1975) study. However, in many international studies of energy demand the lack of data on materials necessitates that authors, such as Fuss (1977b), assume weak separability of $K$, $L$ and $E$ from $M$ so that the cost function can, in general terms, be written $C = C(Q, C_1(P_K, P_L, P_E), P_M)$. Weak separability places restrictions on the parameters of (3.18) such that $b_i/b_j = b_{iM}/b_{jM}$ for $i, j \neq M$ which implies that the marginal rate of substitution between $i$ and $j$ is independent of $M$ (see Fuss *et al.* 1978). One particularly useful consequence of applying separability, as outlined by Fuss, is the concept of two-stage modelling which allows for the estimation of interfuel substitution and is used in several of the studies considered in Section 3.2.

Assume the existence of a homothetic aggregate $(C_1)$ containing coal, oil, gas and electricity which is weakly separable from other non-energy inputs. The non-homothetic cost function is, in general terms,

$$C = C(Q, C_1(P_C, P_O, P_G, P_{El}), P_K, P_L) \tag{3.20}$$

If the homothetic sub-function $C_1$ has a translog form it provides a consistent instrumental variable for the aggregate price of energy $P_E$ (which is usually formed as a Divisia index). Economic optimization can therefore proceed in two stages: first, optimize the levels of the fuels in the separable sub-function and then optimize the levels of the aggregates in the higher stage problem.

Varying types of technical progress are considered in the literature but our concern here is limited to Hicks-neutral and non-neutral constant exponential technical change. Consider the homothetic constant returns to scale translog cost function:

$$\ln C = b_0 + \sum_i b_i \ln P_i + \sum_i \sum_j b_{ij} (\ln P_i)(\ln P_j) + \ln Q + \gamma t + \sum_i \gamma_i t \tag{3.21}$$

where $t$ is a linear time trend. Equation (3.21) has Hicks-neutral technical change iff $\gamma \neq 0$ and $\gamma_i = 0$ $\forall i$. Hicks non-neutral technical change occurs iff $\gamma_i \neq 0$, in which case the share equation for factor $i$ becomes

$$S_i = b_i + \sum_j \ln P_j + \gamma_i t \tag{3.22}$$

The presence of Hicks non-neutral technical change in fuel-share equations is sometimes referred to as 'fuel-efficiency bias'.

The overwhelming majority of the empirical work surveyed in Section 3.2 has utilized versions of the basic static framework outlined above, while recent developments have extended these models to consider dynamic optimization over time explicitly. One such paper is that by Pindyck and Rotemberg (1983) in which the translog functional form is employed to consider the effects of energy price shocks on the four factors $K$, $L$, $E$ and $M$. Energy and materials are assumed to be fully flexible but capital and labour are assumed quasi-fixed. Thus the production technology is represented by a restricted cost function, conditional at time $t$ on $K_t$, $L_t$ and $Q_t$:

$$C = C(P_{Et}, P_{Mt}; K_t, L_t, Q_t, t) \tag{3.23}$$

It is also assumed that changes in capital and labour involve adjustment costs represented by convex functions $c^1(I)$ and $c^2(H)$ where, for simplicity, I is investment and H is net hirings. Firms are assumed to minimize the expected sum of discounted costs:

$$
\min_{\{K,L\}} \mathscr{E}_t \sum R_{t,\tau} [C(P_{E\tau}, P_{M\tau}; K_\tau, L_\tau, Q_\tau) + P_{K\tau}K_\tau
$$
$$
+ P_{L\tau}L_\tau + c^1(I_\tau) + c^2(H_\tau)] \tag{3.24}
$$

where $\mathscr{E}_t$ is the expectation operator and $R_{t,\tau}$ is the discount factor applied at $t$ for values at time $\tau$. The first-order conditions provide the two-variable factor input demand equations

$$
E_t = \partial C/\partial P_{Et} \tag{3.25a}
$$

$$
M_t = \partial C/\partial P_{Mt} \tag{3.25b}
$$

and the Euler conditions give expressions for the anticipated evolution of the quasi-fixed factors over time. The full solution to these equations is a path for $K$, $L$, $E$ and $M$ that depends on the current states of $L$, $K$, $P_E$ and $P_M$, as well as the expected future prices and output. Equations (3.25a) and (3.25b) and the two Euler conditions form regression equations to estimate the parameters of $C$, $c^1$ and $c^2$. Pindyck and Rotemberg assume that the restricted cost function (3.23) is a homogeneous and symmetric translog function in $P_M$, $P_E$, $K$, $L$, $Q$ with neutral technical change, but the choice of function in the dynamic approach is arbitrary.

The relationship between these 'third generation' and the early 'first generation' dynamic models is considered in Watkins (1991). 'First genera-tion' models are not based on explicit dynamic optimization and follow from the Balestra–Nerlove distinction between 'captive' and 'flexible' demands. Typically, a 'first generation' energy demand equation has a simple form:

$$
E_t = \alpha_0 + \alpha_1 P_t + \sum_j \alpha_j Z_{jt} + \beta_1 E_{t-1} \tag{3.26}
$$

where $Z$ is an exogenous vector. This approach has been applied in many of the more *ad hoc* studies discussed in Section 3.2.4 below. The relationship between the two classes of model centres around the interpretation of the $\beta_1$ coefficient in the above input demand equation for a fully flexible factor. Effectively, the first generation model coefficient $\beta_1$ summarizes the complex speed of adjustment relationships modelled in the explicit optimization procedures of the third generation models. Estimation of $\beta_1$ in equation (3.26) cannot identify the structural parameters of the underlying third generation model since the explanatory variables in (3.26) are not 'super exogenous' (see Maddala 1992), and equation (3.26) will only give equivalent predictions to a third generation model if the underlying determinants of speeds of adjustment in the third generation model are constant. Watkins's empirical work is discussed below in section 3.2.

### 3.1.3 Econometric methodology employed

*System-wide approaches*

The main body of the literature review distinguishes between single-equation and system-based models which require the use of system-wide estimators such as full-information maximum likelihood (FIML), seemingly unrelated regression (SUR), Zellner-efficient estimation and iterative seemingly unrelated regression (IZEF).

These methods estimate the system as a whole – in effect, the SUR approach uses OLS to estimate each equation of the system in turn and then uses the derived residuals from equations $i$ and $j$ to estimate elements of the variance–covariance matrix $\Omega_{ij}$. The estimated $\Omega$ matrix is then used as a weighting matrix and the individual equations of the system are stacked and estimated by generalized least squares. The iterative methods repeat this two-stage estimation-weighting procedure until parameter convergence criteria are satisfied. These system methods facilitate imposition of cross-equation restrictions implied by theory and allow for correlation between the residuals from different equations in the system. Both of these aspects are crucial in the estimation of singular demand systems in which expenditure shares sum to unity. This implies the redundancy of one share equation in the complete system and induces correlation between the residuals from the various equations given the adding-up property of the system overall (see McElroy 1987).

In a clear majority of cases, the stochastic performance of such systems is poor in terms of autocorrelation of disturbances but the systems may have vector autoregressive 'corrections' applied. This approach is not commonly applied in the literature on energy demand elasticities, however. Many studies of the demand for energy use a pooled cross-section time-series data set from a group of countries over a period of time. The above system methods are applied to the pooled data and frequently a uniform vector of factor-price coefficients is specified with fixed effects being employed to account for country-specific factors. This approach ignores the problem of contemporaneous correlation of disturbances between the residuals from countries included in the cross-section, although the system estimators naturally allow for such contemporaneous correlation between the individual factor-share equations in the singular demand system. Some evidence on the importance of this form of 'spatial' autocorrelation is presented in Section 3.3.1 below. Application of covariance analysis to these 'pooled' models is typically selective – the slope coefficients are usually specified as uniform across countries and formal tests are not performed. Furthermore, the interpretation of results from such 'pooled' models has been hotly debated (see Section 3.4).

*Stationarity and cointegration*

The methodology discussed above concentrates on the specification of complete demand systems and pays relatively little attention to the properties of the time series being modelled. A rather different modelling approach applies recent advances in time-series econometrics to the estimation of single-equation models of energy demand. (See Nachane *et al.* (1988), Hunt and Manning (1989) and Hunt and Lynk (1992) for applications.)

Economic time series rarely conform to the statistical assumption of stationarity which implies constancy of mean and variance over time. Frequently, such data are trending and possess a unit root. A simple example would be a random walk: $E_t = \Phi_1 E_{t-1} + v_t$ where $\Phi_1 = 1$. In this case, it is clear that no meaningful long-run solution between $E$ and any other variable can exist. The cointegration approach is concerned with the investigation of relationships between such non-stationary series and the confirmation of whether a long-run solution actually exists. As such, it would seem to be a natural candidate for the estimation of long-run energy elasticities in the instance where all variables specified possess common stochastic trends and are non-stationary and yet a linear combination of these non-stationary series is stationary.

The application of the cointegration approach typically involves three stages. First, the order of integration of the time series being modelled is investigated to classify them as level stationary, trend stationary or difference stationary. A level stationary process would not progressively diverge from a mean level and the trend stationary process would similarly oscillate around a deterministic trend. The difference stationary process conforms to neither of these situations and requires differencing to render the series stationary. Series may require progressive differencing to achieve stationarity: if $\Delta^d E_t$ is stationary or integrated of order zero, then $E_t$ is non-stationary and is integrated of order $d$, or $E_t \sim I(d)$ (see Engle and Granger 1987).

In the most straightforward case, the series which are entered into a hypothetically cointegrating regression need to be integrated of the same order – cointegration is found if a linear combination of these series is integrated of a lower order. Thus a linear combination of a number of I(1) series may be stationary. If the series cointegrate, the relationship between the variables does not diverge over time and therefore represents a long-run equilibrium relationship between individually non-stationary series. Conventional applications of this approach employ the Engle–Granger two-step method (Engle and Granger 1987) where prior static regression is used to estimate the cointegrating vector. The specification of such a vector is arbitrary, but conventionally the 'dependent' variable would be regressed on the independent variables plus a constant. The residuals from this regression can then be applied as 'equilibrium errors' in subsequent estimation of dynamic error correction mechanisms since the Granger representation theorem states that, if series cointegrate, a valid error correction mechanism exists. However, such cointegrating vectors need not be unique since the appropriate dependent variable in the prior static regression is not specified.

Such a situation, however, is rarely encountered in empirical applications of the cointegration approach since in practice many economic time series have different stochastic properties. Nonetheless, if the set of variables includes a number of I(1) and at least two I(2) series, cointegration may still be possible even though the properties of the series differ. This would follow if the I(2) series sub-cointegrate to provide an I(1) linear combination. This could then be combined with other I(1) series to provide an I(0) linear combination should cointegration occur.

Recent developments have provided the economist with a wider range of test statistics. The Johansen maximum likelihood procedure (see Johansen 1988; Johansen and Juselius 1990) can be used to assess the number of cointegrating vectors present in a vector autoregression (VAR). In this approach, all $k$ variables under investigation are considered as jointly endogenous in a VAR. In principle, therefore, a multiplicity of cointegrating relationships may exist in the data. A long-run solution is defined for each variable in the VAR as a linear combination of the cointegrating vectors (see Johansen and Juselius 1990). Although these time-series methods are appealing, they are difficult to apply to complete demand systems. Nevertheless, investigation of the time-series properties of the series could provide evidence to assess the likelihood that estimated relationships in such systems are spurious.

## 3.2  A REVIEW OF THE LITERATURE

As noted, the literature review is divided into four sections. Initially applications of the translog model are considered in Section 3.2.1. Subsequently, two studies based upon the Cobb–Douglas and CES production functions are discussed in Sections 3.2.2 and 3.2.3, while Section 3.2.4 surveys a number of disparate and more *ad hoc* studies. Section 3.2.5 presents a summary highlighting the main conclusions and areas which remain controversial.

### 3.2.1  Studies based on the translog specification

The following studies all employ variations of the basic translog framework briefly outlined in Section 3.1.2. For further details on the (static) translog framework see Fuss and McFadden (1976).

One of the first and most influential of the translog-based studies of energy demand is that of Berndt and Wood (1975), who analyse the derived demand for energy and non-energy inputs in American manufacturing between 1947 and 1971. The paper uses time-series data to consider the substitution possibilities between energy and non-energy inputs (capital, labour and all other materials). They employ a four-factor static translog system and make the assumptions that there are constant returns to scale and that any technical change is Hicks-neutral.

In many studies of international energy elasticities, the assumption of separability of factor inputs is necessitated by data deficiencies, as discussed in Section 3.1. Previously, the literature had made one of a number of assumptions. First, it may be assumed that there is a perfect correlation between the (quantity) ratios energy–income and materials–income. This may follow from technological non-substitutability of energy and materials ($\sigma_{EE} = \sigma_{EM} = \sigma_{MM} = \sigma_{KE} = \sigma_{LE} = \sigma_{KM} = \sigma_{LM} = 0$) or result from coincidental shifts in supply and demand, and is commonly known as the 'Leontief aggregation condition'. Second, it may be assumed that some of the models assume the 'Hicksian aggregation condition' which states that $P_E$, $P_M$ and $P$, the output deflator, always move in fixed proportions since either $E$ and $M$ are perfect substitutes or coincidental shifts occur in supply and demand. However, Berndt and Wood consider the situations in which it is valid to analyse substitution possibilities between capital and labour independently of energy and materials. They suggest that neither the Leontief nor the Hicksian aggregation conditions for a value-added specification are satisfied by their data on manufacturing in the United States.

Alternatively, the inputs $K$ and $L$ may be weakly separable from $E$ and $M$. The production function is therefore

$$Y = f[f_1(K, L), E, M] \tag{3.27}$$

This assumption of weak separability places restrictions on the AES; the linear value-added separability restrictions imply that $\sigma_{KE} = \sigma_{LE} = \sigma_{KM} = \sigma_{LM}$ = 1.0, which produces a partial Cobb–Douglas structure. The non-linear value-added separability restrictions imply that $\sigma_{KE} = \sigma_{LE} \neq 1.0$ and that $\sigma_{KM} = \sigma_{LM} \neq 1.0$. The former implies that the sum of $S_K$ and $S_L$ is constant, while the latter implies constancy of the ratio of $S_K$ and $S_L$. Berndt and Wood conclude that the separability conditions for the value-added specification (3.27) are not satisfied by their data. However, the separability of $K$ and $E$ from the other inputs could not be rejected so that $Y = f[f_1(K, E), L, M]$. (This is discussed at greater length below. In addition, see Berndt and Wood (1979).) Clearly, these findings are of broader significance for international studies and not solely of relevance to the data analysed by Berndt and Wood.

A further methodological issue arises from the fact that, since the level of aggregation employed is aggregate manufacturing, Berndt and Wood suggest it may be inappropriate to assume that prices are exogenous and that the regressors in the input-cost-share equations are uncorrelated with the disturbances. Few other translog-based studies have considered the *endogeneity of prices*. In Berndt and Wood, each of the regressors in the input-cost-share equations is regressed on a set of variables considered exogenous to US manufacturing and the fitted values from these first-stage regressions replace the original regressors in the input-cost-share equations.

Positivity of the input demand functions and concavity of the cost function are both satisfied so the translog cost function is well behaved for their data set. Energy demand is found to be responsive to changes in its own price, the own-price elasticity being around $-0.47$, and energy and labour are found to be slight substitutes, the AES being around 0.65 while the cross-price elasticities for $\eta_{LE}$ and $\eta_{EL}$ are about 0.03 and 0.08 respectively. Energy and capital are complements with an AES of approximately $-3.2$ while the cross-price elasticities $\eta_{KE}$ and $\eta_{EK}$ are about $-0.15$ and $-0.18$. Moreover, capital and labour are substitutes with an AES of 1.01, while the own-price elasticities $\eta_{KK}$ and $\eta_{LL}$ are $-0.48$ and $-0.45$ (see Tables 3.1 and 3.2 for summary details). Although the elasticities seem stable over the period, they are calculated from time-invariant second-order coefficient estimates and the actual factor expenditure shares are fairly constant over their data period (see Berndt and Wood 1975).

The study by Griffin and Gregory (1976) also uses a static translog cost function to study energy substitution responses in the manufacturing sector but uses data from Belgium, Denmark, France, West Germany, Italy, the Netherlands, Norway, the United States and the United Kingdom. As is common in many similar studies, three factors – capital, energy and labour – are explicitly analysed and are assumed to be weakly separable from material inputs despite the earlier findings of Berndt and Wood (1975). This assumption is partly necessitated by an absence of reliable data on materials. However, it should be noted that separability of $(K, E)$ from $L$ is supported by the data used in Berndt and Wood (1979).

Griffin and Gregory note that higher energy prices might induce short-run substitution towards the labour and material inputs and away from capital. This follows from the technological relationship between energy inputs and a given stock of capital equipment. Thus in the short run labour and materials are likely to be substitutes for energy whilst capital and energy are complementary. However, in the long run, capital and energy are more likely to be substitutes as more recent vintages of capital embody energy-saving technological advances. Griffin and Gregory therefore point to the possibility of sign reversals in elasticity estimates depending on whether the short run or long run is being analysed.

Their interest in long-run elasticities leads to their consideration of only four cross-sections (1955, 1960, 1965 and 1969) while post-1969 information was rejected on the grounds that energy prices had started to rise. In effect, substantial time-series relative-price variation is explicitly excluded and elasticities identified by cross-sectional variation within the data are interpreted as long run. As noted, this interpretation of cross-section studies providing long-run elasticity estimates and time-series studies providing short-run estimates pervades much of the literature.

In common with many studies of this type, Griffin and Gregory estimate variants on the basis of a pooled translog model including country-specific intercepts and, to allow fully for heterogeneity between countries, they also estimate separate translog models for each country. Given their choice of sample, the latter results are based on very few degrees of freedom, as the authors admit. The system of factor-share equations estimated by iterative Zellner efficient techniques fails to reject the symmetry, positivity and concavity assumptions regardless of whether country-specific intercepts are present in the estimated factor-share equations. Furthermore, the assumption of uniform $b_{ij}$ coefficients cannot be rejected although this is hardly surprising given that only four observations per country are used in estimation. In effect, the data set investigated by Griffin and Gregory necessitates the use of a uniform price coefficient matrix despite the presence of idiosyncratic country-specific effects within the data. These effects, they state, 'will also capture a variety of disequilibrium factors relating to differences in industrial structure amongst countries' (our emphasis). Given uniformity of the $b_{ij}$ values, similarity of elasticities must follow for countries having similar cost shares but the underlying estimates are based on very few observations for each country. They find that energy and labour are substitutes with $\eta_{EL} \approx 0.45$ but, in contrast to Berndt and Wood, energy and capital are also substitutes since $\eta_{EK} \approx 0.30$, while both $\sigma_{KE}$ and $\sigma_{LE}$ are not statistically different from unity. Griffin and Gregory's main findings are summarized in Tables 3.1 and 3.2. The accuracy of Griffin and Gregory's data on capital and labour expenditure in the United States has been questioned by Wood and Hirsch (1981) who note incompatibilities with the sources documented in the appendix.

Griffin and Gregory conclude that their model provides a reasonable long-run alternative to the pre-existing time-series literature on energy, capital and labour substitution and price elasticities such as Berndt and Wood (1975) and Hudson and Jorgenson (1974). They admit to potential measurement error, simultaneous equation bias and specification error problems in their approach, but conclude 'that translog applications to pooled international data represent fruitful lines of inquiry into the issue of energy, capital and labour substitution'.

The demand for energy in the Canadian manufacturing sector is analysed in Fuss (1977b) who assumes that the production structure is weakly separable in the categories of labour, capital, materials and energy. According to Denny and Fuss (1977), the assumption of weak separability implies aggregates which are homothetic in their components, and this is sufficient for an underlying two-stage optimization procedure to exist. First, the mix of components within each aggregate is optimized, followed by the level of each aggregate (see Pindyck (1979a) for further details). Under these assumptions, the cost function can be expressed as

$$C = g[P_E(P_{E1}, \ldots, P_{EN}), P_L, P_M, P_K, Q]$$ (3.28)

Table 3.1 Energy demand elasticities with respect to income and price

| Study | Sector analysed | Data period | Model and estimation technique | $\eta_{EQ}$ | $\eta_{EE}$ | $\eta_{EL}$ | $\eta_{EK}$ | $\eta_{EM}$ | Notes |
|---|---|---|---|---|---|---|---|---|---|
| Berndt and Wood (1975) | Time series for US manufacturing | 1947–71 | KLEM translog by I3SLS | N/A | −0.45 to −0.49 | 0.16 to 0.20 | −0.17 to −0.18 | 0.46 to 0.49 | |
| Griffin and Gregory (1976) | Pooled manufacturing data for nine nations | 1955–69 | KLE translog by IZEF | N/A | −0.79 (−0.77 to −0.80) | 0.48 (0.40 to 0.64) | 0.31 (0.15 to 0.40) | N/A | |
| Kouris (1976) | Pooled cross-section time series for eight nations | 1955–70 | Ad hoc logarithmic model | 0.84 | −0.77 | N/A | N/A | N/A | |
| Smil and Kuz (1976) | Aggregate time series for twenty-six nations | 1950–60 | Ad hoc | 0.60 to 2.00 | N/A | N/A | N/A | N/A | |
| Smil and Kuz (1976) | Aggregate time series for twenty-six nations | 1960–70 | Ad hoc | 0.82 to 1.63 | N/A | N/A | N/A | N/A | |
| Fuss (1977b) | Pooled cross-section time series for Canadian manufacturing | 1961–71 | KLEM translog by iterative minimum distance estimation | N/A | −0.49 | 0.55 | −0.05 | −0.02 | Figures for Ontario |

| Study | Data | Period | Model | | | | | | Comments |
|---|---|---|---|---|---|---|---|---|---|
| Nordhaus (1977) | Cross-section time series for seven nations | 1955–72 | KLE dynamic Cobb–Douglas production function | 0.29 to 1.11 (short run) 0.26 to 1.42 (long run) | −0.03 to −0.68 (short run) −1.94 to 1.45 (long run) | N/A | N/A | N/A | Koyck and Almon distributed lag schemes used |
| Berndt and Wood (1979) | Time series for US manufacturing | 1947–71 | KLEM translog by I3SLS | N/A | −0.13 (gross elasticity) −0.57 (net elasticity) | N/A | 0.13 (gross elasticity) −0.33 (net elasticity) | N/A | Results for 1971 |
| Pindyck (1979a) | Pooled industrial time series for ten nations | 1963–73 | KLE translog by IZEF | N/A | −0.84 (−0.83 to −0.87) | 0.02 to 0.08 | 0.02 to 0.08 | N/A | The United States and Canada are pooled separately |
| Pindyck (1979b) | Pooled residential time series for ten nations | 1960–74 | Translog by IZEF | N/A | −1.05 to −1.15 | N/A | N/A | N/A | |
| Field and Grebenstein (1980) | Pooled cross-section for US manufacturing | 1971 | KLE translog | N/A | −0.54 to −1.65 | −0.32 to 1.21 | −1.76 to 0.89 | N/A | |

Table 3.1 continued

| Study | Sector analysed | Data period | Model and estimation technique | $\eta_{EQ}$ | $\eta_{EE}$ | $\eta_{EL}$ | $\eta_{EK}$ | $\eta_{EM}$ | Notes |
|---|---|---|---|---|---|---|---|---|---|
| Beenstock and Willcocks (1981) | Aggregate time series for developed market economies | 1950–78 | KLE dynamic error correction model | 1.78 | −0.06 | N/A | N/A | N/A | Long-run elasticities reported |
| Turnovsky et al. (1982) | Time series for Australian manufacturing | 1946–75 | KLEM translog by FIML | N/A | −0.22 | −0.64 | 0.44 | 0.42 | |
| Kouris (1983) | Aggregate time series for the OECD | 1961–81 | Dynamic ad hoc logarithmic model | 1.08 (short term) | −0.15 (short term) −0.43 (long term) | N/A | N/A | N/A | Koyck distributed lag scheme used |
| Pindyck and Rotemberg (1983) | Time series for US manufacturing | 1948–71 | KLEM dynamic translog by 3SLS | N/A | −0.36 (short run) −0.58 (inter-run) −0.99 (long run) | −1.37 (short run) 1.07 (inter-run) 1.03 (long run) | 0.47 (short run) 0.46 (inter-run) −1.34 (long run) | 0.36 (short run) 0.13 (inter-run) 1.31 (long run) | Capital and labour quasi-fixed |
| Pindyck and Rotemberg (1983) | Time series for US manufacturing | 1948–71 | KLEM dynamic translog by 3SLS | N/A | −0.66 (short run) −0.93 (long run) | 0.88 (short run) 0.70 (long run) | 0.35 (short run) −1.01 (long run) | −0.22 (short run) 1.15 (long run) | Capital quasi-fixed |
| Prosser (1985) | Aggregate time series for the OECD | 1960–82 | Dynamic ad hoc logarithmic model | 1.02 | −0.22 (short run) −0.40 (long run) | N/A | N/A | N/A | Koyck distributed lag scheme used |

| Study | Data | Period | Method | | | | | |
|---|---|---|---|---|---|---|---|---|
| Hesse and Tarkka (1986) | Pooled cross-section time series of electricity for nine nations | 1960–72 | KLE translog by FIML | N/A | 0.09 (0.31 to −0.35) | 0.69 (0.49 to 0.77) | −0.39 (0.20 to −1.14) | N/A |
| Hesse and Tarkka (1986) | Pooled cross-section time series of electricity for nine nations | 1973–80 | KLE translog by FIML | N/A | −0.30 (0.14 to −0.49) | 0.24 (0.04 to 0.50) | 0.47 (0.18 to 0.69) | N/A |
| Hesse and Tarkka (1986) | Other fuels | 1960–72 | KLE translog by FIML | N/A | −0.16 (0.13 to −0.40) | 0.49 (0.35 to 0.65) | 1.29 (1.12 to 1.51) | N/A |
| Hesse and Tarkka (1986) | Other fuels | 1973–80 | KLE translog by FIML | N/A | −0.23 (−0.06 to −0.44) | 0.02 (0.36 to −0.18) | 0.68 (0.37 to 1.61) | N/A |
| Fiebig et al. (1987) | Cross-section for thirty nations | Not stated | Ad hoc logarithmic | 1.33 (1.24 to 1.64) | −0.66 to −0.88 | N/A | N/A | N/A |
| Apostolakis (1987) | Aggregate time series for five nations | 1953–84 | KLE translog | N/A | −0.11 to −0.60 | 0.05 to 0.53 | 0.16 to 0.33 | N/A |
| Siddayao et al. (1987) | Cross-section time series for manufacturing in the Far East | 1970–80 | KLE translog by IZEF | N/A | −0.31 to −2.60 | N/A | N/A | N/A |
| Saicheua (1987) | Cross-section time series for manufacturing in Thailand | 1974–7 | KLE translog by IZEF | N/A | −1.50 to −2.60 | −0.44 to 1.33 | 0.88 to 2.06 | N/A |

Table 3.1 continued

| Study | Sector analysed | Data period | Model and estimation technique | $\eta_{EQ}$ | $\eta_{EE}$ | $\eta_{EL}$ | $\eta_{EK}$ | $\eta_{EM}$ | Notes |
|---|---|---|---|---|---|---|---|---|---|
| Welsch (1989) | Aggregate time series for eight nations | 1970–84 | Dynamic *ad hoc* linear and logarithmic models | 0.24 (short term) | −0.13 (short term) | N/A | N/A | N/A | Koyck distributed lag scheme used |
| Welsch (1989) | Aggregate time series for eight nations | 1970–84 | Dynamic *ad hoc* linear and logarithmic models | 0.634 (long term) | −0.338 (long term) | N/A | N/A | N/A | Koyck distributed lag scheme used |
| Lynk (1989) | Time series for the UK manufacturing sector | 1948–81 | KLE translog by FIML | N/A | −0.23 (short run) −0.69 (long run) | 0.20 | −0.26 | N/A | Dynamic maximizing model with costs of adjustment used |
| Hunt and Manning (1989) | Aggregate time series for the UK | 1967–86 | Dynamic error correction model Cointegration analysis | 0.80 (short run) 0.38 (long run) | −0.08 (short run) −0.30 (long run) | N/A | N/A | N/A | |
| Patry *et al.* (1990) | Industrial time series for seven OECD nations | 1960–87 | Dynamic logarithmic specification with multinominal logit by IZEF | −0.34 to 1.50 | −0.22 to −0.91 | N/A | N/A | N/A | Long-run elasticities reported |

| Study | Data | Method | | | | | | Notes |
|---|---|---|---|---|---|---|---|---|
| Watkins (1991) | Time series for Canadian textiles | 1957–82 | KLEM dynamic specifications | N/A | −0.48 (short run) −0.50 (long run) | −0.12 (short run) 0.21 (long run) | N/A | 0.60 (short run) 0.54 (long run) | Third generation dynamic results reported |
| Hunt and Lynk (1992) | Time series for UK industry | 1952–88 | KLE dynamic error correction model Cointegration analysis | 0.46 to 0.48 (short run) 0.63 to 0.70 (long run) | −0.08 to −0.13 (short run) −0.29 (long run) | 0.08 to 0.10 (short run) 0.13 to 0.15 (long run) | 0.00 to 0.03 (short run) 0.14 to 0.16 (long run) | N/A | |
| Boone et al. (1992) | Time series for nine nations | 1978–89 | VAR system by Johansen (FIML) | N/A | −0.09 to −0.62 | N/A | N/A | N/A | Energy = fossil fuels A time trend is included in the VAR Quarterly data used |
| Bentzen et al. (1993) | Time series for Denmark | 1948–90 | VAR system with ECM by Johansen (FIML) | 0.67 (short run) 1.21 (long run) | −0.14 (short run) −0.47 (long run) | N/A | N/A | N/A | Temperature variable included |

Table 3.2 Partial elasticities of substitution

| Study | Sector analysed | Data period | Model and estimation technique | $\sigma_{EE}$ | $\sigma_{LE}$ | $\sigma_{KE}$ | $\sigma_{ME}$ | $\sigma_{KL}$ |
|---|---|---|---|---|---|---|---|---|
| Berndt and Wood (1975) | Time series for US manufacturing | 1947–71 | KLEM translog by I3SLS | −10.63 to −10.70 | 0.61 to 0.68 | −3.09 to −3.53 | 0.74 to 0.77 | 1.01 |
| Griffin and Gregory (1976) | Pooled manufacturing data for nine nations | 1955–69 | KLE translog by IZEF | N/A | 0.72 to 0.87 | 1.02 to 1.07 | N/A | 0.06 to 0.50 |
| Pindyck (1979a) | Pooled industrial time series for ten nations | 1963–73 | KLE translog by IZEF | −10.88 to −27.21 | 0.05 to 1.23 | 0.36 to 1.77 | N/A | 0.64 to 1.43 |
| Özatalay et al. (1979) | Pooled aggregate time series for seven nations | 1963–74 | KLEM translog by FIML | −24.60 to −32.25 | 1.03 to 1.05 | 1.15 to 1.22 | 0.42 to 0.65 | 1.06 to 1.14 |
| Turnovsky et al. (1982) | Time series for aggregate manufacturing | 1946–75 | KLEM translog by FIML | −8.73 | −2.66 | 2.26 | 0.79 | 2.00 |
| Prywes (1986) | Pooled cross-section time series for US manufacturing | 1971–6 | KLEM CES | N/A | N/A | −4.53 to 0.33 | N/A | N/A |
| Apostolakis (1987) | Aggregate time series for five nations | 1953–84 | KLE translog | −4.52 to 4.44 | 1.00 to 1.18 | 0.40 to 0.95 | N/A | 0.86 to 0.97 |
| Siddayao et al. (1987) | Cross-section time series for the Far East | 1970–80 | KLE translog by IZEF | N/A | −3.76 to 5.97 | −0.30 to 2.36 | N/A | 0.26 to 1.71 |
| Saicheua (1987) | Cross-section time series for Thailand | 1974–7 | KLE translog by IZEF | N/A | −3.76 to 5.97 | 1.52 to 2.66 | N/A | 0.57 to 1.85 |

where $P_E$ forms an aggregate price index. The price of energy is represented by a translog unit cost function and familiar share equations are estimated. Fuss incorporates a total of nine inputs: capital, labour, materials and six different energy inputs. The two-stage approach allows for the analysis of both interfuel substitution and substitution among energy and non-energy factors of production.

The model is estimated on a combined time-series cross-section data set for four areas of Canada from 1961 to 1971. The six types of fuel analysed in the lower stage are coal, liquid petroleum gas, fuel oil, natural gas, electricity and petrol. The own-price elasticity estimates are negative and, apart from petrol, significant at the 1 per cent level. Considerable interfuel substitution is apparent with the exception of electricity and, possibly, petrol. The demand for liquid petroleum gas, coal, fuel oil and natural gas are all price elastic but, as found in other studies, the demand for electricity is price inelastic. See Table 3.3 for details of the elasticities of individual fuel demands.

For the higher-stage model, total cost is assumed to be a constant or a smoothly changing percentage of gross output in current dollars, whilst exponentially smooth Hicks-neutral technical change is also assumed. Although Fuss finds significantly negative own-price elasticities of demand, all factors have price-inelastic demand, for instance $\eta_{EE}$ is $-0.5$. In general, factors are substitutes, although slight complementarity between energy and materials and between energy and capital exists. However, the cross-price elasticities are all small, typically below 0.3 in absolute value when evaluated with output held constant. Although there is substantial interfuel substitution in the Canadian manufacturing sector, only slight substitution exists between aggregate energy and other aggregate inputs.

Fuss also considers the effects on production costs in Canadian manu-facturing of increases in the price of energy relative to prices of other factors of production. A 1 per cent increase in the aggregate energy price is found to lead to a 0.03 per cent increase in average production costs. Therefore, substantial increases in the price of energy seem to be accommodated by only a moderate increase in the price index of manufacturing output. This finding is related to recent work on the implications of imposing carbon taxes on energy – recent econometric work also finds a very small impact on total production costs of tax-induced increases in energy prices. (See Ingham et al. (1991b) for a summary of recent econometric work on carbon taxes.)

The analysis of capital/energy substitution in American manufacturing is also considered by Field and Grebenstein (1980) who specify the cost function $C = C(P_K, P_W, P_L, P_E)$, where $P_K$ and $P_W$ refer to the prices of physical capital and working capital respectively while $P_L$ and $P_E$ represent the prices of labour and energy. Because of data deficiencies, they assume that these four inputs are separable from inputs of all non-energy intermediate materials and the standard static translog cost function is used for estimation purposes over a cross-section of ten two-digit manufacturing industries in

Table 3.3 Own- and cross-price partial fuel elasticities

| | Fuss (1977b) | Pindyck (1979a) | Turnovsky et al. (1982) | Lynk (1989) | Atkinson and Manning (this chapter)[a] |
|---|---|---|---|---|---|
| Sector analysed | Pooled cross-section/time series for Canadian manufacturing | Pooled industrial time series for ten nations | Time series for Australian manufacturing | Time series for the UK manufacturing sector | Pooled time series of the industrial sector for fifteen nations |
| Data period | 1961–71 | 1959–73 | 1946–75 | 1948–89 | 1960–89 |
| Model and estimation technique | Static translog by iterative minimum distance estimation | Static translog by IZEF | Static translog by FIML | Static translog interfuel by FIML | Statics translog by FIML |
| Notes | Homothetic and symmetric figures for Ontario | Homothetic and symmetric | Homothetic and symmetric | Homothetic and symmetric | Homothetic and symmetric |
| $\eta_{CC}$ | −1.41 | −1.04 to −2.17 | −0.75 | −0.20 | −0.64 |
| $\eta_{CO}$ | 0.30 | 0.15 to 0.99 | 0.46 | N/A | 0.19 |
| $\eta_{CG}$ | 0.71 | 0.43 to 1.66 | −0.06 | N/A | 0.19 |
| $\eta_{CE}$ | 0.09 | −0.48 to 0.49 | 0.35 | N/A | 0.26 |
| $\eta_{OC}$ | 0.32 | 0.12 to 0.97 | 1.16 | 0.61 | 0.12 |
| $\eta_{OC}$ | −1.22 | −1.10 to 0.03 | −0.99 | −0.29 | −0.16 |
| $\eta_{OO}$ | 0.17 | −0.03 to −0.72 | 0.16 | 0.10 | 0.02 |
| $\eta_{OG}$ | 0.27 | −0.22 to 0.85 | −0.33 | 0.27 | 0.03 |
| $\eta_{OE}$ | 0.85 | 0.72 to 4.98 | −0.59 | 0.47 | 0.12 |
| $\eta_{GC}$ | 0.20 | −0.06 to −0.83 | 0.68 | N/A | 0.26 |
| $\eta_{GO}$ | −1.21 | −0.33 to −2.31 | −1.45 | −0.69 | −0.57 |
| $\eta_{GG}$ | 0.02 | −1.82 to 0.12 | 1.37 | N/A | 0.13 |
| $\eta_{GE}$ | 0.27 | −0.06 to 0.25 | 0.31 | −0.35 | 0.06 |
| $\eta_{EC}$ | 0.77 | −0.05 to 0.28 | −0.12 | N/A | 0.01 |
| $\eta_{EO}$ | 0.04 | −0.02 to −0.10 | 0.11 | 0.25 | 0.06 |
| $\eta_{EG}$ | −0.52 | −0.07 to −0.16 | −0.31 | 0.10 | −0.10 |
| $\eta_{EE}$ | | | | | |

Notes: C, coal; O, oil; G, gas; E, electricity.
[a] See Section 3.3.

1971. Field and Grebenstein define physical capital as the stock of capital structures and equipment. The expenditure on physical capital is estimated as the product of user cost and the capital stock. The cost of working capital is calculated by subtracting the cost of physical capital from that of total capital, which is taken as value-added minus labour costs.

The results obtained vary over sectors but a 'very large proportion' of the second-order coefficients are insignificant. In conclusion, they find that physical capital is statistically significant as a complement to energy in four sectors, in three sectors there are weak signs of complementarity and for the remaining three sectors the estimates are insignificant. With respect to working capital and energy the results indicate that they are significant substitutes for five sectors, while insignificant results are found for the other five sectors. Virtually all other cross-price elasticities signify substitutability and all own-price elasticities are of the correct sign.

Finally, they state that for the aggregate manufacturing sector a value-added approach as used by Griffin and Gregory (1976) and Pindyck (1979a) 'would be expected to show capital/energy substitutability, while a service-price approach to capital cost would show complementarity'. Thus, according to Field and Grebenstein, the very definition of 'capital' influences empirical results. For example, the own-price elasticities of demand for physical capital are considerably higher than the equivalent estimates for working capital. Similarly, energy and physical capital are typically complements but energy is a substitute for working capital.

International time-series data for manufacturing in seven countries (the United States, Canada, West Germany, Japan, the Netherlands, Norway and Sweden) from 1963 to 1974 are analysed by Özatalay et al. (1979). A static KLEM translog cost function is assumed to display constant returns to scale and no separability assumptions are made. As in Griffin and Gregory, country dummies are employed with a pooled sample; results are presented for Germany, Japan and the United States. Although they find that all factors are substitutes, the elasticity of substitution between energy and materials is not significantly different from zero. The elasticities of substitution vary very little between countries except for $\sigma_{KK}$ and the large absolute values of $\sigma_{LL}$ for Japan and $\sigma_{EE}$ for the United States. Özatalay et al. conclude that this is due to the historically low prices paid for labour in Japan and for energy in the United States. The own-price elasticities of substitution in the United States, West Germany and Japan average $-2.69$ for capital, $-4.67$ for labour, $-0.91$ for materials and $-27.33$ for energy. The cross-price elasticities of substitution average 1.09 for capital and labour, 0.87 for capital and materials, 1.18 for capital and energy, 1.00 for labour and materials, 1.04 for labour and energy and 0.55 for materials and energy. Summary details are presented in Table 3.2.

Pindyck (1979a) analyses interfuel substitution and the industrial demand for energy on an international data set using a two-stage approach similar to that of Fuss. Capital, labour and energy are assumed to be weakly separable from materials as a group because of a lack of material price data. The underlying cost function can therefore be written as

$$C = G\,[\,g(P_K, P_L, P_E(P_{F1}, P_{F2}, P_{F3}, P_{F4}), Q);\, P_M, Q]$$    (3.29)

where $P_E$ is the aggregate price of energy derived from the homothetic sub-function of the four fuels. This static non-homothetic translog model is estimated using pooled time-series data for a cross-section of ten countries: Canada, France, Italy, Japan, the Netherlands, Norway, Sweden, the United Kingdom, the United States and West Germany. Pindyck estimates the model allowing the second-order coefficients to vary across countries but, as with Griffin and Gregory (1976), inadequate degrees of freedom exist to give satisfactory results. Country-specific intercepts are included and Pindyck specifies separate slope coefficients for the United States and Canada, but does not appear to conduct any formal covariance analysis on the data. The separation of the North American economies is justified on the basis of their historically lower fuel prices. The share equations for the energy cost sub-function are estimated from 1959 to 1973 by standard IZEF methods while the share equations for the total cost function are estimated from 1963 to 1973.

The results for the share equations of the energy cost sub-function indicate that thirteen of the sixteen second-order coefficients are statistically significant. The partial fuel price elasticities given in Table 3.3 are all substantial except for electricity — Pindyck states that electricity is a much more expensive fuel on a thermal basis and so is only used when necessary. For Europe and Japan natural gas own-price elasticities are large while those for oil are small. For the higher-stage cost function most of the second-order parameters are also found to be significant. The elasticities of substitution in Table 3.2 indicate that all other factors are substitutes for energy. Significantly, the largest values for $\sigma_{KE}$ and the smallest values for $\sigma_{LE}$ are found for Canada and the United States.

Elasticities of the average cost of output with respect to the price of energy and the prices of the individual fuels are also estimated. A 10 per cent increase in the price of energy is found to lead to a 0.3 per cent increase in average production costs for the United States and a 0.7 per cent increase for Italy, Japan and Sweden, which echoes the conclusion in Fuss (1977b) discussed above. Pindyck also considers scale economies (see Christensen and Greene 1976) and the elasticity of energy demand with respect to output changes. Even if energy prices remain constant relative to other prices, Pindyck finds that there will be substitution away from energy as output increases, and thus non-homotheticity could not be rejected.

The demand for energy in three separate sectors – industry, residential and transport – is analysed at some length in Pindyck (1979b), but the discussion here is primarily concerned with results for the residential sector. For this sector, data from nine countries are included: the Netherlands, Belgium, Canada, France, Italy, Norway, the United Kingdom, the United States and West Germany, and data span the period from 1960 to 1974. A static translog indirect utility function with time-dependent preferences (see Jorgenson and Lau 1975) is specified with energy being weakly separable from other inputs and the standard two-stage approach is employed. National dummy intercepts are used but the data are otherwise pooled.

Pindyck estimates the models on both the pooled time-series data and on pooled cross-sections at four-year intervals: 'if the resulting estimates are nearly the same, we can conclude that most of the explanation in the data is cross-sectional, so that we are more likely to have obtained long-run estimates of the elasticities' (Pindyck 1979b: 106). Clearly, this approach follows the empirical procedure in Griffin and Gregory (1976). For the translog model of consumption expenditures, the assumptions of stationarity (in this case meaning the absence of time dependence in expenditure share equations), homogeneity, separability and additivity are all rejected. The final model is 'non-stationary', based on a non-additive indirect utility function with country-specific first-order coefficients which account for a good proportion of the explanatory power of the equations. However, twenty-five of the thirty-six second-order coefficients are significant at the 5 per cent level. None of the own-price elasticities for energy are significantly different from $-1$ and most of the cross-price elasticities are approximately zero, although there is a significantly positive value for food and energy and a negative value for energy and transport, which is intuitive. All income elasticities are constrained to unity since the model is homothetic. An equivalent translog approach is discussed by Jorgenson (1977).

The restrictions of regional homogeneity, (time) stationarity and additivity are all rejected in the fuel sub-model which, like the higher-stage equivalent, is homothetic in energy expenditure. Pindyck argues that, as fuel prices have been lower and incomes higher in the United States and Canada, they should be treated separately from the other countries. The corresponding liquid fuel and gas elasticities for the United States and Canada are about half the size of those for the other countries. However, the opposite is true for electricity, the demand being more price elastic in North America and many own-price elasticity estimates for electricity demand in Europe being positive. This may follow from the effective omission of income in the homothetic specification.

For the transport sector a different approach is taken. Detailed data are available on the stock of energy-using durables – motor cars – so that familiar stock and utilization effects can be distinguished. Pindyck pools data from 1955 to 1974 from eleven countries which have car stock information: Belgium, Canada, France, Italy, the Netherlands, Norway, Sweden, Switzerland, West Germany, the United Kingdom and the United States. Country dummy variables account for regional heterogeneity and simple regressions explain new registrations, the depreciation rate, traffic volume per car and average fuel efficiency. However, the performance of the derived car stock is poor in subsequent petrol demand equations. The price of cars and petrol both have significant negative effects and per capita GDP has an insignificant positive effect on petrol demand. Pindyck also estimates transport demand for aviation gasoline, jet fuel, diesel fuel and petrol with simple log-linear models with a Koyck lag adjustment. For Europe, the long-run price elasticity for petrol is −1.61 and the income elasticity is 0.66. The estimated long-run price elasticity of diesel fuel is −0.62, −0.3 for jet fuel and −0.4 for aviation gasoline, while the long-run GDP elasticities are above 2.

Turnovsky *et al.* (1982) analyse factor substitution using a standard static KLEM translog cost function and employ data on aggregate manufacturing in Australia from 1945 to 1975. In common with Fuss (1977b) and Pindyck (1979a, b), they also model interfuel substitution in a two-stage translog model with coal, oil, gas and electricity in the weakly separable homothetic lower-stage sub-function. As elsewhere, the aggregate energy price used in the higher stage is formulated using a Divisia price index and the usual symmetry and homogeneity restrictions are imposed. They employ two specifications of time trend variables to proxy technical change, and favour a linear function over an alternative logarithmic form in the upper stage, while the logarithmic form is preferred in the energy sub-model. Although the cost functions at the higher stage are concave in input prices and the predicted shares are non-negative at each observation, the estimates reject both symmetry and homogeneity. The AES and price elasticities estimated at six points over the time period show that capital and energy as well as materials and energy are substitutes, and that labour and energy are complements, see Table 3.2. The elasticities of substitution imply that coal and gas as well as oil and electricity are complements but all the other fuels are substitutes for each other. As found elsewhere, electricity is the least price-responsive fuel with gas and oil being the most responsive. These estimates are quite sensitive, however, to the treatment of the time trend. Furthermore, if complementarity were found between fuels, Welsch (1989) would reject the specification as theoretically inadmissible (see Section 3.4).

Hall (1986) estimates a range of static and *ad hoc* dynamic translog cost function models for individual fuels (liquid fuels/petroleum products, gas, solid fuels/coal and electricity) for the industrial sector in seven OECD countries (Japan, West Germany, France, Italy, Canada, the United States and the United Kingdom) from 1960 to 1979. The data are not pooled and Hall does not consider the demand for energy in aggregate. The following restrictions are initially imposed in Hall's empirical work: homotheticity, symmetry, homogeneity in prices and neutral fuel-efficiency bias. Consideration of non-homotheticity follows from inclusion of post-1973–4 observations; he argues that the absence of cyclical influence could be a source of misspecification in the estimated share equations.

The results show that all four restrictions cannot be accepted for any country in a static framework. In order to assess whether rejection is due to dynamic misspecification, Hall estimates some simple dynamic models in which the lagged expenditure share of the fuel in question is included. Although this model is consistent with both partial adjustment and adaptive expectations, Hall provides little by way of theoretical justification. The coefficients on these lagged shares are both unconstrained and given a common value in each share equation. However, the imposition of symmetry, for instance, would be rather easier with a uniform parameter on the lagged shares, as discussed below in Section 3.3.1. The treatment of these restrictions is rather unclear. Hall tests the least restricted model for both uniformity and significance in its dynamic process and, once again, rejects the imposition of all four of the above restrictions for any country. According to Hall, it seems unlikely that the absence of any dynamic modelling is responsible for the failure of the four restrictions implied by economic theory. However, the dynamic model employed by Hall is not derived theoretically and expectational terms are absent.

The preferred model varies by country: for the United States, France and Canada a static model cannot not be rejected, for Japan and the United Kingdom the unrestricted dynamic model is preferred, while for West Germany and Italy Hall suggests a uniform coefficient dynamic model. In no instance are all four own-price elasticities significant and of the expected sign. On average the results for the constrained static model indicate that the demand for coal and gas are elastic ($\eta_{CC} = -1.9$ and $\eta_{GG} = -1.4$) while the demand for petroleum products and electricity are inelastic ($\eta_{OO} = -0.8$ and $\eta_{EE} = -0.2$). The corresponding results for the non-homothetic model are coal ($-0.9$), gas ($-0.5$), petroleum products ($-0.5$) and electricity ($-0.5$). The cross-price elasticities vary from model to model and the only firm conclusion is that there is evidence that coal and gas are substitutes in the United Kingdom and France.

Hall concludes that the specification preferred, the static non-homothetic non-symmetric model allowing for the possibility of individual fuel-efficiency bias, indicates that for all countries (excepting possibly the United Kingdom and Canada) both sectoral energy volumes and fuel-efficiency bias have been significant – indeed, they may be more significant than individual fuel prices – as factors explaining individual fuel expenditure shares. Given these results, Hall states that 'more satisfactory results should be obtained from pooled time series/cross-section data and from engineering-based studies' and that the translog functional form is 'theoretically more appealing' than either the single-equation or simultaneous-equation multinominal conditional logit approach (see Fuss *et al.* 1977) or the single-equation approach (see Pindyck 1979b).

Hesse and Tarkka (1986) analyse the demand for capital, labour and energy in European manufacturing industry using the static translog form. They study two periods using annual observations from 1960 to 1972 and from 1973 to

1980, the first period being characterized by relatively stable energy prices while the second period experienced sharply rising energy prices. Time-series data for nine West European countries (Belgium, Finland, France, West Germany, Italy, the Netherlands, Norway, Sweden and the United Kingdom) are pooled and energy is divided into primary fuels (coal, gas, oil plus fuel oils) and electricity. Because of a lack of reliable data, Hesse and Tarkka are forced to assume that materials are weakly separable from other inputs. Thus a unit cost function can be written as follows: $C^* = C/Q = f[h(P_K, P_L, P_{E1}, P_F); P_M]$, where $h$ is a homothetic function of the four inputs explicitly modelled by Hesse and Tarkka.

In estimating the share equations, the data are pooled with country-specific intercepts included and Hicks-neutral technical change is rejected for both periods. When non-neutral technical change is allowed, all the first-order terms are significant and seven of the nine slope coefficients are significant for the first period and only five for the second. Concavity of the cost function is found at almost every point between 1973 and 1980 but there were several deviations from concavity between 1960 and 1972. In general, the industrial demand for a particular factor is inelastic with respect to changes in its own price and there is some tendency for elasticities to be rather lower in absolute value in the second period (see Table 3.1 for details). Although many of the cross-price elasticities are insignificant, the results do indicate the sensitivity of elasticity estimates to the time period chosen. However, Hesse and Tarkka do not seem to present any evidence of structural breaks between the two periods which would have added further empirical weight to their argument.

As noted, cross-country or cross-sectional studies are conventionally interpreted to produce long-run results. However, Hesse and Tarkka question 'how long' the long run really is – particularly as it relates to the period after 1973, which saw sharply rising oil prices and low output growth. They also question whether the results reflect long-run adjustments and whether the observed relationship between the factor inputs will continue once 'normal' levels of economic growth return.

Apostolakis (1987) analyses the role of energy in production functions for southern European economies and applies a static translog model to annual data from 1953 to 1984 from Greece, Italy, France, Spain and Portugal. Output is taken to be the sum of the gross value-added in the consumption and investment goods sectors and capital, labour and energy are inputs. Apostolakis estimates the system of share price equations by SUR but uses Cochrane–Orcutt and Hildreth–Lu corrections for autocorrelation. Further separability tests are possible since Apostolakis has data on two components of aggregate output. The separability tests show that only in the case of Portugal is separability rejected between the inputs and outputs; however, complete global separability is rejected for all countries. This implies that, first, gross value-added is not produced by just capital and labour, second that Cobb–Douglas production functions are inappropriate and third that capital and labour inputs are not separable from energy, which confirms the role of energy in a standard production function. The rejection of non-linear separability means that CES specifications are also inappropriate to the data set.

Energy is a substitute for capital and labour, the AES being close to 0.95 for all countries over the sample. Furthermore, the AES for labour and energy are also close to unity, while the elasticities for capital and energy vary from 0.4 in 1965 for Greece to 0.95 in 1953 for Italy. The own-price elasticities for energy vary from −3.72 for France in 1979 to +4.44 for Greece in 1972 (see Table 3.2). Out of the ninety estimates of own-price elasticities of substitution, fifteen are of unexpected sign. The majority relate to energy and capital expenditures in Greece and for capital in Italy in the initial half of the period. All input demands are inelastic, the own-price elasticities ranging from −0.11 for energy in 1984 in Spain to −0.80 for capital in 1953 in Italy (see Table 3.1). In general, there is a declining trend in the estimated elasticities over time.

Most of the studies cited above have concentrated on 'Western' economies; the following presents some evidence from Far Eastern economies on factor demands in manufacturing industry. Saicheua (1987) analyses input demand and substitution elasticities for five manufacturing industries in Thailand from 1974 to 1977. A static translog cost function is estimated with three inputs: capital, labour and energy. The price of energy is aggregated using a Divisia index and any technical progress is assumed to be Hicks-neutral. The five industries are food processing, textiles and apparel, metals and machinery, export-oriented and import-competing industries.

The results for the own-price elasticities show that the demand for capital is very inelastic, labour has close to unit elasticity, while energy own-price elasticities vary from −1.50 to −2.60. The AES and the cross-price elasticities of substitution show that both capital and energy as well as capital and labour are always substitutes. Labour-intensive industries tend to show energy–labour substitutability while the more capital-intensive industries exhibit energy–labour complementarity.

Siddayao et al. (1987) analyse energy and non-energy input demand elasticities for the food processing and textile industries in Bangladesh, the Philippines and Thailand. A static translog cost function with capital, labour, energy and material inputs is fitted to data from 1970 to 1980 for Bangladesh, 1970 to 1978 for the Philippines and 1974 to 1977 for Thailand. A time trend is included to account for technical progress and returns to scale are assumed to be constant. Data on materials are only available for Bangladesh. Three other industries are included for Thailand: metals and machinery, manufactured exports and import-competing products.

The results indicate that the price elasticities of demand for capital, labour and energy are negative and inelastic, and they compare reasonably with other studies done on similar data sets (see Williams and Laumas 1981). The AES for the Philippines indicate that capital, labour and energy are all substitutes.

For Thailand, the results indicate substitutability, apart from the more capital-intensive industries which, protected from international competition, exhibit labour–energy complementarity. The estimates for Bangladesh fail to reach significance, but reveal energy–capital and energy–labour complementarity in the textile industry. It is interesting that both AES and full elasticities of substitution (FES) are estimated (see Section 3.1.1). As noted, the FES are used to compare results when there are three or more inputs. All FES are positive, as expected from previous studies, but vary considerably from 0.03 for capital and labour in the textile industry of the Philippines to 2.65 for capital and energy in the same industry.

The dynamic translog model, outlined in Section 3.1.2 above, is applied by Pindyck and Rotemberg (1983) to the data set used by Berndt and Wood (1975) for American manufacturing. The translog restricted cost function has symmetry and homogeneity of degree one in prices imposed. Short-, intermediate- and long-run elasticities are computed – the short run being where both capital and labour are quasi-fixed, the intermediate run being when only capital is quasi-fixed, and the long run being when all factors are assumed to be fully variable.

Using three-stage least squares they simultaneously estimate the cost function, the energy-cost-share equation and the Euler equations for capital and labour. The instrument set is varied to assess robustness of the results. The adjustment costs for capital are much greater than those for labour, in line with intuition. All the own-price elasticities are negative. They note that their short-run value for energy ($-0.36$) is close to that of Berndt and Wood, while their long-run value ($-0.99$) is close to those of Griffin and Gregory, as well as Pindyck. This is consistent with the commonly held view that the Berndt and Wood elasticities are short run, while the last mentioned are long run. Pindyck and Rotemberg find that both capital and energy and capital and labour are long-run complements (Berndt and Wood also found long-run $E$–$K$ complementarity). In fact, they find very small adjustment costs of labour and results are similar if labour is treated as flexible. The results reported are very similar (see Table 3.1).

The dynamic translog model is also used by Lynk (1989) to study the industrial demand for energy in the United Kingdom from 1948 to 1981 using capital, labour and energy. A standard translog interfuel model is used to analyse the short-run and long-run demand elasticities for coal, gas, electricity and petroleum where capital is assumed to be fixed in the short run. Both partial and total elasticities are presented. He finds that coal, gas and petroleum have a negative but inelastic relationship with their own price and that all fuels are complements for each other apart from electricity and coal. As expected total elasticities are larger than the partial elasticities with the total own-price elasticity of gas and petroleum being greater than one, but the demand for electricity and coal are both found to be positive and price inelastic. The energy model shows that both the partial and total own-price elasticities for energy are negative and inelastic. Labour is found to be a substitute for energy and capital is found to be a complement for energy. Lynk concludes that his results 'closely approximate earlier studies', namely the total own-price of elasticity is similar to that of Pindyck (1979b) and Nordhaus (1977) although a different methodology is used.

### 3.2.2 Studies based on Cobb–Douglas specifications

In contrast to the translog models discussed above, Nordhaus (1977) analyses international energy demand using a Cobb–Douglas production function. Thus, he specifies a general production function for product $i$ as

$$Q_i = F^i(Q_{i1}, \ldots, Q_{in}, L_i, K_i, E_i, t) \tag{3.30}$$

where $Q_{ij}$ is the input of product $j$ into the production of $i$ and $L$, $K$, $E$ are familiar. Nordhaus takes a Taylor series expansion to (3.30) but disregards the second-order terms which figure prominently in the translog form. The energy demand functions which follow are particularly simple

$$E = a_0 + a_1 P + a_2 Q \tag{3.31}$$

and are estimated with a single lag in $Q$ or an Almon lag in $P$, where $E$ is per capita net energy consumption, $P$ is relative energy price and $Q$ is per capita real GNP.

Nordhaus uses data from seven countries for 1955–72: Belgium, France, West Germany, Italy, the Netherlands, the United Kingdom and the United States. Four sectors are analysed: the energy, transport, industrial and residential sectors. The demand for net energy is calculated using efficiency data for each fuel and it is assumed that all fuels are perfect substitutes within each sector.

Results are given for all possible levels of aggregation and disaggregation, for the long run and short run and for different lag structures. Aggregating across sectors, the long-run income elasticities $\eta_{EQ}$ vary from 0.26 (the United States) to 1.42 (West Germany) and the long-run price elasticities $\eta_{EE}$ from −1.94 (the United States) up to an implausible +1.45 (West Germany) when the countries are analysed separately. The transport sector has the largest average income elasticity of 1.68 and the domestic sector has the greatest absolute average price elasticity of −1.14. Use of a linear five-year lag on the energy price and country-specific intercepts produces a long-run price elasticity estimate of −0.66 and a long-run income elasticity estimate of 0.84. The results are not that sensitive to specification of the lag structure. In general, Nordhaus admits that individual country estimates are not robust, but this may be due to the short sample size of twenty-two years. When the data are pooled, the price and income elasticities are all of the expected sign, the long-run average price elasticity is −0.85 and the income elasticity is 0.79, both of which are plausible.

### 3.2.3  Studies based on constant elasticity of substitution specifications

Prywes (1986) uses the CES production function to estimate elasticities of substitution between capital, labour, energy and materials for American manufacturing over the period 1971–6. Two differing concepts of elasticities are used: the engineering elasticity, which measures 'the ease with which capital is substituted for energy holding the joint contribution to production of capital and energy constant' and the economic elasticity which measures 'the ease with which capital is substituted for energy holding only final output constant'.

The following separability assumptions are made: the sub-function $Q_{KE}$ is nested within $Q_{KEL}$ which is nested within the overall function. Thus, $F$, $Q_{KE}$ and $Q_{KEL}$ are defined as nested CES production functions:

$$Q = F\{Q_{KEL}[Q_{KE}(K, E), L], M\} \tag{3.32}$$

The function $Q_{KE}$ models the joint contribution of $K$ and $E$ to production but is only valid as a representation of production under certain separability conditions. Prywes considers this to be plausible as energy requirements are often technically built into capital, the argument echoing the earlier discussion of 'utilized capital' by Berndt and Wood. Total factor productivity change is Hicks-neutral within each sub-function, but for the overall nested CES production function it is non-neutral. The economic elasticities of substitution depend upon the engineering elasticities and the input shares.

Prywes uses data for twenty two-digit American manufacturing sectors and CES production functions are estimated separately for each industry. As the data only cover the period 1971–6, and the technical energy requirements per unit of output had insufficient time to adjust to the first oil crisis, Prywes suggests that the data might produce short-run elasticities. The majority of the capital/energy engineering elasticities of substitution between $K$ and $E$ are positive but below 0.5 and those between $Q_{KE}$ and $L$ are all positive and somewhat larger numerically. The few negative engineering elasticities are at variance with theory. However, the economic elasticities for capital and energy are negative for sixteen out of the twenty sectors indicating complementarity, and the remaining four elasticities are all below 0.33. Thus, although $E$ and $K$ were slight engineering substitutes over the period 1971–6, they were economic complements.

### 3.2.4  Studies based on other specifications

Many studies of energy demand may be termed essentially *ad hoc* since they are not based on an explicit model of economic optimization. Although many of these studies may be criticized on the grounds of simplicity, the use of alternative methodologies – such as error correction mechanisms – may shed light on issues ignored in the largely static literature surveyed in sections 3.2.1–3.2.3.

The energy–output relationship in Germany, Belgium/Luxembourg, France, Italy, Denmark, the Netherlands and the United Kingdom over the period 1955–70 is studied in Kouris (1976). The basic static model is as follows:

$$E = \beta_0 \, Y^{\beta 1} \, P^{\beta 2} \, T^{\beta 3} \tag{3.33}$$

where $E$ is primary energy consumed, $Y$ is income (GDP), $P$ is an energy price index and $T$ is average annual temperature.

The energy–GDP elasticity estimates vary from 0.32 in the United Kingdom up to 1.79 in Italy, while the price elasticity of energy has a positive sign in four countries and is only of the expected sign and significant in Denmark, with a value of $-0.44$. Although this may be due to the slight price variation in the data, the equations are simplistic and tend to suffer serial correlation. The 'temperature elasticity' is on average about $-0.35$ but notably higher in Italy at $-0.70$, which is intuitively appealing.

Re-estimation with a pooled data set with country-specific intercepts produces an income elasticity of 0.84, a price elasticity of $-0.77$ and a temperature elasticity of $-0.25$. The changes in the elasticity estimates are not consistent with the conventional argument that cross-section studies produce long-run results since increases occur in the price elasticity but not in the income elasticity. Kouris also finds evidence of instability by calculating the elasticities in eleven six-year overlapping intervals. The income elasticity falls from 1955–60 to 1957–62 and subsequently rises, while the price elasticity rises in magnitude from 1955–60 to 1958–63, declines in magnitude until 1962–7, and then achieves stability. Although Kouris believes that these variations over time reflect structural phenomena (changes in the efficiency of capital, labour/capital substitution, growth of sectors, industrial mix, electricity share and energy-saving campaigns), they probably reflect omitted dynamics. The significance of this instability is further considered in Section 3.3.1 below.

Kouris also estimates a two-equation model in which GDP is endogenous: $E = f(Y, P, T)$ and $Y = g(E, L, t)$, where $L$ is the proportion of the labour force in employment and $t$ is a time trend assumed to account for disembodied Hicksian technological progress. Two-stage least squares estimation yields $\ln E = 1.28 \ln Y - 0.31 \ln P - 0.29 \ln T + \text{constants}$, so the differences compared with the one-equation model are minimal. Kouris uses a variety of such models to forecast energy consumption over the period 1971–4 and concludes that no fundamental change in the energy market has occurred due to the oil crisis and all that is observed is a movement along the demand curve, not a shift of the demand curve. However, this is at variance with Hesse and Tarkka (1986) and the evidence presented in Section 3.3.1.

Energy consumption and economic activity in a group of industrialized countries is analysed in Beenstock and Willcocks (1981) using error correction models and treating all countries as a crude aggregate. The consumption of energy by firms is dependent upon the prices of energy, labour and capital together with the level of output, but the prices of labour and capital are assumed away for the empirical work. Household demand depends upon the price of energy, income levels and taxes, which are assumed to be constant. In effect, Beenstock and Willcocks derive a simple long-run energy demand equation:

$$\ln E = a_1 + b_1 \ln P_E + d_1 \ln Y + e_1 t \tag{3.34}$$

where $b_1$ is the reduced form price elasticity, $d_1$ is the income elasticity and $e_1$ is the time trend parameter. The price of imported oil $(P)$ is used as a proxy for the price of energy. The long-run demand equation can then be nested within an error correction mechanism:

$$\Delta \ln E_t = \alpha_0 + \alpha_1 \Delta \ln P_t + \alpha_2 \Delta \ln Q_t - \alpha_3 \ln(E/Q)_{t-1} + \alpha_4 \ln Q_{t-1}$$
$$+ \alpha_5 \ln P_{t-1} \tag{3.35}$$

which has the familiar steady-state solution discussed above. The generalized version of (3.35) includes lags of up to three years in all first differenced variables but also includes contemporaneous first differences, which raises questions over the exogeneity of the regressors used by Beenstock and Willcocks.

Results are given for the collective of what the United Nations defines as 'developed market economies' – approximately the OECD countries. After 'testing down' from the unrestricted model, the long-run income elasticity estimate is 1.78 with a price elasticity estimate of $-0.06$, the time trend coefficient being $-0.04$. For the commercial sector, the equivalent estimates are 1.55, $-0.03$ and 0.03 respectively. The price elasticity estimate is below that found in other studies, but the data are aggregated across countries in a rather heroic fashion and the energy price proxy is crude. Reservations remain over the validity of this type of modelling and are discussed in Section 3.4 below. Nevertheless, the study represents an early example of attempts to apply this technique to energy economics and is a unique application of the approach to international data.

The results, however, are criticized in Kouris (1983), chiefly because of strong evidence of multicollinearity between the time trend variable and the GDP variable (the correlation coefficient was close to 0.99). Indeed, when the time trend variable is absent, the income elasticity estimate is close to 0.9. Kouris also criticizes the proxy for the price of energy and states that 'the correct way of estimating elasticities is at the country level and for each energy demand sector separately'. No doubt Griffin and Gregory, as well as others, would disagree with this view.

Kouris sets up an alternative logarithmic model with a Koyck lag scheme where energy consumption is a function of the price of energy and GDP. Data on the OECD as a whole are used in thirteen-year overlapping periods from

1961 to 1981 and, not surprisingly, the results vary substantially. Although the income elasticity varies slightly from 0.96 to 1.12, long-run price elasticity estimates range from $-0.26$ to $-0.84$, generally increasing in magnitude between 1964–76 and 1969–81. In a reply to Kouris's criticism, Beenstock and Willcocks (1983) assert that Kouris has estimated short-term elasticities which are consistent with their original results. However, neither study is particularly sound in terms of methodology or data set analysed.

Energy demand elasticities in seven OECD countries (Canada, West Germany, France, Italy, Japan, the United States and the United Kingdom) from 1960 to 1982 are analysed in Prosser (1985). He also uses *ad hoc* logarithmic models to express final energy demand as a function of real GDP and average energy price and employs differing lag structures:

$$\ln E = a_0 + a_1 \ln \text{GDP} + b_0 \ln P_t + b_1 \ln P_{t-1} + b_2 \ln P_{t-2} + \cdots$$

$$+ b_m \ln P_{t-m} \tag{3.36}$$

Both Koyck and Almon lag schemes are employed and the derived long-run price elasticity is found to be insensitive to dynamic specification change ($-0.4$ to $-0.41$). The income elasticities are approximately unity (see Table 3.1).

Following Kouris, Prosser also considers the stability of these estimates by using seven overlapping twelve-year periods and finds a trend in both the price and income elasticities. The price elasticity declined until 1970 as the price of energy fell, whilst income elasticities also declined over the period as economies became less energy intensive, an assertion which Chow tests confirm. The estimates show that some 80–90 per cent of the price effect takes place in the year of the price change and that the process is virtually complete within two years. He concludes that consumers respond to price changes relatively quickly, although there appears to be a slow conservation effect that is not necessarily driven by price changes. Moreover, he suggests that by 1982 the trend of falling income and price elasticities may have come to an end. However, the present study presents some rather different findings for individual fuel elasticities in Section 3.3.1. Given our results, it is difficult to believe that energy cross-section elasticities remained constant over the 1980s.

A cross-country demand system is used in Fiebig *et al.* (1987) to estimate income and own-price elasticities of demand for energy. They estimate a complete system of demand equations for broad groups of consumer goods which include energy, and use comparable price and income data for a wide range of thirty countries.[1] Eleven commodities are analysed, comprising food, beverages and tobacco, clothing and footwear, gross rent, energy, household furnishing and operations, medical care, transport and communications, recreation, education and other. They specify a linear relationship between the budget share $w_{ic}$ for good $i$ and the logarithm of income, $\log Q_c$, in country

$c$ (i.e. $w_{ic} = a_i + b_i \log Q_c$). Cross-country price variation is incorporated by assuming that the function holds at the geometric mean of prices and by including a substitution term. The model thus takes the form

$$y_{ic} = a_i + b_i \log Q_c + \sum_j \pi_{ij} \log\left(\frac{p_{jc}}{p_j^*}\right) + \varepsilon_{ic} \tag{3.37}$$

where

$$y_{ic} = w_{ic}\left[1 - \log\left(\frac{p_{ic}}{p_i^*}\right) + \sum_j w_{jc} \log\left(\frac{p_{jc}}{p_j^*}\right)\right] \tag{3.38}$$

and where $p_{ic}$ is the price of the $i$th commodity in country $c$ and $p_i^*$ is the geometric mean price of the $i$th commodity. As such, equation (3.37) incorporates a country-specific price deviation from the mean international change in prices. The constraints associated with Slutsky symmetry and homogeneity are also linear; thus $\pi_{ij} = \pi_{ji}$ and $\sum_j \pi_{ij} = 0$. As the commodities represent broad aggregates, it is assumed that consumers' preferences can be represented by a utility function that is additive in these aggregates. Thus the final model is as follows:

$$y_{ic} = a_i + b_i q_c + H(w_{ic} + b_i)\left[x_{ic} - \sum_j (w_{jc} + b_j)x_{jc}\right] + \varepsilon_{ic} \tag{3.39}$$

where $q_c = \log Q_c$ and $x_{ic} = \log(p_{ic}/p_i^*) - \log(p_{nc}/p_n^*)$. The $n$th equation is deleted and so $2(n-1)$ parameters $a_i$, $b_i$, the $\pi_{ij}$ and $H$ are estimated.

The income and price elasticities are calculated at the geometric means using maximum likelihood estimates. The estimated income elasticities are between 1.2 and 1.3 in the richer countries rising to 1.64 for India and the own-price elasticities vary over countries and methodologies from $-0.60$ to $-0.88$, with the majority being close to $-0.7$. Fiebig et al. separately consider developing countries whose per capita income is between 3 and 6 per cent of the US level to obtain an income elasticity of around 2 and own-price elasticities of around $-1$.

The energy–GDP relationship is considered in Nachane et al. (1988) who analyse the energy–GDP relationship in sixteen countries[2] over the period 1950–85. Cointegration techniques are applied to examine whether long-run relationships exist between the per capita energy consumption (PCEC) of a country and per capita gross domestic product (PCGDP). (The cointegration approach has been briefly outlined in Section 3.1.3.) However, they are chiefly concerned with determining the direction of causality between PCEC and PCGDP. In sixteen out of a total sample of twenty-five countries, Nachane et al. conclude that PCEC cointegrates with PCGDP so that a long-run energy–GDP relationship exists. If the more appropriate critical values obtained in Engle and Yoo (1987) and Phillips and Ouliaris (1990) are used in place of the values in Fuller (1976), only five countries appear to cointegrate.

Welsch (1989) examines the unbiasedness and efficiency of various energy elasticity estimates for eight industrialized countries (the United States, Germany, Japan, France, the United Kingdom, Italy, the Netherlands and Canada) using annual data from 1970 to 1984. He estimates forty different types of model which are evaluated by applying Ramsey's reset test for non-linearity of functional form and Box–Jenkins time-series techniques to assess potential dynamic inadequacies of these specifications which would lead to inefficient estimation. The basic framework includes various lag structures in income, energy price and the price of other goods but Welsch attempts to examine the short- and long-run effects on energy consumption by considering both the trend and cyclical components of income. In effect, Welsch argues that the long-run income elasticity is measured with respect to the trend component. The data are considered on both a single country and a pooled basis.

In order to be 'acceptable' to Welsch, the estimates have to be consistent with economic theory in that models which produce positive own-price elasticities or negative cross-price elasticities are rejected. (Consider the estimates by Pindyck and Turnovsky et al. in Table 3.3.) In addition, the regressions have to pass the reset test and Lagrange multiplier tests for autocorrelation and have to represent parsimonious simplifications of a more general specification with unrestricted dynamics and time trends included. Although the individual country results vary widely, simple models with a single lagged dependent variable with income split into the two components are accepted for all countries except Canada and the United Kingdom. However, there does not seem to be any clear model applicable to all countries, e.g. time trends are only appropriate for some countries.

When the data are pooled, only a double logarithmic form with a single lagged dependent variable, and without the assumption of homogeneity of degree zero in prices, is accepted. The average short-term and long-term price elasticities for the pooled sample are $-0.13$ and $-0.34$, while the equivalent income elasticities are 0.24 and 0.63 respectively. The average short-term price elasticities (for each country, averaged across models) vary from $-0.10$ (the United Kingdom) to $-0.73$ (Italy), and in the long term from $-0.11$ (the United Kingdom) to $-1.09$ (Canada); short-term income elasticities vary from 0.03 (the United States) to 1.86 (Germany), and in the long term from 0.09 (the United States) to 5.55 (France). In general, the elasticity estimates tend to fall when time trends are incorporated to proxy technical progress and are of reasonable magnitude except for the income elasticity in the United States and France. The wide variation in results may be due to differing specifications between countries. Welsch concludes that attempts 'to obtain uniform consistent and efficient elasticity estimates for all countries is in itself not compatible with the data and that energy demand elasticities should be modelled in a country-by-country framework' (Welsch 1989: 291). This observation would reflect the importance attached to structural factors.

Patry *et al.* (1990) analyse energy demand in the residential, industrial and transport sectors of seven OECD countries (Canada, France, Germany, Italy, Japan, the United Kingdom and the United States) and set out to explain the relative importance of factors contributing to the observed fall in energy consumption in these countries over the period 1960–87. The usual two-stage approach is applied to data on the residential and industrial sectors, and the demands for four fuels – oil, gas, electricity and coal – are considered in the lower stage. The real price of energy is defined as a Divisia price index of all energy fuel prices normalized by the GDP deflator. However, energy demand in the transport sector is taken to comprise solely the demand for oil. The demands of the three sectors are estimated together for each country by SUR. They use a multinominal logit specification (see Fuss *et al.* 1977: 158), which is more flexible than a static translog model in the sense that lags can be introduced and easily interpreted, but it has certain drawbacks such as the fact that all cross-price elasticities with respect to one fuel have to be equal.

The model assumes that decision-makers have value functions such as $V_i = I(z_i) + u(z_i)$ where $z_i$ represents characteristics of fuel $i$ and $u(z_i)$ are random. The probability that fuel $j$ will be adopted is given by $\exp[I(z_i)]/\sum_j \exp[I(z_j)]$ where they specify $I(\cdot)$ as a log-linear function of fuel prices, lagged fuel shares, income and other variables. In the upper stage, all but one of the estimated parameters which are statistically significant at the 5 per cent level are of the expected sign and twenty-four out of thirty-five coefficients for the residential sector, twenty-two out of thirty-five coefficients for the industrial sector, and sixteen out of twenty-eight coefficients for the transport sector are significant. A majority of the price coefficients are significant except for the transport sector, for which elasticity estimates are low. Long-run price elasticities of total energy demand vary from $-0.22$ in Japan to $-0.91$ in the United Kingdom for the industrial sector; from $-0.09$ in the United Kingdom to $-1.27$ in Germany for the residential sector; and from $-0.01$ in Japan to $-0.40$ in Italy for the transport sector. Overall, the long-run demand for energy seems to be price inelastic except in the United States and Germany. Income elasticities also vary widely and tend to be lowest for the residential sector and higher as well as more variable for transport. The estimates for the residential sector in Germany and industry in Japan have unexpected negative signs.

Interfuel substitution over the period primarily reflects the slow decrease in the market share of oil and the corresponding increase in the market share of electricity. Correspondingly, Patry *et al.* find that the cross-price elasticity of demand for electricity with respect to the price of oil is substantial for many countries in both the industrial and residential sectors. In order to attempt to account for the impact of conservation and technological change after the oil shocks, Patry *et al.* include a truncated time dummy variable which equals unity only for 1974–80. 'Conservation' is estimated to have reduced the level of sectoral energy demand by an annual average of between 2 and 3 per cent at constant price and income levels, and to have chiefly affected the market share of oil. The inclusion of the trend approximately reduced the estimated price elasticities by approximately half when the trend was significant.

Boone *et al.* (1992) use vector autoregressions (VARs) to study the demand for fossil fuels in nine OECD countries from 1978 to 1989, employing quarterly data. They model fossil fuel demand in individual countries as a function of the energy price relative to the GDP deflator, real GDP and time. They also use the Johansen procedure to determine the time-series properties of the variables. They find that fuel consumption and GDP are both I(1). However, the relative prices of fuels are generally 'very close to the frontier between I(1) and I(2)' and they make the simplifying assumption that they are all I(1). The Johansen procedure is employed with varying lag lengths to determine the number of cointegrating vectors that exist within the VAR system. Three specifications of the VAR are used: first without a constant (a random walk), second with a restricted constant (a random walk with drift) and third as an unrestricted constant (a deterministic trend). In order to assess the impact of the time trend variable the eigenvector of interest is regressed on time, which produces a negatively signed time trend. They find that the results 'vary greatly between countries'. When there is more than one cointegrating vector and they display a negative relationship between consumption and price, the most significnt vector is used within an error correction mechanism (ECM). If they do not display the same properties, they are both utilized and their significance is considered within the ECM. The results for the 'best' cointegrating relationship varies across countries. Some include an unrestricted constant, some a restricted constant and, in the case of Italy, no constant. The lag length varies from two (Italy) to six (Japan). Only elasticities with the 'expected results' are presented. For Canada, Japan and the Netherlands the most significant cointegrating vector produces a positively signed price coefficient. The relative price elasticity is on average −0.18 and for the time trend elasticity the value is −0.01.

The estimated long-run elasticities of fossil fuel consumption with respect to relative prices and the time trend from an ECM are very similar to the results reported from the VAR above. They vary across countries and it is in this regard that Boone *et al.* relate their results to stabilizing fossil fuel consumption. Assuming that the price and time elasticities remain constant, they estimate the growth rate in the price of fossil fuels necessary to stabilize fossil fuel consumption under different GDP growth rates. The results vary across countries, and if GDP grew at 2 per cent per annum relative fossil fuel prices would have to rise from between 0.48 per cent (Belgium) to 10.14 per cent (the United States) in order to stabilize consumption.

### 3.2.5 Summary of estimates of energy elasticities

It is difficult to uncover evidence of any sort of consensus in the direction and magnitude of the various energy elasticities in the literature discussed above. Moreover, differences in the scope of the analyses and the methodologies applied would suggest that caution is required when comparing estimates from different studies. Nonetheless, some of the more salient features of the estimates with respect to the implications for policies to address global warming can be discussed. In aggregate terms, the average $\eta_{EQ}$ varies roughly around unity and $\eta_{EE}$ around $-0.5$. In addition, $\eta_{EL}$ and $\eta_{EM}$ are both generally positive and approximately $+0.5$. However, wide variations exist – e.g. the estimates of $\sigma_{EE}$ vary from $+4.44$ to $-32.25$. There are also notable differences in the estimates of $\eta_{EK}$, ruling out neither substitutability nor complementarity between the two factors.

The results for individual fuels show that coal, oil and gas have partial own-price elasticities of approximately $-1.0$, while electricity has an elasticity of somewhere between $+0.10$ and $-0.52$. Equivalent estimates from VAR systems are $\eta_{CC} = -0.82$, $\eta_{OO} = -0.43$, $\eta_{GG} = -0.92$ and $\eta_{EE} = -0.26$. The partial cross-price elasticities for fuels are generally inelastic and positive, but exceptions exist where negative values indicate complementarity between fuels. According to Hall (1986) this would imply that the model is misspecified.

A variety of reasons have been advanced to explain the differences in results between studies. For instance, the interpretation of estimated elasticities is problematic – are they short-run or long-run estimates? Conventionally, pure time-series studies such as Berndt and Wood (1975) are thought to produce short-run elasticities, and pooled inter-country or cross-section studies such as Griffin and Gregory (1976), long-run estimates. This might explain why Berndt and Wood find $E/K$ complementarity, yet Griffin and Gregory $E/K$ substitutability. Indeed, these two sets of results have been the basis upon which many authors attempt to provide explanations for the conflicting estimates. Pooled inter-country or cross-section data sets tend to display much greater variation in relative factor prices than do pure time series. This is particularly true prior to 1973. Furthermore, since such cross-section variations in structural characteristics may have existed for substantial periods of time, a long-run equilibrium may be reflected in inter-country or cross-section studies. The variation in estimated elasticities is illustrated in Griffin (1981a), who reports the ratio of the highest to the lowest relative price for the Berndt and Wood (1975) and the Griffin and Gregory (1976) data sets:

| Relative price | Berndt and Wood | Griffin and Gregory |
|---|---|---|
| $P_K/P_E$ | 1.68 | 4.12 |
| $P_L/P_E$ | 2.03 | 9.42 |
| $P_K/P_L$ | 2.30 | 7.24 |

Many micro-units will be in a state of disequilibrium at any one point in time but when a cross-section is taken these disequilibrium states may tend to average out and the typically greater cross-section slope estimates can be interpreted as long-run coefficients. However, this argument cannot be upheld in periods of extreme flux such as post-1973, 1979 or 1986 for the energy market. In these situations, all micro-units, be they firms, households, regions or countries, simultaneously experience similar rapid movements in relative prices. Cross-section studies may therefore produce results which are neither short-run nor long-run estimates; rather they are biased due to omitted (dynamic) factors. This would seem to explain the variation in (primarily) cross-section estimates in Section 3.3.1 below.

In addition, most studies which pool short-run time-series data from a number of countries include country-specific first-order terms but few test the assumption of common coefficients on relative prices since the sample sizes are usually insufficient. According to Section 3.3.1 below, such pooling is statistically invalid yet is essential if estimation of standard translog systems is to exploit relative price variation between countries.

A second explanation for divergent results is the treatment of the omitted factor, intermediate materials. However, when materials are excluded they are assumed to be separable from $K$, $L$ and $E$, an assumption which is often necessitated by data limitations and which may affect estimates of substitutability between other factors. The case for omitting materials rests on the relationship between $M$ and the other factors $K$, $L$ and $E$ (see the discussion of Berndt and Wood in Section 3.1.1). As noted earlier in the text, Berndt and Wood (1979) show that energy and capital can be gross substitutes in a production sub-function, but net complements in the aggregate production function. The evidence in the literature is inconclusive. Berndt and Wood (1975) find $E/K$ complementarity but others such as Özatalay et al. (1979), Turnovsky et al. (1982) and Pindyck and Rotemberg (1983) find substitutability when including materials. Both Prywes (1986) and Field and Grebenstein (1980) find that energy and capital display strong signs of complementarity, although materials are not included as an explicit factor in either study.

Berndt and Wood (1979) state that explicit $KLE$ studies only produce gross elasticities $\eta^*_{ij}$ (see Section 3.1.1). They show that the net elasticity $\eta_{EK}$ depends upon the gross elasticity $\eta^*_{EK}$, the cost share of capital in the $KLE$ aggregate $A$ $(S_{KA})$ and the own-price elasticity of the aggregate $A$ $(\eta_{AA})$ in the aggregate function as

$$\eta_{EK} = \eta^*_{EK} + S_{KA}\eta_{AA} \tag{3.40}$$

Therefore it is clear that the gross price elasticity will tend to overstate the substitutability between $E$ and $K$ since $\eta_{AA}$ is negative. Griffin (1981a) applies equation (3.40) to the Griffin and Gregory (1976) data and concludes that 'the omission of $M$ is not a sufficient explanation, and probably not even a major explanation for the disparity of findings' (Griffin 1981a: 1100).

A third reason put forth to reconcile the diverse results is the treatment and definition of capital. As mentioned in Section 3.2.1, Field and Grebenstein (1980) distinguish between two types of capital: working capital and physical capital. Working capital is commonly excluded from the 'capital' variable despite it being difficult to separate the production and sales/financial activities of a firm. However, the distinction is important since they find that energy and physical capital tend to be complements, and energy and working capital are substitutes. However, some debate over the precise definition of working capital exists. Griffin (1981b) considers results from Kopp and Smith (1978) who disaggregate capital into physical and working components. They construct an index of working capital from cash balances, government securities, 'accounts receivable' and inventories. This is in contrast to Field and Grebenstein, who define working capital as a residual from value-added. Not surprisingly, Kopp and Smith find contrasting results to those of Field and Grebenstein: energy and working capital complementarity and substitutability between energy and physical capital. None of these definitions is without fault, as pointed out in Griffin (1981b).

Similar difficulties over data measurement are discussed in Wood and Hirsch (1981) who believe that the incompatibility between the results in Berndt and Wood (1975) and Griffin and Gregory (1976) is attributable to differences in the measurement of capital and labour expenditure. Unlike Berndt and Wood, Griffin and Gregory do not account for taxes in the price of capital; Griffin and Gregory measure capital service expenditure as value-added minus the wage bill, while Berndt and Wood calculate independent measures of capital to measure the capital service expenditure. Wood and Hirsch re-estimate the capital service expenditures using the Griffin and Gregory procedure, together with the Berndt and Wood wage bill, and find that the revised Berndt and Wood $S_K$ has doubled, $S_L$ has fallen by just under 20 per cent and the $S_E$ has fallen by just over 20 per cent compared with the original Berndt and Wood (1975) shares. They find significant substitutability between all inputs. In addition, Wood and Hirsch reconstruct Griffin and Gregory's capital and labour shares for the United States using the sources given in Griffin and Gregory's data appendix and find that the results are comparable with the revised Berndt and Wood results.

Another important measurement problem occurs in the pricing of energy. Taylor (1977) considers the problem of decreasing block pricing in the residential demand for electricity. Should studies use marginal or average price? Is it valid to aggregate over consumers to obtain an aggregate price when the marginal block varies? The problem is confounded as international energy price data sources do not always state their precise definitions and many authors do not accurately report sources or definitions.

The discussion above is primarily concerned with definitions of variables and the interpretation of the elasticities. However, results are also sensitive to the estimated model and functional form chosen. For instance, Fuss and Waverman (1975) obtain an estimated $\sigma_{KE}$ of 0.42 using a translog cost function, but when a generalized Leontief function is used they find $\sigma_{KE} = -11.91$ using identical Canadian data. Furthermore, the treatment of technical change typically revolves around the specification of the time trend variable, yet Ingham and Ulph (1990) point out that technical change is itself endogenous.

The clear majority of theoretically based studies of the international demand for energy have used static models which cannot incorporate the evolution of quasi-fixed factors over time, as considered in Pindyck and Rotemberg (1983) and Watkins (1991). The results may be sensitive to the assumption of the quasi-fixity of factors. For instance, when Pindyck and Rotemberg specify capital and labour as quasi-fixed, they estimate $\eta_{EK}$ at 0.47 in the short run and $-1.34$ in the long run, which is at variance with the convention that capital is a complement to energy in the short run and a substitute in the long run. The equivalence between simple (single-equation) dynamic models of energy, factor prices and output and so-called 'third generation' dynamic models is investigated in Watkins (1991). In general, results of the two classes of model are only equivalent under certain restrictive assumptions – in effect, the lagged energy terms summarize the omitted theoretical dynamics. Dynamic error correction models can also be used to obtain long-run results – see Hunt and Lynk (1992) who employ the cointegration approach. (This approach is applied to international data in Section 3.3.2 below.) Investigation of the time-series properties of the data is largely absent in most of the work on international energy elasticities and some evidence is presented in Section 3.3 below. However, simple applications of error correction models which ignore the quasi-fixity of factors will inevitably, despite econometric rigour, suffer the problems of interpretation raised in Watkins.

In conclusion, a majority of the studies suggest that labour and materials are substitutes for energy but there is still no clear-cut evidence regarding the substitutability of capital and energy. This may follow from the nature of capital itself. Although capital and energy are certainly technically complementary in that capital is energy-using, capital equipment may also be energy-saving. Future research must therefore be concerned with the provision and utilization of data at a more disaggregated level in terms of capital–energy relations. This point is reinforced by Solow (1987), who uses a general equilibrium approach to analyse $E/K$ complementarity. He shows that even when no technical substitution is possible, aggregate data can show substitution or complementarity among the inputs solely as a result of changes in the composition of final output. Assume factor prices are exogenous and firms use fixed-coefficient production technologies. Two consumption goods exist, one of which is energy intensive. Both are normal goods and partial substitutes in consumption. Were the relative price of energy to increase, consumers would substitute away from the energy-intensive good. If aggregate data were used, the econometric results would imply that factor substitution had occurred, yet in a sense this is an illusion. Technologies are fixed-coefficient – the apparent factor substitution solely reflects compositional effects in final output.

## 3.3  FURTHER ESTIMATES OF ENERGY ELASTICITIES

This section briefly presents details of exploratory analysis of data from fifteen countries over thirty years from 1960 to 1989 on the demand for energy in the industrial sector.[3] The data sources are detailed in Appendix 3A. Given the relative importance of elasticities for individual fuels and interfuel substitutability for the issue of global warming, relatively more attention is paid to lower-stage optimization than has been the case in most previous studies. Most of the conclusions from the time-series analyses, however, must be qualified by the limited sample available.

### 3.3.1  Evidence on the demand for individual fuels

Given the discussion of cointegration and stationarity in Section 3.1.3, the time-series properties of the balances of the individual fuels coal, oil, gas and electricity are presented in Table 3.4. The series are classified as level stationary, difference stationary or trend stationary following the procedure

*Table 3.4* Types of stationarity, fuel balances

| Country | Coal | Oil | Gas | Electricity | Total balance |
|---------|------|-----|-----|-------------|---------------|
| Austria | LS | DS | DS | DS | DS |
| Belgium | DS | DS | DS | DS | DS |
| Canada | DS | DS | DS | TS, DS | DS |
| Denmark | DS | DS | DS | DS | DS |
| France | DS | DS | DS[a] | DS | DS |
| Germany | DS | LS | DS | DS | DS |
| Greece | DS | LS | DS | LS[a] | LS |
| Italy | DS | LS | DS | LS | LS |
| Japan | DS | LS | LS | TS | LS |
| Netherlands | DS | LS | LS | LS | DS |
| Norway | DS | LS | DS[a] | LS | LS |
| Spain | DS | LS | DS | LS | LS |
| Sweden | LS | DS | DS | LS | DS |
| United Kingdom | DS | TS, DS | DS | LS | DS |
| United States | DS | DS | DS | LS | DS |

*Notes*: LS, level stationary; TS, trend stationary; DS, first difference stationary; 2DS, second difference stationary.
[a]Classification is somewhat ambiguous.

*Table 3.5* Types of stationarity, fuel prices

| Country | Coal | Diesel | Gas | Electricity | HFO |
|---|---|---|---|---|---|
| Austria | DS | DS | DS | DS | DS |
| Belgium | DS | DS | DS | DS | DS |
| Canada | DS | DS | DS | DS | DS |
| Denmark | DS | DS | DS | DS | DS |
| France | DS | DS | DS | DS | DS |
| Germany | DS | DS | DS | DS | DS |
| Greece | DS | DS | DS | 2DS | DS |
| Italy | DS | DS | DS | DS | DS |
| Japan | DS | DS | DS | DS | DS |
| Netherlands | DS | DS | DS | DS | DS |
| Norway | DS | DS | DS[a] | DS | DS |
| Spain | TS, DS | DS | DS | DS | DS |
| Sweden | DS | DS | DS[a] | DS | DS |
| United Kingdom | DS | DS | DS | DS | DS |
| United States | DS | DS | 2DS | DS | DS |

*Notes*: TS, trend stationary; DS, first difference stationary; 2DS, second difference stationary; HFO, heavy fuel oil.
[a]Interpolated from German and Danish data; see Appendix 3A.

*Table 3.6* Types of stationarity, fuel expenditure shares

| Country | Coal | Oil | Gas | Electricity |
|---|---|---|---|---|
| Austria | DS | DS | DS | DS |
| Belgium | DS | DS | DS | DS |
| Canada | DS | DS | DS | DS |
| Denmark | DS | DS | DS | TS, DS |
| France | LS | DS | DS | DS |
| Germany | LS | DS | DS | DS |
| Greece | LS | DS | DS | DS |
| Italy | DS | DS | DS | DS |
| Japan | LS | DS | DS | DS |
| Netherlands | DS | LS | DS | DS |
| Norway | DS | DS | LS[a] | DS |
| Spain | DS | DS | DS | DS |
| Sweden | DS | DS | DS[a] | DS |
| United Kingdom | LS | DS | DS | DS |
| United States | DS | DS | DS | DS |

*Notes*: LS, level stationary; DS, first difference stationary.
[a]Interpolated from German and Danish data; see Appendix 3A.

*Table 3.7* Lower-stage fuel-expenditure-share equations, long-run own-price
elasticities from five specifications: coal

| | 1 | 2 | 3 | $4_2$ | $4_3$ | DW3 | DF4 | $J4_2$ | $J4_3$ |
|---|---|---|---|---|---|---|---|---|---|
| Austria | −0.68 | −0.66 | −0.40 | −13.19 | −1.64 | 0.27 | −4.11 | 3 | 2 |
| Belgium | −0.68 | −0.66 | −0.22 | −0.97 | −0.39 | 0.27 | −3.21 | 1 | 2 |
| Canada | −0.66 | −0.62 | −0.23 | −1.86 | −0.72 | 0.32 | −3.68 | 1 | 2 |
| Denmark | −0.63 | −0.58 | −0.34 | +17.96 | +10.46 | 0.75 | −3.65 | 1 | 1 |
| France | −0.69 | −0.66 | +0.01 | [a] | −3.80 | 0.12 | −2.13[b] | 0 | 2 |
| Germany | −0.68 | −0.66 | −0.77 | −1.76 | −1.02 | 0.18 | −3.25 | 2 | 4 |
| Greece | −0.58 | −0.51 | −0.44 | −1.22 | −1.02 | 1.15 | −3.22 | 2 | 2 |
| Italy | −0.59 | −0.53 | +0.19 | −0.69 | −0.71 | 0.21 | −4.83 | 2 | 2 |
| Japan | −0.65 | −0.60 | −0.42 | −1.36 | −0.82 | 0.28 | −3.37[b] | 1 | 2 |
| Netherlands | −0.65 | −0.60 | −0.46 | −0.66 | +0.21 | 0.48 | −3.14 | 1 | 5 |
| Norway | −0.45 | −0.35 | +0.08 | −0.19 | −0.18 | 1.26 | −4.83 | 4 | 2 |
| Spain | −0.69 | −0.66 | −0.13 | −1.78 | −2.01 | 0.28 | −5.27 | 1 | 2 |
| Sweden | −0.36 | −0.25 | +0.27 | −1.38 | −9.68 | 0.34 | −5.57[b] | 2 | 2 |
| United Kingdom | −0.69 | −0.66 | +0.05 | −0.44 | +1.50 | 0.47 | −2.24[b] | 2 | 3 |
| United States | −0.65 | −0.61 | −0.14 | −0.37 | −0.76 | 1.65 | −5.30 | 2 | 4 |

*Notes*: Sample period 1960–89; elasticities evaluated at the sample means.
Model 1: translog model, uniform price coefficients, pooled data.
Model 2: translog model, uniform price coefficients, symmetry imposed, pooled data.
Model 3: translog model, symmetry imposed, non-pooled data.
Model 4: single translog fuel-share equation estimated as a VAR system where the number
of vectors utilized is that in column J4. Models estimated separately for each country. The
subscripts 2 and 3 refer to the number of lags incorporated.
DW3: Durbin–Watson statistic for single equation in model 3 system.
DF4: Dickey–Fuller statistic for static fuel-share equation equivalent to model 4.
J4: number of cointegrating vectors identified by the Johansen maximum likelihood
procedure used to estimate model 4.
5 per cent critical values: DF4 = −4.11 (ADF = −3.75) (from Engle and Yoo 1987: sample
size 50).
[a]Zero cointegrating vector identified.
[b]Augmented Dickey–Fuller tests: autocorrelation in the DF equation.

outlined in Dolado *et al.* (1991). The Dickey–Fuller, augmented Dickey–
Fuller and Phillips–Perron tests (see Phillips 1987; Phillips and Perron 1988;
Perron 1988) are used to classify the series. The distinction between level
stationary and trend stationary processes relates to the absence or presence of
a deterministic trend. If a series is level stationary after de-trending, then the
original series must be trend stationary. As discussed in Section 3.1.3, if series
are collectively to possess a stable long-run relationship, the time-series
properties should be similar. A linear combination of one stationary or I(0)
series with one difference stationary or I(1) series cannot represent a long-run
equilibrium since the two series will tend to diverge. The same is true for

*Table 3.8* Lower-stage fuel-expenditure-share equations, long-run own-price elasticities from five specifications: oil

| | 1 | 2 | 3 | $4_2$ | $4_3$ | DW3 | DF4 | $J4_2$ | $J4_3$ |
|---|---|---|---|---|---|---|---|---|---|
| Austria | +0.02 | +0.09 | −0.49 | −0.36 | −0.26 | 0.23 | −3.36 | 5 | 2 |
| Belgium | −0.15 | −0.10 | −0.45 | −2.29 | −0.44 | 0.52 | −3.55 | 1 | 2 |
| Canada | −0.10 | −0.04 | +0.01 | −0.71 | −4.43 | 0.22 | −3.97[a] | 3 | 3 |
| Denmark | −0.23 | −0.20 | +0.18 | [b] | [b] | 1.56 | −4.96 | 0 | 0 |
| France | −0.20 | −0.16 | −0.34 | [b] | −0.36 | 0.35 | −2.49 | 0 | 2 |
| Germany | −0.01 | +0.06 | −0.28 | −1.11 | +0.14 | 0.16 | −2.96 | 1 | 3 |
| Greece | −0.25 | −0.22 | −0.32 | −0.30 | −0.32 | 0.67 | −2.90 | 5 | 3 |
| Italy | −0.08 | −0.02 | −0.37 | −0.73 | −1.22 | 0.32 | −4.68 | 3 | 5 |
| Japan | −0.15 | −0.10 | −0.48 | −0.88 | −1.03 | 0.22 | −2.41 | 4 | 4 |
| Netherlands | −0.24 | −0.20 | −0.26 | −0.68 | −1.12 | 0.80 | −4.36 | 1 | 3 |
| Norway | −0.23 | −0.19 | +0.12 | −7.90 | +0.13 | 0.68 | −3.81 | 3 | 5 |
| Spain | −0.18 | −0.13 | −0.26 | −0.10 | −0.34 | 0.24 | −5.02 | 1 | 1 |
| Sweden | −0.22 | −0.18 | +0.06 | −4.65 | +0.86 | 0.13 | −4.41 | 3 | 2 |
| United Kingdom | −0.18 | −0.14 | +0.16 | −0.39 | −0.61 | 0.23 | −3.86 | 2 | 3 |
| United States | −0.22 | −0.18 | −0.05 | −0.44 | +0.29 | 1.26 | −3.88 | 3 | 3 |

*Notes:*  Sample period 1960–89; elasticities evaluated at the sample means.
Model 1: translog model, uniform price coefficients, pooled data.
Model 2: translog model, uniform price coefficients, symmetry imposed, pooled data.
Model 3: translog model, symmetry imposed, non-pooled data.
Model 4: single translog fuel-share equation estimated as a VAR system where the number of vectors utilized is that in column J4. Models estimated separately for each country. The subscripts 2 and 3 refer to the number of lags incorporated.
DW3: Durbin–Watson statistic for single equation in model 3 system.
DF4: Dickey–Fuller statistic for static fuel-share equation equivalent to model 4.
J4: number of cointegrating vectors identified by the Johansen maximum likelihood procedure used to estimate model 4.
5 per cent critical values: DF4 = −4.11 (ADF = −3.75) (from Engle and Yoo 1987; sample size 50).
[a]Augmented Dickey–Fuller tests: autocorrelation in the DF equation.
[b]Zero cointegrating vector identified.

combinations of I(1) and I(2) series although sub-cointegration is possible (see, for example, S.G. Hall 1986).

The results in Table 3.4 illustrate how energy balances have time-series processes which differ between fuels or, for a given fuel or the total energy balance, between countries. For instance, the total energy consumption in the industrial sector is an I(1) series in ten countries but is stationary in the remaining five. Fuel prices, however, are typically difference stationary as Table 3.5 illustrates, and Table 3.6 provides a similar classification of the time-series properties of shares in total fuel expenditure. In the latter case, the coal share $S_C$ is I(1) in ten countries and stationary in the remaining five. The

*Table 3.9* Lower-stage fuel-expenditure-share equations, long-run own-price
elasticities from five specifications: gas

| | 1 | 2 | 3 | $4_2$ | $4_3$ | DW3 | DF4 | $J4_2$ | $J4_3$ |
|---|---|---|---|---|---|---|---|---|---|
| Austria | −0.58 | −0.62 | +0.08 | −0.86 | −0.05 | 1.58 | −5.12[a] | 2 | 2 |
| Belgium | −0.54 | −0.59 | −0.40 | +2.29 | −1.36 | 0.17 | −4.12 | 1 | 1 |
| Canada | −0.60 | −0.63 | +0.27 | −0.04 | −0.26 | 0.58 | −4.93 | 3 | 2 |
| Denmark | −0.30 | −0.38 | +3.45 | −11.40 | −8.75 | 1.13 | −3.79 | 1 | 2 |
| France | −0.57 | −0.61 | −0.21 | −0.45 | −0.71 | 1.37 | −4.44 | 5 | 2 |
| Germany | −0.47 | −0.53 | −0.03 | −0.69 | −0.74 | 0.25 | −3.00 | 2 | 3 |
| Greece | +2.56 | +2.12 | −1.37 | −0.35 | −0.23 | 1.09 | −3.46 | 5 | 3 |
| Italy | −0.55 | −0.59 | −0.41 | −1.14 | −0.58 | 0.77 | −2.74 | 2 | 5 |
| Japan | −0.12 | −0.22 | −0.45 | +1.02 | +3.51 | 0.30 | −1.59 | 1 | 2 |
| Netherlands | −0.61 | −0.63 | −0.81 | −1.50 | −1.73 | 0.39 | −3.72 | 1 | 5 |
| Norway | +9.47 | +8.17 | +0.56 | −1.01 | −3.32 | 0.70 | −5.02[a] | 4 | 5 |
| Spain | +0.36 | +0.20 | −1.67 | −1.90 | −1.84 | 0.40 | −5.11[a] | 2 | 5 |
| Sweden | +5.30 | +4.53 | +0.10 | −12.18 | −19.25 | 0.67 | −5.15 | 2 | 4 |
| United Kingdom | −0.58 | −0.61 | −0.82 | +0.07 | −0.53 | 0.32 | −3.64 | 2 | 4 |
| United States | +1.20 | +0.93 | +0.46 | [b] | +0.34 | 0.69 | −3.25 | 0 | 3 |

*Notes*: Sample period 1960–89; elasticities evaluated at the sample means.
Model 1: translog model, uniform price coefficients, pooled data.
Model 2: translog model, uniform price coefficients, symmetry imposed, pooled data.
Model 3: translog model, symmetry imposed, non-pooled data.
Model 4: single translog fuel-share equation estimated as a VAR system where the number
   of vectors utilized is that in column J4. Models estimated separately for each country. The
   subscripts 2 and 3 refer to the number of lags incorporated.
DW3: Durbin–Watson statistic for single equation in model 3 system.
DF4: Dickey–Fuller statistic for static fuel-share equation equivalent to model 4.
J4: number of cointegrating vectors identified by the Johansen maximum likelihood
   procedure used to estimate model 4.
5 per cent critical values: DF4 = −4.11 (ADF = −3.75) (from Engle and Yoo 1987; sample
   size 50).
[a]Augmented Dickey–Fuller tests: autocorrelation in the DF equation.
[b]Zero cointegrating vector identified.

other shares $S_O$, $S_G$ and $S_E$ are difference stationary in an overwhelming
majority of cases.

As a general rule, therefore, we can take individual fuel prices and
expenditure shares as difference stationary, and therefore single 'translog'
share equations form potential cointegrating vectors. Tables 3.7–3.10 present
long-run own-price elasticities and summary details of estimation results for
the four fuels. The four tables all present results from five models. Models 1,
2 and 3 are all homothetic static translog models estimated with country-
specific dummies and allow for country-specific non-neutral technical
progress. Column 1 presents elasticities from share equations with individual

*Table 3.10* Lower-stage fuel-expenditure-share equations, long-run own-price elasticities from five specifications: electricity[a]

|  | 1 | 2 | 3 | $4_2$ | $4_3$ | DF4 | $J4_2$ | $J4_3$ |
|---|---|---|---|---|---|---|---|---|
| Austria | +0.02 | −0.10 | +0.02 | +0.95 | +1.02 | −3.23 | 3 | 1 |
| Belgium | +0.02 | −0.11 | −0.02 | +0.46 | b | −3.77[c] | 1 | 0 |
| Canada | +0.02 | −0.09 | +0.17 | +0.20 | −0.14 | −3.63 | 3 | 3 |
| Denmark | +0.06 | −0.10 | +0.35 | b | b | −2.68 | 0 | 0 |
| France | +0.10 | −0.11 | +0.22 | +0.37 | −3.73 | −3.03 | 2 | 1 |
| Germany | +0.02 | −0.09 | −0.19 | +1.61 | −0.04 | −3.42 | 1 | 4 |
| Greece | +0.02 | −0.10 | −0.18 | −0.46 | −0.31 | −3.00 | 5 | 1 |
| Italy | +0.04 | −0.06 | +0.01 | +0.13 | +0.15 | −6.17 | 2 | 3 |
| Japan | +0.04 | −0.06 | −0.14 | b | +0.01 | −2.60 | 0 | 2 |
| Netherlands | +0.06 | −0.11 | −0.19 | −0.79 | +1.14 | −3.45 | 5 | 3 |
| Norway | +0.05 | −0.04 | +0.01 | +0.49 | −0.01 | −4.00 | 1 | 5 |
| Spain | +0.02 | −0.09 | −0.04 | b | −0.08 | −4.83 | 0 | 2 |
| Sweden | +0.05 | −0.04 | +0.05 | +0.33 | +0.17 | −4.22 | 3 | 2 |
| United Kingdom | +0.02 | −0.11 | +0.21 | −0.12 | −1.38 | −6.03 | 1 | 3 |
| United States | +0.03 | −0.07 | +0.13 | +0.28 | −0.04 | −4.02 | 2 | 5 |

*Notes*: Sample period 1960–89; elasticities evaluated at the sample means.
Model 1: translog model, uniform price coefficients, pooled data.
Model 2: translog model, uniform price coefficients, symmetry imposed, pooled data.
Model 3: translog model, symmetry imposed, non-pooled data.
Model 4: single translog fuel-share equation estimated as a VAR system where the number of vectors utilized is that in column J4. Models estimated separately for each country. The subscripts 2 and 3 refer to the number of lags incorporated.
DW3: Durbin–Watson statistic for single equation in model 3 system.
DF4: Dickey–Fuller statistic for static fuel-share equation equivalent to model 4.
J4: number of cointegrating vectors identified by the Johansen maximum likelihood procedure used to estimate model 4.
5 per cent critical values: DF4 = −4.11 (ADF = −3.75) (from Engle and Yoo 1987; sample size 50).
[a]Since the electricity equation was redundant in the translog model, the Durbin–Watson statistic for a single equation in model 3 system was not estimated.
[b]Zero cointegrating vector identified.
[c]Augmented Dickey–Fuller tests: autocorrelation in the DF equation.

intercepts and time trend coefficients. (See equation (3.22) but with uniform second-order parameters, the $b_{ij}$.) Symmetry is imposed in column 2, while column 3 presents results where symmetry is again imposed but non-pooled data are used, i.e. the $b_{ij}$ are not uniform.

The following estimates are from models 1 and 2. The coal elasticities $\eta_{CC}$ in Table 3.7 vary slightly between countries from −0.25 in Sweden with symmetry imposed up to −0.69 in the United Kingdom, but without symmetry imposed elsewhere. The data reject symmetry, but imposition does not affect the estimates materially. Slight variability is also evident in the $\eta_{OO}$

estimates in Table 3.8 which vary around $-0.15$ but the estimates are positive for Austria both with and without symmetry and for Germany when symmetry is imposed. The $\eta_{GG}$ estimates in Table 3.9 indicate the inability of the pooled translog form to provide sensible results for Greece, Norway and Sweden where the industrial usage of gas is very limited. Of greater concern is the positive own-price elasticity estimated for the United States, both with and without symmetry imposed. Finally, Table 3.10 presents $\eta_{EE}$ estimates which are all approximately zero. When symmetry is imposed the unweighted average is $-0.09$ but it is slightly positive when symmetry is not imposed with an unweighted average of $+0.04$.

The hypothesis of uniform $b_{ij}$ coefficients across the countries sampled is decisively rejected by these data. In column 3, therefore, the results of translog systems estimated separately for each country are presented. The results are generally unsatisfactory for all fuel shares equations with at least five countries having positive elasticities for each fuel. The Durbin–Watson test for the relevant equation in the country-specific systems, denoted DW3, is indicative of substantial serial correlation as is frequently found when estimating such static systems. The data are generally difference stationary and the DW3 values do not suggest that cointegration occurs in a majority of these equations. Country-specific single-equation share equations are also estimated and the Dickey–Fuller test values, denoted DF4, are also not generally supportive of cointegration. The 5 per cent critical value with five regressors and fifty observations is $-4.76$ for the DF and $-4.15$ for the ADF tests (see Engle and Yoo 1987: 157–8). However, the (unreported) resultant elasticity estimates are no more 'plausible' than those in column 3.

In order to assess further the possibility that cointegration occurs, an unrestricted vector autoregressive (VAR) system is used as in Boone *et al.* (1992) and Bentzen *et al.* (1993). Long-run parameter estimates are not invariant to the chosen normalization (i.e. the left-side variable) in OLS regression used in the two-step approach. When there are at least three variables it is possible that more than one cointegrating relationship exists and up to $n-1$ cointegrating relationships may exist where $n$ is the number of variables included. The Johansen (1988) and Johansen and Juselius (1990) multivariate maximum likelihood approach to cointegration is used when the number of cointegrating relationships can be identified in a VAR system. As mentioned earlier, a long-run solution is estimated for each variable in the VAR as a linear combination of the cointegrating vectors as outlined below. The Johansen procedure can be represented as

$$X_t = \delta + \Pi_1 X_{t-1} + \ldots + \Pi_k X_{t-k} + e_t \tag{3.41}$$

where $X_t$ is a $p \times 1$ vector of non-stationary variables, $\delta$ is a $p \times 1$ vector of constant terms, $\Pi_1, \ldots, \Pi_k$ are $p \times p$ coefficient matrices and $e_t$ is a $p \times 1$ vector of Gaussian error terms. This can be reparameterized into an ECM as

$$\Delta X_t = \delta + \Gamma_1 \Delta X_{t-1} + \ldots + \Gamma_{k-1} \Delta X_{t-k-1} + \Pi X_{t-k} + e_t \qquad (3.42)$$

where $\Gamma_i = -1 + \Pi_1 + \ldots + \Pi_i$ and $\Pi = -1 + \Pi_1 + \ldots + \Pi_k$. Subject to the variables within $X_t$ cointegrating (thus implying the reduced rank $r < p$ of the matrix $\Pi$), the Johansen procedure estimates equation (3.42) and can be written as $\Pi = \alpha\beta'$ where $\beta'$ is the $p \times r$ matrix of cointegrating vectors and $\alpha$ is the $p \times r$ matrix of corresponding factor weightings.

The levels of the fuel expenditure share and the logarithm of the four fuel prices are entered into separate VARs for each fuel share equation. An intercept and time trend are also included. The order of the VAR or the lag length utilized is chosen following Hall's (1991) approach where he suggests starting with a high-order VAR system and reducing the lag length subject to the VAR passing a likelihood ratio test. The test chosen is that of Sims (1980) where he attempts to overcome the problem of inadequate degrees of freedom due to small sample size by using the following statistical test: $(T - k)$ $(\log|D_R| - \log|D_U|) \sim \varkappa^2(k)$, where $T$ is the sample size, $k$ is the total number of regression coefficients estimated divided by the number of equations, $D_R$ is the matrix of cross-products of the residuals when the model is restricted and $D_U$ is the matrix of cross-products of the residuals when the model is unrestricted. This procedure identifies a lag length of three years for all equations. Results are also presented for a lag length of two years to see how sensitive a VAR system is to the chosen lag length. With three lags there are only 10 degrees of freedom, whilst with two lags there are 15.

Following the Johansen procedure, the results of applying the Johansen–Juselius tests for the number of cointegrating vectors, denoted J4, are presented in Tables 3.7–3.10, where the subscripts 2 and 3 refer to the respective number of lags incorporated in the VAR. Eigenvalues and trace test statistics are used to determine the number of cointegrating vectors. The results indicate that generally at least one, and often more than one, cointegrating vector exists, but ten out of the 120 cases have zero cointegrating vectors. The long-run solution to the VAR comprising a linear combination of the cointegrating vector(s) and the long-run parameter estimates for the fuel share equation in the VAR produce the elasticities reported in column 4, where the subscripts refer to the number of lags. In the instances where zero cointegrating vectors are identified, no elasticities are reported as it is implied that cointegration does not take place. These elasticities vary widely across countries for all four fuel shares and are of the expected sign in forty-three out of the fifty-seven cases when three lags are included, and forty out of the fifty-three cases when two lags are included. Electricity accounts for 52 per cent of these unexpected positive elasticities. Indeed, the electricity results have a positive elasticity in 56 per cent of cases and the majority of the electricity elasticities in models 1 and 3 are positive. There are also some large implausible elasticities. As a general rule, these 'dubious' elasticity estimates are associated with a very small expenditure share, i.e. the largest elasticity in magnitude is $-19.25$ for gas in Sweden with three lags where gas has an expenditure share of only 0.6 per cent. The unweighted averages of the long-run own-price elasticities with three lags across the fifteen countries are $-0.82$ for coal (excluding Denmark, France, Sweden and the United Kingdom), $-0.43$ for oil (excluding Canada and Sweden), $-0.92$ for gas (excluding Denmark, Japan and Sweden) and $-0.26$ for electricity, all of which are close to the consensus discussed in Section 3.2.5 apart from the low estimate for oil. When only two lags are included the results are $-1.06$ for coal (excluding Austria and Denmark), $-0.73$ for oil (excluding Norway and Sweden), $-0.62$ for gas (excluding Belgium, Denmark and Sweden) and $+0.25$ for electricity. These results are not as close to the consensus as those with three lags.

Generally the elasticity results from the VAR system show that they are sensitive to the order of the VAR chosen although they show no consistent variation comparing two with three lags. In general, as the order of the VAR decreases, the number of cointegrating vectors decreases. Comparing two lags with three, 55 per cent of the cases have a larger number of cointegrating vectors with three lags, 23 per cent have a lower number while 22 per cent have the same number. When a lag length of one is considered, there is a large increase in the number of cases where zero cointegrating vectors are found. The reason for the elasticities being sensitive to the number of lags could be the number of cointegrating vectors changing as the lag length varies. Casual inspection of the results suggest that this is not the case, as there are several cases where the elasticities reverse sign although the number of cointegrating vectors remains unchanged, and also cases where the elasticities are virtually identical with different numbers of cointegrating vectors. It could be the case that when elasticity sign reversal occurs with a constant number of cointegrating vectors, the vectors which cointegrate are varying as the lag length varies, although the net change in the number of cointegrating vectors is zero.

The small sample size available limits the number of degrees of freedom. If more than three lags are incorporated in the VAR there are too few degrees of freedom for estimates to be computed. It is therefore possible that the appropriate model should include more than three lags which would imply that the results reported with three lags are biased as the complete lag structure is not incorporated into the VAR in levels, i.e. equation (3.41). The results vary over countries with some countries performing 'better' than others. Out of Denmark's eight possible results, four show zero cointegrating vectors and, of the four reported elasticities, the smallest magnitude is 8.75. Sweden also has 'poor' results, while other countries such as Greece have results that are more consistent with the consensus, e.g. Greece's eight elasticities vary from $-0.23$ to $-1.22$.

Generally the VAR results are unsatisfactory due to the positive own-price elasticities and the large magnitude of some of the elasticities. Comparing the

*Table 3.11* Lower-stage fuel expenditure equations: cross-price elasticities for a static homothetic and symmetric model with fuel efficiency bias terms included

| Coal | C | O | G | E | Oil | C | O | G | E |
|---|---|---|---|---|---|---|---|---|---|
| 60–63 | −0.34 | −0.07 | 0.23 | 0.19 | 60–63 | 0.20 | −0.04 | 0.16 | 0.01 |
| 64–67 | −0.70 | −0.45 | 0.12 | 1.03 | 64–67 | 0.15 | −0.72 | −0.10 | 0.66 |
| 68–71 | −0.59 | −0.18 | −0.01 | 0.78 | 68–71 | 0.13 | −0.46 | 0.12 | 0.17 |
| 72–75 | −0.61 | 0.01 | −0.03 | 0.64 | 72–75 | 0.12 | −0.43 | 0.14 | 0.17 |
| 76–79 | −0.17 | −0.00 | −0.15 | 0.32 | 76–79 | 0.10 | −0.72 | 0.29 | 0.33 |
| 80–83 | 0.01 | 0.04 | −0.22 | 0.09 | 80–83 | 0.08 | −0.90 | 0.46 | 0.37 |
| 83–85 | 0.32 | −0.37 | −0.09 | 0.14 | 83–85 | 0.08 | −0.69 | 0.41 | 0.21 |
| 86–89 | −0.04 | −0.44 | 0.01 | 0.48 | 86–89 | 0.08 | −0.09 | 0.04 | −0.02 |
| 60–89 | −0.64 | 0.19 | 0.19 | 0.26 | 60–89 | 0.12 | −0.16 | 0.02 | 0.03 |
| 60–89[2] | −0.78 | 0.28 | 0.22 | 0.28 | 60–89[2] | 0.12 | 0.00 | −0.05 | −0.08 |
| 60–89[3] | −0.55 | 0.20 | 0.14 | 0.20 | 60–89[3] | 0.12 | −0.17 | 0.02 | 0.03 |
| 60–89[4] | −0.73 | 0.15 | 0.09 | 0.50 | 60–89[4] | 0.12 | −0.40 | 0.06 | 0.22 |
| 60–89[5] | −0.85 | 0.24 | 0.08 | 0.53 | 60–89[5] | 0.12 | −0.67 | 0.07 | 0.47 |

| Gas | C | O | G | E | Electricity | C | O | G | E |
|---|---|---|---|---|---|---|---|---|---|
| 60–63 | 0.20 | 0.22 | −0.67 | 0.26 | 60–63 | 0.07 | 0.00 | 0.07 | −0.05 |
| 64–67 | 0.15 | 0.24 | −0.98 | 0.58 | 64–67 | 0.29 | 0.28 | 0.29 | −0.44 |
| 68–71 | 0.13 | 0.26 | −1.53 | 1.14 | 68–71 | 0.17 | 0.08 | 0.17 | −0.24 |
| 72–75 | 0.11 | 0.29 | −1.53 | 1.12 | 72–75 | 0.14 | 0.10 | 0.14 | −0.29 |
| 76–79 | 0.10 | 0.31 | −1.71 | 1.30 | 76–79 | 0.06 | 0.21 | 0.06 | −0.40 |
| 80–83 | 0.08 | 0.03 | −1.87 | 1.47 | 80–83 | 0.01 | 0.25 | 0.01 | −0.51 |
| 83–85 | 0.08 | 0.29 | −1.71 | 1.34 | 83–85 | 0.02 | 0.12 | 0.02 | −0.34 |
| 86–89 | 0.08 | 0.18 | −0.94 | 0.69 | 86–89 | 0.06 | −0.01 | 0.06 | −0.10 |
| 60–89 | 0.12 | 0.26 | −0.57 | 0.13 | 60–89 | 0.06 | 0.01 | 0.06 | −0.10 |
| 60–89[2] | 0.12 | 0.26 | −0.48 | 0.09 | 60–89[2] | 0.04 | 0.02 | 0.04 | −0.07 |
| 60–89[3] | 0.12 | 0.26 | −0.47 | 0.09 | 60–89[3] | 0.06 | −0.04 | 0.06 | −0.07 |
| 60–89[4] | 0.12 | 0.26 | −0.81 | 0.43 | 60–89[4] | 0.10 | 0.11 | 0.11 | −0.26 |
| 60–89[5] | 0.12 | 0.26 | −0.90 | 0.52 | 60–89[5] | 0.12 | 0.23 | 0.12 | −0.42 |

*Notes*: For the homothetic and symmetric model estimated over 1960–89, log $L$ = 2463.19.
60–89[2]: non-homothetic model, log output included in share equations, log $L$ = 2516.44.
60–89[3]: non-homothetic model, log total energy balance included in share equations, log $L$ = 2535.36.
60–89[4]: non-homothetic dynamic model, log total energy balance and lagged own-share included in share equation, log $L$ = 3310.4, short-run elasticities.
60–89[5]: as 4, long-run elasticities presented.

VAR results with those of model 3 (the non-pooled translog model), the VAR has fewer positively signed elasticities and they are generally more price responsive. The VAR system estimates also generally indicate greater price-responsiveness than do those from a static translog system applied to the pooled data set, presented in Table 3.3. If elasticities are evaluated at the sample mean of the fuel expenditure shares, the latter estimates produce long-run $\eta_{CC} = -0.64$, $\eta_{OO} = -0.16$, $\eta_{GG} = -0.57$ and $\eta_{EE} = -0.10$.

Now consider the result of re-estimating a restrictive translog system on relatively short periods, which typically comprise four cross-sections from, say, 1960 to 1963 (see Table 3.11 for details). Given these relatively short time periods, a majority of the price variation should occur in the cross-section. If cross-section results produce long-run elasticities, the estimates should only vary marginally as the data period changes. This is clearly not the case in Table 3.11 where there is a clear trend in the magnitude of the elasticities over time when the elasticities are evaluated at the sample mean of the pooled data. The own-price elasticity for coal generally falls over the period 1960–89 and is positive for 1980–85. For oil, gas and electricity, the elasticities are lower at either end of the overall sample period, and fall noticeably after 1986.

Table 3.11 also presents the results of a limited sensitivity analysis following Hall (1986). The evidence is mixed: the imposition of homotheticity is clearly rejected by the data, despite being necessary for consistent two-stage modelling (see Fuss 1977b). However, the relaxation of the homotheticity assumption changes the estimated elasticities marginally in the case of gas and electricity, although more substantial differences exist in the estimates for the coal and oil share equations. The final specification considered in Table 3.11 is the *ad hoc* dynamic translog model which appends a single lagged share term to otherwise static translog share equations. The coefficient on the lagged share is constrained to be equal across the fuel share equations which facilitates the imposition of symmetry. Both the estimated long-run and short-run elasticities are greater when the dynamic model is considered, which indicates perhaps that static demand systems may not produce long-run elasticity estimates. However, this dynamic approach is rather *ad hoc*. Furthermore, the sample average long-run elasticities presented in the note to Table 3.11 approximate the averages from the atheoretical VAR systems discussed above.

Many of the studies discussed in Section 3.2 also pool time-series information together but ignore cross-country contemporaneous correlation in estimation. This spatial correlation can be quite significant. Consider the regression for $S_C$ in country $i$, period $t$:

$$S_{Cit} = \alpha_i + \sum_j \beta_j \ln P_{jit} + \gamma_i t + \varepsilon_{Cit} \tag{3.43}$$

Spatial correlation concerns the covariance $E(\varepsilon_{Cit}\,\varepsilon_{Cjt})$ and approximate Lagrange multiplier tests provide $\chi^2(105)$ values of 1015, 865, 1020 and 757 for the $S_C$, $S_O$, $S_G$ and $S_E$ equations of the form (3.43) above (see Greene 1990). This source of estimation inefficiency has not been considered in the literature reviewed in Section 3.2.

### 3.3.2  Evidence on the demand for aggregate energy

In this brief section we consider the total demand for energy in the industrial sector of the fifteen countries. The aggregate fuel price is a Divisia index of the individual fuel price data and details of the prices of labour and capital together with the output data are given in Appendix 3A.

*Table 3.12* Types of stationarity

| Country | Q | PL | PK | PL/PE | PK/PE | PE |
|---|---|---|---|---|---|---|
| Austria | DS | 2DS | DS | DS | DS | DS |
| Belgium | LS | 2DS | DS | DS | DS | DS |
| Canada | LS | 2DS | DS | DS | DS | DS |
| Denmark | LS | 2DS | DS | DS | LS | DS |
| France | LS | 2DS | DS | DS | DS | DS |
| Germany | LS | 2DS | TS, DS | DS | DS | DS |
| Greece | LS | 2DS | DS | DS | DS | 2DS |
| Italy | LS | 2DS | DS | DS | DS | DS |
| Japan | TS, DS | 2DS | TS, DS | DS | DS | DS |
| Netherlands | DS | 2DS | DS | DS | DS | DS |
| Norway | LS | 2DS | TS, DS | DS | TS, DS | DS |
| Spain | LS | 2DS | TS, DS | DS | TS, DS | DS |
| Sweden | LS | 2DS | TS, DS | DS | DS | DS |
| United Kingdom | DS | 2DS | DS | DS | DS | DS |
| United States | TS, DS | 2DS | DS | DS | DS | DS |

*Notes*: LS, level stationary; TS, trend stationary; DS, first difference stationary; 2DS, second difference stationary.

Table 3.12 presents evidence on the time-series properties of the data and, somewhat reminiscent of Nachane *et al.* (1988), differences are found in the classification of the series between countries. Of crucial significance to the analysis are the clear differences between the properties of the output series and the price of labour which are generally I(0) and I(2) respectively. The prices of capital and energy are generally difference stationary, as is the total energy balance (see Table 3.4). However, given that theoretically price relativities affect demand, it may be appropriate to include price ratios in energy demand equations despite the price of labour being I(2). In general, the price ratios, with a few exceptions, are difference stationary.

Table 3.13 presents the results of estimating (static) cointegrating regressions of the functional form

$$\ln E = \alpha_0 + \alpha_1 \ln Q + \alpha_2 \ln(P_K/P_E) + \alpha_3 \ln(P_L/P_E) + \alpha_4 t + \text{residual} \quad (3.44)$$

where the $\alpha$ are the elasticities presented in the table. This functional form, together with the Engle–Granger two-step approach, has been applied to a longer time series of British data in Hunt and Lynk (1992). If the Engle–Granger two-step approach is appropriate to international data, the regressions should cointegrate and, implicitly, sub-cointegration should occur in those instances where output is stationary. However, the evidence for cointegration in the sample of fifteen countries is weak as the diagnostics in Table 3.13 illustrate. The statistics presented are the Dickey–Fuller and augmented Dickey–Fuller tests (DF and ADF) and the Phillips–Perron $Z_{\hat{\alpha}}$ and

*Table 3.13* Upper-stage results – cointegrating regressions: long-run elasticities and summary diagnostics

| Country | $\eta_{EQ}$ | $\eta_{EE}$ | $\eta_{EL}$ | $\eta_{EK}$ | DW | DF | $ADF_1$ | $ADF_2$ | $\hat{\alpha}$ | $Z_{\hat{\alpha}}(2)$ | $Z_{\hat{\alpha}}(5)$ | $Z_{t\hat{\alpha}}(2)$ | $Z_{t\hat{\alpha}}(5)$ |
|---|---|---|---|---|---|---|---|---|---|---|---|---|---|
| Austria | 1.08 | 0.06 | 0.04 | −0.10 | 0.66 | −2.62 | −3.83 | −3.66 | 0.64 | −11.78 | −10.57 | −2.71 | −2.60 |
| Belgium | 1.46 | −0.34 | 0.31 | 0.04 | 1.13 | −3.33 | −3.97 | −3.32 | 0.43 | −17.38 | −14.05 | −3.35 | −3.13 |
| Canada | 0.86 | −0.12 | 0.20 | −0.08 | 0.74 | −2.87 | −2.51 | −1.72 | 0.58 | −12.85 | −13.78 | −2.98 | −3.05 |
| Denmark | 1.28 | −0.35 | 0.31 | 0.04 | 1.38 | −1.04 | −3.63 | −3.34 | 0.29 | −22.07 | −20.14 | −4.07 | −3.98 |
| France | 0.77 | −0.33 | 0.15 | 0.16 | 1.76 | −4.70 | −4.20 | −4.31 | 0.12 | −25.90 | −23.05 | −4.69 | −4.62 |
| Germany | 0.76 | −0.10 | 0.07 | 0.03 | 1.25 | −3.59 | −4.47 | −4.36 | 0.37 | −19.24 | −15.63 | −3.61 | −3.40 |
| Greece | 1.27 | −0.21 | 0.48 | −0.27 | 1.65 | −4.85 | −4.89 | −2.79 | 0.12 | −25.31 | −24.10 | −4.83 | −4.81 |
| Italy | 0.46 | −0.10 | 0.08 | 0.02 | 1.21 | −3.69 | −2.72 | −3.16 | 0.37 | −18.87 | −18.00 | −3.68 | −3.64 |
| Japan | 0.30 | −0.19 | 0.09 | 0.10 | 0.51 | −1.81 | −1.89 | −2.04 | 0.75 | −8.00 | −8.08 | −1.87 | −1.88 |
| Netherlands | 0.27 | −0.10 | −0.11 | 0.21 | 0.73 | −1.97 | −3.36 | −3.25 | 0.66 | −12.10 | −9.38 | −2.20 | −1.88 |
| Norway | 1.15 | 0.04 | −0.29 | 0.25 | 0.60 | −1.88 | −2.42 | −2.12 | 0.71 | −9.57 | −9.33 | −2.01 | −1.98 |
| Spain | 0.59 | −0.00 | −0.01 | 0.01 | 0.74 | −2.23 | −2.40 | −3.87 | 0.64 | −12.62 | −10.70 | −2.42 | −2.22 |
| Sweden | 0.33 | −0.18 | 0.16 | 0.02 | 1.00 | −3.29 | −2.47 | −1.90 | 0.46 | −16.63 | −17.28 | −3.22 | −3.36 |
| United Kingdom | 0.42 | 0.00 | −0.03 | 0.03 | 1.22 | −3.69 | −3.64 | −3.18 | 0.36 | −19.30 | −17.71 | −3.69 | −3.60 |
| United States | 0.22 | −0.01 | −0.04 | 0.05 | 1.27 | −3.75 | −3.45 | −2.03 | 0.35 | −19.95 | −20.41 | −3.71 | −3.81 |

*Sources:* $Z_{\hat{\alpha}}$, $Z_{t\hat{\alpha}}$, Phillips and Ouliaris 1990 (sample size 500); DF, ADF, Engle and Yoo 1987 (sample size 50); DW, Sargan and Bhargava 1983 (five series, sample size 31)

*Notes:* 5 per cent critical values: $Z_{\hat{\alpha}} = −37.73$; $Z_{t\hat{\alpha}} = ADF = −3.73$; DF = −4.11; ADF = −3.75; DW, lower, 0.65; DW, upper, 2.16.

$Z_{t\hat{\alpha}}$ tests (see Phillips and Ouliaris 1990); $\hat{\alpha}$ is estimated from $\varepsilon_t = \alpha\varepsilon_{t-1} + \upsilon_t$, where $\varepsilon_t$ is the residual in (3.44).

Only the regressions for Denmark, France, Greece and the United States reject the null hypothesis that $\varepsilon_t \sim I(1)$ according to the $Z_{t\hat{\alpha}}$ test at the 5 per cent level, while those for the United Kingdom and Italy only marginally fail to reject the null hypothesis. However, the estimated long-run elasticities for these countries are hardly encouraging: $\eta_{EQ}$ varies from 1.28 in Denmark to 0.22 in the United States, $\eta_{EE}$ varies from $-0.35$ in Denmark to 0.00 in the United Kingdom, and the cross-price elasticities $\eta_{EK}$ and $\eta_{EL}$ show no uniform sign pattern in all countries.

## 3.4 CONCLUSIONS

The assessment of long-run elasticities of energy demand is clearly problematic, there being no single theoretical model, econometric technique or set of data definitions which would receive universal support. The assertion that cross-section studies typically produce long-run elasticities and time-series studies short-run elasticities seems hopelessly simplistic in view of the discussion above, the estimation results, and recent econometric developments in the area of cointegration. Few of the studies reviewed in Section 3.2 thoroughly consider the pooling restrictions they implicitly impose, yet when countries are analysed separately, as in Hall (1986) for example, the estimates are highly country-specific and frequently implausible. If countries are to be modelled separately, might not useful gains in estimation efficiency be obtained by taking account of 'spatial correlation' which seems to be significant according to results in Section 3.1.3?

Very few authors consider the time-series properties of their data and where this has been done for international data sets the results are far from uniform across countries (see Nachane *et al.* 1988 and results in Section 3.3.2). Few studies use error correction mechanisms and the results in Section 3.3.2 are generally unsatisfactory. Furthermore, the estimated speeds of adjustment towards long-run equilibrium are all rapid (see Beenstock and Willcocks 1981; Hunt and Manning 1989; Hunt and Lynk 1992). Is it plausible that two-thirds of any short-run disequilibrium is eliminated after one year?

It seems reasonable to conclude that the existing literature on international energy elasticities remains incomplete. Neither applications of static theoretically based factor demand systems nor fairly simple error correction models seem adequately to consider the implicit dynamics. Watkins (1991) convincingly argues that simple dynamic models, frequently used on international energy data, cannot capture the dynamics of adjustment of all inputs which jointly produce final output. Perhaps even more disconcerting is Solow's (1987) argument that econometric estimates based on aggregate data cannot capture technical substitution possibilities since variations in output mix are not observed at the aggregate level. The relevance of both Watkins' and

Solow's arguments is irrefutable. The final question is, therefore, from where does one obtain internationally comparable data of sufficient quality from a number of countries over a reasonable period of time?

## APPENDIX 3A

### Data definitions and sources

All data used are annual and energy prices are constructed from two basic sources. First, industrial energy prices are obtained from *Energy Prices and Taxes* published by the IEA/OECD. This generally covers the period 1978–1990, but for some fuels in some countries data are available before 1978. When these are available they are utilized. Second, industrial energy prices are obtained from *International Energy Prices* published by the US Department of Energy which covers the period 1955–78 and is used if data from the IEA/OECD are unavailable. The former data are considered to be more accurate as the US Department of Energy now sources data from the IEA/OECD in its more recent publications.There are occasions where data are unavailable from these two sources. Gas price data for Denmark from 1981 to 1990 are obtained from Eurostat, while for Greece gas price data from 1981 to 1990 are taken as the world export price of gas obtained from the *UN Statistical Yearbook*. Gas price data for Norway and Sweden over this period are estimated using OLS regressions based on available German and Danish data. The coal price in Greece from 1981 to 1990 is taken as the international coal price obtained from the *UN Statistical Yearbook*. Energy prices are expressed in Btu equivalents in national currencies. Energy balances are taken from *Energy Balances of OECD Countries* published by the IEA/OECD. This covers the period 1960–89 and the balances are measured in million tonnes of oil equivalent for the industrial sector.

An output index is calculated from the *UN Yearbook of National Accounts Statistics*. This index expresses manufacturing output in constant prices expressed in national currencies. The price of capital is formulated following Christensen and Jorgenson's (1969) derivation: $P_K = r_t q_{t-1} + dq_t - (q_t - q_{t-1})$, where $P_K$ is the price index of capital, $r_t$ is the yield on long-term government bonds taken from *IMF International Financial Statistics*, $q_t$ is the implicit price deflator for gross fixed capital formation for year $t$ calculated from the *UN Yearbook of National Accounts Statistics*, $d$ is the depreciation rate assumed to be constant at 5 per cent and $q_t - q_{t-1}$ is the capital gain during each year. The yield on long-term bonds is not available for some countries, so for Finland and Greece the discount rate is used and for Spain the Bank of Spain rate is used. The price of capital is found to be relatively insensitive to different values of the depreciation rate. The price of labour for 1960–89 is taken as an index from *IMF International Financial Statistics*. The definition varies over countries from hourly manufacturing earnings to monthly earnings.

**NOTES**

1   Comprising India, Pakistan, Sri Lanka, the Philippines, Thailand, Malaysia, Korea, Brazil, Colombia, Syria, Iran, Romania, Yugoslavia, Mexico, Poland, Uruguay, Ireland, Hungary, Italy, Japan, Spain, the UK, the Netherlands, Belgium, Austria, Germany, France, Denmark, Luxembourg and the United States.
2   Argentina, Brazil, Chile, Colombia, France, West Germany, Greece, Guatemala, India, Israel, Italy, Japan, Mexico, Portugal, the UK and Venezuela.
3   The countries comprise Austria, Belgium, Canada, Denmark, France, (West) Germany, Greece, Italy, Japan, the Netherlands, Norway, Spain, Sweden, the United Kingdom and the United States.

Chapter 4

# Long-run demand elasticities for gasoline

*Mikael Franzén and Thomas Sterner*

**ABSTRACT**

This chapter is an overview comparing time-series and cross-section estimates of gasoline demand elasticities, drawing on a major study for all OECD countries prepared for the Swedish Road Research Board and subsequent published work.

**INTRODUCTION**

The purpose of this chapter is to discuss long-run elasticities of demand for gasoline in OECD countries. In so doing a number of alternative modelling strategies will be compared. The results can be understood as a further illustration of some of the methodological results on the inherent differences between various estimators analysed by Pesaran and Smith in Chapter 2. There are several reasons for choosing to model gasoline demand:

*   Economically the most important petroleum products are the transport fuels. On the international scene these are the subject of two distinct but interconnected debates. On the one hand, there is the inevitable conflict between producers and consumers over prices. On the other hand there is the fact that increased transportation of goods and passengers causes various environmental problems, ranging from local congestion, noise and smog to global warming due to carbon (and other) emissions. Numerous technical, institutional and legal mechanisms are currently being assessed for their ability to mitigate such problems. For the economist the most natural approach is, presumably, to use the price mechanism in one form or another – be it through carbon taxes, road or zone fees, other special charges or simply gasoline taxes. On the issue of gasoline taxation and pricing in various countries, see Angelier and Sterner (1990) and Sterner (1989a, b). In the context of these debates, policy-makers in both producing and consuming countries have an obvious interest in obtaining good estimates of the elasticity of gasoline demand.

- Gasoline is also a relatively homogeneous product – at least compared with aggregate energy, which contains such inherently different energy carriers as oil, coal, wood and electricity. Homogeneity in this case makes it easier to compare between countries, to aggregate, to calculate average prices, and so forth.
- As a result of these two factors, gasoline demand has already been heavily researched, with a vast literature on this single subject. In a recent survey over a hundred published studies with several hundred individual estimates were discussed (see Dahl and Sterner 1991a, b). This survey showed that, although individual estimates do vary considerably, with a suitable stratification by type of data and methodology used the estimates become more similar. Since there are so many estimates and these estimates have such an immediate policy relevance there is also quite an interest in trying to resolve and explain the differences found. Therefore, in this study a large number of different modelling strategies have been applied on the same data.

## 4.1 THE METHODOLOGY

### 4.1.1 Data

The data used in this paper cover the OECD from 1960 to 1988 and come from the Gothenburg Energy Data Bank. Gasoline consumption is total (apparent) consumption of gasoline per capita, taken from UN data. Income is GDP per capita and prices are domestic consumer prices of regular gasoline, taken from the International Energy Agency and the US Energy Information Administration. All prices and incomes have been converted to a common base by using purchasing power parities from Summer and Heston (1988). And finally, vehicle data are from the International Road Federation.

### 4.1.2 Modelling strategies

A modeller must make a series of choices as to how to build his model. Some, but not all, of these choices can be guided by formal testing and not all of them can be discussed within the scope of a single chapter. Among the major decisions the modeller of gasoline demand faces are the selection of variables to be included, of appropriate functional form, and the level of aggregation. Among the many 'minor' decisions are, for instance, how to convert prices and incomes to a common currency.

This chapter discusses models that are already at a very aggregate level. The data set used is a panel of yearly data for a number of countries and years. It is therefore a large T panel or 'field' as defined in Chapter 2. The focus of the chapter is to compare time-series, cross-section and pooled estimators for this field. All the models discussed use the log-linear functional form and wherever necessary purchasing power parity conversions to constant US dollars are made.[1] Furthermore, only two exogenous variables, gasoline prices and income levels, will be used.

The principal difficulty in modelling gasoline demand stems from the fact that it is a derived demand, depending heavily on the characteristics of the stock of relevant capital equipment, vehicles and transport infrastructure. But it also depends crucially on everyday decisions as to utilization. Thus, both current prices and incomes, as well as historic ones, have an influence on demand and the lags in adjustment to changing prices and incomes are long and may be complicated. One of the reasons for this is the omission of such variables as vehicle stock and infrastructure,[2] which, in turn, have been affected by historic income levels and gasoline prices.

At the same time, however, it is found that there is relatively little variation in gasoline prices between years within each country (see for instance Sterner 1990). Most of the variation (for income, gasoline price and consumption alike) in the data set comes from the variation between countries. Some countries, such as the United States, have had 'cheap' gasoline throughout most of the time period studied, while others, such as Italy, have had 'expensive' gasoline. It thus seems reasonable, *a priori*, to expect that cross-sectional evidence will be needed to pick up effectively the long-run effects of adaptation to these two different price regimes.

### 4.1.3 Model selection

The exogenous variables included, the type of model and lag structure chosen, as well as the functional form used, have been the subject of much debate. For a detailed discussion of gasoline demand modelling the reader is referred to Bohi (1981) or Sterner and Dahl (1991). The purpose of this section is briefly to present the functional forms and models chosen, concentrating primarily on the issue of lag structure.

The simple static model ($M_0$) in which $G$ is gasoline consumption per capita, $Y$ is deflated per capita income and $P$ is deflated gasoline price is chosen initially. All the variables are in logarithms.

$$G_{it} = c + \alpha P_{it} + \beta Y_{it} + \mu_{it} \tag{4.1}$$

where $i = 1, \ldots, N$ are the countries; $t = 1, \ldots, T$ are the years. However, static models cannot in general (i.e. at least not with time-series data) be relied upon to capture the complex process of adaptation to changes in prices and income. The way dynamic adaptation is modelled depends upon the lag structure assumed. One particular form of lag structure is the geometrically declining lag. By using the Koyck transformation, geometric lags on the exogenous variables can be modelled through the inclusion of a lagged endogenous variable:

$$G_{it} = c + \alpha P_{it} + \beta Y_{it} + \lambda G_{i,t-1} + \mu_{it} \tag{4.2}$$

This is referred to as the lagged endogenous model $M_1$. Although geometrically decreasing lags may be a fairly strong restriction,[3] the ease of estimation and the difficulty of obtaining sufficiently long series of data for the estimation of other more complicated lag structures have given the lagged endogenous model considerable popularity.

A slightly less restrictive lag structure can be obtained through the further inclusion of lagged exogenous variables as in (4.3). Model $M_2$ is often referred to as an inverted-V lag[4] because it allows for an adjustment that is first low but increasing (because of a 'perception lag') and then geometrically decreasing.

$$G_{it} = c + \alpha P_{it} + \beta Y_{it} + \beta G_{i,t-1} + \gamma P_{i,t-1} + \delta Y_{i,t-1} + \mu_{it} \tag{4.3}$$

Equation (4.4) is another form of inverted-V lag that will be referred to as model $M_3$ and which can be derived by assuming that the lags follow a Pascal distribution.

$$G_{it} = c + \alpha P_{it} + \beta Y_{it} + \beta G_{i,t-1} - \tfrac{1}{2}\beta^2 G_{i,t-2} + \mu_{it} \tag{4.4}$$

The final form of dynamic model used here is the polynomial distributed lag model $M_4$ in which only lagged observations of the exogenous variables are included but the $\alpha_i$ and $\beta_i$ are constrained by some form of polynomial.

$$G_{it} = c + \sum_\tau \alpha_\tau P_{i,t-\tau} + \sum_\tau \beta_\tau Y_{i,t-\tau} + \mu_{it} \tag{4.5}$$

In this model the short-run elasticities are $\alpha_0$ and $\beta_0$ while the long-run elasticities are given by the sums of all the $\alpha$s and $\beta$s. In the lagged endogenous model $M_1$ the short run is given by $\alpha$ and $\beta$ while the long run is given by $\alpha$ and $\beta$ divided by $1 - \lambda$.

### 4.1.4 Time series, cross-sections and pooled estimators

All the above models can be seen as special cases of a general gasoline demand model with error components such as

$$G_{it} = \sum_k \beta_{kit} X_{kit} + \mu_{it} \tag{4.6}$$

where $\mu_{it} = u_i + \upsilon_t + \varepsilon_{it}$ and $k = 1, \ldots, K$ are various explanatory variables (exogenous or endogenous, current or lagged). In (4.6) the logarithm of gasoline demand depends on the vector $X$ of explanatory variables but may also be affected by time-invariant country-specific effects $u_i$ and time-specific effects for particular years, $\upsilon_t$.

Turning to the issue of how best to use the data, it can be seen that one possibility is to assume that $\beta_{kit} = \beta_{ki}$ and estimate separate elasticities $\beta_k$ for each country. This is the time-series approach in which each country data set is analysed separately. This approach highlights the individual country specifics but does not fully use the information implied by the comparison between countries. Another method of estimating is the pure cross-section which amounts to assuming that $\beta_{kit} = \beta_{kt}$. Thus separate elasticities $\beta_{kt}$ are estimated for each year on a cross-section of countries.

However, many researchers, such as Baltagi and Griffin (1983), have asserted that the most efficient way to use the variation both along time and across countries in a data set simultaneously is to base estimations on combined cross-section time-series analyses. This can be done by assuming that $\beta_{kit} = \beta_k$, such that there is one unique elasticity for each explanatory variable estimated for the whole data set. There are many ways of doing this, however (for instance, with or without common intercepts), and furthermore, as should be clear from the analysis by Pesaran and Smith in Chapter 2, the choice of model must take into account the character of the data used. The use of dynamic models such as $M_1$ and $M_2$ with pooled estimators may result in large biases. The approach here will follow that of Chapter 2 and a number of different estimators will be considered, such as the mean group estimates which are averages of individual country time series along with pure cross-section estimates and various pooled estimators.

## 4.2 THE RESULTS

### 4.2.1 Cross-section estimates

Table 4.1 shows a series of cross-section estimates for different years. The model used is the simple static model $M_0$ and the values obtained average around $-1$ for price and $+1$ for income, which concurs rather well with earlier estimates of long-run elasticities (see Dahl and Sterner 1991a). One advantage with the pure cross-section studies is that they permit the use of such simple models that still appear to pick up long-run elasticities. Note also that the use of dynamic models (the lagged endogenous model $M_1$) with cross-section data gives rather strange values (see Table 4.1, note).

It is interesting to note that the development of the elasticities over time turns out to be moderately stable between most individual pairs of years but that over longer intervals of time there are some appreciable variations. In particular, between 1972 and 1977 there is a constant decline in price elasticities, which reverses after 1977 and increases thereafter, particularly until 1982. One possible explanation is that the international price increase in 1972–3 had strongly varying effects on the domestic price levels in different OECD countries. These differences depended on the degree of energy self-sufficiency and on whether or not the government tried to accommodate price changes through tax policy. In any event, consumption adjusted very slowly for two reasons: first, lags are always important as has already been emphasized, and second, there was less preparedness for this first oil shock. Between 1972 and 1977 price differentiation between countries increased

*Table 4.1* Elasticity estimates with pure cross-sections

| Year | Price elasticity | t | Income elasticity | t | N | $R^2$ |
|------|------------------|---|-------------------|---|---|-------|
| 1970 | −1.27 | −4.92 | 1.15 | 6.16 | 23 | 0.91 |
| 1971 | −1.14 | −4.84 | 1.25 | 6.86 | 23 | 0.91 |
| 1972 | −1.19 | −5.28 | 1.23 | 7.15 | 23 | 0.91 |
| 1973 | −0.95 | −4.55 | 1.39 | 8.50 | 23 | 0.89 |
| 1974 | −0.91 | −4.80 | 1.28 | 6.95 | 23 | 0.88 |
| 1975 | −0.87 | −3.69 | 1.20 | 5.62 | 23 | 0.85 |
| 1976 | −0.78 | −3.79 | 1.25 | 6.12 | 23 | 0.85 |
| 1977 | −0.77 | −4.27 | 1.26 | 6.80 | 23 | 0.86 |
| 1978 | −1.08 | −5.31 | 0.92 | 4.68 | 23 | 0.90 |
| 1979 | −1.13 | −4.33 | 0.92 | 3.96 | 23 | 0.88 |
| 1980 | −1.25 | −6.24 | 0.88 | 4.83 | 23 | 0.91 |
| 1981 | −1.20 | −5.10 | 1.08 | 5.93 | 23 | 0.89 |
| 1982 | −1.34 | −5.64 | 0.82 | 3.98 | 23 | 0.89 |
| 1983 | −1.05 | −4.78 | 1.00 | 4.90 | 23 | 0.87 |
| 1984 | −1.20 | −4.93 | 0.82 | 3.79 | 22 | 0.88 |
| 1985 | −0.98 | −3.92 | 1.02 | 4.60 | 19 | 0.85 |
| Mean[a] | −1.09 | | 1.08 | | | |

*Notes*: These results were obtained using the simple static model.
[a]This is the weighted mean (using the inverse of standard deviations as weights). The simple averages were −1.07 and 1.09 respectively. When using a static vehicle model $G = f(Y, P, V)$, where $V$ is the vehicle stock, the mean price elasticity was −1.18 but the mean income elasticity was practically zero, this effect being picked up by the vehicle variable. When using the dynamic model $M_1$ the mean short-run price elasticity was −0.15 and the income elasticity 0.04. $\lambda$ was 0.85 and thus long-run elasticities can be calculated as −1.0 and 0.27. The values varied markedly between individual years.

with little immediate effect on consumption. After 1977 this process was gradually reversed with consumption finally adjusting but price policies (in most OECD countries) becoming increasingly harmonized in line with international price levels (although with large differences remaining due to fiscal and environmental considerations).

### 4.2.2 Time-series estimates

Using the data as time series allows for the study of possible variations between different countries, which may be very useful in itself since there is no particular reason why the elasticities should be identical between countries. If, however, an overall estimate for the whole group of countries is still considered desirable, there are two ways of using the time-series estimates to give such a global estimate, as pointed out in Chapter 2. First, data for all the individual countries can be aggregated and an aggregate time-series analysis can be conducted. (Note that this is, in a sense, no different from treating the United States as a single-country observation since it is already an aggregation of the various states.) Second, (weighted) averages of the individual time-series estimates for each country can be taken, yielding the 'mean group estimates'.

Table 4.2 lists a set of such individual estimates and the corresponding averages for the lagged endogenous ($M_1$) model. A quick glance at Table 4.2 will convince the reader that there is a considerable difference between the time-series and the cross-section results. The time-series estimates of long-run price elasticities (+0.1 and −2.3) vary more between countries than the cross-section estimates (−0.8 to −1.3). The significance levels are also generally lower.

For some countries the results are rather unexpected. This is the case, for instance, with the positive price elasticity in Switzerland. However, it appears that transit traffic and cross-border purchasing of gasoline between Switzerland, Austria, Germany and Italy is very significant and distorts the results for the relatively small Swiss market. Another country with which problems were encountered was Japan, where an unrestricted estimate of 0.93 for $\lambda$ and (insignificantly) negative income elasticities was obtained. Since such a value for the lagged endogenous variable implies an unreasonably slow adjustment (adjustment would be only 75 per cent complete twenty years after a change in gasoline price!) this parameter was arbitrarily set to 0.8 (which is still higher than the average of 0.69).

Naturally there are many other country particularities that may help to explain variations for individual countries. The case of Sweden, which has been analysed in greater detail elsewhere (see Sterner 1990), will be discussed. Throughout most of the period under discussion Sweden has had uniquely high rates of marginal income taxation. These have been combined, however, with very generous allowances for deducting driving expenses, and thus the companies have had a strong incentive to give their employees cars instead of cash and the latter have had a strong incentive to drive long distances to work. Naturally the incentive effect of gasoline prices has been relatively low and thus also the price elasticities were low (see Table 4.3).

In spite of the variations discussed above, as well as others that are apparent from the table, one may want to consider, with more or less confidence, the mean group estimates as an overall estimate for the OECD as a whole during this period. As noted in Chapter 2 there are two ways of calculating such averages: either by taking (weighted) averages of the long-run elasticity estimates directly or by taking averages of the individual country parameters (short-run elasticities and $\lambda$s) and then calculating a long-run elasticity from these means using, as usual, $\varepsilon_{sr}/(1 - \lambda)$. The choice depends on which hypothesis is made about the distribution of $\alpha$, $\beta$ and $\lambda$ (see Chapter 2).

As it turns out the results do not vary very much between these two hypotheses, but the income elasticity is very sensitive to the difference between weighted and simple means. The simple average of the price elasticities is −0.85, or −0.81 when calculated as the mean of the short-run

Table 4.2 Individual country elasticities (model $M_1$)[a]

| | $\varepsilon_p$(sr) | $\varepsilon_p$(lr) | $\varepsilon_y$(sr) | $\varepsilon_y$(lr) | $\lambda$ | DF | $R^2$ | DH |
|---|---|---|---|---|---|---|---|---|
| Canada | -0.25 (-4.48) | -1.07 (0.35) | 0.12 (1.34) | 0.53 (0.17) | 0.77 (7.05) | 19 | 0.97 | -1.01 |
| United States | -0.18 (-6.59) | -1.00 (0.41) | 0.18 (2.62) | 1.00 (0.17) | 0.82 (12.44) | 21 | 0.98 | 0.11 |
| Austria | -0.25 (-2.30) | -0.59 (0.26) | 0.51 (2.19) | 1.19 (0.19) | 0.57 (3.69) | 18 | 0.97 | -0.52 |
| Belgium | -0.36 (-7.54) | -0.71 (0.17) | 0.63 (3.24) | 1.25 (0.06) | 0.49 (3.54) | 21 | 0.99 | 0.14 |
| Denmark | -0.30 (-7.94) | -0.64 (0.08) | 0.25 (4.63) | 0.52 (0.05) | 0.52 (8.32) | 20 | 0.97 | b |
| Finland | -0.32 (-2.90) | -1.23 (0.39) | 0.32 (2.17) | 1.22 (0.18) | 0.74 (8.31) | 20 | 0.98 | b |
| France | -0.36 (-4.60) | -0.70 (0.17) | 0.64 (2.83) | 1.23 (0.07) | 0.48 (3.00) | 21 | 0.99 | 0.00 |
| Germany | -0.05 (-0.68) | -0.57 (1.01) | 0.04 (0.25) | 0.48 (1.43) | 0.92 (11.86) | 21 | 0.99 | 0.63 |
| Greece | -0.23 (-2.15) | -1.12 (0.74) | 0.41 (2.19) | 2.03 (0.26) | 0.80 (7.56) | 16 | 0.99 | 0.20 |
| Ireland | -0.21 (-4.88) | -1.68 (1.14) | 0.12 (0.88) | 0.93 (0.44) | 0.87 (9.70) | 21 | 0.99 | 0.82 |
| Italy | -0.37 (-2.94) | -1.15 (0.33) | 0.40 (2.41) | 1.25 (0.28) | 0.68 (8.40) | 21 | 0.97 | -0.97 |
| Netherlands | -0.57 (-5.01) | -2.29 (0.76) | 0.14 (1.09) | 0.57 (0.30) | 0.75 (6.97) | 21 | 0.98 | -1.43 |
| Norway | -0.43 (-3.22) | -0.90 (0.31) | 0.63 (3.13) | 1.32 (0.11) | 0.52 (3.64) | 21 | 0.97 | -0.83 |
| Portugal | -0.13 (-1.96) | -0.67 (0.38) | 0.37 (2.05) | 1.93 (0.36) | 0.81 (11.18) | 15 | 0.98 | b |

| | | | | | | | |
|---|---|---|---|---|---|---|---|
| Spain | -0.14 (-0.82) | -0.30 (0.46) | 0.96 (2.12) | 2.08 (0.27) | 0.54 (2.92) | 13 | 0.97 | c |
| Sweden | -0.13 (-2.07) | -0.46 (0.21) | 0.33 (3.10) | 1.16 (0.11) | 0.72 (10.38) | 32 | 0.99 | -1.41 |
| Switzerland | 0.05 (0.32) | 0.09 (0.28) | 0.85 (2.92) | 1.54 (0.15) | 0.45 (3.08) | 22 | 0.98 | 1.30 |
| Great Britain | -0.11 (-1.66) | -0.45 (0.37) | 0.36 (1.81) | 1.47 (0.24) | 0.75 (6.37) | 21 | 0.98 | -0.87 |
| Australia | -0.05 (-2.57) | -0.18 (0.08) | 0.18 (2.44) | 0.71 (0.09) | 0.75 (9.97) | 20 | 0.99 | 0.10 |
| Japan | -0.15 (-4.37) | -0.76 | 0.15 (11.86) | 0.77 | 0.80[d] | 21 | 0.90 | d |
| Turkey | -0.31 (-5.31) | -0.61 (0.22) | 0.65 (4.01) | 1.29 (0.17) | 0.50 (3.91) | 15 | 0.95 | -0.90 |
| Mean | -0.25 | -0.85 | 0.37 | 1.15 | 0.69 | | | |
| Weighted mean[e] | -0.76 | -0.76 | | 0.79 | | | | |
| Aggregate time series | -0.31 | -1.28 | 0.29 | 1.19 | 0.76 | 25 | 0.99 | |

*Notes:* The long-run standard deviation for the OLS estimations is calculated using the Bardsen (1989) method.
[a] The time period is 1960–86; for Sweden 1950–86; for Spain 1965–86.
[b] Re-estimated with GLS because of high degree of autocorrelation.
[c] Durbin H could not be calculated.
[d] The Japanese results are estimated with the restriction that the speed of adjustment is 0.2. Hence the missing *t* values.
[e] Weighted by the inverse of the standard deviation for long-run elasticities. Switzerland not included. Japan given average weights.
Note that long-run elasticities can also be calculated from the means of the short-run elasticities and the lag-end parameter. With unweighted means this method give us values of -0.81 and 1.19 respectively.

elasticities divided by (one minus) the mean of the $\lambda$s. The weighted average of the long-run elasticities is $-0.76$. For the income elasticities the corresponding figures are 1.15, 1.19 and 0.79 respectively. The reason the weighted estimate is so much lower is mainly the effect of Germany which has a very low long-run income elasticity combined with very high levels of significance (and thus a very heavy weight). The unweighted income elasticity, however, concurs well with the cross-sectional evidence found above, while average long-run price elasticities are, as expected, somewhat lower. The same also applies to the aggregate estimates (time series on the sum of all observations) of $-1.28$ and 1.19 respectively; however, in this case the price elasticity is very high.

As noted earlier a number of other dynamic[5] models $M_2$, $M_3$ and $M_4$ can be postulated. $M_2$ is the only functional form for which any tests could be readily conducted (since $M_1$ is nested in $M_2$). In fact it was found that the addition, in $M_2$, of the lagged exogenous variables did not appear to add much, and the more restricted model $M_1$ could not be rejected. The results for $M_2$, which were similar to the other 'inverted-V' lag model ($M_3$) in any case,

Table 4.3 Comparison of long-run elasticities

| | Price elasticities | | | Income elasticities | | |
|---|---|---|---|---|---|---|
| | $M_4$ | $M_1$ | $M_2$ | $M_4$ | $M_1$ | $M_2$ |
| Canada | $-2.0$ | $-1.1$ | $-0.9$ | 0.6 | 0.5 | 0.6 |
| United States | $-1.2$ | $-1.0$ | $-0.6$ | 1.2 | 1.0 | 0.8 |
| Austria | $-1.2$ | $-0.6$ | $-0.7$ | 0.9 | 1.2 | 1.2 |
| Belgium | $-1.5$ | $-0.7$ | $-0.6$ | 1.0 | 1.3 | 1.3 |
| Denmark | $-0.8$ | $-0.6$ | $-0.6$ | 0.3 | 0.6 | 0.6 |
| Finland | $-1.2$ | $-1.0$ | $-0.9$ | 1.2 | 1.4 | 1.4 |
| France | $-0.4$ | $-0.7$ | $-0.6$ | 0.9 | 1.2 | 1.1 |
| Germany | $+0.1$ | $-0.6$ | $+0.3$ | 1.6 | 0.5 | 1.9 |
| Greece | $+0.2$ | $-1.1$ | $-0.6$ | 1.8 | 2.0 | 1.9 |
| Ireland | $-1.0$ | $-1.7$ | $-0.8$ | 1.3 | 0.9 | 1.3 |
| Italy | $-0.7$ | $-1.2$ | $-0.9$ | 0.9 | 1.3 | 1.2 |
| Netherlands | $-3.2$ | $-2.3$ | $-1.5$ | 0.4 | 0.6 | 0.8 |
| Norway | $-2.5$ | $-0.9$ | $-0.8$ | 1.3 | 1.3 | 1.3 |
| Portugal | $-0.7$ | $-0.3$ | $-0.1$ | 1.1 | 2.1 | 2.2 |
| Spain | $-1.2$ | $-0.3$ | $-0.1$ | 1.4 | 2.1 | 2.4 |
| Sweden | $-0.1$ | $-0.45$ | $-0.43$ | 1.2 | 1.2 | 1.3 |
| Switzerland | $+0.15$ | $+0.1$ | $+0.1$ | 1.8 | 1.5 | 1.6 |
| Great Britain | $-1.4$ | $-0.5$ | $-0.4$ | 1.6 | 1.5 | 1.6 |
| Australia | $-0.2$ | $-0.2$ | $-0.1$ | 1.2 | 0.7 | 0.8 |
| Japan | $-0.3$ | $-0.8$ | $-0.8$ | 0.8 | 0.8 | 0.8 |
| Turkey | $-1.1$ | $-0.6$ | $-0.5$ | 1.1 | 1.3 | 1.2 |
| Mean | $-1.0$ | $-0.8$ | $-0.6$ | 1.1 | 1.2 | 1.3 |

will not, therefore, be reported. Table 4.3 summarizes the long-run elasticities for the remaining models $M_1$, $M_3$ and $M_4$, again indicating that the estimates are not all that robust to changes in functional form and showing that more work is required on at least some of the individual countries.

### 4.2.3 Pooled estimates

And finally, the results obtained from the use of pooled estimators will be discussed and the results will be compared with the averages obtained from cross-sections and time series. Table 4.4 contains a number of estimates. These include the ordinary pooled OLS estimator with common intercepts, the fixed effects or so-called 'within' estimator[6] that allows for individual country intercepts, and the generalized least squares estimator (GLS). For the last-mentioned the results of several models are reported. For comparison, the aggregate cross-section or so-called 'between' estimator is also reported, together with both the aggregate time-series and the mean group estimates.

One of the principal points raised in Chapter 2 concerned the risks for sizeable bias when using the lagged endogenous dynamic model with pooled data. The $\lambda$ will tend to be biased towards unity and the short-run elasticities towards zero. This is indeed clearly found in the OLS estimate even if the results are somewhat less dramatic than in the empirical example used in Chapter 2. A $\lambda$ estimate of 0.91, however, implies that only one-tenth of the adaptation occurs in the first year and is indeed difficult to justify intuitively. In addition, the short-run income elasticity has an implausibly low value of 0.05. As in Chapter 2 both these results remain largely true, but to a somewhat lesser extent, with the fixed effects estimator.

The estimated price elasticity, listed in Table 4.2, is $-1.3$, which is in fact higher than the typical time-series values. To illustrate graphically, the relationship between pooled and time-series estimates is complicated by the fact that there are two exogenous variables (as well as lagged variables). However, the assumption that the income elasticity is close to unity (which it tends to be) allows price elasticities to be more closely examined. Figure 4.1 is intended to capture the difference (under this assumption) between different types of estimates by plotting $Q/Y$ against $P$. The figure shows that the pooled (OLS) estimate will indeed be steeper (more price elastic) than the individual time series for the two countries selected, Sweden and Canada.

The 'between' estimator highlights, as the name suggests, the variation between countries. It is a cross-section of the averages over time for each country. The results are not far from the pure cross-section estimates in Table 4.1. The reason why this estimate is lower than the 'within' estimate in Table 4.2 is that the 'between' estimate is based on a static model. Indeed, 'within' estimation of the static model gives values of around $-0.4$.

OLS estimation takes variation both within and between countries into account. However, as pointed out by Baltagi and Griffin (1983), it may be

Table 4.4 Summary of long-run elasticity estimates for the OECD[a]

| Estimation technique | Model | SR price elasticity | LR price elasticity | SR income elasticity | LR income elasticity | Lag-end | DFE | $R^2$ |
|---|---|---|---|---|---|---|---|---|
| Pooled OLS[b] | $M_1$ | −0.12 (−9.3) | −1.39 | 0.05 (3.8) | 0.58 | 0.91 (97.7) | 479 | 0.99 |
| Pooled (fix effects) 'within'[c] | $M_1$ | −0.22 (−10.4) | −1.27 | 0.13 (4.2) | 0.75 | 0.83 (43.1) | 459 | 0.99 |
| Pooled GLS (Fuller and Battese method) | $M_1$ | −0.18 (−10.2) | −1.35 | 0.10 (4.1) | 0.73 | 0.87 (62.0) | 479 | |
| | $M_2$ | −0.22 (−8.5) | −1.34 | 0.25 (2.4) | 0.69 | 0.89 (61.4) | 477 | |
| | $M_3$ | −0.15 (−11.4) | −1.16 | 0.14 (11.0) | 0.63 | 0.87 | 491 | |
| Pooled GLS (Yule–Walker method) | $M_4$[d] | −0.38 (−7.5) | −1.05 | 1.13 (27.0) | 1.63 | | 406 | 0.96 |
| *To compare* | | | | | | | | |
| Between[e] cross-section | Static $M_0$ | | −1.19 (−5.4) | | 1.09 (6.08) | | 18 | 0.90 |
| Mean group estimates | $M_1$ | | −0.76 | | 0.79 | | | |
| Aggregate time series | $M_1$ | −0.31 | −1.28 | 0.29 | 1.19 | 0.76 | 21 | |

Notes: [a]OECD except Luxembourg, Iceland and New Zealand, 1963–85. Purchasing power parity used for conversion.
[b]Even for the static model, OLs produces high price elasticities: −0.98 and 1.26.
[c]For the static model, 'within' estimates do give a typical 'intermediate' value of −0.4 for price.
[d]PDL of second degree, with eight price and four income lags for 1970–85.
[e]'Between' is a cross-section for the static model on average data.

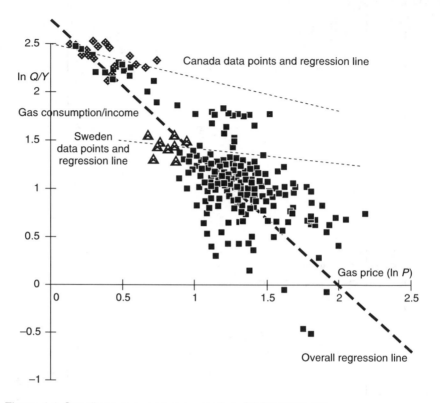

*Figure 4.1* Gasoline prices and consumption, OECD 1960–88

influenced too much by 'between' variation since both within-country (between years) and between-country variation are given equal weight, despite the fact that the between-country error term would be expected to have much greater variance. Therefore, the GLS estimator is proposed in order to take into consideration the respective variances of the error components so as to provide a better estimate. Baltagi and Griffin use five different two-stage GLS estimators that give different estimates, but state that there is no suitable way to choose between them. In this case only one estimator has been chosen (following Fuller and Battese 1974; see Drummond and Gallant 1979). Attention is concentrated, instead, on variation due to the model used and the region or time period analysed.

For the lagged endogenous model, a significant gap between the 'within' and the OLS estimators is found. Furthermore the GLS estimate fits neatly in between the two for both price and income elasticities.[7] The inverted-V lag, $M_3$, gave slightly lower (and more plausible?) price elasticities.[8] This model is subject to the same type of bias as discussed above, however. Of particular interest is the polynomial distributed lag model $M_4$, since it has no lagged endogenous variable. $M_4$ was estimated with a Yule–Walker GLS auto-regressive procedure (see Gallant and Goebel 1976). This gives lower price elasticities but much higher income elasticities. It must be noted, however, that the period used for estimation is much shorter owing to the data required for the lags on price and income.

To sum up all the pooled estimates, very low income elasticities (except in the PDL) and high long-run price elasticities ($-1.2$ to $-1.4$) are found. Compared with the cross-section estimates the price (but not income) elasticities seem to concur rather well. Compared with aggregate or mean time-series results, however, the price elasticities are indeed higher but the income elasticities still considerably lower.[9]

And finally, it should be pointed out that the estimates are considerably higher than those reported by Baltagi and Griffin. This has already been discussed by Sterner (1991) who noted two factors explaining the difference. First, Baltagi and Griffin used gasoline per vehicle as an endogenous variable. As they rightly point out this assumes that the number of vehicles is insensitive to the price of gasoline and thus their price elasticities were correspondingly biased. Second, and more interestingly, in the present study a 'moving window' approach was used to show that the pooled estimates were rather sensitive to the exact composition of countries and years included. With longer time periods the price elasticities tended to increase and for some,

*Table 4.5* Elasticities for different regions and time periods

|  | LR price elasticity | LR income elasticity | Lag-end |
|---|---|---|---|
| *1963–78* | | | |
| OECD | −1.15 | 0.98 | 0.84 |
| EU | −1.01 | 0.72 | 0.87 |
| North Europe | −0.78 | 0.95 | 0.78 |
| Scandinavia | −0.93 | 1.06 | 0.68 |
| Non-Europe | −1.74 | 0.91 | 0.83 |
| *1963–85* | | | |
| OECD | −1.35 | 0.73 | 0.87 |
| EU | −1.41 | 0.38 | 0.89 |
| North Europe | −1.28 | 0.65 | 0.84 |
| Scandinavia | −1.08 | 0.96 | 0.74 |
| Non-Europe | −2.12 | 0.58 | 0.88 |

*Notes*: This is a generalized 'moving window' approach allowing regions and time periods to vary. The model is $M_1$ estimated with GLS (Fuller and Battese). Regions are defined as follows: OECD except Iceland, Luxembourg and New Zealand; EU is defined as above except Norway, Sweden, Findland and Switzerland; North Europe is defined as above except Spain, Portugal, Belgium, France, Austria and Italy; Scandinavia is Norway, Sweden, Denmark and Finland; Non-Europe is Canada, United States, Australia, Japan and Turkey.

smaller, samples of countries the price elasticities even increased quite dramatically, as shown in Table 4.5.

## 4.3 CONCLUSIONS

In this chapter the focus has been on the long-run price sensitivity of gasoline demand. By comparing time-series, cross-section and pooled estimators using different models it is hoped that yet another empirical illustration of the systematic sources of differences between the estimators analysed in Chapter 2 has been provided. Although pooled estimators appear to be an attractive way of using all the available information, Pesaran and Smith have shown that pooled estimators with dynamic model specifications give biased values and the modeller thus has to turn to other estimators. The findings in this study are, in this respect, fully in accord with those in Chapter 2. Furthermore it was found, as expected, that cross-sections tend to give higher price elasticities than time series. Moreover, they do so even with simple static models, whereas time-series data require the modeller to use dynamic specifications. And finally, the potential importance of which countries and years are actually included in the data set analysed is discussed.

## NOTES

1   Other approaches are discussed in Sterner (1990).
2   The main reason for their exclusion is lack of data on vehicle prices, public transport availability and road infrastructure variables etc.
3   This model can be derived by assuming that desired consumption is $G_t^* = c + \alpha P_t + \beta Y_t + \varepsilon_{t1}$ but that adaptation is partial: $G_t - G_{t-1} = s(G_t^* - G_{t-1}) + \varepsilon_{t2}$. Note that this implies that $\mu_t = s\varepsilon_{t1} + \varepsilon_{t2}$.
4   The static model and the models $M_1$ and $M_2$ are the same as in Chapter 2 but models $M_3$ and $M_4$ defined here are not used in Chapter 2.
5   The static model could also be used but, as shown in Chapter 2 or in Sterner (1990), static estimates will be biased if the true model does indeed include some form of lag structure. See also Table 4.4, note c.
6   'Within' is basically an estimator designed to pick up elasticities due to variation within countries. It is estimated as an OLS with country dummies on the intercept (for the lagged endogenous model specification).
7   In a single explanatory variable model the GLS estimator must fall between the OLS and the 'within' estimator but this does not necessarily apply in models with several explanatory factors.
8   Note that nested tests cannot be carried out comparing (4.5) and (4.4) because of the restriction on the parameters of $G_{t-1}$ and $G_{t-2}$.
9   Except when compared with the weighted average which, however, as we saw above was very heavily influenced by one single country.

# Chapter 5

# Responses of energy demand in UK manufacturing to the energy price increases of 1973 and 1979–80

*Alan Ingham*

## ABSTRACT

This chapter presents estimates of energy elasticities based on a vintage model of UK manufacturing (excluding the iron and steel industries). Energy price changes affect energy demand in the model in two ways. The first is through the design of newly installed equipment. This depends on expectations of future factor prices. The second is though changing the use of existing equipment. This depends upon actual factor prices. The model thus allows for differing *ex ante* and *ex post* responses. The magnitude of the first response will determine the long-run elasticity.

The chapter takes an estimated model for the period 1971–90 and considers how the observed changes in the energy–output ratio over that time can be decomposed into that part explained by technical progress, that part explained by changes in the level of production, that part explained by changes in wage rates and that part explained by changes in energy prices in terms of (i) the expectation of future energy prices and (ii) their realized value. In particular the effect of energy price changes in 1973 and 1981 will be decomposed into that part which worked through changing expectations and that part which worked through changing current factor prices.

## INTRODUCTION

The discussion of the proposed European Union carbon/energy tax has led to considerable interest in energy demand elasticities, as they are vital to an understanding of the economic and environmental impact of such policies. The purpose of this chapter is to consider what insights might be obtained from a dynamic model based on economic structure rather than of a statistical time-series nature. Ideally, such a model would be used to separate out short-run from long-run consequences and to estimate the length of adjustment to taxes, especially if environmental problems arising out of energy use need to be addressed within a particular time period. Furthermore, an analysis of the effect of the announcement of future taxes on present energy consumption would be desirable. Ideally, the model should be structural as the use of a purely statistical model might run into regime shift problems.

In order to answer these questions, the use of a vintage model, such as that which has been constructed for the Department of Trade and Industry (formerly the Department of Energy) to assist in the evaluation of long-run forecasts, is appropriate. The original motivation for the study was to explain the changes in energy demand that resulted from the large energy price changes of 1973 and 1980. Box–Jenkins type studies had not been able to explain the fall in energy demand after the 1980 price rise. By considering a more detailed structural model of the decisions made by industry it was hoped that the delays in reacting to price changes could be explained. The model has been moderately successful in this respect and the purpose of this chapter is to consider what the price elasticities of energy demand were during periods of large price changes. This will allow for the estimation of the extent to which energy demand falls both in the short run immediately following price rises and in the long run if these price rises continue into the future.

One disadvantage of the model used is that the specification of the model does not allow for a simple answer to this question. The first reason for this is that there are no simple closed-form solutions dependent upon a few parameter estimates, so it is generally necessary to undertake simulations. The second problem is that the magnitude of the response depends potentially on all the exogenous variables. Thus it is necessary to undertake a series of *ceteris paribus* simulations. This is handled by considering several scenarios, varying the magnitude of the price rise and the growth of output.

An early version of the model was described by Ingham *et al.* (1988). More recently, work has concentrated on the simulation of possible carbon/energy taxation policies. These simulations are reported in Ingham and Ulph (1991a, b) and Ingham *et al.* (1991a). In this chapter the concern is strictly with energy demand changes by United Kingdom manufacturing during the period 1971–90, in particular in the years of the two oil shocks.

The effect of an increase in the rate of growth of price increases on the economy works through several channels. There will be the immediate substitution out of energy, depending on the degree of substitutability. Next the increase in energy prices will cause certain plants to become uneconomic. They will be closed down and possibly replaced. Any new plants will embody more energy-saving technology, with the extent of energy saving dependent upon the expected price increase. Faster growth in price increases will change expectations more rapidly and so more rapid transformation of the capital stock and a greater degree of adjustment would be expected.

The degree of adjustment will also affect the extent to which new investment is taking place, irrespective of new investment caused by premature scrapping. While some of this investment occurs because of routine replacement of depreciated equipment, the rest is determined by the need for extra capacity. The faster this new capacity is installed the faster the effects of increasing prices should be felt. This will be considered by simulating the effects of increasing energy prices for different growth rates of output for the manufacturing sector. This is an important question for energy and environmental policy since policies which increase energy prices may slow down the rate of growth of output and lead to less, rather than more, substitution.

These effects depend upon the expectational mechanism. The mechanism employed in the model is an adaptive process where expected prices are extrapolations of trends calculated from linear regressions using past observations. The length of the data set for these regressions determines the extent to which the past is incorporated as an estimated parameter in the model. Expectations enter into the model through a present value expression, which means that the changed expectations are very slow to take effect. Two alternative possibilities are also considered. One is that of perfect foresight, which is similar to a rational expectations formulation. Given the data sets available, this formulation can only be applied in so far as there are sufficient observations. The existence of missing observations is overcome by extending the data using existing trends. The calculation of the effect of such a formulation is important since a likely policy would be to announce, in a credible way, increased energy taxes in the future, thereby obtaining immediate energy reductions through changes in the design of newly installed equipment.

A second alternative is to consider a purely myopic form of expectations, wherein the current real energy price is expected to rule for ever. As will be seen this has, at first sight, some surprising effects. A final set of simulations looks at the effect of a sudden increase in energy prices. This is carried out under two scenarios, one wherein the increase is expected by industry and the other where it is unexpected. The first case corresponds to the perfect foresight scenario, with the second case corresponding to perfect foresight until the price increase, adaptive expectations in the period following the increase, and perfect foresight thereafter. It is hoped that this gives an impression of the extent to which perfect foresight anticipates future price changes, and the delay before which the effect of an unanticipated price change wears off.

The chapter proceeds in the following manner. Section 5.1 considers the specification of the vintage model. This is done in a descriptive and intuitive way. A more formal mathematical specification of the model is provided in Appendix 5A, and details of the estimated parameters are provided in Appendix 5B. Section 5.2 considers data availability on the nature of vintage changes over time, and the consequent implications of such changes for the short-run and long-run behaviour of the model. Section 5.3 considers the results from applying the model to simulations. This is divided into two parts. The first set of simulations is designed to calculate energy price elasticities and to consider the various factors that will influence them. The second set of simulations looks at the role that price expectations may have played in determining changes in energy demand. Finally Section 5.4 provides conclusions.

## 5.1  A DESCRIPTION OF THE VINTAGE MODEL

An important aspect of a vintage model of factor demands is that it allows for the analysis of the dynamics by which producers will respond to price changes. In the short run, producers can respond either by adjusting the mix of variable factors employed on machines already installed (e.g. there may be some scope for fuel switching) or by varying the output produced on machines of different ages (vintages). But in the long run there is the more important response of changes in the capital stock by scrapping old machines and investing in new ones employing different factor proportions.

In early developments of the vintage model (e.g. Salter 1966; Malcomson and Prior 1979), it was assumed that technology had a structure characterized as 'putty-clay'. Thus it was assumed that the scope for varying the mix of factors (e.g. labour, raw materials, energy) employed on a machine installed at a particular time (vintage) occurred only at the design stage (an *ex ante* decision), and once the machine was installed factors such as labour or energy would be employed on that machine in fixed proportion to the output produced; the only way in which firms could vary the mix of factors they employed on machines which were already available would be to vary how much output was produced on different machines (an *ex post* decision).

In the model employed, based on Fuss (1977a), there is some scope for varying the input–output ratios even at the *ex post* stage, though the scope for doing so will in general be less than at the *ex ante* stage; moreover producers decide at the *ex ante* stage how much *ex post* substitution (flexibility) they wish to have (within technology limits) depending on how much they expect relative prices to vary over the design life of the machine. This structure is called putty-semi-putty. The full details of this model are provided in Appendix 5A.

The model can be characterized in simple terms as follows. Begin with the producer's choice of design of machine *ex ante* and choice of actual factor mix *ex post*, assuming that there are only two factors, labour and energy, and that the producer knows what output level will be produced on a machine once it is operational. At the time of designing the machine the prices of labour and energy are expected to be $\hat{W}$ and $\hat{P}$ respectively, while actual factor prices turn out to be $W$ and $P$. Figure 5.1 depicts the situation with putty-clay technology. AA is the *ex ante* isoquant, representing the mixes of labour and energy that the machine could be designed to operate with. Given expected factor prices, the producer chooses to operate with the mix represented by point X. *Ex post* there is no scope for varying the mix of factors, so the *ex post* isoquant is BB, and if actual factor prices turn out to be $W$ and $P$ the producers will be operating with a mix of factors which is considerably more expensive than would have been the case if they had predicted relative factor prices correctly (point Y). The putty-semi-putty model is illustrated in Figure 5.2. The situation is more complicated, so the description will be rather more intuitive.

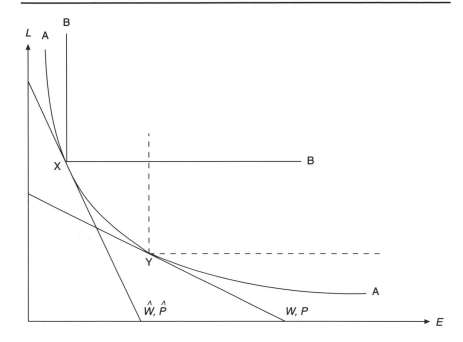

*Figure 5.1  Ex ante* technology putty-clay

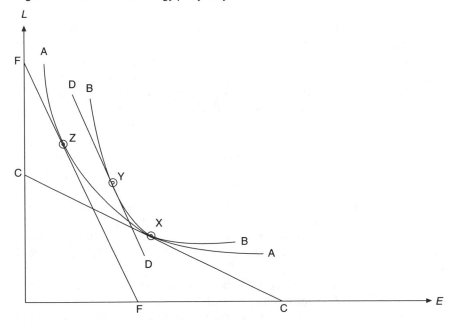

*Figure 5.2  Ex ante* technology putty-semi-putty

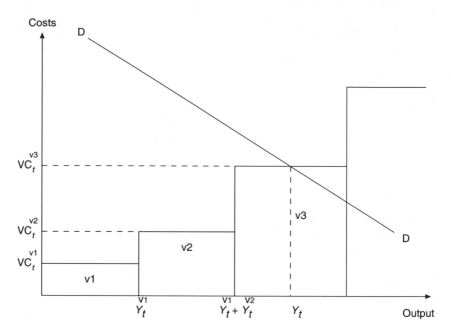

*Figure 5.3  Ex post decision*

Again given the ratio of expected future prices the producer must choose from the *ex ante* isoquant AA the ratio of labour to energy that would be employed *ex post* if actual factor prices equalled expected prices; this is shown by the point X, or more precisely the entire set of such prices is shown by the ray through X. Corresponding to this point is a family of *ex post* isoquants (BB and CC are two examples) with differing degrees of *ex post* factor substitution. Depending on the extent to which relative factor prices are expected to change over the life of the machine (i.e. the expected variability in factor prices), the producer will select the appropriate *ex post* isoquant. If it is expected that factor prices will not differ much from the ratio represented by $\hat{P}$ and $\hat{W}$, an isoquant such as CC is chosen, with little potential for *ex post* substitution, since that will minimize production costs; however, if quite wide variations are expected, e.g. $P$ and $W$, then it will be cheaper to have an isoquant like BB which allows for some degree of *ex post* substitution. In that case when actual prices are $P$ and $W$ the firm could move from factor mix X to factor mix Y.

   In order to see how producers decide how much output to produce from each vintage at each point in time, note first that given the *ex post* choice of input–output coefficients for variable factors firms can first calculate the unit variable cost of production on each available vintage and then rank them in increasing order of unit cost, as shown in Figure 5.3, where the maximum amount of output that can be produced on each vintage depends on the original installed capacity and any subsequent depreciation, which is assumed to be reflected solely in terms of reduced available capacity, as if some fraction of machines become obsolete each period while the rest continue operating at their design efficiency. This gives the supply curve of producers and Figure 5.3 shows two ways in which overall output is determined. In the first case, total output $Y_t$ is simply specified exogenously, in which case vintages will be employed in order of increasing unit variable cost until aggregate available capacity exceeds output required. In the figure, vintages 1 and 2 will be fully employed, vintages 4 onwards will not be employed and vintage 3 will be the marginal vintage, with the machine operating at less than full capacity.

In the second case, the output produced depends on the price of output (e.g. as shown by the demand curve DD), and in this case price and output are determined simultaneously by supply and demand. Specifically, price is set equal to the variable cost of the marginal vintage employed plus a mark-up reflecting the fact that the output market may not be fully competitive. In fact, output and price are not determined simultaneously; rather, a model of price adjustment, which is described shortly, is employed.

And finally, the determination of rates of investment and scrapping must be addressed. Producers use their expectations of future factor prices to compare the present value of operating costs on existing vintages over the planning horizon with the present value of total production costs (operating and capital costs) on a new machine. Old machines have the advantage that their capital costs have been sunk, but new machines have the advantage of being designed specifically to meet the relative factor prices expected to prevail in the future and of embodying any improvement in technology. Old machines which are more expensive than a new machine are scrapped. Firms compare the capacity that they plan to have available on old machines at the date a new machine could be installed with the output they expect to have to produce at that date in order to meet demand; if capacity falls short of expected demand, new machines are commissioned to provide the additional capacity; if capacity exceeds expected demand, there is no new investment, and the more expensive of the old machines will be scrapped until some specific margin of excess capacity remains. It should therefore be clear that a sharp change in expected factor prices relative to those which were expected to prevail when old machines were built is likely to lead to a lot of old machines being scrapped and new ones ordered. The capital stock parameters have been estimated on quarterly data for the UK manufacturing sector for the period 1971Q1–1989Q4. Details are provided in Appendix 5B.

## 5.2  THE ESTIMATED MODEL AND ITS USE IN SIMULATION

### 5.2.1  The goodness of fit

The tables and figures which follow are the results obtained from the best fit over the sample period. Turning first to the labour, energy and investment series, displays of the actual and fitted series are produced in Figures 5.4–5.6. Figure 5.4 shows that employment is fitted quite well. Turning points and sharp declines are predicted well. The model tends to react more quickly than the economy actually does, and the upturn in 1973 and the decline in 1975 are predicted to have happened one quarter too early. The fitted series is more variable than the actual path, even though the employment series is taken to be hours worked multiplied by the PUL index of labour utilization (see Smith-Gavine and Bennett 1993). Neither of these effects is too surprising. There is nothing in the model which prevents manufacturing from responding immediately to changes in factor prices and demand, apart from the nature of the capital stock. Hence the fitted employment series will be that level of labour services which manufacturing would like to employ, rather than that level which it has to employ because of hiring and firing costs, redundancy legislation and other labour market characteristics.

The other main comment to be made on the performance of the model in explaining labour demand is that the model tends to underpredict labour

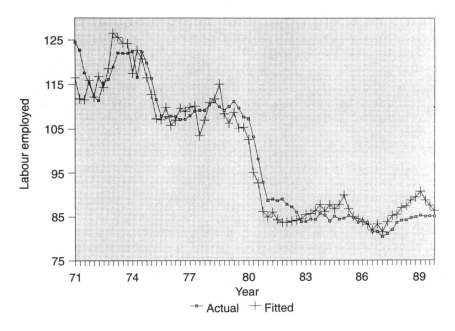

*Figure 5.4* Fit of model: labour

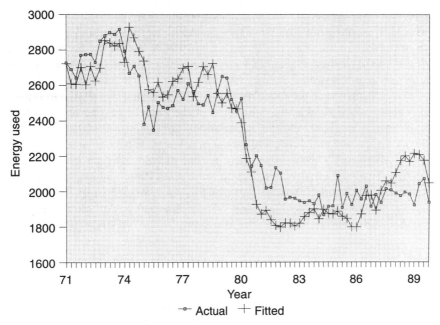

*Figure 5.5* Fit of model: energy

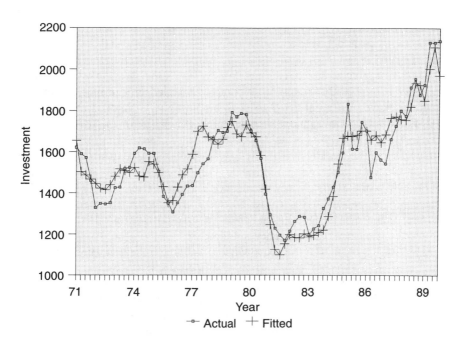

*Figure 5.6* Fit of model: investment

demand for the period up to 1983 and overpredict demand for the period after 1983. This is consistent with the notion that there was a structural break in the labour market and industrial relations in the 1980s, following the legislative programme of the first Thatcher Conservative government and the increase in credibility that followed from the resolution of the miners' strike.

The performance of the model in fitting energy demand is shown in Figure 5.5. This is not as good as the estimation of the model over previous, shorter, sample periods. However, the model does capture the decline in energy demand in 1974–5 and 1981, while other models have been unable to capture these phenomena. The main problem is that the data display a remarkably constant level of energy demand through the 1980s whilst output was increasing. The model explains some of this decreasing energy–output ratio but fails to capture the decline after 1986. It appears that, in minimizing the error over this period, the model distorts the fit for the other part of the sample period.

Investment is displayed in Figure 5.6. The fit here is quite good. The fitted values tend to smooth out the cycle in the early 1970s and then to anticipate the increase in investment in the 1976–80 period. Post-1979 the model fits the series well and captures period-by-period fluctuations. Table 5.1 gives the number of vintages used and available, and this gives an indication of the extent of capacity utilization. The latter numbers are somewhat low, certainly compared with the length of service lives used in the capital stock series produced by the CSO, but they are consistent with the length of life found in other countries. A possible reason for the shortness of life, and the rather high rate of depreciation that goes with it (see the parameter estimates in Appendix 5B), is the aggregation across firms. For an individual firm, investment may be rather lumpy in that plants may only be installed in a limited number of years. However, different firms will exhibit 'lumpiness' in different years, so that the pattern of investment will be much smoother for the economy as a whole than for individual firms.

By treating the manufacturing sector as a representative firm it appears that capital is being replaced much faster than is actually the case. For the purposes of forecasting energy demand due to price rises or tax changes this would not be particularly serious if firms were alike in their energy-using characteristics or the aggregation problem was not serious. However, it is known that this is almost certainly not the case and therefore there will be an aggregation error in our results, which could be in either direction. The reaction to an energy tax will be rapid if it occurs just as a high-energy-using firm is replacing its equipment and slow if it occurs just after high-energy-using firms have replaced their equipment. The analysis employed here is only concerned with temporal disaggregation. Whilst it would be most desirable to disaggregate across sectors of industry, if not firms, the data are not available to allow this to be done.

*Table 5.1* Number of vintages available and used

| Date | Used | Available | Date | Used | Available |
|------|------|-----------|------|------|-----------|
| 1971.1 | 22 | 59 | 1980.3 | 26 | 79 |
| 1971.2 | 22 | 60 | 1980.4 | 24 | 80 |
| 1971.3 | 22 | 61 | 1981.1 | 24 | 81 |
| 1971.4 | 22 | 62 | 1981.2 | 25 | 81 |
| 1972.1 | 21 | 63 | 1981.3 | 26 | 81 |
| 1972.2 | 23 | 64 | 1981.4 | 28 | 82 |
| 1972.3 | 24 | 65 | 1982.1 | 28 | 83 |
| 1972.4 | 26 | 65 | 1982.2 | 29 | 84 |
| 1973.1 | 28 | 66 | 1982.3 | 30 | 85 |
| 1973.2 | 28 | 67 | 1982.4 | 31 | 84 |
| 1973.3 | 29 | 68 | 1983.1 | 33 | 84 |
| 1973.4 | 29 | 69 | 1983.2 | 34 | 83 |
| 1974.1 | 26 | 70 | 1983.3 | 36 | 84 |
| 1974.2 | 29 | 71 | 1983.4 | 38 | 83 |
| 1974.3 | 28 | 72 | 1984.1 | 40 | 83 |
| 1974.4 | 26 | 73 | 1984.2 | 41 | 80 |
| 1975.1 | 25 | 74 | 1984.3 | 42 | 81 |
| 1975.2 | 23 | 75 | 1984.4 | 43 | 82 |
| 1975.3 | 22 | 76 | 1985.1 | 44 | 80 |
| 1975.4 | 23 | 77 | 1985.2 | 45 | 80 |
| 1976.1 | 24 | 78 | 1985.3 | 44 | 81 |
| 1976.2 | 25 | 79 | 1985.4 | 42 | 82 |
| 1976.3 | 25 | 80 | 1986.1 | 42 | 81 |
| 1976.4 | 27 | 81 | 1986.2 | 42 | 82 |
| 1977.1 | 28 | 82 | 1986.3 | 42 | 83 |
| 1977.2 | 27 | 83 | 1986.4 | 44 | 81 |
| 1977.3 | 27 | 84 | 1987.1 | 43 | 81 |
| 1977.4 | 28 | 85 | 1987.2 | 46 | 82 |
| 1978.1 | 29 | 86 | 1987.3 | 47 | 79 |
| 1978.2 | 30 | 87 | 1987.4 | 47 | 76 |
| 1978.3 | 31 | 86 | 1988.1 | 48 | 74 |
| 1978.4 | 31 | 83 | 1988.2 | 47 | 74 |
| 1979.1 | 30 | 83 | 1988.3 | 49 | 74 |
| 1979.2 | 32 | 80 | 1988.4 | 48 | 73 |
| 1979.3 | 30 | 81 | 1989.1 | 48 | 73 |
| 1979.4 | 31 | 80 | 1989.2 | 46 | 74 |
| 1980.1 | 30 | 81 | 1989.3 | 42 | 73 |
| 1980.2 | 27 | 78 | 1989.4 | 39 | 72 |

## 5.2.2 Differences in vintages

In considering an estimated econometric model it is usual to consider the magnitude of the parameter estimates and to interpret their value. The putty-semi-putty vintage nature of the model with generalized Leontief technology does not allow this to be done as easily as the basic estimated parameters from the matrix $A$, which drives the *ex ante* and *ex post* substitution.

As is shown in Appendix 5A, each vintage is characterized by the (derived) parameters $b_1^v$, $b_2^v$, $b_3^v$, $b_4^v$ (equations (5.3a) and (5.3b)) which depend on the parameters in the matrix $A$. These are more easily interpreted as the *ex post* input–output coefficients. These coefficients are important in answering the question of the extent to which it is possible to aggregate different vintages of capital, which in turn depends on how similar the different vintages are. If these parameters were constant, then all vintages would be the same in terms of the factor input–output ratios, and so quality change in the sense of Denison would not occur. As noted earlier, this is an important question from the point of view of trying to investigate the long-run response of energy demand to changes in energy prices.

If there is substantial quality change in capital then simple aggregation will be inappropriate. The extent to which $b_1^v$, $b_2^v$, $b_3^v$, $b_4^v$ vary measures the size of the aggregation problem. The values of these parameters for vintages from 1955 to 1989 are shown in Figures 5.7–5.10. For all of the $b$s there is an initial 'settling-down' period since they depend upon expected prices, which within the model are extrapolations of past fitted trends. At the beginning of the sample period, as there are only a few observations over which to calculate these trends, expected future prices show considerable fluctuation. This should not affect the model over the period for which factor demands are fitted as these early vintages are not used.

For the period after 1960 the figures show that the $b$s vary over time. $b_1^v$ – the constant in the labour–output ratio *ex post* (see equation (5.1a) of Appendix 5A) – declines slowly up to 1975, reflecting the effect of exogenous technological progress. However, it shows a more marked decline in the next ten years, generating increases in labour productivity. It could be claimed on the basis of this that improvements in labour productivity, purported to be a consequence of decisions taken in the 1980s, started much earlier. It appears to be relatively constant again after 1985. $b_2^v$, the constant in the energy–output ratio, follows the expected pattern in that it increases up to 1975, decreases thereafter to a minimum in 1985 after which it increases again. $b_3^v$, the capital–output ratio for investment of different vintages, is perhaps the parameter of most interest. It appears to be less variable than the other two. Nevertheless, within the period 1960–89 it varies between 0.3 and 0.2, a quite substantial variation. This means that output per unit of investment is going to be quite different for different periods. As a final (derived) characteristic of vintages the retirement pattern for vintages is considered. Vintages retire in two ways. The first is that depreciation reduces the amount of each vintage in operation in successive quarters. The second is that vintages are deleted from the list of those available. This means that all the equipment of that vintage is obsolete, and as such this phenomenon will be referred to as the 'scrapping' of that vintage. However, in terms of the conventional use of the concept of scrapping, it will probably be the case that some of the retirement allocated to depreciation will in fact be machinery which is scrapped. In particular, the effect of exponential depreciation, even when the rate

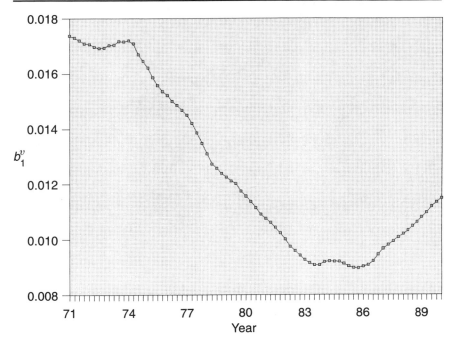

*Figure 5.7* $b^v_1$ coefficient

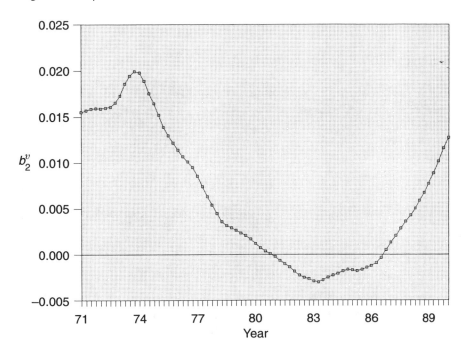

*Figure 5.8* $b^v_2$ coefficient

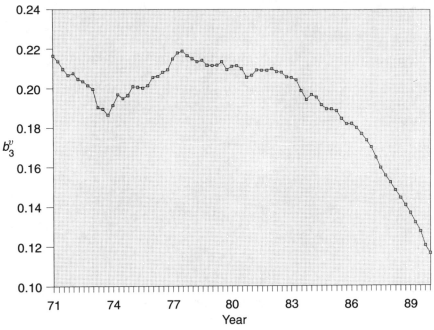

Figure 5.9 $b^v_3$ coefficient

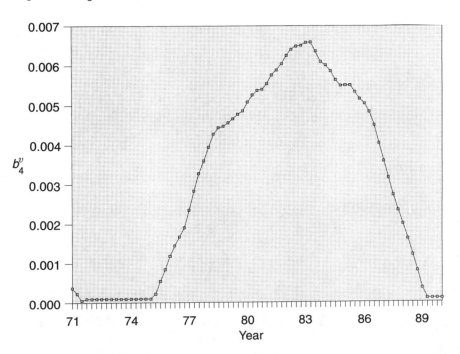

Figure 5.10 $b^v_4$ coefficient

estimated is relatively modest, is to reduce the quantity of a particular vintage to zero relatively rapidly. In the next section there will be a discussion of the estimates of depreciation rates, but for the moment the question of the dates at which different vintages are retired will be considered.

Table 5.2 lists the dates at which each vintage is retired. This shows that whilst scrapping is not consecutive at the start of the sample period, it becomes so later. The scrapping out of order of the first twenty vintages may be due to the model 'settling down' in the initial periods. In particular, the results of the expectation-formation submodel will be relatively unstable for the first vintages. Once the initial period of instability is passed, vintages are scrapped consecutively, although not in a particularly even pattern. There are quarters when no vintages are scrapped and others, such as quarter 131, when four vintages are scrapped. It can also be seen that there has been a slight decline in the life of vintages, from approximately eighty quarters down to approximately seventy quarters.

*Table 5.2* Scrapping dates for vintages (period 1 = 1955Q1)

| Vintage | Scrapping date | Vintage | Scrapping date | Vintage | Scrapping date |
|---------|----------------|---------|----------------|---------|----------------|
| 1 | 65 | 24 | 107 | 47 | 131 |
| 2 | 65 | 25 | 112 | 48 | 131 |
| 3 | 65 | 26 | 112 | 49 | 131 |
| 4 | 65 | 27 | 113 | 50 | 131 |
| 5 | 72 | 28 | 114 | 51 | 132 |
| 6 | 95 | 29 | 114 | 52 | 132 |
| 7 | 102 | 30 | 116 | 53 | 132 |
| 8 | 96 | 31 | 116 | 54 | 132 |
| 9 | 95 | 32 | 117 | 55 | 133 |
| 10 | 102 | 33 | 118 | 56 | 133 |
| 11 | 102 | 34 | 118 | 57 | 133 |
| 12 | 98 | 35 | 118 | 58 | 134 |
| 13 | 98 | 36 | 118 | 59 | 135 |
| 14 | 96 | 37 | 121 | 60 | 136 |
| 15 | 96 | 38 | 121 | 61 | 136 |
| 16 | 96 | 39 | 122 | 62 | 137 |
| 17 | 98 | 40 | 121 | 63 | 139 |
| 18 | 100 | 41 | 125 | 64 | 139 |
| 19 | 98 | 42 | 125 | 65 | 140 |
| 20 | 97 | 43 | 128 | 66 | 140 |
| 21 | 100 | 44 | 128 | 67 | 141 |
| 22 | 102 | 45 | 128 | 68 | 142 |
| 23 | 106 | 46 | 129 | 69 | 142 |
| | | | | 70 | 142 |

*Note*: Vintages installed after quarter 71 (1972Q3) are still available at the end of the sample period.

### 5.2.3  Relative merits of the vintage model approach

The main advantage of the vintage approach is that it captures the effects of both history and the future on current decisions. This means that price changes may not have immediate effects. The speed at which price effects feed through the economy is based on optimization, rather than being due to an unexplained cost of adjustment. This adjustment reflects two effects, which can be separated out one from the other. The first is delay in adjusting due to the quantity of capital stock, its depreciation and normal life. The second is the role of price expectations which determine the factor use coefficients of newly installed equipment.

It is important to distinguish between these two factors as they have quite different policy implications. For the first, adjustment to price changes will occur faster the faster the economy is growing. Thus energy taxes that slow growth of the economy will slow down the response to them. A further consequence of this is that there will be a cost of energy taxes in the extra investment due to replacement of capital earlier than would otherwise be the case. An estimate of this cost can be obtained, and will depend on how fast taxes are imposed. The cost can therefore be minimized by imposing the taxes in such a way that capital is replaced no faster than would otherwise be the case. This implies that a policy designed to reduce energy should be implemented substantially in advance of the date at which the reduction in energy use is required. For some calculations of this see Ingham *et al.* (1991a). The second effect, the response which is dependent upon expectations, implies that adjustment would be faster the closer the new path of prices is to the old. Taxes may need to be high in order to induce correct design. Alternatively if price expectations can be changed by announcements then taxes may only be needed to obtain the correct usage of factors *ex post*, and not to influence the *ex ante* design.

The first disadvantage of the model arises from the complexity of the likelihood function. There are a large number of parameters, and because of the vintage structure the likelihood function for the model is of a non-standard form. Maximizing the likelihood is not possible by the usual 'hill climbing' techniques and is undertaken using the Nelder–Mead algorithm. This ensures convergence to a maximum, and the use of a variety of starting points is used to investigate the possibility that a local rather than a global maximum is obtained. The Nelder–Mead algorithm requires a large number of iterations, each of which requires the calculation of the costs in order to sort the vintages by cost. To minimize the computations required, a specification with linear calculations is used as far as possible. This can be done by using the generalized Leontief functional form. Although this is a flexible form, studies such as that of Lau (1986) suggest that it may not be as good as other functional forms in approximating the data.

A second disadvantage arises from the type of simulations that one might want to undertake. Typically in considering long-run responses one would want to consider how an economy moves from one steady state to another. So one might consider a simulation in which exogenous variables are either held constant or grow at some specified rate. Energy prices are then increased and the reaction of the model to this is observed. Eventually the economy adjusts to the new long-run state. This adjustment depends on the parameters of the model, especially those determining the shape of the *ex post* isoquant. As outlined in the previous section *ex post* substitution is determined by $b_4^v$, in connection with the relative price of the variable factors.

It is expected that *ex post* substitutability will come at a cost and, indeed, this is the case. Situations in which $b_4^v$ is high and $b_2^v$ is low, such as in the period around 1983, correspond to a higher energy–output ratio than situations in which the reverse is the case, such as in the period around 1971. Whilst the specification of the *ex ante* technology does not allow for recording variability in prices or changes in their trends, it is the case that, if factor prices follow a trend similar to that which occurred over the sample period, then $b_4^v$ is driven down to zero and, if permitted, even becomes negative. Driving $b_4^v$ to zero is consistent with intuition. If relative factor prices behave in a predictable way then there should be no desire for *ex post* flexibility. However, if there is a linear trade-off between flexibility and overall input level then $b_4^v$ will become negative. However, this is not consistent with intuition as it suggests perverse input demand. Falls in the actual price of a factor will lead to increases in its use. The problem is that there is no guarantee that the generalized Leontief cost function will be concave. Functional forms which guarantee a concave cost function have been developed, such as the modified Barnett (see Diewert and Wales 1987). As this is too complex, computationally, to be incorporated, a simple device of prohibiting $b_4^v$ from falling below zero is adopted. The model is estimated with this constraint. However, it also restricts the use of the model for simulation. Simulations for which $b_4^v = 0$ correspond to simulations with a putty-clay technology, and this loses the point of having estimated a putty-semi-putty technology. Consequently, the simulations undertaken use data on exogenous variables for the period 1971–90, and as such contain some price variability.

## 5.3 THE RESULTS OF THE SIMULATIONS

Figure 5.11 shows the path of a Divisia index of real energy prices over the period 1965–85. This shows three periods of basically constant prices with two periods of sudden increases. The relative factor cost of energy prices to wage costs in United Kingdom manufacturing, displayed in Figure 5.12, also shows considerable variability. The fact that the United Kingdom has experienced such large price changes in 1973 and 1979–80 suggests that it might be possible to calculate the sort of taxation levels that might be needed

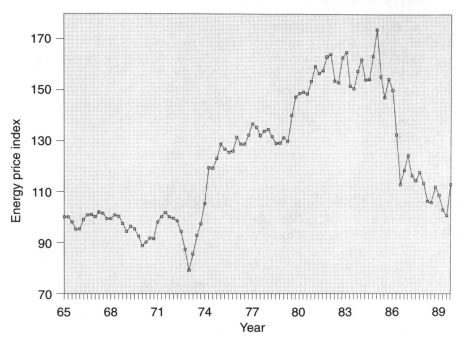

*Figure 5.11* Divisia index of real energy prices, 1965 = 100

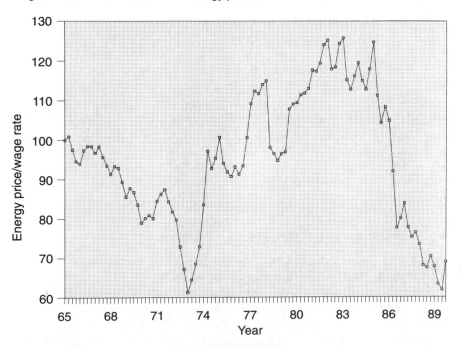

*Figure 5.12* Energy price/wage costs, 1965 = 100

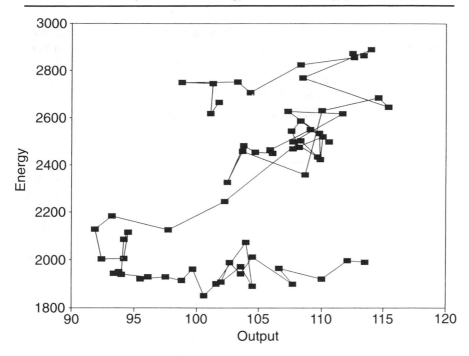

*Figure 5.13* Energy–output ratio

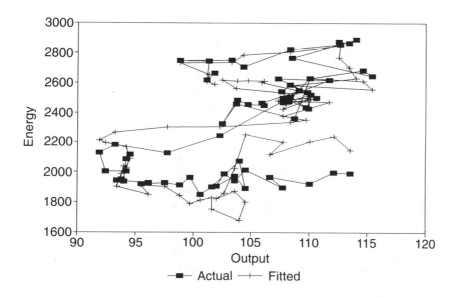

*Figure 5.14* Fit of model: energy–output ratio

if reductions in energy use by manufacturing are required. However, whether or not the experience of the oil shocks is a useful indicator depends on both the perceived durability of a cartel (OPEC) and the perceived credibility of government policy (a carbon tax). Even if the price increases are equal in magnitude, firms may adjust their capital and fuel expenditures in a very different manner depending on the perceived permanence of the increase.

From Section 5.2 it can be seen that the important aspect of the model is that long-run adjustments to price changes are modelled endogenously, rather than long-run adaptation being due either to a cost of adjustment, which is not modelled or explained, or to some dynamic statistical specification. The first set of simulations calculates energy elasticities from the model by considering different scenarios for energy prices after 1973. Energy prices showed a dramatic increase at that time after having fallen, in real terms, for much of the previous two decades. After this, real energy prices were almost constant until 1979 when they rose again, quite sharply, during the next nine quarters, again reaching a plateau. Meanwhile the energy–output ratio declines over time, although closer inspection reveals that this is not a constant decline. The period from 1975 to 1980 shows an almost constant ratio.

An interesting way of depicting this is that of Semple (1989), who graphed energy usage against output and obtained a Z-like pattern as shown in Figures 5.13 and 5.14. Figure 5.13 plots the actual relationship, and Figure 5.14 plots the relationship corresponding to actual energy demand and as fitted by the model. The decline in the energy–output ratio before 1975 and after 1980 corresponds to the horizontal parts of the Z, whereas the diagonal corresponds to the period between 1975 and 1980 when the energy–output ratio was relatively constant.

The base scenario is one in which all exogenous variables, apart from fuel prices (i.e. factor prices and interest rates), follow their actual values up to 1990 after which they are extended by using the trend growth rate throughout the period 1955–90. Fuel prices after 1973 are taken as growing at the trend growth rate for the period up to 1973, which corresponds to a quarterly decline of −0.4 per cent. This provides the base case in which the energy–output ratio rises slowly at first but more rapidly as factor substitution takes place. Different scenarios are considered for output growth. The first is that output remains constant, the others are that output grows at either 0.5 per cent per quarter or 1 per cent per quarter. This should enable an assessment as to whether more growth in output would allow the capital stock to respond more rapidly to energy price changes.

A growth factor of 1, 1.5, 2 and 2.5 per cent is then added to fuel prices. All the resulting energy–output ratios, shown in Figures 5.15 and 5.16, exhibit marked declines. The most remarkable feature is that the difference between the base case and 1 per cent is much greater than the difference between the other cases. In consequence the elasticities are much greater for small price increases than for larger ones. The elasticities for the various scenarios are

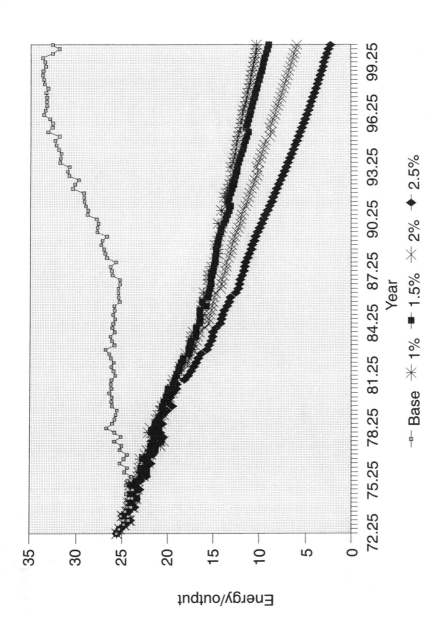

*Figure 5.15* Energy–output ratio: output constant

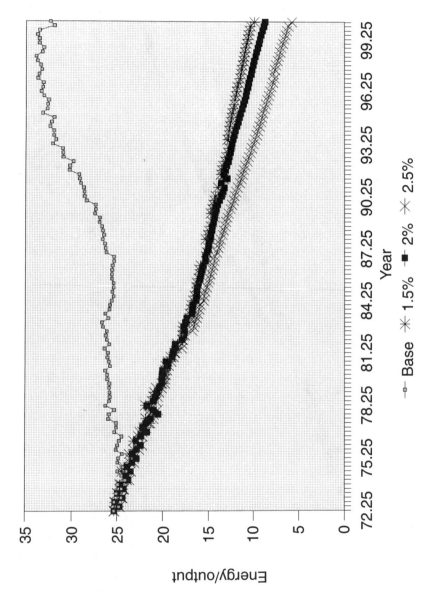

*Figure 5.16* Energy–output ratio: 0.5 per cent growth

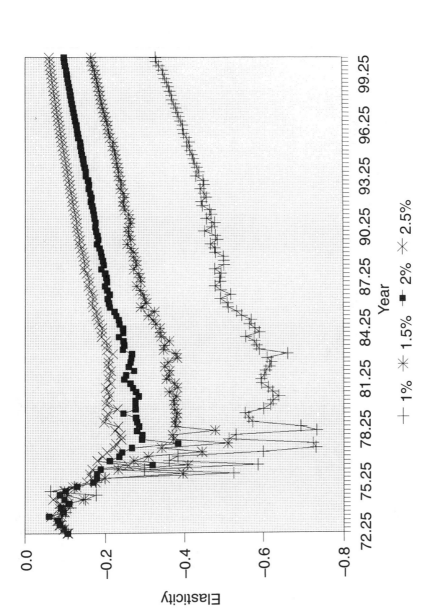

*Figure 5.17* Price elasticities: output constant

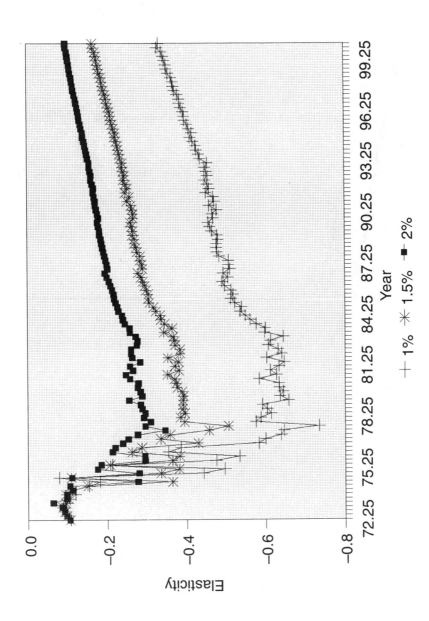

*Figure 5.18* Price elasticities: 0.5 per cent growth

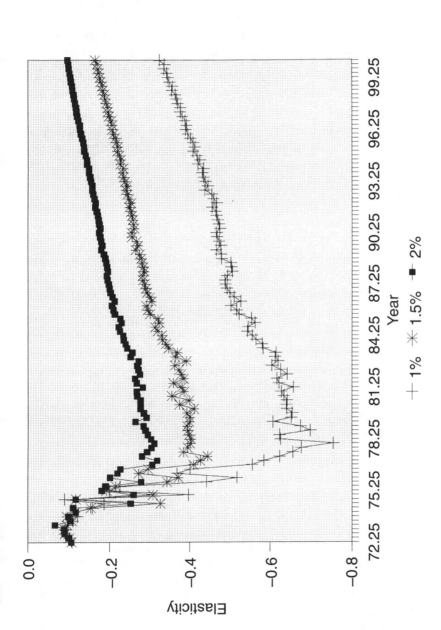

*Figure 5.19* Price elasticities: 1 per cent growth

shown in Figures 5.17, 5.18 and 5.19. These elasticities are calculated by taking the base energy demand to be $\{E_t^0\}$ for the path of prices $\{P_t^0\}$, and by taking the simulation of the path for energy demand of $\{E^1\}$ for the path of prices $\{P^1\}$. The elasticity is then given by $\eta_t = (E_t^1 - E_t^0)P_t^0/(P_t^1 - P_t^0)E_t^0$.

The pattern of the elasticities, as shown in Figure 5.17, tells the expected story. To start with there is not much reduction in energy use with an estimated elasticity of around $-0.1$. This does not vary much with the rate of increase in prices. The elasticity starts to increase in magnitude after five quarters as this change starts to affect expected factor prices and *ex ante* substitution takes place. As is to be expected this now depends on the rate at which prices are rising. Energy demand is determined by the exogenous technological progress as well as factor prices so that the effect of the price change is attenuated by technological change eventually and the elasticity starts to fall. This represents the transition to long-run phenomena from the short run. The greater the rate of price increase the earlier this transition takes place, as expected. The faster prices rise the faster expectations will adjust. If this interpretation is correct, adjustment to the long run takes around twenty quarters. This seems to depend very little on output growth. Thus, for the fastest growth in prices and 1 per cent growth in output per quarter full adjustment takes place two quarters earlier.

The second task is to assess the role of expectations. As noted before, the importance of this arises from the possibility that taxes on energy may not be imposed immediately but may be announced for implementation at some future date. If this policy is credible it might be thought that this will lead to a lower tax being required than if a tax were implemented without announcement, or if there were doubts about the credibility of the policy.

To consider this, some simulations are run in which the technical parameters of the model remain unchanged but the manner in which prices enter into expectations changes. The first is to consider what energy demand would have been if prices had been perfectly anticipated. Given that the present value of future prices is calculated over a horizon of forty-five quarters, this can only be done for the period 1971–88, for the extended data set. This is contrasted with the formation of expectations within the estimated model and a situation in which expectations are myopic in the sense that the current real price is expected to rule indefinitely. The results of doing this are presented in Figures 5.20–5.24.

Figures 5.20 and 5.21 depict the base case where all variables are at their actual values up to 1990 and trend values thereafter. There is little difference between the three for much of the sample period. At first this might seem rather surprising, but two explanations can be put forward. The first is that at the start of the period in 1971 real energy prices were falling, so that the extrapolated expectations of the model would have also predicted a decline in real prices. As real prices were in fact rising, myopic expectations would be closer to the prices actually realized, i.e. perfect foresight. Thus myopic

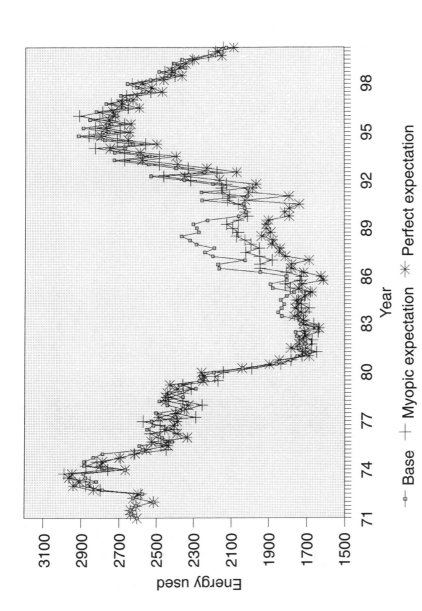

Figure 5.20 Energy demand: different expectations

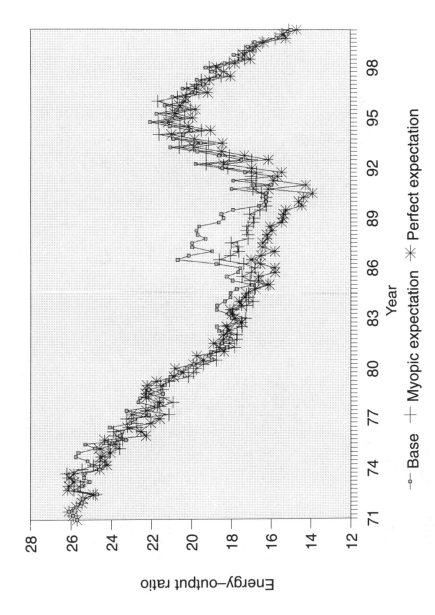

*Figure 5.21* Energy–output ratio: different expectations

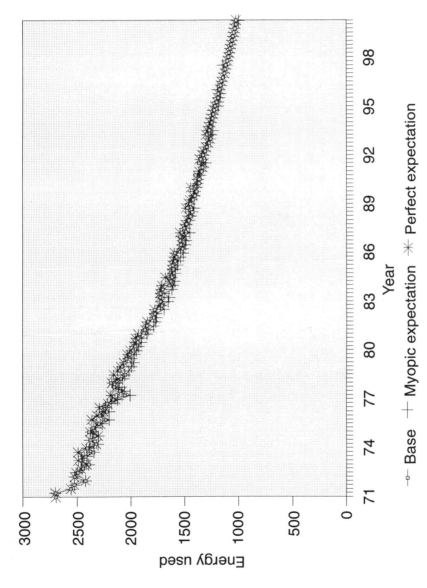

*Figure 5.22* Energy demand: 1 per cent price increase

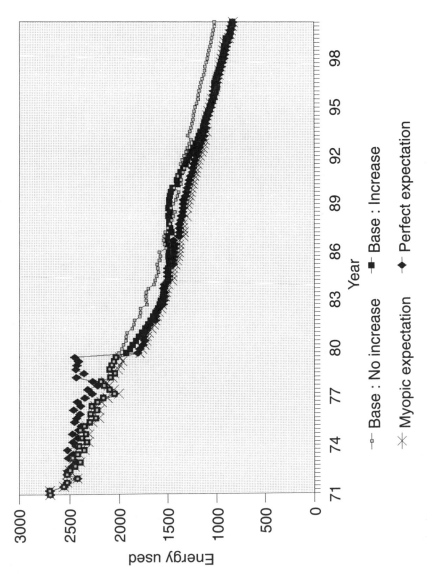

*Figure 5.23* Effect of sudden increase in 1980

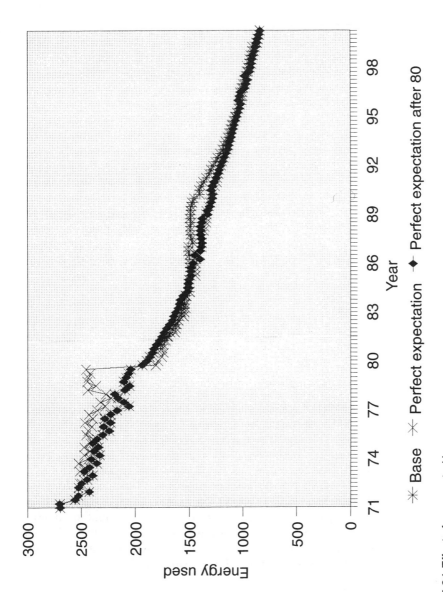

※ Base  ※ Perfect expectation  ◆ Perfect expectation after 80

*Figure 5.24* Effect of unexpected increase

expectations lead to lower energy use in the period of increased prices because myopia turns out to be closer to what actually occurred than expectations under the model assumptions. Substantial change in energy demand between the simulations appears during the 1986–90 period. In fact, this is a period in which the model, as estimated, overpredicts energy usage. So whereas extrapolative expectations seem to explain behaviour well in the 1970s and early 1980s, it seems that perfect foresight may be more appropriate for the late 1980s. The second explanation is related to the *ex post* flexibility built into the capital stock. This may well be fairly large, making incorrect expectations relatively unimportant in terms of factor usage.

As before, the effect of price increases on expectations is considered. Figure 5.22 considers the case wherein fuel prices increase at their 1955–73 trend plus 1 per cent per quarter. This causes trend expectations, perfect foresight and myopic expectations to move together, and so there is really very little difference between them. However, suppose some lack of smoothness is incorporated into this scenario. The scenario assumed is that of a large price increase in 1980, such as an energy tax of the magnitude some have proposed. In the scenario real energy prices are doubled and the effects of different expectations formation are considered. These are shown in Figure 5.23. The first series is the base case corresponding to Figure 5.22. The second is the base case with a doubling of prices in 1980. This leads to a reduction in energy usage which gradually increases to around 20 per cent. The myopic expectations path is close to the others up to 1980 where the price increase is built into newly installed machinery immediately. Perfect foresight leads to quite an interesting path in that it does not reduce energy use below that of myopic expectations, as might have been expected. There is an increase in energy usage in the period before, however, with a large adjustment when the increase takes place. The reason for this increase is the plateau in prices that occurs after the 1973 increase. This means that with perfect foresight investment will have been determined by a constant real energy price, whereas under trend expectations the energy price will have been expected to increase. So under trend expectations less-energy-using equipment would be installed.

Figure 5.24 considers the case where expectations are adaptive before the increase but perfect foresight is assumed thereafter. In this case, the doubling in price is unanticipated, but the effect of future price changes is fully accommodated. Comparing this with the case of perfect foresight throughout shows that perfect foresight makes a noticeable difference to the reduction that takes place when prices increase, and to the level. Although the two paths converge after the increase, it takes four years for the two to become indistinguishable.

## 5.4  CONCLUSIONS

Although many other simulations could be carried out, it is hoped that those conducted give an indication of the estimation of the model interpreted in both a short-run and long-run elasticity format. The magnitude of the elasticity depends upon the magnitude of the price increase, and there is a non-linear relationship of a concave nature. This is not surprising, given the generalized Leontief cost function employed. Elasticities increase just after price increases take place; starting from a value of $-0.1$ they increase to $-0.8$ depending on the price increase envisaged. This elasticity falls over time as the magnitude of the price increase rises and technological progress takes place. These numbers are not inconsistent with those found from other studies. It should be emphasized that a wide range of own-price elasticities for energy have been calculated. For example, Waverman (1992) reports elasticities ranging from $-0.08$ to $-1.56$ for industrial use of different fuels in the United States.

The effect of changing output growth is to speed up adjustment, but not significantly. This is again not surprising as the basic model incorporates constant returns to scale. A conclusion which could be drawn is that the energy–output ratio is much more dependent on the energy price than on the output level. The effect of changing expectations is surprising. The lack of much noticeable effect seems to depend on the pattern that energy prices have followed in the past. For much of the sample period myopic expectations have, perhaps, been a better predictor than an adaptive model. Although it should be added that it is possible for the estimated model to select this, and a crude test (because of its non-nested nature) for this favoured the adaptive model. A clearer indication of the effect of different expectations is obtained from the comparison of an expected and an unexpected doubling of energy prices. In this simulation it takes some sixteen quarters for the effect of incorrectly anticipated prices to dissipate.

## APPENDIX 5A: MATHEMATICAL SPECIFICATION OF THE MODEL

### Factor utilization decisions

At any point in time $t$, producers have available to them a set of machines of different vintages, indexed by $v < t$. (Not all possible past vintages will necessarily be available.) A machine of vintage $v$ is characterized by five parameters – four design parameters, $b_i^v$, $i = 1, \ldots, 4$, and its available capacity $\bar{y}_t^v$. Given current variable factor prices, $p_t$, $w_t$ for energy and labour respectively, the input–output ratios can be calculated for labour, energy and capital that will be chosen for this machine, namely:

$$\lambda_t^v = b_1^v + b_4^v \, (p_t/w_t)^{\frac{1}{2}} \tag{5.1a}$$

$$\varepsilon_t^v = b_2^v + b_4^v \, (w_t/p_t)^{\frac{1}{2}}$$

$$\kappa_t^v = b_3^v \tag{5.1b}$$

It will be recognized that these are the input–output ratios for a generalized Leontief production function, a flexible functional form. Two further points need to be made, following from what was said in the introduction. First, this model allows for *ex post* substitution between variable factor inputs. Second, the degree of *ex post* substitution, as reflected in the parameter $b_4^v \geq 0$, is chosen endogenously by producers, as described shortly, and can be varied vintage by vintage.

The unit variable cost of vintage $v$ at time $t$ can then be defined as

$$VC_t^v = \lambda_t^v w_t + \varepsilon_t^v p_t \tag{5.2}$$

where the assumption of constant returns to scale has implicitly been introduced. Vintages are then ranked in order of increasing unit variable cost and, given that a level of output $y$ has to be produced at time $t$, will be employed in that order until total available capacity exceeds required output. All previous infra-marginal vintages will be employed at full capacity; all subsequent extra-marginal vintages will not be employed at all; the marginal vintage will produce sufficient output to meet required output exactly. Given the level of output for each vintage, and their input–output coefficients, the total demand can be calculated for variable factor inputs at each period.

### Design parameters for new vintage

At time period $t$, a new machine of vintage $t$ is to be designed. It will be installed at time period $t + LD$, and the firm has a planning horizon of $[t + LD, t + LD + LT]$ (LD and LT are to be estimated). Let $P_t^\tau$, $W_t^\tau$, $R_t^\tau$ be the expected values of the energy price, wage rate and real interest rate at time period $\tau$, $t + LD \leq \tau \leq t + LD + LT$, expectations being formed at $t$ (in a manner to be discussed shortly); let $Z_t^\tau$ be the expected value at $\tau$ of $(P_t^\tau W_t^\tau)^{1/2}$; finally, let $K_t$ be the price of a machine at time $t$, known with certainty.

Then the following pseudo-factor prices can be defined; let $\omega_1^t$ be the present value of the stream of $W_t^\tau$ over the planning period, using the $R_t^\tau$ as discount rates; let $\omega_2^t$ be the corresponding present value of expected energy prices over the planning period; let $\omega_3^t$ be $K_t$; let $\omega_4^t$ be the present value of the stream of $Z_t^\tau$ over the planning horizon; finally, let $\omega_5^t$ be $(\omega_1^t \omega_3^t)^{1/2}$ and $\omega_6^t$ be $(\omega_2^t \omega_3^t)$. These pseudo-factor prices are essentially the present values of the expectations of all the basic factor prices and the square roots of the products of these factor prices; the latter capture the extent of correlation between (variable) factor prices over the planning horizon.

Then the four design parameters of a new machine of vintage $t$ are calculated as follows. Let $A$ be a $4 \times 6$ matrix of parameters $[\alpha_{ij}]$ which describe the structure of production; these are parameters to be estimated. It is now possible to calculate, for $i = 1, \ldots, 4$,

$$B_i^t = \sum_{j=1}^{j=6} \alpha_{ij} \left( \frac{\omega_j^t}{\omega_t^t} \right)^{\frac{1}{2}} \tag{5.3a}$$

$$b_i^t = \frac{B_i^t}{(1 + \upsilon_i)^t} \tag{5.3b}$$

where the $\upsilon_i$ are the exogenous rates of technological progress. Equation (5.3a) shows that the design parameters are themselves outputs from a form of generalized Leontief production function using the pseudo-factor prices and so depend on both the expected level and correlation between basic factor prices. The level of factor prices will determine the extent to which producers design their machines to economize on factors which are expected to become relatively more expensive over the planning horizon, and thus represent a form of endogenous technological progress. The correlation between variable factor prices is important for assessing the extent to which producers will need to design more *ex post* flexibility into their machines to protect against future fluctuations in relative prices of variable factors. Equation (5.3b) introduces exogenous, factor-augmenting, technological progress; technological progress also applies to the parameter representing *ex post* flexibility.

### Scrapping and investment

It is important to recognize that in this model existing machines are assumed not to deteriorate in efficiency over time (i.e. their running costs do not change unless variable factor prices change, so there is no increase in maintenance costs) and in principle can last indefinitely; depreciation takes the form of a certain proportion of machines 'evaporating' each period – see below. So existing machines need to be evaluated over the same future time horizon as new machines. There are therefore two reasons why producers might scrap existing machines – because they are likely to be more expensive to operate over the future planning period than a new machine, or because producers have excess capacity.

To be precise, at time $t$ there will be a certain number of past vintages of machines which producers will expect still to be available at time $t + $ LD. For each of these the expected present value unit operating cost over the planning period is calculated as

$$EV^v_t = b^v_1 \, \omega^t_1 + b^v_2 \, \omega^t_2 + 2b^v_4 \, \omega^t_4 \tag{5.4a}$$

For a new machine the expected present value unit total cost is calculated as

$$ET^t_t = EV^t_t + b^t_3 \, \omega^t_3 \tag{5.4b}$$

Producers will scrap any existing machine for which $EV^v_t > ET^t_t$; i.e. producers scrap old machines which are expected to be more expensive to run over the planning period than a new machine. This is the excess cost reason for scrapping old vintages.

For any remaining old machines, producers calculate the total capacity likely to be available from such old machines at time $t + LD$, say $\bar{Y}_t$. They also calculate what they expect to have to produce at time period $t + LD$, $Y_t$. They then decide to invest in new machines so as to be able to produce output level

$$\bar{y}^t_t = \max[(Y_t - \bar{Y}_t), 0] \tag{5.5}$$

If no investment is undertaken because producers expect to have excess capacity, they will scrap some of their existing capacity in order of decreasing expected present value unit operating costs until a margin, XCF, of capacity over expected output is reached. This is the excess capacity reason for scrapping old vintages.

The investment decision requires some elaboration. Equation (5.5) provides an output measure of investment. From this the number of machines of vintage $t$ planned at time $t$ is calculated:

$$I_t = b^t_3 \, \bar{y}^t_t \tag{5.6}$$

Then the (historic cost) investment expenditure on vintage $t$ is calculated as

$$E_t = K_t I_t$$

where $K_t$ is the real price of capital goods at time $t$ (deflated by the price index for manufacturing output). It is assumed that total expenditure $E$ is not all incurred in one period, but rather is spread over the LD periods between planning and bringing into commission a new machine. The pattern of distribution over the LD periods can be modelled as a beta distribution function with parameters $p$ and $q$ (to be estimated). This allows for a wide range of patterns of such expenditure. Accordingly for $l = 1, \ldots, LD$ define $\sigma_l$ by:

$$\sigma_l = B\left(p, q, \frac{l}{LD}\right) - B\left(p, q, \frac{l-1}{LD}\right) \tag{5.7}$$

Then total investment expenditure in period $t$ will be given by

$$TE_t = \sum_{l=1}^{LD} \sigma_l E_{t+1-l} \tag{5.8}$$

$TE_t$ will be comparable with the quarterly series on investment expenditures.

**Miscellaneous aspects**

Two final aspects are needed to complete the description of the model. First, the determination of the capacity of machines after the date of installation needs to be discussed. This is done by assuming that depreciation takes the form of a particular proportion $\delta$ of existing capacity being taken out of operation each period (until it is scrapped). Thus:

$$\bar{y}^v_\tau = \frac{\bar{y}^v_v}{(1 + \delta)^{t-v-LD}} \qquad t > v + LD$$

Second, it is necessary to make assumptions about how expectations of output and factor prices are formed. A simple form of adaptive expectations is assumed, whereby at time $t$ producers use the past LT observations on the variable to fit a linear trend, which is then extrapolated forward the appropriate number of periods.

**Estimation**

The model has been estimated using full-information maximum likelihood on quarterly data for the UK manufacturing sector (excluding iron and steel) over the period 1955Q1–1989Q4. The estimated parameters are the matrix $A = [a_{ij}]$, $v_1, \ldots, v_4$, LD, LT, XCF, $p$, $q$ and $\delta$. Because the likelihood function cannot be assumed to be differentiable in parameters, a simplex algorithm (Nelder–Mead) was used to maximize the likelihood function.

**APPENDIX 5B  PARAMETER ESTIMATES**

Matrix of parameters $A =$

| | | | | | |
|---|---|---|---|---|---|
| 0.0572 | −0.0500 | 0.0256 | −0.0413 | −0.0679 | 0.0312 |
| 0.0477 | −0.1024 | −0.0381 | 0.0385 | 0.0408 | −0.0230 |
| −0.0161 | 0.0719 | −0.0377 | −0.1612 | −0.1321 | 0.2572 |
| −0.0410 | 0.1471 | 0.1944 | −0.0678 | −0.2686 | 0.0803 |

Depreciation rate 0.041
Investment period 2
Expected life of vintages 45
Excess capacity factor 1.37
Technical progress rates: $v_1 = 0.0064$, $v_2 = 0.0072$, $v_3 = 0.0029$, $v_4 = 0.0109$
weights for investment: period 1, 0.51; period 2, 0.49
Premium on treasury bill rate to obtain discount rate 0.04525

# Chapter 6

# Elasticities for OECD aggregate final energy demand

*Lakis Vouyoukas*

## ABSTRACT

The IEA model is used primarily for the construction of global long-term energy scenarios that serve as the basis for IEA's *Energy Outlook*. Its global orientation imposes a fairly aggregate treatment of energy demand. In terms of final demand, there are ten regions, four fuels and three consuming sectors. Most of the demand parameters are econometrically estimated over the period 1960–90, with great emphasis being placed on the use of end use prices rather than primary fuel prices. The results indicate that energy price elasticities are generally low and not always well determined. It is suggested that a major explanation of this could be the assumed exogeneity of the economic structure and the technology incorporated in the energy-using capital stock.

## INTRODUCTION

The purpose of this chapter is to present the aggregate activity and price elasticities of OECD final energy demand used in the present version of the IEA energy model. The first section of the chapter gives an overview of the model, as it is currently being developed, and puts the results, aggregation and methodology in the context of the objectives of the model. This is most important since if pure estimation was the only objective a much cleaner and more disaggregated set of data could and should have been used. The second section of the chapter presents the results on elasticities with a very brief evaluation. No effort has been made in this chapter to discuss in detail the key driving forces and historical developments of the major energy-using sectors of OECD economies. The chapter concludes with some comments on the implications for primary energy markets and policy.

## 6.1 THE FRAMEWORK OF ESTIMATION AND DATA

The primary objective of the IEA long-term energy model is to serve as the basic analytical tool for constructing the scenarios that comprise the long-term global energy outlook of the IEA. The essential requirements in terms of model output are regional energy balances so that the underlying trends in energy demand, supply, trade and security of supply can be analysed. Secondary objectives include the analysis of the environmental impact of energy use, and sensitivity analysis of policy action, technological change and resource availability.

The structure and design of the model have, to a large extent, been determined by these objectives in conjunction with available resources. In the context of the present chapter, it should be emphasized that only a small part of the model, that which is concerned with final energy demand in the OECD, will be presented. Most other parts of the demand side of the model as well as most of the supply side and price determination modules are much less reliant on time-series econometric estimates. The models of final demand for non-OECD regions rely mostly on cross-sectional parameters owing to the lack of sufficiently long and high quality time series of end use prices in these regions.

Given the modelling objectives and resource limitations, the econometric results presented here are based on fairly aggregate data in terms of regions, fuels and sectors, as can be seen from Table 6.1. In terms of regions, four groupings have been identified, three of which, North America, Europe (excluding the eastern Lander of unified Germany) and Japan, have been econometrically estimated as reported. The modelling of Australia/New Zealand is based on a different methodology and not reported here. Clearly, for more accurate and better determined results, estimation of individual country parameters would be preferable. In terms of energy data, North America and Europe are rather large aggregates with very large intra-regional differences. However, modelling particular sub-regions would increase the size of the model manyfold given that many of the variables that appear to be exogenous in this chapter are endogenous within the overall model.

The sectoral disaggregation adopted reflects the materiality of the sector, its economic coherence/homogeneity and the ready availability of relevant data. For example, in the case of transportation, given its significance for energy as a whole and its paramount importance for oil demand, three types of inland transportation (road passenger, road freight and air transport) have been distinguished. Bunker fuel demand has also been modelled separately. The

Table 6.1  Aggregation scheme for final energy demand in the OECD

| Regions | Sectors | Fuels |
| --- | --- | --- |
| North America | Transportation | Oil |
| Europe | Industry | Gas |
| Japan | Building | Solids |
| Australia/New Zealand | Non-energy | Electricity |

other two major sectors, industry and the building sector, are far too aggregate and current work aims at further disaggregation. Some of the aggregation issues involved are discussed in the next section. Non-energy use has been modelled through a mixture of econometric and other techniques and the results for this sector are not reported here.

Finally, in terms of fuel aggregation four major aggregates have been adopted. While gas and electricity are fairly homogeneous, oil and solids consist of a very large number of quite different products used for very different purposes. Again given the importance of transportation, three oil products have been separately modelled, namely gasoline, diesel and aviation fuel. In general, where possible, the end use price of the dominant product of each fuel was used in each sector. For example, the price of oil was proxied by the price of residual fuel oil in the industrial sector and by the price of heating oil in the building sector while for transportation the gasoline and diesel prices were directly used. In total, ten energy end use prices are used for each region.

Another very important limitation imposed by the objectives of the model was the selection of explanatory variables. Given that the model is primarily a tool for long-term projections, explanatory variables themselves need to be projected. For example, for each region, activity variables like industrial production, consumer expenditure etc. as well as the end use energy prices used in the model need to be modelled. Given resource considerations this clearly limits the number of explanatory variables that could be used. Furthermore, since primary data are usually generated at country level, the use of regional aggregates necessitated a large number of approximations. In the case of Europe, activity and end use price series and their constituent components (taxes, wholesale prices etc.) for the region have been approximated by the use of the relevant series for only the four or five biggest countries. This should not be a poor approximation given that these countries are diverse and account for the bulk of European energy demand.

Almost all estimation reported here is based on single-equation techniques. No cross-equation restrictions have been attempted because of the presence of very complex and diverse dynamic patterns often running to fifteen years. These arise partly because of the longevity of the energy-using capital stock (e.g. more than forty years for buildings and up to thirty years for some types of industrial plant) and partly because of the potential flexibility in the choice of fuel. Thus, two or three cycles of response to a price change can be detected, namely the instantaneous fuel switching from dual-fired plant, the medium-term retrofitting and the longer-term replacement of the capital stock.

In modelling industrial and residential/commercial energy demand a choice needs to be made between (a) modelling the total energy demand of each sector and then the shares of the fuels or (b) modelling the individual fuels independently. The first approach, on which the results presented here are based, emphasizes the substitutability among different forms of energy while the second approach emphasizes the individuality of each fuel. It is arguable that for most non-transportation energy consumption consumers are simply interested in heating, steam raising etc. and not in the form of the fuel that they use. However, in many applications a specific form of fuel may well be necessary, like coking coal for traditional steel production and specific forms of hydrocarbons for petrochemical feedstocks. These special cases can in principle be isolated and the present version of the model already subtracts feedstock use in Europe and Japan from the energy use in industry. The potentially more serious criticism of the approach adopted is the frequent lack of substitutes for electricity use which is often based on quite specific technological and other characteristics of electricity. For example, the use of electricity for lighting in the building sector or for electrolysis and arc furnaces in many energy-intensive industries is not really subject to competition. Thus, the optimal separation of the problem could well be an initial nesting of electric versus non-electric energy and then a second nesting of non-electric energy into the appropriate fossil fuels.

All energy demand data used for the estimation of the elasticities presented in this chapter are based on the IEA's 'Energy Balances' databases. These data are converted from original units to million tons of oil equivalent. Data on energy prices and taxes since 1978 come from IEA's 'Energy Prices and Taxes' databases. For the period before 1978 a variety of sources has been used and a reasonably consistent set of data has been created back to 1960. All data are annual. The most common estimation period for the results reported here is 1965–90. In equations with severe parameter instability, the results from the latter part of the sample were usually used.

## 6.2 ESTIMATED ELASTICITIES[1]

### 6.2.1 Transportation sector

The transportation sector is the best documented, in terms of data, and the most heavily researched area in energy economics. This to a large extent is due to its importance not only for the energy industry but also for the automotive industry and the economy as a whole. In the case of the demand for gasoline, almost every conceivable modelling approach has been attempted and elasticity results vary according to region and the methodology and data used (for a recent survey see Dahl and Sterner 1991). In the context of the present IEA model, and given its long-term nature, it was considered essential to disaggregate the transportation sector fuel demand into road passenger, road freight and air travel. Both forms of road transport use gasoline and diesel. For the most important sectors, in terms of fuel demand, the preferred approach has been to impose a minimum structure on the problem and model the underlying driving forces of demand rather than model the fuel demand directly.

*Road passenger transportation*

In the case of the United States and Europe equations for the per capita distance travelled by passenger cars have been estimated. The resulting projections of travel are then combined with estimates of efficiency improvements and car turnover rate and diesel/gasoline penetration assumptions in order to arrive at projections of fuel demand. In the case of Japan, owing to the much smaller demand for passenger fuel demand, a gasoline demand equation has been estimated directly. It is beyond the scope of the present version of the model to endogenize the choice of mode of passenger transport between bus, car and rail or the purpose of travel (recreation, work, shopping etc.). This is the domain of specialist transportation models or of much larger energy models. Also, no information on the number of cars has been utilized. It is not clear what the effect of this variable would be on gasoline demand. It could be argued, for example, that, as the number of cars per household increases, consumers could reduce fuel consumption by selecting the most efficient of their cars for a large portion of their driving needs.

The principal driving forces of road passenger transportation would be expected to be income, cost of travel, the cost of alternate means of transport and population. The influence of population is taken care of through defining travel and income in per capita terms and income has been approximated with consumer expenditure. The cost of potential substitutes has not been incorporated owing to lack of readily available price data, but their effect is likely to be very modest as a large proportion of driving is non-discretionary. Estimating the cost of travel presents a major problem since, at least in the long term, it should include the lifetime cost of owning and operating a car. Even the short-run cost of travel is not equivalent to the cost of gasoline or diesel but should take into account the efficiency of the car and other variable costs (Greene 1992). Unfortunately, the data requirements for a proper derivation of the cost of travel are prohibitive in this context. However, in the case of the United States where a reasonable series of the average car efficiency is available, the price series used is the effective fuel cost per mile driven.

As can be seen from Table 6.2, the income effect is generally quite high and varies from 0.8 in the United States to 0.9 in Europe and Japan. The somewhat lower US elasticity could be due both to the higher per capita GDP there and to road transportation being more of a necessity. One surprising result of Table 6.2 is the large price elasticity of European travel where the cost of travel has been approximated by the real price of gasoline. If the same variable had been used for the US equation the estimated elasticity would be even smaller than the reported $-0.26$. This is because changes in the price of gasoline tend to overstate changes in the fuel cost of travel since consumers can reduce the impact of gasoline price changes by driving more or less efficient cars. Thus, in the United States, while the price of gasoline has risen marginally between

*Table 6.2* Long-term[a] transportation demand elasticities

|  | United States | | Europe | | Japan | |
| --- | --- | --- | --- | --- | --- | --- |
|  | *Income* | *Price* | *Income* | *Price* | *Income* | *Price* |
| Distance travelled | 0.76 | −0.26 | 0.92 | −0.75 | | |
| Gasoline demand | | | | | 0.86 | −0.80 |
| Freight ton miles/km | 0.95 | −0.23 | 1.11 | | | |
| Truck share in freight | | −0.10 | | −0.20 | | |
| Truck ton km | | | | | 0.87 | −0.21 |
| Air miles | 1.45 | −0.60 | | | | |
| Aviation fuel demand | | | 1.39 | −0.07 | 1.22 | −0.32 |

*Note*: [a]It is important to note that the size of the estimated long-term elasticities in this table and elsewhere in the chapter should be seen in the context of the length of the estimation period. Since this is usually around twenty-five years, the reported values may well underestimate the 'true' long-term elasticities which will reflect changes in lifestyles, long-term technological innovations and changes in infrastructure, such as roads and railways.

1970 and 1990, the fuel cost per mile has actually fallen as a result of efficiency improvements. One reason for which European car travel might be more price elastic than that of the United States is that it faces potentially much greater competition from the railways and the urban mass transit systems which tend to be much less developed in the States. However, it must be stressed that while the income elasticities of distance travelled are consistently close to unity, the price elasticity estimates are much more unstable and highly sensitive to the time period of estimation. It should also be mentioned that the short-run price effects of car travel are extremely small.

The price elasticity of Japan is not directly comparable with that of the United States and Europe as it refers to gasoline demand rather than distance travelled. Consequently, it includes the second round effects of changes in the price of gasoline on the efficiency of new cars and the average size of new cars selected by consumers. Preliminary work on the effect of price on car efficiency, using US data, indicates very significant price effects with some evidence of asymmetry. However, these results are very unstable and price elasticity estimates vary from −0.2 to −2! There are many potential explanations for this instability including poor data on efficiency, regulatory changes on efficiency standards etc. (Greene (1990) examines the comparative impact of price and regulation on changes in the efficiency of cars in the United States.) The selected value, for projection purposes, for the price elasticity of the efficiency of new cars is −0.4. In conjunction with the figure reported in Table 6.2, the overall long-term price elasticity of gasoline demand becomes −0.66 for the United States, −1.25 for Europe and −0.8 for Japan.

*Freight transportation*

The dependent variable for freight transportation is ton miles/kilometres. For the United States and Europe, total freight equations are first estimated and then an equation for the share of freight carried out by truck (as opposed to railways etc.) is estimated. The real price of diesel oil has been used as a proxy for the relative price of truck freight and GDP has been used as a proxy for economic activity. As expected, the income elasticity is around unity for all three regions. The overall long-term price effect is around $-0.2$. The cost of fuel is almost a negligible proportion of the cost of freight with labour and capital costs being much more significant.

*Air transportation*

Lack of readily available data for air distance and cost of travel in Europe and Japan precluded a more 'structural' approach and equations of total aviation fuel were directly estimated. For the United States passenger air miles was the dependent variable and a series was constructed for the cost of air travel rather than just the cost of fuel.[2] The income effect for all three regions is quite high and between 1.2 for Japan and 1.5 for the United States. This is likely to be due to the luxury nature of air travel. The seemingly very different price elasticities of air travel in Table 6.2 provide a good illustration of the importance of the price series used for interpreting elasticities. In terms of the reaction of fuel demand to the crude oil price all three regions have much more similar elasticities than would appear from Table 6.2. The $-0.6$ US price elasticity relates to the cost of air travel, only a small proportion of which is accounted for by the fuel cost (the 1990 value used in the model is 25 per cent for the United States). The European $-0.07$ elasticity on the other hand is with respect to the price of crude oil which is only part of the cost of aviation fuel, let alone the cost of air travel.

## 6.2.2  Industrial sector

The industrial sector is a very diverse sector requiring energy for a variety of purposes, including motive power, steam raising and process heat. It also includes the large petrochemicals and iron and steel industries where the use of energy products takes place not just for energy purposes but also for their transformation into non-energy products.

In some of these uses, only a unique form of energy is possible (and, consequently only activity effects would be expected) , while in others, like steam raising, almost any form of energy could be used and we would expect a very high price elasticity, at least in the long term. This diversity makes aggregate modelling and the interpretation of parameters exceedingly difficult. However, there is little choice in the absence of a full set of data on the end use of energy. With the exception of North America, petrochemical feedstocks have been modelled separately.

A second problem with modelling industry energy demand is the treatment of own electricity generation. Given that a large part of the inefficiency of electricity takes place in its production stage rather than its use, own generation rather than purchasing of electricity can lead to apparent inefficiency of industrial energy use. What makes this problem worse is that there has been a gradual shift towards electricity, for reasons not always due to the competitiveness of electricity (e.g. mini mills, controllability, technology etc.), which is likely to lead to a trend of apparent improvement in efficiency. One potential solution to this problem would be to consider measuring industrial energy demand in primary energy requirement terms.

Another problem with industrial energy demand is the great scope for relocation of industry. Modelling this would involve modelling individual industries on a global scale. However, it is not clear that the cost of energy is the only or, in some cases, even the major reason for relocation, making modelling of the process quite difficult. Again the phenomenon of relocation and the absence of suitably disaggregated output data can lead to the appearance of great improvements in energy efficiency as industrial countries may import the energy embodied in the products. Finally, the econometric modelling of industrial energy demand is most unlikely to capture the phenomenon of large-scale switching between fuels that depends on the specific configuration of the price vector and on the availability of dual-firing capital stock. This is because this stock has been changing rapidly over the past fifteen years with industry putting more emphasis on flexibility. Within the model, judgemental adjustments are likely to be used to capture this.

*Total industrial energy demand*

In estimating total industrial energy demand the explanatory variables used were (a) an energy weighted industrial production index for Japan and Europe and the ordinary US industrial production index for North America and (b) the real weighted average of industrial fuel prices for each region. In the case of Europe, industrial energy demand, the dependent variable, excludes petrochemical feedstocks for the reasons given above. The results given in Table 6.3 indicate that the impact of industrial activity on energy demand varies from 0.6 in Europe to 0.8 in North America and 0.9 in Japan. Activity elasticities significantly less than unity indicate the well-established trend for energy efficiency improvements in all OECD regions.

For price elasticities, significant asymmetry effects were found for North America and Europe.[3] The short-term reaction to a price increase is almost identical, at just over 0.1, in all three regions. A price fall seems to have a significant short-term impact only in Japan. In the long term, there is a large difference in all regions between the effect of price increases, between −0.35

*Table 6.3* Long-term industrial energy demand elasticities

|  | Activity | Energy price |
|---|---|---|
| North America | 0.78 | −0.40 (+ ve dp) |
|  |  | −0.28 (−ve dp) |
| Europe | 0.61 | −0.35 (+ ve dp) |
|  |  | −0.21 (−ve dp) |
| Japan | 0.89 | −0.50 (+ ve dp) |
|  |  | −0.13 (−ve dp) |

and −0.5, and the effect of price decreases, which vary between −0.13 and −0.28. Over the estimation period Japan, with no significant indigenous energy resources, appears to have become impressively energy efficient, and to the extent that much of this improvement may have been due to the relocation of heavy industry there must be a question mark on whether this high elasticity may not moderate in future. In all three regions significant price effects were found over a period of at least nine years. This is not surprising given the long average lifespan of much industrial equipment.

*Industrial fuel shares*

In modelling fuel shares the major explanatory variable was the price of the appropriate fuel relative to either the total industrial energy price or the price of the major competing fuel, or both. Exceptionally, for the North American and European share of solid fuels the ratio of the industrial production in the iron and steel sector to the total industrial production was also used as a relative activity indicator. The reason for this is the especially large weight of this sector for solids demand and the substantial structural changes that have taken place in it over the past twenty years.

In general, relatively little uniformity would be expected in terms of the elasticities of the fuel share equations across regions owing to the large differences in the industrial structures and comparative economics. One of the few uniform results is the high relative price elasticity of oil which is probably due to the fact that oil has often been the residual fuel in industry and is often used by dual-firing equipment. However, as residual fuel oil has been gradually backed out of industry, and as an increasing proportion of oil goes to premium uses like motive power and feedstocks, it is possible that these elasticities overestimate the potential future flexibility of oil usage. Most other relative price effects tend to be smaller and, almost always, when a short-run/long-term distinction is possible the short-run effects tend to be extremely small. This, of course, is due to the relative inflexibility of the energy-using capital stock in its choice of fuel. No asymmetric effects were investigated in the share equations even though they would be expected to be

*Table 6.4* Long-term price elasticities of industrial fuel shares

|  | Activity | Own price relative to total industrial price | Own price relative to competing fuel |
|---|---|---|---|
| *North America* | | | |
| Electricity | | | Gas: −0.64 |
| Gas | | −0.44 | Oil:  −0.33 |
| Oil | | −1.36 | Gas: −0.37 |
| Solids | 0.64 | | Gas: −0.28 |
| | | | |
| *Europe* | | | |
| Electricity | | −0.55 | |
| Gas | | −0.38 | Oil:  −0.06 |
| Oil | | −1.07 | |
| Solids | 0.27 | −1.04 | Gas: −0.21 |
| | | | |
| *Japan* | | | |
| Electricity | | −0.34 | |
| Gas | | −1.30 | |
| Oil | | −0.96 | |
| Solids | | −0.52 | |

quite significant. For example, there is a long established trend for electricity to increase its share in industrial energy demand and this is almost certainly only partly due to the corresponding trend of declining relative electricity prices. Many other considerations increasingly favour electricity as an industrial fuel, including many technological advances, the greater controllability of electricity and its environmental benefits at the point of use. Consequently, it is possible that the elasticity estimates in Table 6.4 may be too high, especially for a rising relative price of electricity.

### 6.2.3  The building sector

This sector consists primarily of the residential and commercial sectors as well as the small components of the agricultural and 'non-specified' sectors. While the incorporation of these is likely to affect the quality of the data somewhat, the effect is likely to be very small as they only account for about 9 per cent of the energy in this overall sector. The bulk of energy use in this sector is linked to the building stock.

Key influences on the energy-using capital stock in this sector include the longevity of buildings, which leads to an extremely gradual incorporation of new technologies and materials that might arise as a result of higher energy prices, and the five to ten year lifespan of boilers and appliances, with the boilers being a key influence on the extent of inter-fuel competition. Unlike the industrial sector, very little dual firing is available in the residential and commercial sectors. Other key aspects of the sector include the importance of the severity of the winter and, in the case of North America, the heat intensity of the summer (this is likely to become much more important in future for some areas of Europe and Japan as, with rising incomes, more households are likely to install air-conditioning).

## Total building energy demand

The major explanatory variables for the overall per capita energy demand equations were per capita consumer expenditure, as a proxy for household income, the weighted average of end use fuel prices and a series that estimates the degree of the abnormality of weather. In the case of Europe the change in consumer expenditure was also found to be very strongly significant although it is difficult to give an intuitive interpretation to this variable.

As can be seen from Table 6.5, the activity elasticities for aggregate demand in Europe and North America tend to be quite close and, at around 0.5, modest in size, probably reflecting saturation effects given that heating, household appliance use and lighting are necessities and unlikely to be much affected by rising income. The income elasticity for Japan is nearly twice this level, probably because of the scarcity of space in this country which makes the size of homes highly income sensitive. Cross-section work by Hiroshi Sakamaki on the link between residential energy use and income cohort, based on household expenditure surveys, found that the income elasticity in Japan is around 0.3 and in the United States around 0.2. The higher time-series elasticities reported here may be due to the inclusion of the commercial sector, which would be expected to be more sensitive to income effects, and to the inclusion of price effects.

The price elasticities for Europe and Japan tend to be very small in the short term and around 0.3 in the long term. Given that the average life of buildings can be very long, it is quite possible that the length of the data series used, up to thirty years, is not sufficient to capture the long-term price effect which might be somewhat higher. In the short run, of course, only a negligible fraction of the building sector can react to price changes. In the case of North

*Table 6.5* Elasticities for per capita total energy building demand

|  | Per capita consumer expenditure | Energy price |
| --- | --- | --- |
| North America | 0.51 | −0.43 (+ ve dp) <br> −0.15 (−ve dp) |
| Europe | 0.45 | −0.26 |
| Japan | 0.87 | −0.29 |

America the price effects are much stronger as well as asymmetric. This could well be due to the much more common use of air-conditioning which tends to be somewhat more discretionary. As with the industrial sector, the length of lags of price terms is very long.

### Building fuel shares

The fuel share results given in Table 6.6 include activity variables for North America and Japan in the form of the degree of penetration by a specific fuel as the major fuel in housing. Apart from the relative prices of competing fuels, many equations also include time trends. The fuel penetration is currently exogenous to the model as it depends on the available infrastructure which is to a large extent determined by policy, resource availability and price. The long-term price elasticities are likely to underestimate the price effect somewhat as they ignore the impact of price on the selection of fuel for new buildings. Unsurprisingly, almost all cross-price elasticities refer to electricity, as the choice is often between installing a second fuel for heating purposes apart from electricity. The solids category is relevant only for Europe but even here nearly half of solids consumption is in the form of wood rather the traditional coal which is in the process of being backed out of the building sector by cleaner fuels.

Since coal is already being backed out to a large extent, the most common competing fuel in all regions is oil which is the fuel most under threat now in the building sector. No asymmetry effects have been investigated in the fuel share equations even though they would be expected to be significant. For

Table 6.6 Long-term elasticities of building fuel shares

|  | Penetration of fuel | Own price relative to competing fuel | Own price relative to competing fuel |
|---|---|---|---|
| *North America* | | | |
| Electricity | 0.37 | Oil:         −0.13 | Gas: −0.44 |
| Gas | | Oil:         −0.26 | |
| Oil | 1.74 | Electricity: −0.44 | |
| *Europe* | | | |
| Electricity | | Oil:         −0.33 | |
| Gas | | Oil:         −0.58 | |
| Oil | | Electricity: −0.46 | Gas: −0.07 |
| Solids | | Oil:         −1.07 | |
| *Japan* | | | |
| Electricity | | Gas:         −0.22 | Oil:  −0.39 |
| Gas | 0.37 | Oil:         −0.53 | |
| Oil | | Electricity: −0.22 | |

example, the cost of installing a gas network in an all-electric residential area can be prohibitive if it is not done during the initial construction phase.

## 6.3 CONCLUSIONS

The major conclusion to emerge from the results presented here is that, in general, long-term energy price elasticities tend to be small, at least compared with the corresponding income or activity elasticities. This is despite the fact that, in almost all cases, end use prices rather than primary energy prices have been used. This is an important distinction since the link between primary and end use prices is often extremely weak, especially in the transportation and residential sectors. For example, the proportion of the price of gasoline accounted for by the cost of crude oil varies from 61 per cent in the United States to 20 per cent in Europe while only around 10 per cent of the cost of residential electricity is due to the cost of primary fossil fuel energy.

There are two important implications of this combination of relatively low energy demand price elasticities with limited feedback from primary to end use prices. First, primary energy markets would be expected to be rather volatile as moderate supply shocks would lead to large price changes. Second, small additional energy taxes would be unlikely to have a major impact on energy demand. Thus, in the context of the current debate on the effectiveness of carbon taxes to control energy-related $CO_2$ emissions, the results presented in this chapter would suggest that rather large carbon taxes would be necessary in the medium term and in a world where, in the absence of additional taxes, energy demand would be expected to continue to increase (see IEA 1993).

## NOTES

Hiroshi Sakamaki and Teresa Malyshev contributed to the estimation of the domestic and industrial sectors respectively. I am also grateful to Keith Welham for comments on a previous draft. The views expressed here are those of the author and do not necessarily reflect those of the IEA.

1   The results presented here should be seen as work in progress and subject to change as the model is constantly being refined and the data revised and extended. The version of the model described in this chapter was completed in January 1993 and the resulting projections were published in the IEA's 1993 *World Energy Outlook*; see later issues of the *Outlook* for updates of the model and its estimates. Given the coverage of energy sectors, fuels and regions in this chapter the listing of individual equations and the details on data sources are not included. Readers interested in further details should contact the author.

2   This was only possible for the period 1980–90 and the results from this equation must be treated with special caution.

3   For the methodology used to capture asymmetry see Dargay (1992).

# Chapter 7

# Modelling UK energy demand

*Derek Hodgson and Keith Miller*

**ABSTRACT**

This chapter describes recent energy demand modelling by the Economics and Statistics Division of the Department of Trade and Industry (DTI) (formerly the Department of Energy), focusing on some of the ongoing research into the domestic sector's energy demand. Various sectoral long-term own-price energy and output elasticities are reported with particular emphasis on the domestic sector, reflecting the most recent research efforts. These are compared with previous estimates of elasticities and reasons for the differences are suggested. (Long-term cross-price elasticities are not reported here as the fuel splitting tool, the Science and Policy Research Unit's boiler model, is currently being updated.) The results show that the DTI long-term elasticities are broadly similar to those obtained by other researchers. Some differences in the elasticity estimates are inevitable, however, as econometricians have access to different information sources. This is reflected in the different levels of disaggregation used in their final models. In this respect the DTI has good access to disaggregated data sources and consequently its models tend to be more disaggregated than those used by other researchers. Thus the DTI energy model is less likely to suffer from aggregation bias than most other UK energy models.

**INTRODUCTION**

This chapter begins by describing the recent history of the DTI energy model and then proceeds to discuss the current version of the model in terms of the estimation techniques used, the data and the results. The estimated output and price elasticities and their properties are discussed in Sections 7.4 and 7.5. Finally, in Section 7.6, our recent research efforts into domestic sector energy demand are described, with the demand being divided into energy demand for heating, cooking and appliances. The energy demand model structure is presented in diagrammatic form in Appendix 7A and an overview of the model is given in Appendix 7B.

## 7.1 HISTORY

Econometric models of energy demand and supply were originally introduced by the Department of Energy (now part of the DTI) for energy planning reasons. The Sizewell B Inquiry in 1983 was the last occasion on which the model was explicitly used to provide published energy projections for this purpose. Following the Sizewell B Inquiry the role of long-term energy modelling diminished, in line with the market-based approach adopted by the government (see Price (1991) for the background to official energy modelling). However, by the late 1980s a need to produce estimates of future levels of pollutants led to a resurgence of interest in energy modelling and to substantial redevelopment of the Department's model. The results from this model were subsequently published in October 1989 as Energy Paper 58. During 1991 further revisions to the model used in Energy Paper 58 were made and the results from this revised model were published as Energy Paper 59. Based on the 1991 version of the model the then Secretary of State for Energy, in a Parliamentary Question of 6 December 1991, gave the following range of $CO_2$ emissions (in million tonnes of carbon):

| 1990 | 2000 | 2005 | 2020 |
|------|------|------|------|
| 160 | 156–178 | 166–200 | 188–284 |

It should be noted, however, that the model described below (1992 version) includes a new set of domestic sector equations which were estimated during 1992. This did not alter significantly the $CO_2$ ranges reported above.

The last paper describing the government's energy model was published in Helm et al. (1989). That paper essentially described the energy model used for the Sizewell B Inquiry. The equations used in the model were simple partial adjustment equations. Since those equations were estimated econometrics has improved significantly in terms of both modelling techniques and the software available to researchers. The latest version of the energy model takes advantage of these improvements and is based on a set of econometric equations that have been estimated in unrestricted error correction form, e.g.

$$Y_t = a + b_i X_{t-i} + c_j Y_{t-j} + d_i X_{t-i-1}$$

$Y$ is energy demand, $X$ is a vector of exogenous variables such as prices, income and output, $a$ is a coefficient and $b_i$, $c_i$ and $d_i$ are vectors of coefficients. The use of the unrestricted error correction model is preferred to the partial adjustment model since it has three advantages over the latter.

1    It allows for greater flexibility between short- and long-term price and output effects.
2    Energy demand can adjust at different speeds to changes in prices and output.
3    The historic data play a larger role in estimating the equation.

## 7.2  ESTIMATION TECHNIQUE

The unrestricted error correction functional form was applied to annual data derived from the Digest of United Kingdom Energy Statistics (*DUKES*). Since energy demand data are only available on a reliable basis from the early 1950s onwards it was decided not to use cointegration techniques (see Engle and Granger (1991) for a discussion of this technique) to estimate the equations as unit root tests typically require around a hundred observations. The above functional form encompasses the previous partial adjustment functional form and allows the data to play a larger role in the estimation process.

The energy demand data taken from *DUKES* were collected on the basis of the 1968 Standard Industrial Classification (SIC) until 1984 when it was transferred onto the 1980 SIC. Although the Department of Energy did its utmost to put these data on a consistent 1980 SIC basis, a dummy taking the value of 1 from 1984 onwards was inserted into each equation to allow for any inconsistencies in the SICs. A dummy was also used in the equations to allow for the miners' strike in the mid-1980s. Each equation was estimated by ordinary least squares using the econometric software package Microfit (Pesaran and Pesaran 1991). The diagnostics given in this package were used to derive the final equation for each sub-sector. Most of the equations were estimated over the period 1954–88.

## 7.3  ENERGY DEMAND DATA

Energy demand is divided into five sectors:

1    Transport
2    Other industry
3    Service
4    Domestic
5    Iron and steel

These sectors are further subdivided into more appropriate sub-sectors for estimation purposes. Thus the transport sector's energy demand is subdivided into gasoline, Derv and aviation fuel etc. The non-transport sectors are initially subdivided by type of final consumer. Having split the sectoral energy demands into the main categories of final consumers these demands are in turn divided between the principal fuel types. One obvious problem with this approach is that information at this level of disaggregation is often poor. In order to deal with this problem specific sectoral information has been taken from various Energy Efficiency Office (EEO) publications. In the domestic sector end use demands have been derived on the basis of data provided by the Building Research Establishment. Appendix A shows the current level of disaggregation used in the model.

Energy demand within the model is measured and estimated in terms of 'useful therms' rather than delivered therms. There are two reasons for using this numeraire of energy demand. First the switch away from coal to oil and more recently to gas exaggerates, when measured in delivered therms, the reduction in energy intensity since the war. This suggests that what we should be interested in estimating is the *effective demand for energy* or *useful energy* demand. Useful energy demand can be thought of as what the energy consumer actually requires once all the losses and inefficiencies have been deducted from the delivered amount of energy (usually measured in therms). Thus useful energy demand relates to the demand for energy *services* rather than energy demand itself. In order to compute useful energy demands each fuel was converted into therms, and then factors defined between 0 and 1 were applied to these data to produce useful therm data. Note that the factors used to convert from therms to useful therms vary both by fuel and sector.

The second reason for using useful therms rather than delivered therms as the energy numeraire is that when prices of fuels are being compared, for fuel substitution purposes, it is important that their prices are compared on the same basis as the energy consumer would compare them. In other words they must be compared on a useful therm basis. To a certain extent the differing efficiencies of fuels will be reflected in their thermal prices, which is why electricity and gas usually command a premium over coal and oil.

The long-term elasticities resulting from this estimation process are shown below in Section 7.2.[1] It should be noted that industrial and service sector fossil fuel switching is largely determined by the Science Policy Research Unit's (SPRU) model. Using the SPRU model to determine the demand for fossil fuels in the industrial and service sectors is preferred to econometric cross-price elasticities for several reasons.

1 The SPRU model contains specific information about energy contracts such as the minimum quantities of energy that must be purchased, e.g. interruptible gas, information which econometric cross-price elasticity estimates ignore.
2 Over a range of prices one fuel is likely to dominate energy demand and so econometrically based cross-price elasticities are likely to be misleading.
3 The SPRU model incorporates information on when it is economic to replace fuel-specific capital equipment with capital equipment that uses a different fuel.

The above suggests that fuel switching models based on econometric cross-price elasticities could be misleading as the cross-price elasticities themselves may be unstable over time.

## 7.4 LONG-TERM ELASTICITIES

### 7.4.1 Long-term price elasticities

For a discussion of the elasticities given in Table 7.1 with respect to energy taxation and $CO_2$ emissions see Hodgson (1992).

The own long-term price elasticities of the DTI's energy model can be compared with those produced by the Operational Research Executive of British Coal (BC) (see Gregory *et al.* 1991); these are shown in Table 7.2. A comparison of the industrial own-price elasticities shows the average to be identical for both models. The higher DTI oil and gas elasticities are offset by the somewhat higher BC coal and electricity elasticities.

The iron and steel electricity price elasticities differ considerably between the energy models. Whereas the DTI was unable to find any significant price effects, BC found a relatively large elasticity of −0.7. Two reasons are suggested for this difference. First, the BC work appears to use more aggregated data than that used for the DTI model, which specifically relates electricity consumption to arc steel production. Since electricity in this sector is almost wholly used for arc steel production it is possible that the BC work may not capture this relationship adequately. Second, the BC paper suggests that they have used levels type equations rather than the unrestricted error correction equations used by the DTI. It is possible that this difference in modelling technique may explain the rather high electricity elasticity obtained by BC. Interestingly both models estimate the coal elasticity to be −0.2. Since coal, in the form of coke, is the major fuel consumed in this sector this is an important result. Overall the DTI model has a larger average price elasticity than the BC model, −0.35 compared with −0.2.

When comparing elasticities between studies it is important to note that the industrial structure changes over time and so the inclusion or exclusion of a

*Table 7.1* DTI energy model own long-term price elasticities

| Sector | Average | Electricity | Coal | Oil | Gas |
|---|---|---|---|---|---|
| Industry | −0.6 | −0.3 | −0.9 | −1.3 | −2.1 |
| Iron and steel | −0.35 | Negligible | −0.2 | −0.8 | |
| Service | −0.3 | −0.6 | | −0.1 | |
| | | | | | |
| *Domestic* | | | | | |
| Heating | N/A | −0.54 | −0.49 | −0.45 | −0.20 |
| Cooking | N/A | −0.1 | N/A | N/A | −0.1 |
| Appliance | N/A | N/A | N/A | N/A | N/A |
| | *Average* | *Gasoline* | *Derv* | *Aviation fuel* | |
| Transport | −0.2 | −0.3 | −0.2 | −0.1 | |

*Table 7.2* British Coal's own long-term price elasticities

| Sector | Average | Electricity | Coal | Oil | Gas |
|---|---|---|---|---|---|
| Industry | 0.6 | −0.5 | −1.0 | −0.6 | −1.3 |
| Iron and steel | −0.2 | −0.7 | −0.2 | −0.3 | −0.3 |
| Service[a] | −0.35 | −0.1 | −0.3 and −1.1 | −0.2 | −1.5 and −0.4 |
| Domestic | −0.1 | −0.8 | −0.3 | −0.5 | −0.6 |
| | *Average* | *Gasoline* | *Derv* | *Aviation fuel* | |
| Transport | −0.1 | N/A | N/A | N/A | |

*Source*:  Gregory *et al.* 1991
*Notes*:  [a]The British Coal elasticity estimates divide the service sector into public administration and miscellaneous. The former is shown first in these tables.
N/A, not available.

time trend in the energy demand equation can have a crucial impact on the final estimated elasticities/coefficients. In the service sector individual elasticities differ somewhat in both models, although the average price elasticities are virtually identical.

The DTI average transport sector long-term energy price elasticity is twice as large as that found in the BC study. Again this difference may be the result of different levels of aggregation and functional form. Dargay (see Hawdon 1992) using an irreversible model for road transport demand found a long-term price elasticity of −0.1 (although her 'maximum previous price' variable had a long-term elasticity of −1.5) and −0.4 using a reversible model. Since the DTI average elasticity falls between the two Dargay estimates there is some support for it; however, it should be remembered that Dargay's work excludes non-road transport demand.

### 7.4.2  Long-term output elasticities

Hawdon (1992), referring to work done by Beenstock and Dalziel, shows their industrial long-term output elasticity to be 1.1 and their energy price elasticity to be −0.29. Assuming industry refers to both the other industry and the iron and steel sectors, it can be seen from Table 7.3 that the DTI industrial long-term output elasticities are both less than 1.1. The average DTI industrial long-run price elasticity is somewhat higher than −0.29. Beenstock and Dalziel appear to have used log-linear equations and so the comments given for BC's use of this functional form also apply to this work. Since their equations are only estimated between 1953 and 1982 they do not capture the shake-out of manufacturing industry in the 1980s and the long-term impact of the 1979 hike in oil price. Thus the energy price elasticity of −0.29 given by Hawdon may be too low in absolute terms and the output elasticity too high. Lynk (again shown in Hawdon) for the period 1944–81 estimates the

*Table 7.3* DTI energy model own long-term income–output elasticities

| Sector | All fuels | Electricity | Coal | Oil | Gas |
|---|---|---|---|---|---|
| Industry | 0.82 | 1.73 | N/A | N/A | N/A |
| Iron and steel | 1.0 | 1.0 | 1.0 | 1.0 | 1.0 |
| Service[a] | 0.6 | 2.7 | N/A | N/A | N/A |
| Domestic[b] | 0.2 | 0.3 | −2.4 | −0.2 | 0.3 |
| | Average | Gasoline | Derv | Aviation fuel | |
| Transport | N/A | 0.81 | 1.25 | OECD GDP = 2.07 UK RPDY = 0.31 | |

*Notes*: [a]This value is for space and water heating demand only.
[b]Space and water heating only.
RPDY, real personal disposable income; N/A, not available.

long-term industrial output and price elasticities to be 0.44 and −0.69 respectively. The DTIs industrial price elasticities are broadly similar to Lynk's −0.69, although his output elasticity is around half of that found by the DTI.

Dargay, in her work referred to above, found the long-term road transport output elasticity to be either 0.7 or 1.49 depending on whether a reversible or irreversible model was used. Since the DTI's gasoline and Derv long-term output elasticities fall within these two estimates her work again tends to support the DTI elasticities. Dargay also uses unrestricted error correction mechanisms in her work so comparisons with the DTI's model are somewhat easier to make, as one does not need to make an allowance for different functional forms.

## 7.5 PROPERTIES OF ELASTICITIES

Since energy elasticities are often used to evaluate environmental policy measures such as carbon taxes it is important that policy-makers realize that elasticities are not constant over time. Recall the own-price elasticity formula:

$$e_{EE} = \frac{\mathrm{d}EP_E}{\mathrm{d}P_E E}$$

Consider the first ratio in this formula. It can be thought of as representing the possibilities for energy conservation. At low price levels the first ratio will be relatively large, suggesting that the possibilities for energy conservation are plentiful. However, as $P_E$ increases, due say to a carbon tax, the possibilities for energy conservation will decline as they are gradually taken up and so the first ratio will fall. Note, however, that the second ratio will be increasing and so the value of the elasticity is indeterminate.

Own energy price elasticities will also vary considerably depending on the market penetration of the particular fuel being considered. Suppose for instance that a fuel has a low level of market penetration so that the value $E$ in the elasticity formula is relatively small. If the price of fuel $E$ (i.e. $P_E$) now falls, then assuming that the first ratio in the elasticity formula remains constant the elasticity will fall over time as $E$ increases. In the context of UK energy demand an obvious example of this process at work is the introduction of natural gas to the industrial market in the late 1960s.

Essentially similar arguments to those made above for own energy price elasticities can also be made for energy cross-price elasticities. The point to come out of these examples is clear: estimates of elasticities are only valid for a short period of time as changes in market shares etc. will lead to variations in the value of the elasticities. This has obvious implications for those using elasticities in policy-related work.

One important factor which must be remembered when examining individual long-term output–income energy elasticities is that as the energy saturation level is approached this elasticity tends to zero. This is particularly important in the case of modelling work associated with projecting long-term $CO_2$ emissions, as a log log functional form will result in energy demand being greatly overestimated. This overestimation of energy demand/$CO_2$ will increase with time. In order to avoid putting explicit ceilings into the DTI energy model several of the equations have been estimated in linear log form, i.e.

$$Y = a + b \ln X$$

which has the elasticity $b/Y$. Thus the income–output elasticity declines as income rises over time. This functional form has the desirable property that successive equal increments in income–output have less and less impact on the growth in energy demand. Once a saturation level has been reached the impact of energy efficiency measures becomes somewhat clearer to perceive as energy consumption can only decline as the result of energy efficiency measures being introduced. Much of the non-econometric modelling of $CO_2$ emissions is based around saturation levels being reached in the near future, e.g. see the Building Research Establishment's work.

Saturation levels are particularly important for bottom-up models. Bottom-up models are essentially databases of the existing stock of capital equipment. They also usually take account of economic investment in new equipment and the scrapping of existing capital equipment. These databases can be used to determine the level of projected energy consumption by assuming that energy consumers use the most cost-efficient technology to meet their useful energy demand requirements. Although an important approach, the bottom-up approach does suffer from the drawback that it can only capture relative price effects, i.e. switching between fuels, and not absolute price effects. Furthermore at levels of energy consumption below the saturation level bottom-up models have difficulty in capturing the impact of increases in income–output on energy demand. In recognition of the importance of bottom up effects on energy consumption the DTI energy model incorporates a number of capital stock features which help to limit the future growth in energy consumption. Probably the most important of these is the SPRU model. As Appendix 7A shows, the SPRU model is used to determine the boiler fuel shares in the industrial and service sectors.

## 7.6 DOMESTIC SECTOR MODELLING

### 7.6.1 Domestic sector energy demand for heating purposes

Another sector where stock effects and saturation levels are important is in the domestic sector. In order to capture the impact of saturation effects logit models are used to project the proportion of households owning central heating (CH). Initially a logit model is used to project the percentage of households owning central heating, with a saturation level of 100 per cent. This percentage is then divided amongst households with different types of CH; gas, electricity, oil and solid fuel. Once again this is achieved by using logit models. Relative price effects play an important part in determining which fuels are used for CH purposes in the logit equations. Since a large portion of households will never have access to gas, because of the high connection charges in remote areas, the percentage of households who can have access to gas is limited to 90 per cent of all households.

Having estimated the percentage of households owning each type of CH the next step is to use this information to estimate energy consumption. This is done by estimating space and water heating equations for each fuel type, with the above CH stock variables included in these equations as regressors. It should be noted that CH energy demand is only one part (admittedly the major part) of total domestic sector space and water heating demand. Thus additional regressors are also added to the space and water heating energy demand equations in order to capture the impact of non-CH stock factors such as portable gas heaters. Some of the space and water heating equations have been estimated in linear log form. Thus any remaining saturation effects not captured by the CH stock logit equations are dealt with in the demand equations.

Recent DTI research suggests the domestic sector space and water heating elasticities given in Table 7.4. Currently we are evaluating SURE and multinomial estimation techniques to see if they can significantly improve upon these preliminary results.

The domestic sector also uses energy for two other reasons:

*Table 7.4* Domestic sector heating price elasticities

|   |   | Energy demands | | | |
|---|---|---|---|---|---|
|   |   | Gas | Oil | Coal | Electricity |
| P<br>r<br>i<br>c<br>e<br>s | Gas | −0.2 | +0.55 | +0.30 | +0.54 |
|   | Oil | +0.1 | −0.45 | Negligible | Negligible |
|   | Coal | Negligible | Negligible | −0.49 | Negligible |
|   | Electricity | Negligible | +1.36 | +0.52 | −0.54 |

1   Cooking
2   Appliances

### 7.6.2  Domestic energy demand for cooking purposes

Energy consumption for cooking purposes is dominated by gas and electricity. Some oil and solid fuel is also used for cooking purposes but the amounts involved are so small that it makes more sense to enter them as exogenous assumptions rather than as separate equations. The split between gas and electricity is approximately 55:45. Although a small number of cookers are dual fired most are not and so it is important to model the stock of cookers prior to estimating individual fuel demands. In order to do this we begin by modelling the percentage of households with gas cookers, again applying the above 90 per cent ceiling. Using the assumption that each household owns one cooker it is then possible to derive the total fuel demands by multiplying the number of households using a given fuel for cooking purposes by the average annual fuel consumption per cooker for that fuel.

Total gas cooker fuel demand is obtained by assuming that a typical gas cooker consumes some 50 therms a year. This estimate of average per annum gas cooker consumption can be adjusted during the projection period in line with likely improvements in gas cooker efficiency.

Average electric cooker consumption per annum is estimated via an equation that has a lower limit of 370 kW h. Thus average annual electric cooker consumption cannot fall below this limit during the projection period. This lower limit was obtained from Energy Efficiency Series 13 (DEN 1990b).

Using the above domestic cooker equations the long-term price elasticities given in Table 7.5 were obtained. Note that we were unable to find a significant real personal disposable income term in any of the equations. This lack of significance can be attributed to the fact that total cooker energy demand long ago saturated and so the only remaining item of interest is which fuels meet this saturated level of energy demand. Saturation effects aside, one would expect that increasing real incomes would tend to reduce cooker

*Table 7.5* Domestic sector cooking price elasticities

|  |  | Energy demands | |
|---|---|---|---|
|  |  | Gas | Electric |
| P | Gas | −0.06 | +0.05 |
| r | | | |
| i | Electric | +0.06 | −0.10 |
| c | | | |
| e | | | |
| s | | | |

demand since households will increasingly eat out rather than eat at home. Thus domestic sector cooker consumption will to a certain extent be substituted by additional service sector cooker consumption, e.g. restaurants and cafeterias.

### 7.6.3  Domestic appliances energy demand

The amount of energy consumption attributable to appliances is a particularly difficult area to model as the econometrician is trying to model the energy consumption of appliances that may not even exist yet. An example will perhaps illustrate the problems involved in estimating this type of energy consumption. Suppose in 1950 we were trying to prepare forecasts of appliance energy consumption. We would have found it difficult (if not impossible) to forecast the energy consumption of appliances not yet invented, such as video recorders and personal computers. Furthermore, although many new domestic appliances would appear to have great energy-saving potential, this is not always the case. A case in point is microwaves which are thought to be energy efficient. What is often missed, however, is the additional uses to which microwaves can be put, as they can be used to defrost food as well as cook it. When this type of additional energy consumption is taken into account the savings obtainable from new appliances is often very much smaller than originally thought. Thus the sudden introduction of a new appliance does not always invalidate projections of energy demand made prior to that new appliance being introduced.

It is precisely these considerations that today's energy econometricians are required to incorporate into their models if $CO_2$ emissions are to be meaningfully projected beyond the year 2000. In fact, both econometric and bottom-up models are deficient in this area. The approach adopted up to now by the DTI is similar to that adopted for space and water heating demand. Initially the stock of appliances is modelled by relating it to income etc. This stock estimate is then entered into an appliance energy demand equation, along with other variables, and the estimate of future appliance energy demand is arrived at by projecting this equation into the future. Because of

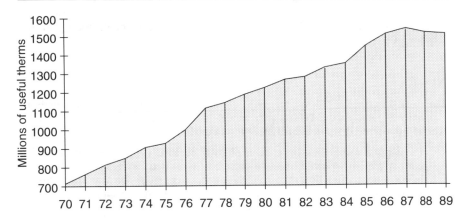

*Figure 7.1* Total domestic sector appliance energy demand
*Source*: Building Research Establishment

the problems outlined above domestic appliance energy consumption is the most difficult part of total domestic energy consumption to model. Fortunately, however, appliance energy consumption is only some 14 per cent of total domestic energy consumption and so relatively large errors in this component of domestic energy consumption do not alter the total greatly. Appliance energy consumption has traditionally been the fastest growing component of domestic energy consumption; since 1986, however, it has shown some signs of saturating (Figure 7.1). We are currently investigating the data shown in the above chart to discover if appliance energy demand has indeed saturated or if there has been some misallocation of total domestic energy demand, resulting in too little demand in this subsector. Once this analysis has been completed it is likely that at least some of the estimated elasticities will alter.

Certainly the energy appliance demand data post-1986 sits uneasily with the growth in real personal incomes over this period, which suggests that appliance demand has not saturated. The latter is also supported by the relatively high electricity–income elasticity shown in Table 7.3 for domestic space and water heating energy demand. Since electricity demand for cooking purposes is relatively well defined, any missing appliance demand must appear in space and water heating electricity demand.

## 7.7 CONCLUSIONS

This chapter has discussed some of the improvements in econometric techniques that have recently been incorporated into the DTI energy model. Several of the equations used in the model are of the error correction model type and the problems encountered in estimating these equations have been described. Future developments to the model will include the introduction of a new model of industrial and service sector boiler heat, incorporating combined heat and power technologies.

## NOTE

The work described in this chapter is based on work in progress and is not therefore a definitive guide to the DTI energy model; interested researchers should contact Keith Miller directly for details of more recent modelling work.

1   Cross-price elasticities have been omitted because the DTI energy model is currently being updated by the inclusion of a revised SPUR boiler model. The boiler model's function is to split the overall demand for heat in the industrial sector into demands for individual fossil fuels. It is therefore a major determinant of cross-price elasticities. It is hoped to report the results of this work in 1994.

## APPENDIX 7A   ENERGY DEMAND MODEL STRUCTURE

## Appendix 7A continued

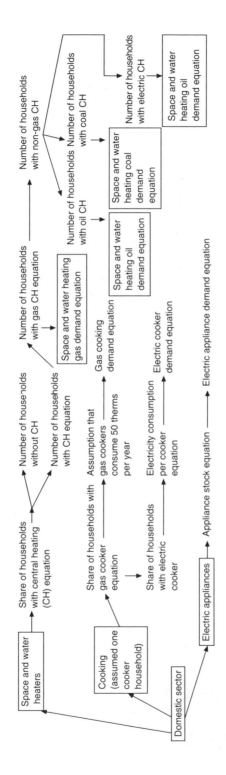

# APPENDIX 7B  DEPARTMENT OF TRADE AND INDUSTRY ENERGY MODEL OVERVIEW

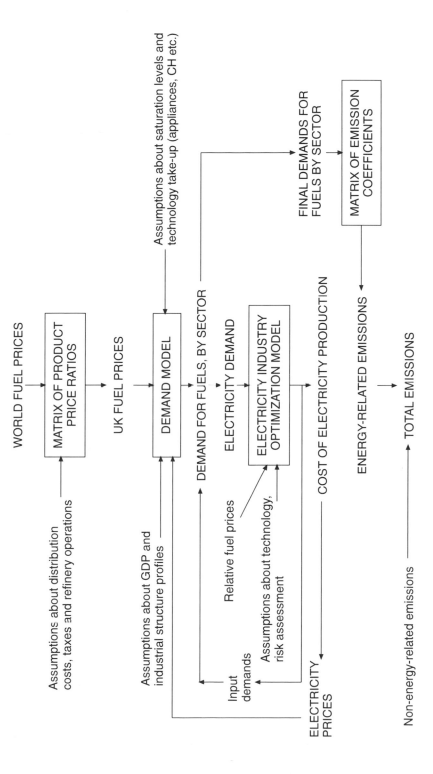

# Part II

# Energy, the economy and greenhouse gas abatement

Chapter 8

# Endogenous technological progress in fossil fuel demand

*Laurence Boone, Stephen Hall, David Kemball-Cook and Clare Smith*

## ABSTRACT

This chapter reports on work to develop energy demand sectors for the Global Econometric Model (GEM), maintained jointly by the London Business School and the National Institute for Economic and Social Research. We have derived data for the total fossil fuel energy consumption, energy prices, GDP and general prices for the main OECD countries (Belgium, Canada, France, Germany, the Netherlands, Italy, Japan, the UK and the United States). We then apply multivariate cointegration tests to test for the presence of cointegration between this set of variables. We find remarkably similar relationships in terms of price elasticities and in terms of trend increases in energy efficiency across all the countries. We then go on to estimate full dynamic models for all the countries. Finally in this chapter we consider the relationship between long-term growth, increasing energy efficiency and energy prices and calculate some illustrative trade-offs which leave $CO_2$ emissions unchanged.

## INTRODUCTION

In recent years concern has increased about the build-up of greenhouse gases in the atmosphere, and in particular emissions of $CO_2$ arising from the burning of fossil fuels. Much analysis has been devoted to assessing the economic cost of stabilizing or reducing $CO_2$ emissions by means of economic instruments such as a special tax on fossil fuels weighted according to carbon content. In this chapter an econometric analysis of the determinants of fossil fuel demand in nine OECD countries is conducted. The chapter poses three questions.

1   What is the historical relationship between fossil fuel consumption, fossil fuel prices and GDP in each country?
2   What is the historical trend in this relationship?
3   If the historical patterns were maintained what would be the economic cost of limiting energy consumption assuming various scenarios for GDP growth?

This is the first part of work which will incorporate the resulting energy demand equations into the Global Econometric Model (GEM) maintained jointly by the National Institute and the London Business School. The focus of the study is on the G7 countries, as well as Belgium and the Netherlands. The overall objectives of the research are to model the international macroeconomic consequences of measures to reduce emissions of $CO_2$, hence shedding light on the benefits and costs of an abatement strategy and the impact of such a policy, not only within a particular country but also throughout the world, while taking into account the effect on trade and competitiveness.

This chapter attempts to build fossil fuel demand equations for nine OECD countries (Belgium, Canada, France, Germany, Italy, Japan, the Netherlands, the United Kingdom and the United States) as a function of gross domestic product (GDP), energy prices relative to the GDP deflator, and time, used as a proxy for technological innovation. First, the time-series properties of the variables, namely fossil fuel consumption, fossil fuel prices relative to the GDP deflator and GDP, are studied under the Johansen procedure. This leads to the construction of a cointegrating relationship which is close to the Cobb–Douglas representation that most previous studies have used. Several possible forms of the potentially cointegrating equation (vector autoregression (VAR) with or without a restricted or an unrestricted constant) are tested with the Johansen procedure in order to get the most accurate long-run relationship. This also allows us to estimate all the different possible relationships between fossil fuel consumption and relative prices, with a negative sign expected. The impact of technology is taken into account via a time trend, whose sign is also expected to be negative.

Recognizing that this treatment of the impact of technology is unsatisfactory, this set of estimates is regarded as only the first step towards a model which fully endogenizes the technological innovation factor so that ultimately it will be possible to assess the effects of policy on the rate of innovation. The following general model is proposed as a means of approaching the problem. First, begin by specifying a standard error correction model for energy demand:

$$\Delta E = \sum_{j=1}^{q} \gamma_j \Delta E_{t-j} + \sum_{j=1}^{p} \alpha_j \Delta X_{t-j} + \beta(E_{t-1} - \gamma X_{t-1} + T_t) + \upsilon_t \qquad (8.1)$$

where $\Delta$ is first difference, $E$ is the log of fossil fuel energy demand, $X$ is the log of price relative to the GDP deflator, $T$ is time, $\alpha$, $\beta$, $\gamma$ are coefficients, $p$, $q$ are maximum number of lags and $\upsilon$ is an error term. If $T_t$ was simply a deterministic trend this would be a conventional model. But if the trend is generated as follows the model is much richer.

$$T_t = T_{t-1} + g_{t-1} + \eta Z_t + e_{t1}$$ (8.2)

$$g_t = g_{t-1} + e_{t2}$$

where $g$ is the rate of increase of the trend (possibly stochastic) and $Z$ represents a vector of other explanatory variables. A restricted form of this model (when both the error terms are set to zero and the coefficients on $Z$ are zero) gives the special case of a standard deterministic time trend. More generally, when this restriction is relaxed the time trend becomes stochastic and its determination can be modelled through the set of extra explanatory variables $Z$ (e.g. structural changes, investment, expansion in non-fossil fuel consumption). This model, when it is fully implemented, will allow for the endogenous treatment of technological progress within an empirical econometric model.

Most of this chapter will be concerned with a preliminary analysis of the model with deterministic progress. The intention is to build a set of error correction models for each country. This leads to a reduced dynamic representation of fossil fuel consumption whose congruence is tested through a set of diagnostic tests. From the error correction models the long-run equilibrium equations can be investigated. A simulation of the movement in the relative price of fossil fuel required to maintain constant fuel consumption in the nine countries is then considered under different assumptions about GDP growth. This highlights differences across countries and the various costs that such a goal implies. There are two main conclusions. First, it is possible to derive broadly similar cointegrating relationships between fossil fuel consumption and prices for the nine countries studied. Second, according to these estimates, and assuming that there is no policy intervention, the annual increases in fossil fuel prices necessary to stabilize consumption would vary considerably between countries. For instance, assuming growth in real GDP of 3 per cent *per annum* across the G9, required annual price rises would need to be as high as 17.8 per cent in the Netherlands but zero in France, Belgium and Japan. The chapter concludes with a brief initial exploration of the full stochastic technological progress model.

## 8.1 ENERGY DEMAND AND GROSS DOMESTIC PRODUCT IN GLOBAL MODELS[1]

In energy economy models the link between energy use and macroeconomic variables is typically represented by the *energy intensity* coefficient, defined as energy consumption per unit of GDP. In industrialized countries energy intensity has been in steady decline since the early 1970s or before, and the rate at which it is expected to continue to decline is critical to the predictions of models concerning greenhouse gas emissions. All models simulate the effect of policies to control greenhouse gas emissions by constructing a 'business-as usual' *base-case scenario* and then making departures from it by means of policy changes such as the introduction of carbon taxation. The main global models concerned with greenhouse gas emissions, reviewed by Boero *et al.* (1991), are summarized in Table 8.1.

The general equilibrium models and the optimal growth models make use of a constant elasticity of substitution (CES) aggregate production function of the form

$$Y = H \left( aF^{\rho} + bE^{\rho} \right) \frac{1}{\rho}$$

where $Y$ is final output, $E$ is energy input and $F$ represents other factor inputs. $H$, $a$ and $b$ are parameters. The elasticity of substitution $\sigma$ between energy and other factors is then given by $\sigma = 1/(1 - \rho)$, where $0 < \sigma < \infty$, $-\infty < \rho < 1$.

In parameterizing the models to yield paths for energy intensity in the base-case scenario, Whalley and Wigle (1990), Nordhaus and Yohe (1983) and Nordhaus (1990a) assume neutrality in technological change (i.e. it affects all factors of production equally, with only the $H$ parameter being affected). The other studies allow for energy-saving technological progress, as modelled by parameters $a$ and $b$.

In almost all studies, GDP growth is treated exogenously in the base case. Various assumptions are then made about the base trend of energy intensity (i.e. the trend it would follow in the absence of policy changes). The standard assumption of declining energy intensity is attributed to a number of factors, and here it is important to separate the factors that are not connected with movements in energy prices from those which are. The non-price factors which affect energy use are summarized by Boero *et al.* (1991) as follows:

1   'exogenous' energy-saving technological progress (i.e. that which would happen anyway, regardless of price changes);
2   policy-induced technological change;
3   elimination of inefficient technologies or 'no regrets' changes (i.e. measures which are already cost effective in their own right, such as certain energy conservation measures);
4   changes in the composition of GDP.

Boero *et al.* point out that almost all studies amalgamate the non-price factors into a single 'exogenous energy-efficiency' parameter, which applies equally in the base case and in the simulations. For instance, Manne and Richels (1990) use the term 'autonomous energy-efficiency improvements' (AEEI), modelled by a decline in the coefficient $b$. The problem with this approach, which Boero *et al.* point out, is that non-price factors do not apply equally in the base and the constrained cases because policies to constrain emissions will affect non-price factors 2 and 3 above. It would therefore be unwise to assume that policy-induced changes were equivalent in the base case and the simulations. Indeed, a strong case has been made for the merits

Table 8.1 Summary of features of global models

| Study model | Period | Type of model | Particular features | Regions |
|---|---|---|---|---|
| Edmonds and Reilly (1983a, b) IEA-ORAU | 1975–2050 | Partial equilibrium | Detailed energy sectors | Nine regions |
| Nordhaus and Yohe (1983) | 1973–2100 | General equilibrium | Nested CES for energy inputs | Global |
| Edmonds and Barnes (1990a, b) revised IEA-ORAU[a] | 1973–2025 | Partial equilibrium | Two strategies: global agreements and OECD unilateral | Nine regions |
| Manne and Richels (1990) ETA-MACRO | 1990–2100 | Partial equilibrium energy model Optimal growth macro model | Solves sectoral and macro models interactively. CES production function with nested Cobb–Douglas | Five regions |
| Nordhaus (1990a) | 1990–2100 | Optimal growth | Cobb–Douglas function. Interaction between emissions and growth | Six regions |
| Whalley and Wigle (1990) | 1990–2030 | Static computable general equilibrium | Simple energy sector with two types of energy. CES production functions | Six regions |
| Burniaux et al. (1991a, b) GREEN | 1990–2025 | Dynamic computable general equilibrium | Fully clearing markets. Mix of CES and Leontief production functions | Seven regions |

Note: [a]The IEA-ORAU model has also been used by Reilly et al. (1987), Mintzer (1987), Darmstadter and Edmonds (1988) and Waide (1992).

Table 8.2 Assumptions made by studies about energy elasticity and energy intensity

| Study | Energy demand own-price elasticity | | Energy intensity 'autonomous' rate of decline (% p.a.) | | | | |
|---|---|---|---|---|---|---|---|
| | | | | 1975 | 2050 | | |
| Edmonds and Reilly (1983a, b) | OECD Residential | −0.9 | | 0.0 | 0.0 | | |
| | Commercial | −0.9 | | 1.0 | 1.75 | | |
| | Industrial | −0.8 | | 0.0 | 0.0 | | |
| | Transport | −0.7 | | | | | |
| | Non-OECD | −0.8 | | 1.0 | 1.3 | | |
| | | | | | | 1975–2000 | 2000–25 | 2025 on |
| Nordhaus and Yohe (1983) | Residential | −0.9 | (Neutral technological progress) Productivity growth | | | | | |
| | Transport | −0.8 | | | | | | |
| | Industrial | −0.7 | High | | | 3.4 | 0.9 | 0.1 |
| | | | Middle | | | 2.3 | 1.6 | 1.0 |
| | | | Low | | | 1.2 | 2.3 | 1.9 |
| Edmonds and Barnes (1990a) | −0.7 | | | 1.0 | | | |
| Edmonds and Barnes (1990b) | Low | −0.2 | | 0.0 | | | |
| | Reference | −0.7 | | 1.0 | | | |
| | High | −1.2 | | 2.0 | | | |
| Reilly et al. (1987) | −0.65 (mean) −0.70 (median) | | | 1.0 | | | |
| Mintzer (1987) | High emissions | −1.1 | | 0.2 | | | |
| | Base | −0.8 | | 0.8 | | | |
| | Modest policy | −0.7 | | 1.0 | | | |
| | Slow build-up | −0.7 | | 1.5 | | | |

| | | | 1990–2050 | 2050–2100 |
|---|---|---|---|---|
| Manne and Richels (1990) | USA | −0.4 | | |
| | Other OECD | −0.3 | | |
| | Rest of world | −0.3 | | |
| | USA | | 0.5 | 0.5 |
| | Other OECD | | 0.5 | 0.5 |
| | CIS/EE | | 0.25 | 0.5 |
| | China | | 1.0 | 0.5 |
| | Rest of world | | 0.0 | 0.5 |
| | (Neutral technological progress) | | | |
| | Productivity growth | | | |
| | Oil exporters | | 2.5 | |
| | OECD | | 2.3 | |
| | Rest of world | | 2.7 | |
| Whalley and Wigle (1990) | Approximately −0.7 (substitution elasticity between energy and other inputs) | | | |
| Burniaux et al. (1990a, b) GREEN | Between −0.3 and −0.6 (substitution elasticities with capital, labour respectively) | | 1.0 | |

of supply-side measures such as tightened energy standards and government spending on energy conservation to complement demand-side measures, such as a carbon tax to stabilize greenhouse gas emissions (Lazarus *et al.*, 1992). In particular, the issue of revenue recycling or the use of carbon tax revenue to fund supply-side measures is not adequately addressed in this approach.

If 'exogenous' changes in energy intensity are assumed to apply equally in base cases and simulations, this may understate the potential for energy saving and overstate the costs of abatement. For example, Williams (1990) argues that the annual autonomous decline in energy intensity of 0.5 per cent to 1.0 per cent postulated by Manne and Richels (1989) is too low because it underestimates the potential for policy-induced conservation measures. A single parameter which has the same value in base and constrained cases is likely either to underestimate energy efficiency on one side or overestimate energy efficiency on the other. Table 8.2 (taken from Tables 4.3 and 4.4 of Boero *et al.*) lists the assumptions made by various studies about the 'autonomous' or 'base-case' path of energy intensity.

Hogan and Jorgenson (1990) criticize what they call the 'conventional wisdom' behind the assumption that, in the absence of relative price changes, energy intensity should decline. This is reflected in Table 8.2 by the various assumptions for autonomous decline in energy intensity. Hogan and Jorgenson report estimates of sectoral productivity trends for the United States and find that, contrary to conventional wisdom, most sectors are becoming more energy intensive rather than less so, i.e. there is an autonomous tendency for the share of energy relative to output to rise rather than decline. Such a trend, they say, has been swamped in the last twenty years by the effects of large changes in the relative price of energy, but in the long term it could prove to be significant. The implication of their findings, if true for countries like the United States, is that the studies are substantially underestimating the costs of greenhouse gas abatement. Indeed, they suggest that the studies may underestimate the cost of abatement by as much as half the total cost. This illustrates the importance of isolating the relative price effects on energy demand from those of autonomous technological change.

Table 8.2 also summarizes the assumptions made about the long-run own-price elasticity of demand for energy, or the elasticity of substitution between energy and other inputs as an approximation to the former when the energy share of GDP is small. Most studies make assumptions that the elasticity is less than unity but quite high nevertheless, with most assuming that it is greater than 0.5.

## 8.2  CONSTRUCTION OF CONSUMPTION AND PRICE VARIABLES

### 8.2.1  Consumption data

Since the present study is concerned with emissions of $CO_2$, and the carbon content of different fuels varies, consumption of different fossil fuels is the focus rather than aggregate energy. The UN Energy Database (United Nations 1992) for the period 1950–89 (annual data) was used to define the consumption of coal, gas and oil[2] for each of the nine main countries of the GEM, namely the G9.[3]

Consumption of coal has decreased over the past forty years, but much more slowly since the first oil crisis. While consumption in the United Kingdom, Germany and France is still steadily diminishing, consumption in Japan and the United States has risen slightly over the period 1950–90. The United States is the biggest consumer of the G9, consuming around three times the level in the United Kingdom, which has been the second highest consumer since 1976. Since 1983, Japan seems to have reached British levels of coal consumption. Consumption in Belgium, Italy, the Netherlands and Canada is far below France, which is itself a relatively small consumer with about a third of British levels over the past fifteen years.

Consumption of petroleum products increased dramatically until the first oil price shock in 1973, and remained remarkably stable at very high levels over the following six years. However, the second oil crisis in 1979 led to a fall in consumption in all G9 countries. Thus, in 1982 the aggregate level of consumption was nearly half the 1979 level. And finally, since 1987 an increasing trend in consumption for the G9 as a whole can be discerned. Japan is the greatest consumer of petroleum after the United States, consuming more than twice the level of Germany, the United Kingdom or France (all which are roughly the same). In all nine countries except the United States, the path followed by consumption is almost the same, characterized by two dips corresponding to the two oil shocks, followed by a slight upward trend in the late 1980s. It is only in the United States that consumption of petroleum products had recovered to pre-1973 levels by 1990. This is illustrated in Figures 8.1 and 8.2 for the United States, Japan, Germany, the United Kingdom and France.

Natural gas consumption in all countries shows the same features – a constant path until 1968, then a dramatic increase to 1979. Since the second oil price shock, consumption of natural gas has tended to stay at 1979 levels. The United States consumes much more natural gas than the rest of the G9. The United Kingdom is the second largest consumer, considerably above the rest of the G9, and exhibits the most dramatic rising trend. However, it is still significantly behind the United States. Germany is the smallest consumer, with the path of consumption remaining unchanged between 1950 and 1990.

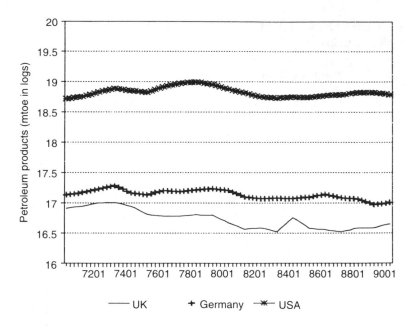

*Figure 8.1* Consumption of petroleum products (log of t.o.e.) for the United States, United Kingdom and Germany

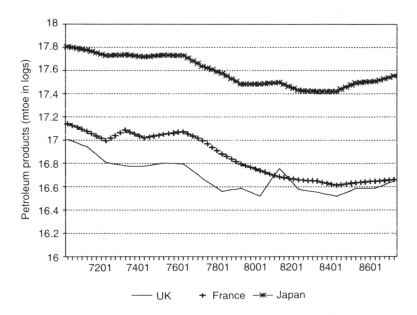

*Figure 8.2* Consumption of petroleum products (log of t.o.e.) for France, Japan and the United Kingdom

## 8.2.2  Price data

Data on both prices and taxes were obtained from the International Energy Agency (IEA 1991a) for the period 1978–90 (annual data). Oil and natural gas prices followed the same path over the whole period. Roughly speaking, they rose dramatically after the second oil price shock in 1979 until the mid to early 1980s, after which they decreased for about five years before a new increasing trend can be discerned. Coal prices remained constant between 1978 and 1991 and were generally lower than petroleum prices over the whole period. However, in France coal becomes the most expensive energy commodity after the two oil price shocks.

Oil had the highest tax, while taxes on coal and gas were at roughly the same lower level. In nearly all the countries, oil taxes rose steadily between 1978 and 1991. In Belgium, there was a short break in this increasing path between 1987 and 1989. In the United States, the rising trend started only in 1983. Prices before and after tax of oil for the United States and France are illustrated in Figures 8.3 and 8.4.

Data for the average (after-tax) price of fossil fuel were obtained by weighting by consumption the prices of oil, coal and gas.[4] This average price of fossil fuels relative to the price deflator of GDP exhibits the same features for the whole G9 – a dramatic increase from 1979 to the beginning of 1982,

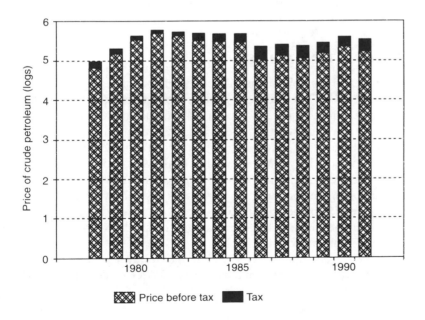

*Figure 8.3* Price and tax of petroleum products in the United States

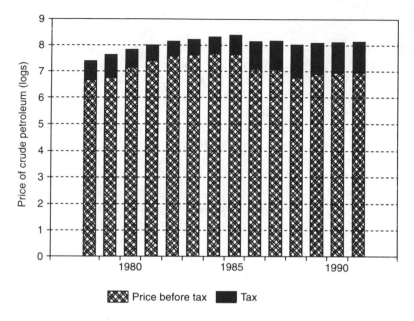

*Figure 8.4* Price and tax of petroleum products in France

then the relative price stays at this very high level until the end of 1985 when the relative price decreases steadily.

## 8.3  COINTEGRATION ANALYSIS

The seminal paper in the development of cointegration analysis was that of Engle and Granger (1987), who developed the concept of cointegration under the assumption that the cointegrating vector was unique and who proposed a range of tests for assessing whether a set of variables cointegrate, as well as discussing the estimation of a cointegrating vector of parameters. An early example of this methodology may be found in Hall (1986). Johansen (1988) proposed a more general framework for considering the possibility of multiple cointegrating vectors and this framework also allows questions of causality and general hypothesis tests to be carried out in a more satisfactory way. This is described in Hall (1989) and a more detailed textbook account may be found in Cuthbertson *et al.* (1992).

Johansen (1988) sets his analysis within the following very general framework. First, define a vector autoregressive (VAR) model of a set of variables *X* as

$$X_t = \pi_1 X_{t-1} + \ldots + \pi_k X_{t-k} + e_t \qquad t = 1, \ldots, T \tag{8.3}$$

where $X_t$ is a vector of $N$ variables of interest, $\pi_i$ are $N \times N$ coefficient matrices, $k$ is the maximum lag length and $e_t$ is a vector of error terms. This is simply an unrestricted dynamic system for the set of variables $X$. Much of the power of this approach can be attributed to the fact that a complete system wherein all the variables have equal status is being considered. There are no exogenous and endogenous variables and so assumptions about the exogeneity of some of the variables do not need to be incorporated into the model right from the beginning, as often happens with more traditional modelling methods. This system may be expressed in vector error correction form (VECM) as

$$\Delta X_t = \Gamma \Delta X_{t-1} + \Pi X_{t-k} \tag{8.4}$$

where

$$\Delta X = [\Delta X_t, \ldots, \Delta X_{t-k+1}]$$

$$\Gamma = [(I + \pi_1), (I + \pi_1 + \pi_2), \ldots, (I + \pi_1 + \ldots + \pi_k)]$$

$$\Pi = I - \pi_1 - \pi_2 - \ldots - \pi_k$$

and $I$ is the identity matrix. Non-stationarity of $X$ implies that $\pi$ will have deficient rank. If there is no cointegration within the system $\Pi$ will be a matrix with rank zero. In general the rank of this matrix will be equal to the number $r$ of distinct cointegrating vectors in the system. The heart of the Johansen procedure is to decompose $\Pi$ into two matrices $\alpha$ and $\beta$, both of which are $N \times r$, such that

$$\Pi = \alpha \beta' \tag{8.5}$$

The rows of $\beta$ may be defined as the $r$ distinct cointegrating vectors and the rows of $\alpha$ show how these cointegrating vectors are incorporated into each equation in the system. Johansen then gives a maximum likelihood estimation technique for both $\alpha$ and $\beta$, based upon canonical correlation, and he outlines a set of suitable tests which allow examination of hypotheses about the matrices and the number of cointegrating vectors which exist. The estimation is based on the solution to a generalized eigenvalue problem where the eigenvectors are shown to be the parameters of the cointegrating vector and the eigenvalues are the basis for the testing procedure. By testing $\beta$, restrictions such as parameter constraints on the long-run properties of the data or price homogeneity may be tested. By testing $\alpha$, the manner in which these long-run relationships affect the variables in the system may be tested.

In the empirical work presented below, the dependent variable is the relative share of fossil fuel consumption to GDP for each country, where fossil fuel consumption is the total of oil, natural gas and coal consumption for that country. The explanatory variables are the average price of fossil fuels relative to GNP (or GDP), where the former is the average of prices after tax of oil, gas and coal weighted by consumption. It is to be expected that total fossil fuel consumption is negatively associated with relative average price. A time trend is included as a proxy for technological progress, leading to a simple equation of proportional fossil fuel demand as a function of price and technological innovation.

### 8.3.1 Time-series properties of the data

For the nine countries, the analysis of the univariate time-series properties of GDP, fossil fuel consumption and relative price is the first step to a cointegrating regression. If successful this should lead to an error correction representation. Each variable was subjected to tests for the presence of a unit root, with the tests being applied to the variables in levels as well as in first and second differences. The augmented Dickey–Fuller (ADF) and the Phillips tests appeared to give results most consistent with each other and with intuition, and so results from these tests are reported.

At each stage the null hypothesis is the presence of a unit root in the variable (as differenced). A sequential testing procedure is undertaken until the null hypothesis is rejected. Thus, failure to reject the null hypothesis on the level of the variable means that the variable is at least integrated of order 1; failure at the next stage implies integration of at least order 2, and so on. A summary of the results is shown in Table 8.3.

For the nine countries results generally indicate fossil fuel consumption to be integrated of order 2 (I(2)), i.e. the second difference is stationary but the first difference is non-stationary. The log of GDP/GNP is generally either I(2) or on the border between I(1) and I(2). One apparent exception is the case of Belgian GDP, where the results indicate I(0) but a glance at the data shows the data to be clearly non-stationary. The relative price of fossil fuels is either I(2) or close to the frontier between I(1) and I(2). Hereafter, the simplifying assumption that these data series are I(2) is made. First and second differences of relative price for Germany and Italy are shown in Figures 8.5 and 8.6.

### 8.3.2 Cointegrating properties of the data

If in the long run two (or more) macroeconomic time series move together, even though they are trended, the difference between them will remain constant. This relationship may characterize a long-run equilibrium. The Johansen procedure, outlined above, provides a maximum likelihood way of estimating these relationships. A number of options are available within the Johansen procedure; in particular the length of the VAR must be chosen and the treatment of the constant within the model will affect the distribution of the test statistics. In the first instance a very general VAR specification was tested. Since the data are quarterly this involved four lags. Differences in the treatment of the constant may be summarized as follows:

1     without a constant;

Table 8.3 Summary of stationarity properties for each variable by country

| | Level | | First difference | | Second difference | | |
|---|---|---|---|---|---|---|---|
| | ADF | Phillips | ADF | Phillips | ADF | Phillips | |
| **Belgium (bg)** | | | | | | | |
| bgcl | −2.87 | −1.44 | −0.96 | −1.92 | −4.09 | −6.84 | I(2) |
| bgrpl | −4.01 | −3.60 | −1.93 | −2.66 | −4.55 | −6.72 | I(2) |
| bgyl | −1.21 | −0.54 | −1.67 | −2.26 | −3.69 | −8.60 | I(2) |
| **Canada (cn)** | | | | | | | |
| cncl | −3.03 | −1.03 | −2.56 | −1.99 | −1.73 | −6.82 | I(2/3) |
| cnyl | −0.14 | −0.04 | −2.18 | −5.70 | −3.92 | −16.2 | I(1/2) |
| cnrpl | −2.32 | −1.67 | −1.91 | −3.51 | −3.56 | −9.90 | I(1/2) |
| **France (fr)** | | | | | | | |
| frcl | −3.35 | −1.25 | −1.44 | −1.93 | −2.93 | −6.80 | I(2) |
| fryl | 1.41 | 1.27 | −2.63 | −7.80 | −3.77 | −20.2 | I(1/2) |
| frrpl | −0.48 | −0.12 | −1.68 | −6.44 | −4.12 | −22.3 | I(2) |
| **Germany (ge)** | | | | | | | |
| gecl | −2.80 | −0.98 | −2.19 | −2.36 | −2.16 | −6.80 | I(2/3) |
| geyl | −2.13 | 0.66 | −2.38 | −8.86 | −3.79 | −22.3 | I(1/2) |
| gerpl | −0.30 | 0.41 | −1.73 | −5.11 | −3.08 | −16.0 | I(1/2) |
| **Italy (it)** | | | | | | | |
| itcl | −0.96 | −0.94 | −1.78 | −2.70 | −4.02 | −6.84 | I(2) |
| ityl | −0.09 | −0.42 | −2.80 | −5.72 | −4.48 | −15.1 | I(1/2) |
| itrpl | −0.40 | −0.43 | −2.19 | −6.22 | −5.42 | −11.9 | I(1/2) |
| **Japan (jp)** | | | | | | | |
| jpcl | −0.21 | −0.18 | −1.94 | −2.58 | −3.68 | −6.81 | I(2) |
| jpyl | 2.23 | 1.17 | −2.52 | −7.87 | −4.34 | −21.2 | I(1/2) |
| jprpl | −0.62 | −0.47 | −2.50 | −6.03 | −4.61 | −17.6 | I(1/2) |
| **Netherlands (nl)** | | | | | | | |
| nlcl | −1.60 | −1.38 | −1.53 | −2.61 | −4.33 | −6.89 | I(2) |
| nlyl | 1.38 | 1.65 | −1.82 | −1.48 | −1.99 | −6.44 | I(2/3) |
| nlrpl | −0.67 | −1.15 | −0.85 | −0.96 | −2.30 | −3.54 | I(2/3) |
| **United Kingdom (uk)** | | | | | | | |
| ukcl | −4.12 | −1.67 | −2.19 | −2.89 | −4.11 | −6.80 | I(2) |
| ukyl | 2.16 | 1.74 | −1.29 | −8.13 | −3.14 | −23.4 | I(1/2) |
| ukrpl | −1.77 | −1.22 | −1.59 | −2.14 | −3.00 | −7.65 | I(2/3) |
| **United States (us)** | | | | | | | |
| uscl | −2.13 | −0.99 | −2.21 | −2.15 | −2.67 | −6.80 | I(2/3) |
| usyl | 0.13 | 0.44 | −2.69 | −5.13 | −4.00 | −12.9 | I(1/2) |
| usrpl | −0.53 | −0.38 | −2.20 | −4.69 | −3.80 | −15.5 | I(1/2) |

Notes: cl, log of consumption of fossil fuels; yl, log of GDP; rpl, log of price of fossil fuels relative to price deflator of GDP.
The critical values at the 5 per cent and 1 per cent levels are −2.8 and −3.4 respectively.
Statistics in italics exceed the 1 per cent levels.
The final column indicates the conclusion, e.g. 'I(1/2)' indicates that the statistics are not unanimous, with one indicating I(1) and the other I(2).

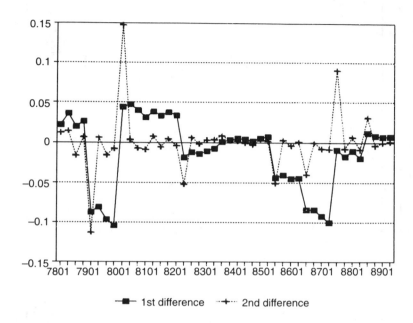

*Figure 8.5* First and second differences for relative price of fossil fuel for Germany

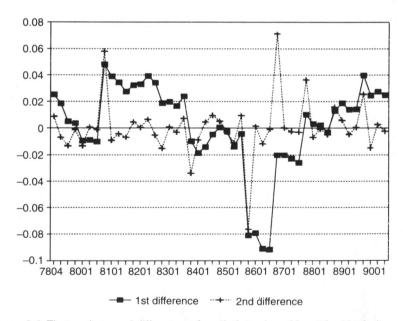

*Figure 8.6* First and second differences for relative price of fossil fuel for Italy

2   with a restricted constant – in that case, the ECM (8.4) contains a constant within the term in the long-run matrix only; in other words, constants are associating with the cointegrating vector;
3   with an unrestricted constant – if the ECM has some equations without cointegrating vector (simple difference equation), these equations will still contain constants.

The two last cases characterize, respectively, the presence of a random walk without drift and the presence of a deterministic trend in the variables.

For each country, the dependent variable is the ratio of fossil fuel consumption to GDP (in logs), where fossil fuel consumption is the total of oil, natural gas and coal consumption for that country. The principal explanatory variable in the cointegrating regressions is the average price of fossil fuels relative to the price deflator of GNP or GDP (again in logs), where the average (after-tax) price is that of oil, gas and coal weighted by consumption. A time trend was included in the VAR as a proxy for technological innovation. It was not possible to estimate its impact during the estimation process since the time trend is within the VAR. This was carried out separately from the procedure by regressing the eigenvector of interest on a time variable and estimating it by ordinary least squares. In all cases, the time trend presented the expected (negative) sign, representing the impact of technological innovation on energy consumption. In addition, it is to be expected that the fossil fuel ratio is negatively associated with relative price. The data are graphed for each G9 country in Figures 8.7–8.15.[5] It can be seen

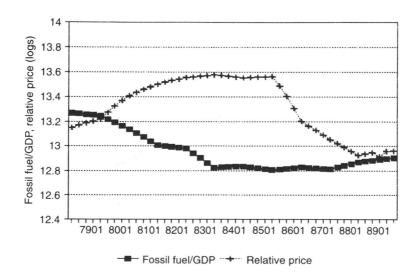

Figure 8.7 Belgium fossil fuel consumption/GDP and relative price of fossil fuel

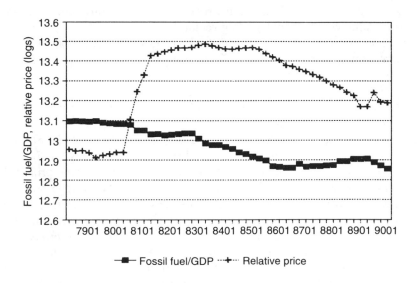

*Figure 8.8* Canada fossil fuel consumption/GDP and relative price of fossil fuel

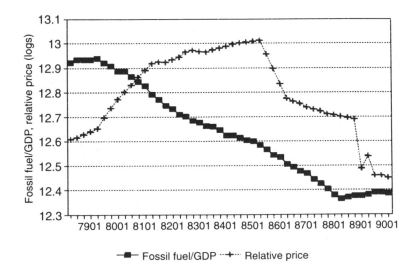

*Figure 8.9* France fossil fuel consumption/GDP and relative price of fossil fuel

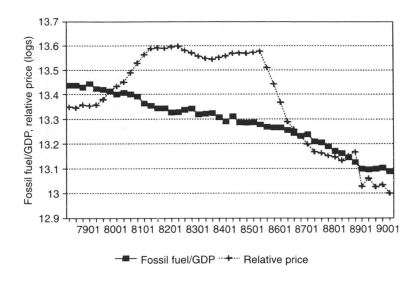

*Figure 8.10* Germany fossil fuel consumption/GDP and relative price of fossil fuel

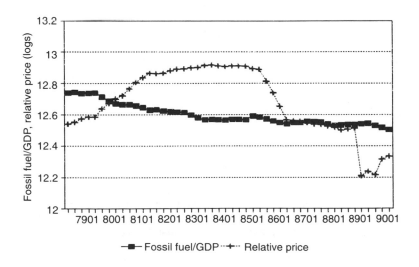

*Figure 8.11* Italy fossil fuel consumption/GDP and relative price of fossil fuel

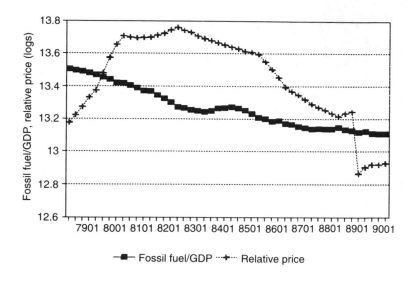

*Figure 8.12* Japan fossil fuel consumption/GDP and relative price of fossil fuel

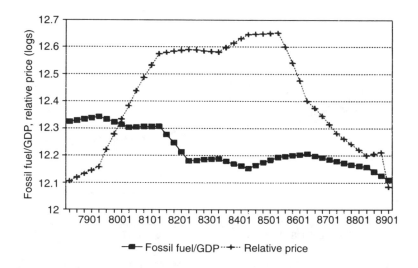

*Figure 8.13* Netherlands fossil fuel consumption/GDP and relative price of fossil fuel

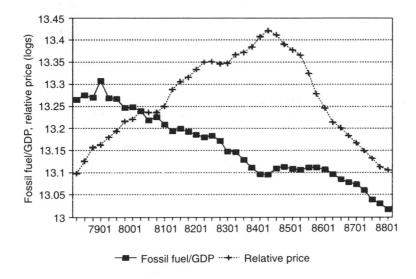

*Figure 8.14* United Kingdom fossil fuel consumption/GDP and relative price of fossil fuel

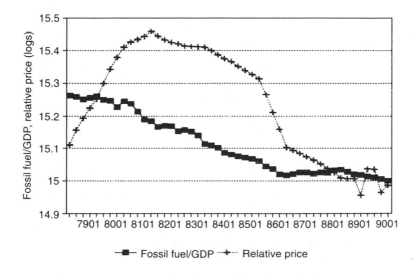

*Figure 8.15* United States fossil fuel consumption/GDP and relative price of fossil fuel

from Figures 8.7–8.15 that all countries tend to exhibit the same characteristic shape. The ratio of fossil fuel to GDP declined since 1978, but with a slowing of the decline, or even an increase, in the late 1980s. The relative price of fossil fuel shows a 'hump', rising sharply after 1979 and then falling back during the mid-1980s.

The results from the Johansen procedure are shown in Table 8.4. In the case of Germany (illustrated in Figure 8.10) there was only a very weak negative cointegrating relationship between the energy consumption ratio to GDP and relative prices. This near-absence of cointegration is due to the almost-linear decline in the consumption ratio throughout the period. The inclusion of more factors is necessary in order to derive long-term relationships which explain consumption, such as the use of non-fossil fuel sources for electricity generation in France. (Indeed, this is being investigated in ongoing research.)

For all G9 countries more than one specification gave rise to significant sets of cointegrating vectors. The vectors from the two best[6] specifications are shown in the table, and the two most significant vectors from each specification are shown, with the most significant presented first. The vector finally selected for use in the dynamic model (see below) is italicized. When both vectors from the same specification exhibited the same (desired) property of having the consumption ratio and the relative price negatively associated, the most significant vector was preferred. When the cointegrating vectors offered two contradictory relationships, i.e. negative and positive relationships between the consumption ratio and the relative price, both representations were retained and their significance was tested in the dynamic model.

The coefficients for relative prices and time trends from the cointegration analysis are shown in Table 8.5. The 'best' cointegrating relationships used to derive these involve lag lengths between four and eight and either restricted or unrestricted constants as described above. The United Kingdom, the Netherlands and Germany show the smallest elasticities of demand with respect to price, all under 10 per cent. Belgium, France and the United States are highest at around 15 per cent with the remainder falling in between. The time trend, or technological innovation factor, varies greatly between countries. France, Belgium and Japan show the highest effect with a time trend of $-4$ to $-5.7$ per cent per annum, which is in part due to large nuclear expansion in these three countries during the estimation period. In most other countries it is around $-2$ per cent per annum. It should be noted that, as this trend represents change in energy intensity, a value of $-2$ per cent implies that with GDP growth of 2 per cent or less, consumption would be stable or decreasing.

For Italy and Japan, the two significant cointegrating vectors presented two different possible relationships between consumption and relative price, either negative (as price rises, consumption decreases) or positive. The latter would mean that if demand is increasing then prices are rising. The impact of these two possible effects was then tested within the dynamic modelling (see below).

*Table 8.4* Cointegrating regressions for each country

| | Specification | First vector | Second vector | Specification | First vector | Second vector |
|---|---|---|---|---|---|---|
| **Belgium** | | | | | | |
| Lags | 4 | | | 6 | | |
| | Restricted | | | Unrestricted | | |
| Constant | | −215.1 | 514.7 | | | |
| bgrpl | | 2.76 | −14.35 | | 18.15 | 18.73 |
| bgc-y | | 17.27 | −37.38 | | 56.54 | 32.43 |
| **Canada** | | | | | | |
| Lags | 7 | | | 8 | | |
| | Restricted | | | Restricted | | |
| Constant | | 726.2 | 52.41 | | −0.51 | 883.0 |
| cnrpl | | −5.21 | −0.310 | | −6.21 | −7.15 |
| cnc-y | | −51.61 | −4.86 | | 4.71 | −62.32 |
| **France** | | | | | | |
| Lags | 5 | | | 6 | | |
| | Unrestricted | | | Unrestricted | | |
| Constant | | | | | | |
| frrpl | | 8.49 | 7.59 | | 8.11 | −9.92 |
| frc-y | | 57.84 | −37.87 | | −50.14 | −63.61 |
| **Germany** | | | | | | |
| Lags | 4 | | | 8 | | |
| | Unrestricted | | | Unrestricted | | |
| Constant | | | | | | |
| gerpl | | 3.97 | 8.33 | | 1.77 | 14.48 |
| gec-y | | 62.66 | −55.88 | | 132.8 | −59.88 |
| **Italy** | | | | | | |
| Lags | 4 | | | 4 | | |
| | Unrestricted | | | Restricted | | |
| Constant | | | | | −1089 | 1157 |
| itrpl | | 16.30 | 5.19 | | 8.53 | −14.73 |
| itc-y | | 125.80 | −9.81 | | 85.01 | −89.56 |

| | | | | |
|---|---|---|---|---|
| *Japan* | | | | |
| Lags | 4 | | 4 | |
| | Unrestricted | | Restricted | |
| Constant | | | 781.8 | −349.2 |
| jprpl | *9.00* | 4.30 | −5.64 | 8.23 |
| jpc-y | *67.63* | −14.74 | −58.15 | 25.83 |
| *Netherlands* | | | | |
| Lags | 8 | | | |
| | Restricted | | | |
| Constant | *−759.5* | −598.5 | −362.9 | |
| nlrpl | *5.14* | 6.24 | −0.254 | |
| nlc-y | *60.48* | 47.15 | 29.76 | |
| *United Kingdom* | | | | |
| Lags | 8 | | | |
| | Restricted | | | |
| Constant | *4189* | 3343 | | |
| ukrpl | *−14.14* | −13.92 | | |
| ukc-y | *−313.4* | −25.00 | | |
| *United States* | | | | |
| Lags | 4 | | | |
| | Restricted | | Unrestricted | |
| Constant | *−766.1* | | | |
| usrpl | *7.95* | | 46.83 | −6.45 |
| usc-y | *50.04* | | 12.08 | 69.22 |

*Notes*: c-y, log of fossil fuel consumption relative to GDP; rpl, log of price of fossil fuel relative to price deflator of GDP.
Only the most significant vectors for a given specification are presented.
The vector in italics is the one which was selected.
A dummy variable is used in the VAR for France, taking the value 1 from 8903 to 9002, and zero otherwise.

*Table 8.5* Own-price elasticities of demand for fossil fuel share of GDP and time
trends

| Country | Relative price coefficient | Time trend (% p.a.) |
|---|---|---|
| Belgium | −0.155 | −4.80 |
| Canada | −0.101 | −2.17 |
| France | −0.147 | −5.67 |
| Germany | −0.063 | −3.12 |
| Italy | −0.130 | −2.19 |
| Japan | −0.133 | −4.06 |
| Netherlands | −0.085 | −1.61 |
| United Kingdom | −0.045 | −2.58 |
| United States | −0.159 | −3.09 |

## 8.4 DYNAMIC MODELLING

The error correction mechanism (ECM hereafter) captures the idea that agents
alter their behaviour according to 'signals' that they are out of equilibrium.
Expressed more formally, an ECM representation allows the long-run
components of the variables to obey equilibrium constraints, while short-run
components have a flexible dynamic specification. Therefore, a typical ECM
relates the change in the dependent variable to past equilibrium errors as well
as to past changes in both the dependent and explanatory variables. Hence, the
change in energy demand would be related to the change in relative prices and
to GDP, as well as to their past changes. It would also take account of the past
deviations from the equilibrium.

The relationship between error correction models and cointegrating
variables is embodied in the Granger representation theorem. Amongst other
things, this states that if an $N \times 1$ vector $x_t$ is cointegrated of order $(1,1)$ with
cointegrating rank $r$, then the following hold.

1  There exists a vector autoregressive moving average (ARMA) repre-
    sentation:

$$A(L)x_t = d(L)\varepsilon_t$$

    where $A(1)$ has rank $r$ and $A(0) = I_n$, $I_n$ being the $N \times N$ identity matrix.
    $d(L)$ is a scalar lag polynomial with $d(1)$ finite, and when $d(L) = 1$ this
    is a VAR.
2  There exists an error correction representation with $z_t = \alpha'x_t$, an $r \times 1$
    vector of stationary random variables:

$$A^*(L)(1 - L)x_t = -\gamma Z_t - 1 + d(L)\varepsilon_t$$

    with $A^*(0) = I_n$.
3  The vector $z_t$ is given by

$$z_t = K(L)\varepsilon_t$$

$$(1 - L)z_t = - a^T \gamma Z_t - 1 + J(L)\varepsilon_t$$

where $K(L)$ is an $N \times r$ matrix of lagged polynomials given by $\gamma^T C^*(L)$,[7] with all elements of $K(1)$. $z_t$ is interpreted as the disequilibrium or error correction term. It represents short-run deviations from the long-run equilibrium.

4    If a finite VAR representation is possible, it will have the form given by (8.3) and (8.4) above, with $d(L) = 1$ and both $A(L)$ and $A^*(L)$ being matrices of finite polynomials. This implies that the error correction model (8.4) will have only stationary variables on both sides of the equation, and so the usual stationary regression theory applies. This renders the model immune from the spurious regression problem, i.e. it provides consistent estimation and testing of the dynamic model, including the cointegrated variables.

In this case, the cointegrating vectors are the estimate of the innovation process $\varepsilon_t$ as defined by

$$a(c_t - y_t) + b(\text{rp}_t) + cT = \varepsilon_t$$

where $c$, $y$ and rp are the logs of, respectively, fossil fuel consumption, GDP and the price of energy relative to the price deflator of GDP and $T$ is the time trend, while $a$ and $b$ are the coefficients of the Johansen cointegrating vector.
Hence the ECM can be written as[8]

$$\Delta c_t = k + a z_{t-1}^1 + b z_{t-1}^2 + \sum_{i=1}^{4} \phi_i \Delta c_{t-i} + \sum_{i=1}^{4} \psi_i \Delta \text{rp}_{t-i} + \sum_{i=1}^{4} \gamma_i \Delta y_{t-i} \qquad (8.6)$$

where $k$ is a constant and the $z_{t-1}^i$ ($i = 1, 2$) are the lagged estimate of the innovation process $\varepsilon_t$.[9] Past forecasting errors are thereby taken into account in forecasting the next change in fossil fuel consumption. This general unrestricted model was estimated for the G9. It was simplified to eliminate the irrelevant parameters and redundant explanatory variables and transformed so that the disturbance term is an innovation process.

Estimates of the ECM for each country are reported in the Appendix together with a set of diagnostic statistics for each equation. The simplified and parsimonious representations of GDP for the G9 present many common features. The first is that they explain about 70–80 per cent of the quarter-by-quarter variance changes in fossil fuel demand. The standard errors of the regression cluster around 0.5 per cent, with the United States the lowest at 0.36 per cent and the Netherlands the highest at 0.68 per cent, indicating confidence ranges of about 1 per cent about the regression line.

*Table 8.6* Significance of the residuals on two competing cointegrating vectors

|  | t ratio for residual with negative relationship | t ratio for residual with positive relationship |
|---|---|---|
| Germany | −2.72 | −3.91 |
| Italy | −4.13 | 1.65 |
| Japan | −3.52 | 0.76 |

Previous changes in fossil fuel consumption have a major impact on the change in current consumption. The coefficient on the previous quarter's change ranges from 0.57 for the Netherlands to 0.88 for Italy, and is always highly significant. In all cases the coefficient on the error correction term is significant. However, for Belgium, Canada and the United Kingdom it is only marginally so. Price movements and recent evolution of GDP seem to play an important role in the evolution of demand for fossil fuels in European countries of the G9, but apparently not so much in the case of Canada, Japan and the United States. The dynamics of the models do not generally go much beyond one lag, except in the case of the Netherlands.

In the cases of Canada, Germany, Italy and Japan, the best specifications gave rise to two possible cointegrating vectors. The more significant vector according to the maximum likelihood criterion of the two was selected, and this exhibited the expected negative relationship between the consumption ratio and relative prices. For the last three countries, the second vector exhibited a positive relationship between relative price and the consumption ratio, which would sustain the hypothesis that, as demand increases, prices rise; in other words there exists a demand effect on prices. When the estimated residuals of these relationships were also estimated and residuals from both vectors were included in a dynamic model, they turned out to be non-significant for Italy and Japan but significant for Germany. Thus, for all countries except Germany, the effect of prices on consumption comes only through the negatively signed energy demand relationship, as one would expect. Germany remains problematic because of the very weak negative cointegrating relationship. The coefficients in the dynamic models after eliminating non-significant variables are shown in Table 8.6.

## 8.5 LONG-RUN ANALYSIS

The equilibrium relationships can be derived from the error correction relationships estimated in the previous section by making the assumption that, in the steady state, variables in levels are constant. The long-run equations for each country have a Cobb–Douglas form, their elasticities with respect to relative price and time (see Table 8.5 for the coefficients) varying between countries. The elasticity with respect to time captures the trend in fossil fuel consumption which is not associated with price movements. As noted in Section 8.2, it would be wrong to assume that it necessarily relates to autonomous technological progress because of the presence of a non-price factor such as policy changes which may be significant. However, for illustrative purposes we make the assumption that there are no changes in non-price factors. Formally we obtain

$$C_t = AT^a RP^b Y$$

where $C$ is total fossil fuel consumption, $T$ is time and RP is the relative price of energy. $A$ is a constant and $a$ and $b$ are parameters.

For all countries, elasticities ($a$ and $b$) are negative, as expected. Hence, energy demand is inversely related to price and time. The 'time' coefficients vary between −5.7 per cent (France) and −1.6 per cent (Netherlands). The relative price elasticities are between 5 per cent (United Kingdom) and 16 per cent (United States and Belgium), with the average being around 13 per cent. However, the impact of price and time vary greatly across countries. Therefore, it appears that the cost of reducing fossil fuel consumption, even given a similar level of GDP growth, is very different among the G9 countries.

Next, some illustrative calculations are carried out to estimate the degree of annual price change that would be necessary in order to stabilize fossil fuel consumption given various GDP growth rates, based on the assumption that both time and price elasticities remain constant. This is shown in Table 8.7, and the calculations involved are summarized in Table 8.8. The results are highly sensitive to the GDP growth rate assumed. For growth of less than 2 per cent in GDP in the G9 as a whole, fossil fuel consumption would *decrease*

*Table 8.7* Growth rate of the relative price of fossil fuels necessary to maintain fossil fuel consumption constant, given assumptions about real GDP growth

| Country | GDP growth rate (% p.a.) | | | |
|---|---|---|---|---|
| | 2.0 | 2.5 | 3.0 | 3.5 |
| Belgium | – | – | – | – |
| Canada | – | 3.3 | 8.6 | 14.1 |
| France | – | – | – | – |
| Germany | – | – | – | 6.2 |
| Italy | – | 2.4 | 6.5 | 10.6 |
| Japan | – | – | – | – |
| Netherlands | −4.7 | 11.1 | 17.8 | 24.9 |
| United Kingdom | – | – | 9.8 | 22.7 |
| United States | – | – | – | 2.6 |

*Note*: –, consumption is stable or decreasing at constant prices.

*Table 8.8* Calculations required to estimate price changes required to stabilize fossil fuel consumption

*How price variations are obtained in Table 8.7*

The equilibrium relationship derived from the dynamic equation is the following:

$$\ln(c_t) = a + b \ln(\text{rp}_t) + \ln(y_t) + dt$$

The variations per annum of both fossil fuel consumption and relative price are derived from this equation, leading to

$$\Delta \ln(c_t) = b \Delta \ln(\text{rp}_t) + \Delta \ln(y_t) + d$$

If the consumption is to remain constant from one year to the other, then $\Delta \ln(c_t) = 0$. Therefore the variations in price can be set equal to

$$\Delta \ln(\text{rp}_t) = -\frac{1}{b} \Delta \ln(y_t) - \frac{d}{b}$$

For example consider the UK with GDP growth of 3 per cent per annum. The coefficient $b$ (that with respect to relative price) is 0.045 and $d$ (time coefficient) is $-0.0258$. This gives

$$\Delta \ln(\text{rp}_t) = (1/0.045)(0.03) - 0.0258/0.045$$

$$\Delta \ln(\text{rp}_t) = 9.8\%$$

if fuel prices remained unchanged. Growth of 2 per cent leads to a tax being required only in the Netherlands.

In the event that trends continue Belgium, France and Japan show no increase in consumption at growth rates up to 3.5 per cent per annum. As discussed previously, this is thought to be due to a combination of increasing nuclear power and structural and technological change. With GDP growth at 3 per cent or more, prices in Germany, the Netherlands, Canada, the United Kingdom and Italy would also have to increase dramatically every year in order to maintain constant consumption. In several cases the required prices are far too high to be implemented, indicating the necessity for supply-side policies to complement price rises.

## 8.6 ENDOGENOUS TECHNOLOGICAL CHANGE

In this section some preliminary results for the United Kingdom which outline and illustrate the power of the endogenous technological progress model given in (8.1) and (8.2) will be presented. Taking the ECM model derived for the United Kingdom (given in Appendix 8A), the general form is

$$\Delta E = \sum_{j=1}^{p} \alpha_i \Delta X_{i,t-j} + \beta(E_{t-1} - \gamma X_{t-1} + T_t) + \upsilon_t \tag{8.7}$$

If $T_t$ was simply a deterministic trend this would be a conventional model. Generating the trend as follows the model is much richer:

$$T_t = T_{t-1} + g_{t-1} + \eta_1 \text{rp}_t + \eta_2 \Delta m/y_t + e_{t1} \tag{8.8}$$

$$g_t = g_{t-1} + e_{t2}$$

where rp, as before, is relative energy prices and $m/y$ is the share of manufacturing output in total GDP. It is to be expected that an increase in energy prices increases the rate of growth of technological innovation and that as manufacturing in the United Kingdom declines the aggregate level of energy use also declines. The estimation of this model can be carried out using the Kalman filter where (8.7) is the measurement equation and (8.8) is the state equation. The formal estimation strategy is given below.

A standard state-space formulation is presented, with the appropriate Kalman filter equations for the univariate case, following Harvey (1987). Let

$$Y_t = \delta' z_t + \varepsilon_t \tag{8.9}$$

be the measurement equation where $Y_t$ is a measured variable, $z_t$ is the state vector of unobserved variables, $\delta$ is a vector of parameters and $\varepsilon_t \sim \text{NID}(0, \Gamma_t)$. The state equation is then given as

$$z_t = \Psi z_{t-1} + \Omega W_t + \psi \tag{8.10}$$

where $\Psi$ and $\Omega$ are parameters, $W$ is extra observed variables (rp and $m/y$) and $\psi \sim \text{NID}(0, Q_t)$; $Q_t$ is sometimes referred to as the hyperparameters.

The appropriate Kalman filter prediction equations are then given by defining $z_t^*$ as the best estimate of $z_t$ based on information up to $t$, and $P_t$ as the covariance matrix of the estimate $z_t^*$, and stating

$$z_{t|t-1}^* = \Psi z_{t-1}^* + \zeta W_t \tag{8.11}$$

and

$$P_{t|t-1} = \Psi P_{t-1} \Psi' + Q_t \tag{8.12}$$

Once the current observation on $y_t$ becomes available, these estimates can be updated using the following equations:

$$z_t^* = z_{t|t-1}^* + \frac{P_{t|t-1} \delta (Y_t - \delta' z_{t|t-1}^*)}{\delta' P_{t|t-1} \delta + \Gamma_t} \tag{8.13}$$

and

$$P_t = P_{t|t-1} - \frac{P_{t|t-1} \delta \delta' P_{t|t-1}}{\delta' P_{t|t-1} \delta + \Gamma_t} \tag{8.14}$$

Jointly, equations (8.9)–(8.14) represent the Kalman filter equations. If the one-step-ahead prediction errors are then defined as

$$v_t = Y_t - \delta' z^*_{t|t-1} \tag{8.15}$$

then the concentrated log-likelihood function can be shown to be proportional to

$$\log l = \sum_{t=k}^{T} \log f_t + N \log \left( \sum_{t=k}^{T} \frac{v_t^2}{N f_t} \right) \tag{8.16}$$

where $f_t = \alpha' P_{t|t-1} \alpha + \Gamma_t$, $N = T - k$ and $k$ is the number of periods needed to derive estimates of the state vector; i.e. the likelihood function can be expressed as a function of the one-step-ahead prediction errors, suitably weighted.

Applying this estimation technique to the model outlined above for the United Kingdom yields the following results:

Measurement equation:

$$\Delta c_t = 2.2828 - 0.1714(c/y)_{t-1} - 0.0077 \mathrm{rp}_{t-1} + 0.8443 \Delta c_{t-1}$$
$$- 0.2636 \Delta c_{t-4} - 0.1800 \Delta y_{t-1} - 0.1500 \Delta \mathrm{rp}_t + T$$

Transition equations:

$$T = 1.0022 T_{t-1} + 1.0055 g_{t-1} - 0.0573 \Delta \mathrm{rp}_t + 0.2366 m/y_t$$
$$g_t = 0.9992 g_{t-1}$$

where $m/y$ is the share of manufacturing output in total GDP.

*Statistical diagnosis*

| | |
|---|---|
| Mean of residuals | −0.0021653 |
| Sum of residuals | −0.0584644 |
| Standard deviation | 0.0060145 |
| Coefficient of skewness | −0.5180972 |
| Coefficient of kurtosis | 0.9626856 |
| Box–Jenkins normality test | 2.2505203 |

The state-space representation does not differ very much from the ECM representation. One remarkable change is the greater weight attached to the share of consumption relative to GDP. Apart from this variable, the other coefficients appear largely the same. However, the share of manufacturing output relative to GDP seems to play a non-negligible role in explaining the declining trend in energy consumption. This representation seems reasonable

*Table 8.9* Autocorrelation function, Box–Pierce statistic and Ljung–Box statistic

| Lag | 1 | 2 | 3 | 4 | 5 | 6 | 7 | 8 |
|---|---|---|---|---|---|---|---|---|
| Coefficient | −0.17 | −0.01 | 0.15 | −0.46 | 0.23 | −0.06 | −0.18 | −0.071 |
| Box–Pierce statistic | 0.80 | 0.80 | 1.44 | 7.11 | 8.49 | 8.58 | 9.47 | 9.60 |
| Ljung–Box statistic | 0.89 | 0.90 | 1.66 | 8.81 | 10.64 | 10.76 | 12.04 | 12.25 |

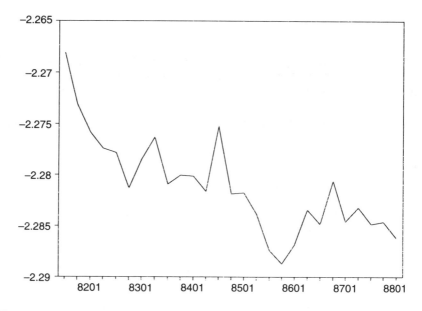

*Figure 8.16* Endogenous technical progress for the UK

with respect to statistical criteria (see Statistical diagnosis). There are signs of non-normality, which was also the case with the ECM representation, although it was much stronger. The Box–Pierce statistic and the Ljung–Box statistic (Table 8.9) suggest some sign of fourth-order autocorrelation of the residuals, which may be due to the use of interpolated data.

Overall, the model seems promising. The path of the endogenous technological progress effect, which is graphed in Figure 8.16, shows a rapid increase in energy efficiency in the early 1980s as manufacturing declined as a share of total GDP and as energy prices were particularly high. As these two effects decline in the late 1980s the rate of increase in trend efficiency falls off dramatically. Clearly, projecting the future growth rate from the later levels will give a very different picture from using either the earlier or average growth rates.

## 8.7  CONCLUSIONS

This chapter has attempted to quantify the long-run relationships between economic activity, the price of fossil fuels and fossil fuel consumption for nine OECD countries. It has highlighted the differences in these influences across countries. Furthermore, it has sought to provide illustrations of how energy prices would have to move in order to stabilize fossil fuel consumption for each country in the G9 according to different scenarios of economic growth.

Price elasticities are generally small and differ greatly between countries. The largest are those of Belgium and the United States (0.16), the lowest that of the United Kingdom (0.05). Germany and the Netherlands also exhibit low values of 0.06 and 0.09 respectively, while the remaining countries range from 0.10–0.15. Elasticities with respect to time, a proxy for technological factor, are rather larger than is often assumed. France and Belgium show the highest at about 5 per cent per annum, and the Netherlands the lowest at 1.6 per cent.

The following section derived the dynamic models for fossil fuel consumption for each country. The dynamics were found to be relatively short in most cases, with only one lag generally significant (although fourth lag terms were highly significant for the Netherlands). Section 8.5 presented some illustrative calculations based upon the results to answer the question: How would fossil fuel price have to vary in order to stabilize fossil fuel consumption for a given rate of growth per annum? The answer varied according to the particular features of each country. The country with the largest declining trends, namely France, Belgium and Japan, would 'suffer' the least, i.e. would have the smallest price increases. On the other hand the Netherlands and the United Kingdom, as a result of low price elasticity, would see fuel prices increase dramatically. Nevertheless, the use of own-price elasticities much smaller than most of those used in other studies should lead one to consider these results cautiously. However, the results obtained on the importance of autonomous technical progress seem to be confirmed by most existing studies. The final section showed how technical progress factors could be treated as endogenous, and gave illustrative results for the United Kingdom.

### APPENDIX 8A:  ERROR-CORRECTION REPRESENTATIONS

(Standard errors for each coefficient are in parentheses.)

### Belgium

$$\Delta c_t = 0.00196 - 0.0566\Delta rp_t - 0.00158 res_{t-1} + 0.644\Delta c_{t-1}$$
$$\quad (0.0011) \quad (0.026) \qquad (0.00083) \qquad (0.073)$$
$$\quad - 0.585\Delta y_t$$
$$\quad (0.14)$$

$R^2 = 0.86$, DW = 1.81, SER = 0.0051, RESET(4, 33) = 0.90, SK = 0.90
EK = 4.92, BJ(2) = 12.13, LM4(4,29) = 0.62

## Canada

$$\Delta c_t = 0.000108 - 0.0450\Delta rp_t + 0.000991 res_{t-1} + 0.761\Delta c_{t-1}$$
$$\quad\ (0.00072) \quad (0.017) \qquad\ (0.00053) \qquad\quad (0.081)$$

$R^2 = 0.77$, DW = 1.78, SER = 0.0047, RESET(4,37) = 0.53, SK = −0.17
EK = 5.14, BJ(2) = 8.77, LM4(4,37) = 0.53

## France

$$\Delta c_t = -0.0021925 - 0.00061 res_{t-1} + 0.803895 - c_{t-1}$$
$$\qquad\ (0.000769) \quad (0.00051) \qquad (0.065)$$
$$\quad -0.01863\Delta rp_t - 0.0212\Delta rp_{t-4} + 0.00234\Delta dum$$
$$\qquad (0.0146) \qquad (0.015) \qquad\ (0.002)$$

$R^2 = 0.87$, DW = 1.59, SER = 0.004, RESET(4,33) = 0.810, SK = −1.40
EK = 7.63, BJ(2) = 52.56, LM4(4,29) = 1.441

## Germany

$$\Delta c_t = 0.000025 + 0.000883\Delta res_{t-1} + 0.856 c_{t-1} - 0.0535\Delta rp_{t-2}$$
$$\quad\ (0.00065) \quad (0.00025) \qquad\quad (0.0836) \quad (0.0152)$$
$$\quad -0.126\Delta y_{t-1}$$
$$\quad\ (0.0510)$$

$R^2 = 0.75$, DW = 1.79, SER = 0.0034, RESET(4,36) = 0.030, SK = −1.01
EK = 4.84, BJ(2) = 13.98, LM4(4,32) = 0.75

## Italy

$$\Delta c_t = -0.000053 - 0.00199 res_{t-1} + 0.878\Delta c_{t-1} - 0.0310\Delta rp_t$$
$$\qquad\ (0.0010) \quad\ (0.00050) \qquad (0.106) \qquad (0.0137)$$
$$\quad +0.0282\Delta rp_{t-2} + 0.163\Delta y_t - 0.187\Delta y_{t-1}$$
$$\qquad (0.0131) \qquad\ (0.1042) \quad (0.1054)$$

$R^2 = 0.69$, DW = 2.07, SER = 0.0046, RESET(4,34) = 0.606, SK = 0.82
EK = 4.10, BJ(2) = 7.29, LM4(4,30) = 0.979

## Japan

$$\Delta c_t = -0.00243 + 0.309\Delta y_t - 0.0024 res_{t-1} + 0.737\Delta c_{t-1}$$
$$\qquad\ (0.00156) \ (0.131) \qquad (0.00064) \quad\ (0.087)$$

$R^2 = 0.71$, DW = 2.19, SER = 0.0055, RESET(4,37) = 0.56, SK =0.17
EK = 3.82, BJ(2) = 1.48, LM4(4,33) = 1.91

## Netherlands

$$\Delta c_t = -\ 0.00767 - 0.00246\text{res}_{t-1} + 0.574\Delta c_{t-1}$$
$$\quad (0.0028) \quad (0.0010) \quad\quad\quad (0.127)$$
$$\quad -\ 0.560\Delta c_{t-4} - 0.0636\Delta\text{rp}_{t-1} - 0.910\Delta t_{t-1} + 2.981\Delta y_{t-4}$$
$$\quad\ (0.152) \quad\quad\ (0.0350) \quad\quad\ (0.553) \quad\quad (0.655)$$

$R^2 = 0.78$, DW = 1.89, SER = 0.0068, RESET(4,29) = 3.96, SK =−0.11
EK = 2.75, BJ(2) = 0.18, LM4(4,25) = 7.41

## United Kingdom

$$\Delta c_t = -\ 0.000426 + 0.000493\text{res}_{t-1} + 0.718\Delta c_{t-1} + 0.318\Delta c_{t-3}$$
$$\quad (0.00110) \quad (0.00023) \quad\quad\ (0.126) \quad\quad (0.148)$$
$$\quad -\ 0.526\Delta c_{t-4} - 0.184\Delta\text{rp}_t - 0.277\Delta y_{t-1} + 0.156\Delta y_{t-4}$$
$$\quad\ (0.156) \quad\quad\ (0.050) \quad\quad (0.074) \quad\quad (0.072)$$

$R^2 = 0.81$, DW = 1.89, SER = 0.0046, RESET(4,24) = 0.66, SK =0.15
EK = 2.99, BJ(2) = 1.58, LM4(4,27) = 2.048

## United States

$$\Delta c_t = 0.00109 - 0.00178\text{res}_{t-1} + 0.816\Delta c_{t-1} - 0.152\Delta y_{t-3}$$
$$\quad (0.00068) \quad (0.00055) \quad\quad (0.084) \quad\quad (0.066)$$

$R^2 = 0.79$, DW = 1.99, SER = 0.0036, RESET(4,37) = 0.067, SK =0.80
EK = 4.91, BJ(2) = 11.62, LM4(4,33) = 0.053

## NOTES

The authors would like gratefully to acknowledge the support of the ESRC (Grant Y320 25 3010).

1 Boero *et al.* (1991) provide a review of the models being used to estimate emissions of greenhouse gases and the consequences of measures to control them. This section is based on their review.
2 Consumption of coal and petroleum products is given in metric tonnes, and natural gas is given in terajoules. The data on crude petroleum, hard coal and lignite were converted to terajoules according to standard conversion factors. The four commodities were then converted into tonnes of oil equivalent (t.o.e.), and the data for consumption of lignite/brown coal and hard coal were added together to produce figures for coal consumption.
3 G7 plus the Netherlands and Belgium.

4    The figure used for the price of oil is the average price weighted by consumption of gasoline, diesel, heavy fuel oil and light fuel oil (domestic currency/t.o.e.). The figure used for the price of coal is that for steam coal. The figure for the price of gas is the weighted average of industry and household prices. All prices were converted to domestic currency per tonne of oil equivalent (*source*: International Energy Agency/OECD).

5    The scales on the graphs correspond to logs of the ratio of fossil fuel consumption to GDP, and hence have no intuitive meaning. A constant has been added to the data for relative price in order to represent them on the same axes.

6    'Best' in the sense of providing the most stationary set of residuals after regressing the cointegrating vector on the time trend.

7    $C(L)$ is defined according to the Wold representation, i.e. if each component of the vector $x_t$ is integrated of order 1, then there always exists a multivariate Wold representation:

$$(1 - L)x_t = C(L)\varepsilon_t$$

where

$$C(L) = In - C_iL_i$$

with each $C_i$ being $N \times N$ multivariate white noise.

8    Up to four lags for both the dependent and the explanatory variables were included because the data are quarterly.

9    There can be up to two cointegrating vectors, which correspond to two different relationships: either consumption is explained by the relative price (negative relationship) or the latter is explained by the level of demand (positive relationship). Those two potential causalities are represented by, respectively, $z^1$ and $z^2$. Since consumption is being estimated, $z^1$ would be expected to be significant.

# Chapter 9

# UK energy price elasticities and their implications for long-term $CO_2$ abatement

*Terry Barker*

## ABSTRACT

A set of aggregate energy demand equations is estimated for the United Kingdom and 'consensus' price elasticities are imposed in the estimation. The relationship between the imposed lags in response and the magnitude of the price elasticities is explored and it is shown that the data do not reject quite substantial long-term responses to price changes for some energy users. The implications of different price elasticities for the analysis of abatement policies is treated in the context of a projection of the effects of the European Union's carbon/energy tax on UK energy demand and $CO_2$ emissions to the year 2005. A fall of 12 per cent is projected in emissions below the level in the business-as-usual projection in 2005, even with zero aggregate energy price elasticities for all users as a result of fuel substitution and early retirement of coal-burning plants in the electricity industry. If high aggregate price elasticities are assumed, the reduction below base is 18 per cent in 2005.

## INTRODUCTION

The objective of this chapter is to show how varying estimates of price elasticities of energy demand (crucial parameters in some price-based models projecting the effects of pollution abatement policy) can be imposed on the aggregate energy equations, what this implies for the lags in the response and how the different estimates affect the results of the model in analysing the effects of the European Union's proposed carbon/energy tax. This work is part of a broader research programme to provide a comprehensive treatment of the responses of the UK economy to fiscal incentives, such as a carbon/energy tax, designed to reduce $CO_2$ emissions over the long term. The comprehensive treatment is achieved through the use of a large-scale model of the economy, the Cambridge Multisectoral Dynamic Model (MDM), which distinguishes output and expenditures in great detail.

The next section of the chapter describes the development of the MDM into an energy–environment–economy (E3) model. This includes an overview of the treatment of secondary energy demand as well as that of energy demand by the energy industries themselves, divided into demand by the electricity supply industry (ESI) for primary fuels and demand by the primary energy industries (coal, gas and oil) for secondary fuels. All these demands may involve the burning of fossil fuels and therefore the emission of $CO_2$ and other pollutants such as $SO_2$ and $NO_x$ into the atmosphere.

One crucial set of equations determining the responses of the model is that concerning aggregate energy demand and this chapter primarily focuses on these equations. Section 9.2 of the chapter takes the UK Department of Energy's (DEn) 1989 specification of these equations (DEn 1989a) and re-estimates it on new data and a group of sectors which fits into the rest of the larger model; the model is then extended to use cointegration procedures. However, in studies of $CO_2$ abatement it is important to allow for substitution between fuels because they can have very different carbon contents, and Section 9.3 reports briefly on the allocation of secondary energy demand between the different energy carriers, coal, oil products, gas and electricity. Finally, Section 9.4 describes some sensitivity tests on the values of long-term price elasticities of secondary energy demand which have been imposed in the model. The tests take five sets of equations each with a different assumption about the size of the price elasticities; a new version of the model is created for each set of equations and is used to project the UK economy over the period 1990–2005 with and without the European Union's carbon/energy tax. The effects of the different sets of elasticities and of the tax can then be measured in terms of changes in $CO_2$ emissions and aggregate energy demand.

## 9.1 AN E3 MODEL FOR THE UK

### 9.1.1 Introduction

The Cambridge Multisectoral Dynamic Model (MDM) (Barker and Peterson 1987), a large-scale model of the UK economy, has been extended to include energy–environment–economy interactions to become an E3 model. The model already contained an energy sub-model (Peterson 1987); this has been replaced by a new version based closely on the DEn specification (DEn, 1989a). The energy sub-model allows a detailed analysis of the demand for energy and the substitution between fuels. The projection of fuel use, distinguished by user and type of fuel, is then available to calculate emissions of $CO_2$, allowing for different qualities of fuels and fuel-burning technologies (e.g. carbon and heat content of fuels; conversion efficiencies of technologies). Previous versions of the Cambridge model have been used to analyse earlier proposals for the imposition of a carbon/energy tax (Barker and Lewney 1991), but the reactions of the energy sector had to be imposed on the model using elasticities derived from work by the UK Department of Energy reported in the Sizewell B Public Enquiry which is now rather dated (see DEn 1987). The new sub-model follows the general approach of the DEn modelling but uses more recent data and adapts the approach to the requirements of a disaggregated industrial model.

### 9.1.2  Extending the Cambridge model

As noted above, the model has been extended by the incorporation of an energy sub-model and a set of equations for environmental emissions. The solution for the economic variables yields changes in economic activity and general price levels to the energy sub-model. The sub-model then calculates energy demand by sector and the use of primary fuels in electricity generation. These results can be expressed as changes in the input–output coefficients for the electricity and other industries, thus providing a feedback to the main model. Finally the burning of fuels implies emissions of $CO_2$ and various pollutants such as $SO_2$ and CO into the atmosphere; these add to other emissions, not directly associated with the burning of fossil fuels, which are generated by agriculture, industry and other human activities, and which are calculated from changes in variables in the economic model.

### 9.1.3  The data

The data sets, the units of measurement and the classifications adopted are in general different in each of the E3 components of the new enlarged model.[1] The unit used in the economic model to measure changes in the volume of activity is million pounds at constant (1985) prices, as adopted in the UK CSO's *National Accounts* and associated data sets such as the *Input–Output Tables for 1985*; the unit used for volumes in the energy sub-model is millions of therms as adopted for the energy balances in the UK Department of Energy's (now the DTI's) *Digest of UK Energy Statistics (DUKES)*; and the unit for air emissions is thousands of tonnes (of carbon in the case of emissions of $CO_2$) as in the Department of the Environment's *Digest of Environmental Protection and Water Statistics (DEPWS)*.

The units of account and general integrity of each of the data sets in these official statistics have been preserved in the modelling. In general the model has been calibrated on the most recent set of data (1991 for the economic data; 1990 for the energy and environmental data), so that the official statistics on particular variables, e.g. $CO_2$ emissions in 1990, are reproduced in the model solution. The equations for the energy sub-model have been estimated on data from successive editions of *DUKES*, which have been made consistent with definitions of industries in the 1980 Standard Industrial Classification (SIC). The prices of energy carriers have been estimated as average prices, pence per therm, using the value data in this source.

### 9.1.4  The classifications adopted in the model

The classifications adopted in the model provide the basis for the collection of data and the organization of the variables in the model. They provide the operational significance for terms such as 'energy', 'environmental emissions' or 'economic activity' and are chosen so as to make the most of the data available on energy use and environmental emissions. The following terms and classifications are included in the model; the letter codes shown, e.g. J, are those adopted in the new version of the model (MDM88) containing the energy sub-model. The environmental emphasis in this new version is on air emissions.

*Economic activity indicators for environmental effects – Fuel users (FU)*

It is convenient to define a much shorter list of economic activities than is usual in a SAM, concentrating on those which are of more direct relevance to environmental protection. The following categories of fuel users are chosen to account for the most serious air pollutants, with extra detail provided by a disaggregation of each type of fuel use into the principal fuels being consumed.

1  Power generation
2  Oil refineries and other own use of energy
3  Iron and steel
4  Non-metallic mineral products (e.g. bricks, glass)
5  Chemicals
6  Other industry
7  Rail transport
8  Road transport
9  Water transport
10  Air transport
11  Domestic use
12  Other final demand, including agriculture, commercial, government and construction

*Energy types (J)*

Another important classification is that of energy types or fuels. Here a balance must be struck between the full detail available, e.g. including coke and creosote as separate categories, and the requirement that the model is primarily concerned with long-term projections, when items such as coke consumed may be negligible. Another criterion for the classification is the emission characteristics of different fuels. The categories adopted for energy carriers are as follows.

1   Coal and coke (solid fuels)
2   Motor spirit
3   Derv
4   Gas oil
5   Fuel oil
6   Other refined oils
7   Gas (natural gas, coke oven gas and town gas)
8   Electricity (all secondary use, plus net trade and pumped hydro)
9   Nuclear electricity (primary supply)
10  Other fuel, including renewable (primary supply)

*Emissions or pollutants (EM)*

These are generated by many types of economic activity, in particular chemical-intensive agriculture, the burning of fossil fuels for electricity or for transport and the processing of metals and chemicals The time-series emissions data in official statistics (*DEPWS*) are mainly for flows into the atmosphere. Data on stocks of pollutants are often not available; however, although these are important for land and water pollutants, they are less important for air pollutants such as $NO_x$ and CO where flows are more important. Although the environmental consequences of $CO_2$ emissions are stock related (i.e. are related to the ambient concentrations of the gas in the atmosphere) the absence of spatial or temporal differentiation in the effects simplifies the stock–flow relationship so that using flow data is not such a problem. (In contrast, to take one example, the role of volatile organic compounds in generating low-level ozone depends on the place and time of emissions.) Since the model is initially concerned with the economic consequences of achieving given environmental targets, in particular a given level of $CO_2$ abatement, and not the targets themselves, it is sufficient to include flows of emissions to the atmosphere, especially those associated with the burning of fossil fuels. The following categories cover the main emissions for which data are readily available.

1   Carbon dioxide $CO_2$
2   Sulphur dioxide $SO_2$
3   Nitrous oxides $NO_x$
4   Carbon monoxide $CO$
5   Methane
6   Black smoke
7   Volatile organic compounds VOC
8   Nuclear – emissions to air
9   Lead – emissions to air
10  Chlorofluorocarbon CFC

### 9.1.5 The structure of the energy submodel

The energy submodel has five components containing solutions for

- electricity supply characteristics (fuel use, generating capacity)
- secondary energy demand by user in aggregate
- fuel use by energy carrier and user
- the prices of fuel use by user
- emissions to the atmosphere

The weather influences energy demand in the model through the average temperature variables in equations for the aggregate demand for energy and those for the substitution between fuels. The dollar oil price is also exogenous, being determined by the world market. And government policy, expressed through direct subsidies to the coal industry and regulations concerning the setting of electricity and gas prices, determines the relative prices of the other principal energy carriers.

On the energy supply side, the electricity industry is assumed to invest in new generating plant and to utilize the existing plant according to the demand for electricity, the plant available and the cost of fuel and capital. The type of plant in the system and its utilization in each year determines the fuels used and the price of electricity to the contract market.

On the energy demand side, secondary energy demand in aggregate by the ten final users is determined by a set of equations very similar to those developed by the UK DEn. These include the effects of economic activity, relative prices, deviations of temperature from normal values and the miners' strike of 1984. These aggregate demands are then allocated across the different fuels by means of a set of share equations. First the share of electricity demand in the total is determined and then the non-electricity demand is divided between coal, oil products and gas. The relative prices for energy and the fuels are derived from world prices, the UK tax structure and the regulatory rules. Finally own use of energy is taken as a fixed proportion of the total by energy type.

The feedback from the energy sub-model to the rest of the model is as follows. Changes in fuel use by the domestic sector determine changes in consumers' expenditures in constant prices on electricity, gas, coal, heating oils and petrol. Changes in fuel use by other final demand are used to determine the share of government expenditure on fuels. For industrial use of fuels, the implied changes in the input–output coefficients are calculated at the nine-industrial-sector level of the energy model and are applied to the coefficients at the full forty-three-industry level of the economic model. The coefficients for fuel use by the electricity industry are entered directly into the full input–output coefficient table. Finally the mix of regulated and contract-market prices for electricity is averaged to give the electricity price in the main model.

### 9.1.6  A submodel of the electricity supply industry

A simple model of the plant profile of the UK electricity supply industry has been constructed to provide a framework in which to make informed judgements about future fuel inputs to the electricity industry. The main inputs from the rest of MDM to the electricity supply industry (ESI) submodel are the projected growth in electricity output and the relative fuel prices given the assumed level of the carbon/energy tax. The ESI model then produces fuel input requirements for the electricity industry, i.e. the amount of each type of fuel used in million therms which is entered in the fuel use table. This treatment allows fuel use in the ESI to be determined by the existing and expected characteristics of the generating stations, including their expected life-time, their efficiency and the type of fuel they burn.

## 9.2  SECONDARY ENERGY DEMAND IN AGGREGATE

### 9.2.1  Research strategy

The research on aggregate energy demand by ten consuming sectors is done in three stages:

1   the estimation of a set of equations (the base equations) closely following DEn methodology (DEn 1989a) and the examination of the statistical, economic and forecasting properties of the equations;
2   re-specification of the equations into two components, a long-term relationship and a short-term dynamic equation, following the cointegration procedure (the cointegrating equations);
3   re-examination of the specification to allow for characteristics of the dwellings, appliance and vehicle stocks and the transport infrastructure.

An important aspect of the research is the ongoing assessment of proposals for environmental policies, e.g. the carbon/energy tax, so at each stage the estimated equations are being tested as part of a long-term solution of MDM assessing the effects of tax and related proposals. This is a continuing programme of research with the emphasis on policy design; thus Barker and Lewney (1991) use an earlier version of MDM to report the possible effects of a carbon tax with the DEn elasticities introduced *ad hoc*, i.e. without any re-estimation of equations on new data. This chapter reports on progress with stages 1 and 2.

### 9.2.2  An equation for total delivered energy by sector

Dynamic equations have been estimated for the demand for energy, defined as total heat supplied,[2] in ten sectors of the economy (i.e. for all the fuel users listed above except for power conversion and the energy industries' own use of energy). Demand is related to economic activity, relative prices and deviations from mean for air temperature; a dummy variable to represent the effects of the miners' strike in 1984 was included but turned out to be insignificant in these equations. The specification of the base equations for a particular sector is as follows (DEn 1989a: 78):

$$
\begin{aligned}
\ln E = a_1 &+ a_2*[\ln Y - a_6*\ln Y(-1)] \\
&+ a_3*[\ln T - a_6*\ln T(-1)] \\
&+ a_4*\ln \text{RPE} - a_5*\text{time} \\
&+ a_6*\ln E(-1) + e
\end{aligned}
\tag{9.1}
$$

where ln denotes natural logarithm, $(-1)$ denotes a lag of one year, $a_1, a_2, a_3, a_4, a_5, a_6$ are parameters, $E$ is total delivered energy in million therms, $Y$ is a measure of economic activity, $T$ is the deviation from trend temperature, RPE is the price of energy relative to that of all goods and services, time is a time trend and $e$ is an error term.

Equations of this form were estimated as non-linear equations (note that parameter $a_6$ appears three times) with the parameter $a_4$ representing the price elasticity and $a_6$ the lag on the price effect, both being imposed at 'consensus' values using the estimation packages MREG (Peterson 1992) and Microfit (Pesaran and Pesaran 1991). A full discussion of the logic behind the equations and their properties is given by the UK DEn (1989a: 77–91); the specification allows for lagged effects of relative prices but not of any other variable. The reasoning behind this lagged response is that the history of energy prices up to the previous year is embodied in the stock of energy-using equipment used in the current year; it is this stock, combined with the economic activity and the average temperature in the current year which determines energy demand.

Table 9.1 shows the estimated or imposed long-term activity and price elasticities for each sector. The low price elasticities agree with those from other studies adopting a single-equation, partial framework (Vernon and Wigley 1982; Westoby and Pearce 1984; Beenstock and Dalziel 1986; Hunt and Manning 1989; Lynk 1989) including the estimates of the DEn. Table 9.2 gives some conventional test statistics, although it is recognized that some of these may not be valid owing to the presence of the lagged dependent variable in the regressions.

These equations have been introduced into MDM to provide a starting point for further analysis, but it should be recognized that there are problems with the specification, some of which are covered in the literature. Indeed the DEn model has been developed in recent years to address one of these, namely the crudeness of estimating a constant lagged response together with time trends to represent improvements in energy efficiency. This has been accomplished by including the influence of the capital stock of fuel-burning appliances (Hodgson 1992) in energy demand. This is certainly an important

Table 9.1 Parameters for the aggregate energy equations – base specification 1970–90

| | Intercept | Economic activity | Short-term price effect | Air temperature | Time trend (% p.a.) | Lag |
|---|---|---|---|---|---|---|
| Iron and steel | 0.015 | 1.006 | −0.07 | 0.0 | −0.8 | 0.8 |
| Mineral products | 0.900 | 0.629 | −0.12 | −0.06 | −0.3 | 0.7 |
| Chemicals | 0.399 | 0.617 | −0.065 | 0.0 | −0.5 | 0.9 |
| Other industry | 0.362 | 0.638 | −0.065 | −0.05 | −0.2 | 0.9 |
| Rail transport | 0.725 | 0.423 | −0.040 | 0.0 | 0.0 | 0.8 |
| Road transport | 3.169 | 0.323 | −0.120 | 0.0 | 0.8 | 0.6 |
| Water transport | 1.249 | 0.034 | −0.020 | 0.0 | 0.0 | 0.8 |
| Air transport | 1.770 | −0.02 | −0.040 | 0.0 | 0.7 | 0.8 |
| Domestic final use | 2.438 | 0.390 | −0.120 | −0.07 | 0.0 | 0.6 |
| Other final use | 1.042 | 0.396 | −0.060 | −0.04 | 0.0 | 0.8 |

Table 9.2 Test statistics for the aggregate energy equations – base specification 1970–90

| | t ratio | | | | $\bar{R}^2$ | DW | SE (%) |
|---|---|---|---|---|---|---|---|
| | Intercept | Economic activity | Air temperature | Time trend | | | |
| Iron and steel | 0.08 | 10.04 | | 3.85 | 0.974 | 1.99 | 5.2 |
| Mineral products | 2.42 | 4.65 | 3.33 | 2.09 | 0.966 | 2.56 | 3.4 |
| Chemicals | 2.55 | 4.05 | | 3.68 | 0.874 | 2.55 | 3.6 |
| Other industry | 1.95 | 4.19 | 3.32 | 1.58 | 0.975 | 1.87 | 2.5 |
| Rail transport | 2.00 | 1.79 | | | 0.848 | 1.78 | 4.6 |
| Road transport | 8.71 | 3.27 | | 5.83 | 0.990 | 2.44 | 1.6 |
| Water transport | 2.66 | 0.13 | | | 0.096 | 1.39 | 8.6 |
| Air transport | 4.72 | 0.09 | | 4.01 | 0.941 | 1.69 | 4.2 |
| Domestic final use | 7.49 | 5.89 | 6.67 | | 0.891 | 2.25 | 2.0 |
| Other final use | 2.88 | 2.73 | 2.96 | | 0.603 | 1.85 | 2.7 |

Table 9.3 Price elasticities for various lags in aggregate energy equations – base specifications 1970–90

| Column | 1 | 2 | 3 | 4 | 5 | 6 | 7 | 8 | 9 |
|---|---|---|---|---|---|---|---|---|---|
| Lag | Unrestricted | Imposed | 0 | 0.2 | 0.4 | 0.6 | 0.8 | 0.9 | 0.95 |
| Iron and steel | 0.108 | −0.350 | 0.110 | 0.125 | 0.142 | 0.155 | 0.170 | 0.195 | 0.248 |
| Mineral products | 0.035 | −0.400 | −0.035 | −0.012 | 0.009 | 0.000 | −0.028 | −0.033 | −0.021 |
| Chemicals | 0.087 | −0.650 | 0.316 | 0.266 | 0.191 | 0.065 | −0.268 | −0.919 | −2.220 |
| Other industry | 0.021 | −0.650 | 0.169 | 0.147 | 0.097 | −0.027 | −0.369 | −0.955 | −2.078 |
| Rail transport | −0.092 | −0.200 | −0.270 | −0.275 | −0.279 | −0.275 | −0.249 | −0.198 | −0.099 |
| Road transport | −0.134 | −0.300 | −0.119 | −0.163 | −0.237 | −0.384 | −0.747 | −1.366 | −2.577 |
| Water transport | 0.096 | −0.100 | 0.083 | 0.093 | 0.112 | 0.158 | 0.310 | 0.580 | 1.045 |
| Air transport | −0.169 | −0.200 | −0.167 | −0.184 | −0.219 | −0.307 | −0.573 | −1.066 | −2.022 |
| Domestic final use | −0.334 | −0.300 | −0.071 | −0.091 | −0.124 | −0.186 | −0.339 | −0.589 | −1.071 |
| Other final use | −0.300 | −0.300 | −0.047 | −0.051 | −0.057 | −0.071 | −0.099 | −0.109 | −0.052 |

Table 9.4 $\bar{R}^2$ for various lags in aggregate energy equations – base specifications 1970–90

| Column | 1 | 2 | 3 | 4 | 5 | 6 | 7 | 8 | 9 |
|---|---|---|---|---|---|---|---|---|---|
| Lag | Unrestricted | Imposed | 0 | 0.2 | 0.4 | 0.6 | 0.8 | 0.9 | 0.95 |
| Iron and steel | 0.99 | 0.98 | 0.987 | 0.987 | 0.987 | 0.985 | 0.982 | 0.979 | 0.978 |
| Mineral products | 0.98 | 0.97 | 0.982 | 0.983 | 0.982 | 0.979 | 0.974 | 0.970 | 0.969 |
| Chemicals | 0.87 | 0.89 | 0.704 | 0.785 | 0.846 | 0.884 | 0.895 | 0.890 | 0.885 |
| Other industry | 0.97 | 0.98 | 0.941 | 0.954 | 0.964 | 0.972 | 0.977 | 0.979 | 0.980 |
| Rail transport | 0.90 | 0.86 | 0.659 | 0.741 | 0.806 | 0.852 | 0.856 | 0.832 | 0.813 |
| Road transport | 0.99 | 0.99 | 0.993 | 0.994 | 0.993 | 0.991 | 0.988 | 0.985 | 0.984 |
| Water transport | 0.65 | 0.14 | 0.323 | 0.423 | 0.455 | 0.417 | 0.301 | 0.208 | 0.155 |
| Air transport | 0.99 | 0.95 | 0.982 | 0.983 | 0.980 | 0.975 | 0.963 | 0.953 | 0.946 |
| Domestic final use | 0.96 | 0.90 | 0.924 | 0.925 | 0.919 | 0.906 | 0.883 | 0.867 | 0.858 |
| Other final use | 0.81 | 0.64 | 0.718 | 0.742 | 0.741 | 0.714 | 0.664 | 0.632 | 0.613 |

development for long-term analysis, but it is much more complex and demanding of data than the original DEn specification.

Another improvement would be the use of the cointegration procedure in estimating responses. There is a problem in the estimation of the DEn equations of identifying the price elasticity when the lagged dependent variable is introduced. This is illustrated by Table 9.3 which shows the unrestricted estimates of the maximum long-term price elasticities when different lags ($a_6$ in (9.1)) are imposed. The first column gives the elasticities calculated from the unrestricted equations; the second column shows the elasticities imposed to obtain the results reported in Table 9.1; column 3 shows the elasticities with zero lag; and columns 4–9 show the elasticities for lags imposed at 0.2, 0.4, 0.6, 0.8, 0.9 and 0.95 respectively. Clearly, for most users, the longer the lag, the more negative the price elasticity. Table 9.4 shows that goodness of fit as measured by $\bar{R}^2$ is not much help and that a range of long-term price elasticities is consistent with high values of $R^2$ in most sectors. The imposed elasticities were found by inspecting the properties of the equations to ensure a reasonable goodness of fit, estimated effects of activity variables and consistency with earlier estimates.

### 9.2.3  Cointegrating energy demand equations

Hunt and Manning (1989) estimate an aggregate energy demand in the UK on data for 1969–86 using cointegration techniques (see Engel and Granger 1991). The cointegration literature recognizes that the time-series properties of a set of observations are affected by their stationarity. In particular, if the variables in (9.1) are not stationary, the $t$ statistics and the $R^2$ are likely to be invalid (Engel and Granger 1987).

When the time-series variables used to estimate (9.1) are tested for stationarity, using the Dickey–Fuller and augmented Dickey–Fuller tests (Pesaran and Pesaran 1991: 48), it appears that all the variables with the exception of temperature must be differenced once to produce stationarity, i.e. they are integrated of order 1, a result also found by Hunt and Manning (1989) for aggregate energy use by all sectors. These results suggest the two-stage procedure (Hall 1986; Engel and Granger 1987, 1991) of (i) estimating a long-term relationship from a set of cointegrating variables ((9.2) below) and testing that the residuals, EC, from the regression are stationary (Pesaran and Pesaran 1991: 96) and then (ii) estimating a dynamic equation, including these residuals lagged one period ((9.3) below).

$$\ln E = a_1 + a_2 * \ln Y + a_3 * \ln \text{RPE} + a_4 * \ln T + a_5 * \text{time}$$
$$+ \text{EC} \tag{9.2}$$

$$d \ln E = b_1 + b_2*d \ln E(-1) + b_3*d \ln T + b_4*d \ln Y$$
$$+ b_5*d \ln Y(-1) + b_6*d \ln RPE + b_7*d \ln RPE(-1)$$
$$+ b_8*EC(-1) + e_2 \tag{9.3}$$

where ln denotes natural logarithm, d ln denotes differences in logarithms, (–1) denotes a lag of one year, $a_1, a_2, a_3, a_4, a_5, b_1, b_2, b_3, b_4, b_5, b_6, b_7,$ $b_8$ are parameters, $E$ is total delivered energy in million therms, $Y$ is a measure of economic activity, RPE is the price of energy relative to that of all goods and services, $T$ is deviation from trend temperature, time is a time trend, EC is the error correction term in (9.3) from the residuals in (9.2) and $e_2$ is an error term.

This more general specification allows for much more possibility of short-term effects than (9.1), including a short-term income elasticity distinct from that in the long term. Table 9.5 shows the long-term equations with the price elasticities imposed at base specification values. In three sectors (chemicals, other industry and rail transport) the activity elasticity was also imposed to prevent negative estimated values. Wrong-signed parameters for temperature were dropped. The parameters and $t$ ratios (in absolute values) for the short-term equations are shown in Tables 9.6 and 9.7; the full specification in (9.3) was estimated first and insignificant parameters were dropped; the tables show the parameters remaining after this procedure was completed. Table 9.8 shows the $\bar{R}^2$ statistic from the difference equation, the Durbin–Watson statistic (DW) and the standard error. There are some econometric problems with these equations, but the estimated parameters are more or less satisfactory.

*Table 9.5* Parameters for the long-run cointegrating energy equations – base long-term price elasticities

| | Intercept | Economic activity | Long-term price effect | Air temperature | Time trend (% p.a.) |
|---|---|---|---|---|---|
| Iron and steel | 4.93 | 0.49 | $-0.35^a$ | 0.0 | $-3.7$ |
| Mineral products | 5.69 | 0.34 | $-0.40^a$ | $-0.05$ | $-1.7$ |
| Chemicals | 4.25 | $0.62^a$ | $-0.65^a$ | 0.0 | $-1.0$ |
| Other industry | 3.79 | $0.64^a$ | $-0.65^a$ | $-0.14$ | $-0.9$ |
| Rail transport | 3.71 | $0.42^a$ | $-0.20^a$ | 0.0 | 0.0 |
| Road transport | 8.65 | 0.24 | $-0.30^a$ | 0.0 | 2.1 |
| Water transport | 5.07 | 0.17 | $-0.10^a$ | 0.0 | 0.0 |
| Air transport | 5.74 | 0.31 | $-0.20^a$ | 0.0 | 3.8 |
| Domestic final use | 6.64 | 0.35 | $-0.30^a$ | $-0.08$ | 0.0 |
| Other final use | 6.30 | 0.31 | $-0.30^a$ | $-0.06$ | 0.0 |

*Note*: $^a$Imposed parameters.

Table 9.6 Parameters for the dynamic cointegrating energy equations – base long-term price elasticities

| Variable | Intercept | d ln Y | d ln RPE | d ln Y(−1) | d ln RPE (−1) | d ln E(−1) | d ln T | EC(−1) |
|---|---|---|---|---|---|---|---|---|
| Iron and steel | −0.04 | 1.07 | | | 0.20 | | | −0.16 |
| Mineral products | −0.02 | 0.66 | | | | | −0.06 | −0.37 |
| Chemicals | −0.01 | 0.49 | | | | | | −0.19 |
| Other industry | −0.02 | 0.79 | | | | | −0.04 | −0.01 |
| Rail transport | −0.01 | | −0.07 | | | | | −0.42 |
| Road transport | 0.02 | | −0.18 | 0.24 | | | | −0.70 |
| Water transport | 0.03 | | | −0.49 | | 0.50 | | −0.65 |
| Air transport | 0.03 | | −0.17 | | | 0.21 | −0.03 | −0.63 |
| Domestic final use | 0.01 | | −0.25 | | | | −0.07 | −0.48 |
| Other final use | 0.01 | | −0.26 | | | | −0.04 | −0.12 |

Note: See equation (9.1) for definitions of variables shown at the head of each column.

Table 9.7 $t$ ratios for the dynamic cointegrating energy equations – base long-term price elasticities

| Variable | Intercept | d ln Y | d ln RPE | d ln Y(−1) | d ln RPE (−1) | d ln E(−1) | d ln T | EC(−1) |
|---|---|---|---|---|---|---|---|---|
| Iron and steel | 3.48 | 10.5 | | | 1.95 | | | 1.02 |
| Mineral products | 2.71 | 3.71 | | | | | 2.87 | 1.48 |
| Chemicals | 0.60 | 2.57 | | | | | | 2.79 |
| Other industry | 3.11 | 3.27 | | | | | 2.45 | 0.13 |
| Rail transport | 1.36 | | 0.99 | | | | | 2.89 |
| Road transport | 4.97 | | 5.01 | 2.09 | | | | 3.49 |
| Water transport | 1.44 | | | 1.63 | | | | 3.52 |
| Air transport | 3.61 | | 7.16 | | | 2.55 | 1.98 | 2.23 |
| Domestic final use | 1.91 | | 2.34 | | | 1.92 | 6.20 | 2.42 |
| Other final use | 1.48 | | 3.75 | | | | 3.23 | 0.80 |

*Table 9.8* Test statistics for the dynamic cointegrating energy equations – base long-term price elasticities

|  | $\bar{R}^2$ | DW | SE (%) |
|---|---|---|---|
| Iron and steel | 0.90 | 2.13 | 4.7 |
| Mineral products | 0.67 | 1.92 | 3.6 |
| Chemicals | 0.55 | 1.73 | 4.3 |
| Other industry | 0.56 | 1.60 | 3.0 |
| Rail transport | 0.36 | 1.64 | 4.8 |
| Road transport | 0.74 | 1.38 | 1.5 |
| Water transport | 0.39 | 2.39 | 6.7 |
| Air transport | 0.77 | 1.34 | 2.4 |
| Domestic final use | 0.74 | 2.22 | 1.9 |
| Other final use | 0.52 | 1.73 | 2.3 |

The results for short- and long-term price elasticities are summarized in Table 9.9 and those for activity elasticities in Table 9.10. The summary includes estimates from a set of equations with lower imposed elasticities following an examination of the freely estimated long-term cointegrating equations which suggested that the imposed price elasticities may be too high. A striking feature of the summary of activity elasticities is the set of insignificant short-term elasticities which are restricted to zero for transport and final use.

### 9.2.4  Prediction tests 1986–90

Since these are forecasting equations, an important set of tests is carried out on the ability of both sets of equations to forecast the last five-year period of data, 1986–90. This coincides with the period of low real energy prices after the 1985 collapse of world oil prices, so the tests are particularly appropriate when the emphasis of the research is on the effects of changes in real prices on energy demand. Table 9.11, column 1, reports the $F$ statistic for a test of predictive failure for the dynamic cointegrating equation estimated over the period 1972–85 and forecasting over the period 1986–90. The 95 per cent value of the $F$ test for the appropriate degrees of freedom is given in column 2; it can be seen that only rail transport fails the test, and then only just. However, it should be noted that the error correction variable in the equation is kept at the estimated values for the whole period 1971–90, i.e. the long-term equation is not re-estimated for the shorter period 1971–85. Columns 3 and 4 show the average absolute static and dynamic forecasting errors respectively from the dynamic cointegrating equation over 1986–90. In order to take account of possible changes in the long-term estimates, the dynamic forecasts were recalculated with the long-term equations re-estimated over the period

Table 9.9 Estimated and imposed *price* elasticities of aggregate secondary energy demand, UK 1970–90

| | Base short term | Base long term | Base cointegrating short term | Base cointegrating long term | Lower cointegrating short term | Lower cointegrating long term |
|---|---|---|---|---|---|---|
| Iron and steel | −0.07 | −0.35[a] | 0.0[a] | −0.35[a] | 0.0[a] | −0.20[a] |
| Mineral products | −0.12 | −0.40[a] | 0.0[a] | −0.40[a] | 0.0[a] | −0.45 |
| Chemicals | −0.06 | −0.65[a] | 0.0[a] | −0.65[a] | 0.0[a] | −0.10[a] |
| Other industry | −0.06 | −0.65[a] | 0.0[a] | −0.65[a] | 0.0[a] | −0.65[a] |
| Rail transport | −0.04 | −0.20[a] | −0.07 | −0.20[a] | −0.12 | −0.20[a] |
| Road transport | −0.12 | −0.30[a] | −0.18 | −0.30[a] | −0.16 | −0.25[a] |
| Water transport | −0.02 | −0.10[a] | 0.0[a] | −0.10[a] | 0.0[a] | −0.10[a] |
| Air transport | −0.04 | −0.20[a] | −0.17 | −0.20[a] | −0.17 | −0.17 |
| Domestic final use | −0.12 | −0.30[a] | −0.25 | −0.30[a] | −0.15 | −0.12[a] |
| Other final use | −0.06 | −0.30[a] | −0.26 | −0.30[a] | −0.23 | −0.06 |

*Note:* [a]Imposed parameters.

*Table 9.10* Estimated and imposed *activity* elasticities of aggregate secondary energy demand, UK 1970–90

| | Base short term | Base long term | Base cointegrating short term | Base cointegrating long term | Lower cointegrating short term | Lower cointegrating long term |
|---|---|---|---|---|---|---|
| Iron and steel | 1.01 | 1.01 | 1.07 | 0.49 | 0.98 | 0.66 |
| Mineral products | 0.63 | 0.63 | 0.66 | 0.34 | 0.77 | 0.73 |
| Chemicals | 0.62 | 0.62 | 0.49 | 0.62[a] | 0.65 | 0.62[a] |
| Other industry | 0.64 | 0.64 | 0.79 | 0.64[a] | 0.70 | 0.64[a] |
| Rail transport | 0.42 | 0.42 | 0.0[a] | 0.42[a] | 0.0[a] | 0.42[a] |
| Road transport | 0.32 | 0.32 | 0.0[a] | 0.24 | 0.0[a] | 0.28 |
| Water transport | 0.03 | 0.03 | 0.0[a] | 0.17 | 0.0[a] | 0.17 |
| Air transport | −0.02 | −0.02 | 0.0[a] | 0.31 | 0.0[a] | 0.36 |
| Domestic final use | 0.39 | 0.39 | 0.0[a] | 0.35 | 0.0[a] | 0.31 |
| Other final use | 0.40 | 0.40 | 0.0[a] | 0.31 | 0.0[a] | 0.18 |

*Note:* [a] Imposed parameters.

Table 9.11 Tests of predictive failure for dynamic cointegrating aggregate energy equations and base specification – 1986–90

| | F statistic | 95 per cent significance level | Average static error (%) | Average dynamic error A (%) | Average dynamic error B (%) | Average dynamic error B, lower price elasticity (%) | Average dynamic error B, base specification (%) |
|---|---|---|---|---|---|---|---|
| Iron and steel | 0.30 | 3.33 | 2.3 | 3.7 | 15.4 | 17.9 | 17.5 |
| Mineral products | 0.29 | 3.20 | 2.2 | 3.5 | 2.6 | 9.3 | 11.8 |
| Chemicals | 1.18 | 3.33 | 4.1 | 7.4 | 8.8 | 10.7 | 2.7 |
| Other industry | 0.78 | 3.20 | 2.4 | 1.8 | 6.1 | 3.5 | 2.4 |
| Rail transport | 3.43 | 3.20 | 6.0 | 6.2 | 6.2 | 1.6 | 15.5 |
| Road transport | 0.40 | 3.33 | 1.0 | 1.2 | 4.3 | 4.2 | 1.4 |
| Water transport | 0.25 | 3.33 | 3.5 | 3.7 | 11.4 | 11.4 | 13.7 |
| Air transport | 0.18 | 3.33 | 3.4 | 4.4 | 6.2 | 7.0 | 14.4 |
| Domestic final use | 0.21 | 3.20 | 1.1 | 1.0 | 4.4 | 1.4 | 6.8 |
| Other final use | 0.35 | 3.20 | 1.3 | 3.6 | 8.2 | 2.4 | 7.3 |

Note: Dynamic error A uses the long-term equation estimated over 1970–90; dynamic error B uses the long-term equation estimated over 1970–85. The last column shows the fully dynamic errors from the equations estimated according to the base specification of Table 9.1 over the period 1970–85.

1970–85. Column 5 shows these results. In general the errors are larger the less information about the predicted period is included in the equation estimates. Finally, the fully dynamic forecasting errors for the other sets of equations are summarized in columns 6 and 7.

## 9.3 SUBSTITUTION BETWEEN ENERGY CARRIERS IN AGGREGATE DEMAND

The total demand for energy by the non-transport sectors is divided between electricity, coal, oil products and gas by means of a set of share equations. The demand by transport sectors is largely fuel specific (except for rail which is switching from oil to electricity) and the shares of each fuel have been fixed exogenously. For the other sectors, the share of total demand taken by electricity is estimated first, on the grounds that electricity demand is generally not in competition with other energy carriers, being used for additional and occasional point heating and for powering appliances. The share is related to economic activity, relative prices of electricity, a temperature variable and a dummy variable for the 1984 miners' strike.

$$\ln(ELEC/E) = a_1 + a_2 * \ln Y + a_3 * \ln T + a_4 * \ln(RPELEC/RPE)$$
$$+ a_5 * \text{time} + a_6 * DUM84 + a_7 * \ln(ELEC/E)(-1)$$
$$+ e \tag{9.4}$$

where ln denotes natural logarithm, $(-1)$ denotes a lag of one year, $a_1, a_2, a_3,$ $a_4, a_5, a_6, a_7$ are parameters, $ELEC/E$ is the share of electricity in total delivered energy, $Y$ is a measure of economic activity, $T$ is deviation from trend temperature, RPELEC is the price of electricity relative to that of all goods and services, RPE is the price of energy relative to that of all goods and

Table 9.12 Long-term price elasticities from the share/ratio equations

|  | Electricity share | Coal share | Oil–coal ratio | Gas–coal ratio |
|---|---|---|---|---|
| Iron and steel | −1.0 | −0.4 | −0.1 | −0.1 |
| Mineral products | −0.1 | −0.2 | −2.3 | −0.4 |
| Chemicals | −1.4 | −5.9 | −2.5 | − |
| Other industry | 0.0 | −0.8 | −3.0 | − |
| Rail transport | −2.3 | − | − | − |
| Road transport | − | − | − | − |
| Water transport | − | − | − | − |
| Air transport | − | − | − | − |
| Domestic final use | −0.2 | −0.3 | −0.3 | − |
| Other final use | −0.2 | −0.5 | −0.3 | − |

Note: −, not calculated.

services, time is a time trend, DUM84 is a dummy variable for the miners'
strike 1984 = 1 and $e$ is an error term. The long-term price elasticities
estimated from these equations are given in column 1 of Table 9.12.

The shares of coal in non-electricity energy demand by some users
(chemicals, other industry, domestic final users and other final users) are
treated on a similar basis, since consumer and government demand for coal
is more closely related to locational, demographic and institutional factors
than to relative prices or income levels (equation (9.5)). For these users, the
ratio of oil to coal demand is estimated by another equation (equation (9.6))
and gas demand is taken as a residual. The share or ratio long-term price
elasticities are shown in columns 2 and 3 of Table 9.12.

$$\ln(\text{COAL/NEE}) = a_1 + a_2* \ln Y + a_3* \ln T$$
$$+ a_4* \ln(\text{PCOAL/PNEE}) + a_5* \ln(\text{PGAS/PNEE})$$
$$+ a_6*\text{time} + a_7*\text{DUM84}$$
$$+ a_8* \ln(\text{COAL/NEE})(-1) + e \qquad (9.5)$$

where the definitions are as for equation (9.4) and COAL/NEE is the share of
coal in total non-electricity delivered energy, PCOAL, PGAS is the price of
coal and gas respectively (pence per therm) and PNEE is the price of non-
electrical energy (pence per therm).

$$\ln(\text{OIL/COAL}) = a_1 + a_2* \ln Y + a_3* \ln T$$
$$+ a_4* \ln(\text{POIL/PNEE}) + a_5* \ln(\text{PCOAL/PNEE})$$
$$+ a_6*\text{time} + a_7*\text{DUM84}$$
$$+ a_8* \ln(\text{OIL/COAL})(-1) + e \qquad (9.6)$$

Finally for two other users (iron and steel and mineral products), the ratio
of gas to coal demand is also estimated, and coal then becomes the residual
fuel:

$$\ln(\text{GAS/COAL}) = a_1 + a_2* \ln Y + a_3* \ln T + a_4* \ln(\text{PGAS/PNEE})$$
$$+ a_5* \ln(\text{PCOAL/PNEE}) + a_6*\text{time}$$
$$+ a_7*\text{DUM84} + a_8* \ln(\text{GAS/COAL})(-1)$$
$$+ e \qquad (9.7)$$

where the definitions are as for equation (9.4) and OIL, COAL and GAS are
delivered energy in these carriers (million therms), POIL, PCOAL, PGAS is
the price of oil, coal and gas respectively (pence per therm) and PNEE is the
price of non-electrical energy (pence per therm).

The price elasticities are much higher for substitution between some of the
fuels than for substitution between energy and other goods and services. Since

the estimating equations are in shares, the elasticities are not constant, but it is clear from the results for share elasticities in Table 9.12 that the own-price and some of the cross-price elasticities are as high as 3, implying a considerable ability for some industries to switch between fuels.

## 9.4 ENERGY PRICE ELASTICITIES AND UK $CO_2$ EMISSIONS: A SENSITIVITY ANALYSIS

### 9.4.1 Introduction

It is clear from the results reported above, and indeed the survey in Chapter 3, that there is considerable uncertainty about the value of the long-term price elasticity of energy demand. Indeed, this is one reason why some of these elasticities were imposed in the estimated equations. Given this uncertainty, it is important to test the effect of changing the imposed elasticities when the model is used in applications, in particular the analysis of the introduction of a carbon tax. MDM, with the inclusion of the DEn specification of the equations, has previously been used to analyse the effects of the European Union's (EU) proposed carbon/energy tax. The research reported here starts from these results as a base and examines the sensitivity of the results to different assumptions about the price elasticities.

### 9.4.2  Modelling the impact on prices of the carbon/energy tax

Before setting out the detail of the sensitivity tests, it is worth explaining how the model predicts the impact of the carbon/energy tax on prices and tax revenues. The effects on total energy consumption and the use of fuels are derived entirely from the effects of the tax on prices. The carbon and energy components of the EU tax are treated separately. The carbon tax is converted from the $1.5 per barrel oil-equivalent in 1993 rising to $5 in the year 2000 (real 1993 prices) to a rate in pounds sterling (using the fixed exchange rate $1.75 = £1) per tonne of carbon emitted for each year 1993–2005. The rate is indexed on UK consumer prices and rises from £8.8 per tonne in 1993 to £37.3 per tonne in 2000 and £45.0 per tonne in 2005. The carbon tax liability of all fuels is calculated on the basis of their carbon content, and is converted into pence per therm on the basis of their heat content. The energy component of the tax is expressed in pence per therm, and again indexed on the consumer price index, so the rate rises from 1.4p/therm in 1993 to 6.1p/therm in 2000 and 7.3p/therm in 2005. A matrix of total carbon/energy tax rates for each fuel and user can be constructed for each year and average rates can be calculated for each fuel and each user. Tax revenues can then be calculated from energy consumption for conversion, own use by energy industries and for secondary uses; the potential revenues will be reduced if consumption falls when the tax is imposed.

The EU proposals are modelled by assuming that imports and domestic supplies of fuels will bear the tax according to their carbon and energy content, with exports exempted from the tax coverage; the treatment is assumed to be very close to that adopted for excise duties on hydrocarbons. If it is also assumed that all the tax is passed on to the user of the fuels, and that the industrial user then passes on the extra costs in the form of higher prices (i.e. perfectly elastic supply conditions), then the new prices for all goods and services in the economy can be calculated. The increase in price will be a result of the direct and indirect carbon and energy content of each of the forty-three commodities and sixty-eight consumers' expenditure categories (to take two important sets of prices in the model). Most of the tax revenues are assumed to be used to reduce value-added tax (VAT) so that there is only a modest effect of the tax on consumer prices. However, some of the revenues are assumed to be used as direct transfer payments to help low-income households and some are allocated to energy-saving schemes, so that there is an overall increase in the consumer price index, implying some extra wage inflation and higher industrial costs and prices.

### 9.4.3  The design of the sensitivity tests

The sensitivity tests were done by imposing a set of long-term price elasticities on the estimating equations for total secondary energy demand and therefore in the solution of the model. (Note that the fuel share equations have been left unchanged in this analysis.) The base specification is that described in Section 9.3 above; the low, high and higher elasticity assumptions change the imposed elasticities across the board by +0.1, −0.1 and −0.2 respectively. These changes are introduced into the estimating equations by varying the imposed lags sufficiently to produce the desired long-term elasticity, i.e. the short-term elasticities remain exactly as before. As a comparison, a set of equations with zero or very low elasticities[3] have also been estimated and included in the model and projections.

### 9.4.4  $CO_2$ emissions and energy demand to 2005

Tables 9.13 and 9.14 show the results for $CO_2$ emissions and total gross energy demand for the year 2005. The emissions for 1990 from the DOE statistics are estimated to be 160 million tonnes carbon (mtc); and the estimated total gross energy demand in 1990 is 94.7 billion therms. The tables show the changes projected over the period 1990–2005 and the estimated effect of the EU carbon/energy tax introduced in 1993 on the emissions and energy demand in 2005.

There are several interesting features in these results. The first is that the differing assumptions about price elasticities affect the $CO_2$ emissions in the absence of any carbon tax. Since real energy prices are expected to be lower

*Table 9.13* UK $CO_2$ emissions 1990–2005 from projections using MDM

| | Price elasticity | | | | |
| --- | --- | --- | --- | --- | --- |
| | *Zero* | *Low (base +0.1)* | *Base specification* | *High (base −0.1)* | *Higher (base −0.2)* |
| $CO_2$ emissions 2005 (mtc) (no carbon/energy tax) | 157.3 | 170.9 | 175.1 | 178.6 | 181.3 |
| $CO_2$ emissions 2005 (mtc) (carbon/energy tax) | 138.2 | 146.8 | 147.2 | 147.7 | 148.1 |
| Change in $CO_2$ emissions (%), 1990–2005 (no carbon/energy tax) | −1.7 | 6.8 | 9.4 | 11.6 | 13.3 |
| Change in $CO_2$ emissions (%), 1990–2005 (carbon/energy tax) | −13.6 | −8.2 | −8.0 | −7.7 | −7.4 |
| Difference from base in $CO_2$ emissions (%) in 2005 (carbon/energy tax) | −12.1 | −14.1 | −15.9 | −17.3 | −18.3 |

in 2005 than in 1990, the higher (more negative) the price elasticity, the higher the energy demand and $CO_2$ emissions. An increase in the absolute values of the elasticities of 0.1 across the board from base values increases energy demand by 3.0 per cent. Comparing the projection when zero price elasticities are imposed with the base case, the reduction in real energy prices for 1990–2005 is calculated to raise energy demand by 12.3 per cent. The second feature is the larger increases in energy demand than in $CO_2$ emissions for any particular set of price elasticities. This is the effect of the substantial increase in the use of gas and the reduction in the use of coal in 2005 compared with 1990. However, when it comes to responses to the carbon/energy tax, the reductions in energy demand are uniformly lower than the reductions in $CO_2$ emissions, because the tax penalizes the high-carbon fuels such as coal. The difference is sufficient to mean that in most of the tax scenarios energy demand in 2005 is higher than in 1990 and at the same time $CO_2$ emissions are lower. The third feature worth noting is that there is a strong response to

Table 9.14 UK total energy demand 1990–2005 from projections using MDM

|  | Price elasticity | | | | |
|---|---|---|---|---|---|
|  | Zero | Low (base +0.1) | Base specification | High (base −0.1) | Higher (base −0.2) |
| Energy demand 2005 (billion therms) (no carbon/energy tax) | 101.4 | 109.9 | 113.9· | 117.3 | 119.8 |
| Energy demand 2005 (billion therms) (carbon/energy tax) | 93.3 | 99.9 | 100.7 | 101.4 | 102.0 |
| Change in energy demand (%), 1990–2005 (no carbon/energy tax) | 7.1 | 16.0 | 20.3 | 23.9 | 26.5 |
| Change in energy demand (%), 1990–2005 (carbon/energy tax) | −1.5 | 5.5 | 6.3 | 7.1 | 7.7 |
| Difference from base in energy demand (%) in 2005 (carbon/energy tax) | −8.0 | −9.1 | −11.6 | −13.6 | −14.9 |

the carbon/energy tax even if the aggregate energy demand elasticities in question are zero. This is because there are at least two other important responses to the tax which are left out of these sensitivity tests, namely substitution between different fuels with different carbon contents and the response of the electricity generators to the new fuel prices. Finally, the estimated effect of the tax on emissions is shown to depend, not surprisingly, on the elasticities imposed. On the basis of these tests, the range of effects is from a reduction in emissions of 12 per cent for zero elasticities (with the effects all coming from fuel substitution and responses in the electricity industry) to 18 per cent for the highest elasticities assumed.

## NOTES

This research has been possible with the assistance of Leda Hahn who has patiently carried out the many estimations and specification searches involved. I am also grateful to participants at the Energy Workshop held at Robinson College, Cambridge, 29–30 September 1992, and to Susan Baylis, Padhraic Garvey and Nick Johnstone for comments on the draft. Finally I would like to acknowledge the support of the ESRC who have funded the project 'Policy options for sustainable energy use in a general model of the UK economy' under Phase 1 of the Global Environmental Change Programme (Project Y320253012). The research reported in this chapter was undertaken as part of this project.

1    In August 1993 the UK CSO published a new set of *National Accounts* based on 1990 prices using an updated input–output table for 1990 and with the industrial detail converted to the 1992 SIC. The Cambridge model has since been re-estimated on this new database.

2    The DEn model takes the measure of aggregate demand to be total useful energy, applying average efficiency factors to each fuel over the data period. These factors are assumed to be constant. Thus those efficiency gains in energy use arising from the fact that different fuels are associated with different efficiencies in combustion are incorporated into the measure of demand, whereas changes in efficiency coming from improvements in appliances and equipment are explained by the equation. By measuring the aggregate on a delivered-energy or heat-supplied basis instead of on a useful-energy basis, all effects of improvements in energy efficiency are treated similarly in the equation reported in this chapter. A test was made of the effect of switching from delivered energy to useful energy, taking the efficiency factors to be 0.5 for coal, 0.55 for oil products, 0.65 for gas and 0.9 for electricity. The changes in the unrestricted estimates of the parameters were very small and did not indicate relatively more elastic price responses; indeed the changes in parameter values were no more than might be expected from a revision to the data.

3    However, an estimate of –0.125 for road transport was necessary to obtain a good equation estimate.

Chapter 10

# Price elasticity and market structure
## Overcoming obstacles to final demand energy efficiency

*Tim Jackson*

**ABSTRACT**

The chapter notes and seeks to explain why some economic models and engineering estimates suggest greatly differing potential for improvements in energy efficiency at current prices, with the low potential suggested by the models expressed by their low price elasticities of demand. The result is that these models indicate that high energy taxes and high costs will be necessary to reduce $CO_2$ emissions significantly. The chapter first distinguishes between the fuels themselves and the energy services – heat, light, power – which they are intended to supply. The supply paths involve different fuels and different capital equipment. The elasticity of demand for basic energy services is likely to be low, but the way this converts into elasticity of demand for fuels depends not only on possible interfuel substitution but, more fundamentally, on possible substitutions between different supply paths. Investments to change the supply paths are the responsibility of different economic agents, who may have widely differing discount rates. The implication of this for energy efficiency is shown by comparing the cost-effectiveness of energy efficiency measures using a single low discount rate characteristic of some agents with the cost-effectiveness of the same measures using the widely varying discount rates of the agents actually responsible for the changes. In the former situation many measures are cost effective. In the latter few are. The take-up of energy efficiency measures can be increased either by changing the structure of the energy market, so that agents with low discount rates become responsible for such measures, or by direct government regulation which overrides inappropriately high discount rates.

**INTRODUCTION**

For a number of reasons, there is an increasing interest in developing macroeconomic and industrial models to include energy demand and supply. In particular such studies are motivated by the call for reductions in greenhouse gas emissions resulting from fossil fuel combustion. Such models might prove useful, for example, in determining the economic impacts of achieving specific emission reduction targets. An appropriate model might also be used to determine the interaction between energy prices and emission levels, and thereby provide a useful tool for the analysis of fiscal policy measures (such as a carbon or energy tax) aimed at reducing greenhouse gas emissions.

However, in the course of the development of such modelling approaches it has become apparent that different kinds of models exhibit significantly different degrees of optimism about achieving given reductions. Macro-economic models have tended to predict the need for very high carbon taxes, implying the possibility of significant macroeconomic disruption if desired greenhouse gas emission reduction targets are to be met. For example, Capros et al. (1990) estimated that tax rates in the European Union in excess of 200 per cent, with a tax rate on coal of almost 600 per cent, would still fail to meet the Toronto target of 20 per cent emissions reduction over 1987 levels. Ingham and Ulph (1990) estimated that tax rates of 123–277 per cent would be required in the UK manufacturing sector. Barker and Lewney (1991) required incremental tax rates reaching 350 per cent on coal in 2005 in order to achieve the Toronto target.

The magnitude of the taxes required to achieve a given reduction is a reflection of the responsiveness of consumers to changes in the price of energy. As such these results are hardly surprising, given that historically determined price elasticities of demand for energy are rather low. For instance, Barker and Lewney (1991) used a price elasticity of demand for electricity of –0.4; long-term elasticities of around –0.3 (varying between different sectors and fuel types) are cited by Barker (1992, 1993b), the UK Department of Trade and Industry (DEn 1989a; Hodgson and Miller 1992) and Gregory et al. (1991). On the basis of these low price elasticities, macroeconomic models have often suggested that significant price changes, and associated economic dislocation, are required to meet environmental objectives.

On the other hand, 'bottom-up' engineering analyses of the technological characteristics of energy consumption in different sectors indicate that considerable potential exists for reductions in the greenhouse gas emissions associated with energy consumption, in particular by the implementation of 'demand-side' energy efficiency measures (DEn 1984, 1988, 1990a, b) as well as fuel substitution. Analysis of these technological options suggests moreover that much of this potential is economically cost effective now, even at current fuel prices, and that more of it becomes economic, given relatively small fuel price increases (Jackson 1989, 1991; Jackson and Roberts 1989; Mills et al. 1991). Figure 10.1 illustrates the results of an analysis of technological options for reducing emissions of greenhouse gases into the atmosphere. Several of these options – in particular those associated with energy efficiency improvements – incur economic savings when assessed on

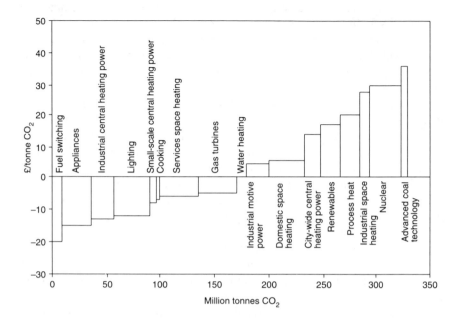

*Figure 10.1* Cost-effectiveness of different $CO_2$ emission abatement options (by the year 2005; 10 per cent assumed discount rate)

a marginal cost basis at a common discount rate of 10 per cent.

In Figure 10.2, a carbon tax has been included in the energy price (Jackson 1992). The magnitude of this tax was chosen to reflect the level of tax deemed necessary according to one of the macroeconomic models (Barker and Lewney 1991) in order to achieve the Toronto target (20 per cent reduction over current levels) by the year 2005. But the results of this microeconomic analysis seem to suggest that such a tax would result in economically viable reductions significantly in excess of those required for a 20 per cent reduction in emissions.

Thus, it is apparent that low energy price elasticities can coexist with unrealized opportunities for improvements in energy efficiency. This has profound repercussions for the interpretation of both macroeconomic models and engineering models of energy demand. If energy efficiency improvements are really economic, why are they not already being implemented? Why is a carbon tax or an energy tax required at all? And why, if there are economic gains to be made by reducing energy consumption through improved energy efficiency, have macroeconomic analyses tended to suggest that reducing greenhouse gas emissions could be both costly and disruptive (Nordhaus 1990; Manne and Richels 1992)?

The answers to such questions rest, in part, with an understanding of the

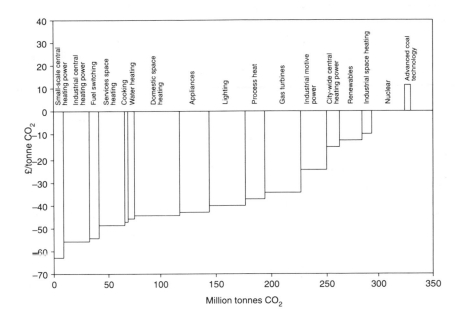

*Figure 10.2* Effects of a carbon tax on microeconomic analysis of $CO_2$ abatement options (by year 2005; 10 per cent discount rate)

different methodological approaches used by the models and the questions that they are attempting to answer. On the one hand, macroeconomic models take the structural characteristics of the economy as given and, as such, are not able to capture the impact of changes in that structure. On the other hand, engineering models tend to adopt an assumption of 'socially optimal' economic decision-making, and therefore fail to reflect the exigencies of actual market behaviour. Thus, although both approaches provide valuable insights into the potential for, and means of, realizing significant gains in understanding energy consumption, the respective insights of the two approaches should be regarded in the light of their methodological foundations when they are used to evaluate appropriate policy interventions.

## 10.1 THE SUPPLY OF 'ENERGY SERVICES': REDEFINING THE ENERGY MARKET

Before answering the questions posed above, it is worthwhile to discuss in some detail the nature of the energy market. First of all, strictly speaking, there is no such thing as the price elasticity of demand for energy, because energy *per se* is not really traded. Electricity is traded; coal, oil, gas and other fuels are traded. But to say that energy is traded is really only a manner of speaking, or a way of measuring the trade in the commodities of primary and secondary fuels.

It makes some sense therefore to speak of the price elasticity of demand for primary and secondary fuels. On the other hand, the 'demand' for fuels is only an intermediate demand for commodities which are required to provide certain kinds of services to consumers. The 'final' demand is not for fuel, nor even for energy, but rather for certain 'energy services' which primary and secondary fuels can help to provide. These energy services include, for instance, thermal comfort, hot water, light, motive power (including transportation) and so on.

In order to meet the demand for these services certain kinds of commodities are traded. These commodities include fossil fuels and electricity. They also include energy conversion appliances (boilers, heaters, lights, cars, power stations). Equally, the provision of a particular level of thermal comfort service, for example, depends upon the level of capital investment in the thermal structure of the dwelling. What is clear from this analysis is that a demand for a particular service is met not by a simple transaction involving the trading of certain quantities of primary and secondary fuels, but rather through a network of transactions involving capital investments in various parts of the network as well as trade in consumable goods (fuels) throughout the network.

There are several points to make concerning this supply network. First, it should be noted that the energy service supply network involves investments at different points by different economic actors. The fuel supply elements of the network require corporate investment in coal production and distribution, and in electricity production and distribution; and the fuel demand elements typically require investment mainly by companies and households in appliances to burn fuels and in insulation and other energy-retention characteristics of buildings (also see Chapter 1 for a discussion of the network). Second, it is important to note that any particular demand for energy services can be met by a number of different 'chains' of investment and transaction, within the energy service supply network. For instance, the demand for thermal comfort in an existing poorly insulated dwelling can be met through a supply chain involving an inefficient open fire using a certain quantity of low-grade coal, and perhaps supplemented by direct electric heating with electricity generated by traditional coal-fired electricity generation. Alternatively, the same demand for thermal comfort could be met by improving the thermal insulation of the dwelling (requiring increased investment in a different part of the network) and thereby reducing the requirement for low-grade coal and electricity (and reducing the fuel cost). This alternative represents a second 'energy service supply chain' providing the same energy service. Equally, the demand for thermal comfort could be met by replacing the open fire with a modern, efficient gas-fired boiler (requiring investment in energy conversion capital goods) and purchasing supplies of domestic gas (at a reduced cost in consumable goods). This represents a third energy service supply chain. Of course, investments in both thermal insulation and energy conversion technologies could be made; and this represents yet another energy service supply chain.

Third, for each particular energy service demand, the level of fuel consumption depends heavily on the particular energy service supply chain which supplies that demand. For example, it is usual to define thermal comfort requirements in terms of internal temperatures. Determination of a specific internal temperature, together with a knowledge of the thermal characteristics of the dwelling and the thermal efficiency of the heat conversion equipment, allows us to determine the quantity of fuel required to satisfy that internal temperature requirement. If the internal temperature requirement is given, then the demand for fuels will be determined by the thermal characteristics of the dwelling and the technical characteristics of the conversion equipment. Each different energy service supply chain will allocate different levels of investment to the thermal infrastructure of the dwelling and to the conversion technologies. Clearly therefore each energy service supply chain will imply different levels of primary fuel consumption, and hence different levels of emission of greenhouse gases.

Finally, it is worth mentioning here that the question of defining energy services is not in itself straightforward. Actually we should not even regard internal temperatures as a fixed definition of thermal comfort levels because thermal comfort depends (for a given internal temperature) on the thermal insulation properties of the clothes a person is wearing. It also depends on the metabolic rate of the person, and this metabolic rate differs not only between individuals but also for each individual depending on their activity level. These considerations suggest that the provision of thermal comfort cannot be defined entirely through technical or economic parameters but includes cultural and behavioural elements.

Irrespective of these finer points, however, the provision of thermal comfort is very distinct from the provision of fuel supplies. The total demand for fuel supplies (and implicitly the total emissions of greenhouse gases when the fuels are burned) can differ widely between different energy service supply chains providing the same final demand, e.g. that for thermal comfort.

## 10.2  PRICE ELASTICITY, SUBSTITUTION AND MARKET STRUCTURE

What are the implications of this analysis for the issue of price elasticity? First, by definition, basic services such as thermal comfort, hot water and cooking (for instance) are likely to be very *inelastic* in demand. As the opening remarks in this chapter suggested, it is also true that *historically* the demand for primary and secondary fuels has been relatively inelastic. However, it does not follow that the low historical price elasticity in primary

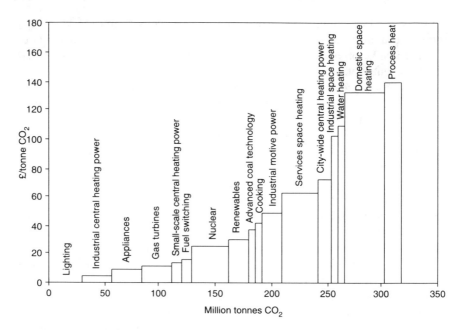

*Figure 10.3* Cost-effectiveness of $CO_2$ emission abatement options when seen from the investor's perspective

and secondary fuels is an inevitable consequence of the low elasticity of demand for basic energy services, for reasons which should by now have become obvious: primary and secondary fuel demand depends heavily on the particular structure of the energy service supply chains. The substitution of one energy service supply chain for another can result in principle in large reductions in demand for energy at no change in the price of fossil fuels.

The issue of substitution does, however, throw considerable light on the price elasticity of demand for fossil fuels. The most important consideration in determining price elasticities of demand for a good or service is the ease with which consumers can substitute another good or service that fulfils approximately the same function. The easier it is to substitute, the higher the elasticity.Thus, for example, it is *not* easy to substitute for basic energy services such as thermal comfort, and therefore we would expect the demand for such services to be price inelastic. Equally, however, the low historical price elasticity of demand for fuels suggests that – despite the existence of different energy service supply chains with radically different associated primary fuel demands – substitution between these different energy service supply chains has not been easy.

It is well documented in the literature (Johansson *et al.* 1989; Grubb 1990; Jochem and Gruber 1990; Jackson and Jacobs 1991; Jackson 1992) that there are a number of fundamental obstacles to energy efficiency improvements. In

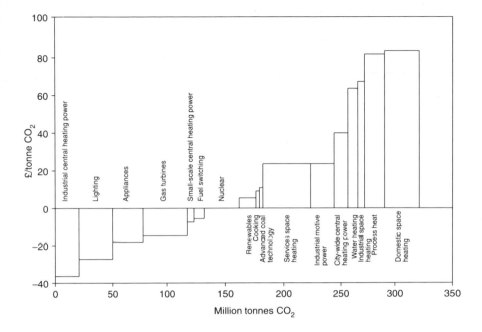

*Figure 10.4* Effects of a carbon tax on microeconomic analysis of $CO_2$ abatement options from the investor's perspective

particular, these obstacles include lack of awareness of energy efficiency measures, lack of information, lack of technical expertise, low availability of technologies, capital constraints, separation of responsibility for costs from benefits (the so-called 'tenant–landlord problem' – Jackson 1992), unfavourability of tariff structures and taxation policies, and the structure and regulation of the fuel supply industries. These obstacles have the result that households typically require very high rates of return before they will invest in energy-saving technologies. Essentially, these market barriers can be thought of as obstacles to substitution between different energy service supply chains. By restricting substitution between fuel-intensive supply chains and fuel-efficient supply chains, these obstacles have the effect of reducing the potential for implementation of cost-effective energy efficiency measures and thereby raising the demand for primary and secondary fuels.

To carry the analysis further, the structure of the energy services market can be characterized in terms of a correspondence between economic actors and energy service supply chains. In each particular market structure, different economic actors are implicated in investments in different parts of the energy service supply chain. Conversely, the set of economic actors investing in each energy service supply chain is determined by a number of economic and institutional factors which in their entirety might be called the structure of the market.

To take a specific example, traditional energy markets are characterized by energy service supply chains in which public-sector monopolistic utilities (now privatized) have invested in the supply and distribution of primary and secondary fuel whilst private agents (manufacturing companies in the industrial sector and individuals in the domestic sector) have invested in energy conversion technology and improvements in the thermal structure of buildings. The utilities have had a major economic interest in keeping the level and growth of energy use as high as possible. This remains true after privatization, although there is increasing pressure for energy efficiency measures from the industry regulators.

The economic implications of market structure arise in particular because different kinds of investor bring different profitability requirements to their economic decision-making. One way of expressing these profitability require-ments is in terms of the discount rate or required rate of return of different investors. The old public-sector utilities had rates of return imposed by central government which approach the social discount rate – traditionally some-where between 5 and 8 per cent. Privatized utilities are likely to have slightly higher required rates of return on capital. In contrast, the required rates of return by private companies for investment in insulation and other energy-saving schemes have varied considerably but can be as high as 30 or 40 per cent. There is evidence that the effective rates of return required by individual consumers are considerably higher even than this (Chernoff 1983; Meier and Whittier 1983).

If the effect of market structure is to allocate specific investors to specific investments within the energy service supply chains, then the economic effect of market structure will be to impose different profitability criteria – different rates of return – on the constituent parts of each energy service supply chain. Thus, investments occurring at different parts of the energy service supply network are not necessarily comparable on an equal footing, and certain energy service supply chains will be preferred over others simply because of the different profitability requirements associated with the different invest-ments in each chain.

The effect of this mapping of investors onto investments in the energy services supply network can be very significant as the following analysis shows.

## 10.3 THE INVESTOR'S PERSPECTIVE: RE-ORIENTING MICROECONOMIC ANALYSIS

In Figure 10.1, different technological options for reducing greenhouse gas emissions were ranked using a common (10 per cent) discount rate applied to the projects. This examination reflects the consensus view of energy efficiency investments under a microeconomic analysis: some investments in energy efficiency are already more cost effective than investment in conventional energy supply even at current energy prices. In Figure 10.2, the effects of a carbon tax deemed necessary under a macroeconomic analysis to reach the Toronto target (Barker and Lewney 1991) were applied to the microeconomic analysis. The microeconomic analysis suggested that this level of taxation would achieve considerably more reduction than the Toronto target.

These figures illustrate very clearly the apparent conflicts between macroeconomic and microeconomic analyses, but it can also be shown why this conflict might arise.

The market structure produces a correspondence between investors and technologies within the energy services supply network, and in so doing apportions different required rates of return to different kinds of technological investments within the network. Using rates of return applicable to different investors under the structure of the existing energy market in the UK, a further analysis was carried out (Jackson 1992) to examine the economic effect of the market mapping of investors onto technological options. Figure 10.3 illustrates the 'investor's perspective' of the same technological options analysed in Figure 10.1. The rates of return on utility electricity supply options were assumed to remain at 10 per cent. Rates of return on industrial investments (industrial combined heat and power, and improved efficiency) were assumed to be higher, however, depending on the kind of investment, to reflect corporate required rates of return in the region of 25–40 per cent. Rates of return for investments by domestic consumers were assumed to reflect the very high effective rates of return applied by these consumers.

In sharp contrast to the previous analysis, *none* of the investments which were already cost effective under the 10 per cent discount rate assumptions look economic under the conditions appropriate to the existing market structure. All of them are perceived under the investor's perspective in the current energy market structure as more expensive than the conventional fuel supply option. This is because different profitability requirements have now been imposed on these different technological options, as a result of the market structure.

What is the effect of an imposed carbon tax under these assumptions? Interestingly, the application of the same level of carbon tax used in the previous analysis (Figure 10.2) now reveals (Figure 10.4) cost-effective emission reductions amounting approximately to a 20 per cent reduction on current levels, roughly in line with the macroeconomic analysis.

Although these results are subject to a number of caveats where exact costs are concerned, and the analysis here must therefore be considered as purely illustrative, the lessons are nonetheless clear. Market structure affects the real economic choices which are made between technologies, because it 'maps' different investors onto different technological options and thereby allocates different profitability requirements to those options. It is this investor's perspective which determines actual transactions in the real world. Under the structure of the existing energy market in the UK, the map is such that technological options which would appear to be socially optimal under a low common discount rate analysis fail to be implemented because of very high effective discount rates operating at that level of investment in the energy services network. Consequently, very high tax rates are required in order to reduce the demand for energy. Although generated through an essentially microeconomic analysis, this accords closely with the conclusions from macroeconomic analyses. The next question is: what can be done about this?

## 10.4 STRUCTURAL CHANGE: THE KEY TO GREATER ENERGY SAVING

Different technological investment options are accorded different financial criteria according to the map imposed by the market structure in energy. In very broad terms, this market structure can be thought of as being determined by a wide variety of different factors including of course regulatory frameworks, tariff structures, ownership patterns, price regulation formulae and the structure of energy institutions. These factors in themselves are often influenced by 'softer' institutional and social factors such as historical preference, received wisdom, corporate practice and so on, as well as by less easily quantifiable but nevertheless economically significant factors like the availability of information and expertise. In other words, almost all of those factors which have frequently been identified as market barriers to the implementation of energy efficiency have a bearing on the structure of the energy market, and therefore on the map which allocates specific profitability criteria to specific technological options. There is also the factor of market uncertainty , i.e. the private sector tends to require higher discount rates than the government because it has less ability to determine the future economic environment.

Do all these factors have to be accepted as inevitable and immutable features of the energy market?

Obviously, the answer to this question is crucial. If the answer is to the effect that all of these factors are inevitable consequences of the operation of a perfect market in energy services, then there are no means of altering market structure in such a way as to remove impediments to energy efficiency improvements; and consequently no changes can be expected in the investment map determined by that structure. In this case, it will have to be accepted that the simple microeconomic analysis of technological preferences on the basis of a common social discount rate has no counterpart in the real world: it relates only to an unattainable ideal. As a corollary, there must in fact be some real economic factors (transaction costs) which can be identified to account for the differences between the apparent social preferences and the actual investor preferences, and these transaction costs must be the reason why the apparent social preferences are simply misguided.

On the other hand, if it is accepted that there are certain historical and institutional contingencies in the existing market structure, then this gives some encouragement to seek out opportunities to alter those contingent factors in such a way as to move investor preferences closer to the social preferences, and thereby unlock the vast apparent potential for improvement in energy efficiency. In other words, there is the possibility that certain kinds of broad structural changes in the market can increase the price elasticity of fossil fuel demand by easing the substitution of more efficient energy service supply chains. Such changes might include new regulatory requirements for buildings and appliances; changes in price regulation formulae; changes in ownership structure; the availability of innovative financing arrangements; improved awareness and education and so on.

In fact, a cursory overview of the possibilities immediately persuades us that there are very real opportunities for such change. For instance, the existing market structure maps private consumers onto investments in improved energy efficiency in the domestic sector (such as domestic appliances and lights). This mapping immediately allocates higher required rates of return for these energy service options, and obscures (Figure 10.4) the benefits which are apparent from the social perspective (Figure 10.1). But this is to some extent a contingent factor arising from the historical development of the fuel supply network. There is no *a priori* reason why energy utilities should not invest capital in energy efficiency except that, under the historical structure of the market, price regulation formulae have prevented them recovering the costs of such investments from consumers. A change in price regulation could free up low-cost capital for energy efficiency investments. This would have the effect of reallocating investors within the market structure map and radically altering the economic preferences between different energy service supply chains. Energy efficiency investments would once more be comparable with energy supply options on the basis of an equal rate of return, and the new energy structure will better reflect socially optimal choices.

Equally there are a number of other broadly structural changes which might be made, with the same effect. Energy efficiency standards in appliances, for example, have the effect of allocating industrial capital to the manufacture of improved energy conversion technologies. Building regulations allocate industrial capital to investment in the thermal structure of dwellings. These regulatory measures force capital into sectors of the energy services supply network which have been subject to over-high discount rates from a social point of view and offset the bias of the discount rate structure towards investments in fuel supply. There can also be cost advantages to be gained through implementing change at the design stage rather than in *post hoc* improvement.

## 10.5 CONCLUSIONS

In summary, therefore, the ability to facilitate substitution between energy service supply chains with different associated fuel demands suggests the possibility of reducing energy demand by removing market imperfections. Clearly, this analysis has important repercussions for macroeconomic modellers because of their critical reliance on reliable long-term price elasticity parameters. If such models are accurately to identify cost-effective solutions to the problem of greenhouse gas emission reduction, it will be important not to rely solely on the use of parameters which only reflect price-dependent responses. Rather it will be necessary to develop models capable of reflecting structural changes in the market.

A number of such structural changes have been identified in the preceding discussion. These include the introduction of appliance efficiency standards, improvement of energy efficiency standards in buildings, and changes in price regulation formulae to allow the flow of 'low-cost' capital into energy efficiency investments. This chapter has argued that the impact of such changes could be significant in improving the efficiency with which energy is consumed by the final user.

Improved market efficiency therefore offers the possibility of substitution to more efficient energy service supply chains and thereby of reduced fuel consumption, irrespective of fuel price changes. But one of the lessons of this chapter has been that price response and market structure are not unrelated aspects of the economy. Changes in market structure are likely to affect price responses. Equally, over the longer term, price changes are likely to have an impact on market structure. Both structural changes and price incentives are likely to be necessary for a cost-effective emission reduction strategy. In particular, of course, there is a role for price incentives in offsetting the 'rebound' or responding effect of improved energy efficiency (Brookes 1990, 1992; Grubb 1990, 1992). But the associated carbon taxes within such a strategy are likely to be significantly lower than those associated with a strategy solely reliant on price responses, and the associated economic disruption will be considerably less.

Chapter 11

# Rethinking the use of energy elasticities

*Stefan P. Schleicher*

the future of energy is much more a matter of choice than of prediction.
Goldemberg *et al.* (1988)

**ABSTRACT**

Energy elasticities seem to be the dominating tool for forecasting energy demand. This chapter explores the microeconomic foundations of energy elasticities and their special problems for econometric estimation. A look into the technological structure of the energy sector, however, suggests that energy elasticities may be a dangerous shortcut for drawing conclusions about long-term developments for energy demand.

An analysis of the forecasting properties of microeconomic energy demand models with econometrically estimated parameters reveals theoretical deficiencies, instability of the estimated parameters and poor forecasting quality over longer forecasting periods. This class of forecasting models is compared with technology-oriented structural models of the energy sector. The main emphasis in these models is given to the identification of technological options for improving the efficiency of the transformation of primary energy to end-use energy and useful energy and the substitution of useful energy and capital for obtaining specific energy services. Finally a statistical methodology is proposed which combines the two approaches taking into account the relative merits of the two types of models depending on the forecast horizon.

## INTRODUCTION

Energy elasticities seem to be a prerequisite for all kinds of analyses related to the energy sector of an economy. Major failures to predict the events on the energy markets of the last two decades and many implausible scenarios for the next two decades produced by conventional energy models offer at least an incentive to rethink the current practices in the use of energy elasticities. The basic theme of this chapter is the proposition that an evolution of paradigms in our understanding of the energy sector of an economy also requires an evolution of methodologies applied to analyse energy systems.

There has been a fairly dramatic change in the focus of energy policy over the past two decades. The early 1970s were marked by the potential threat of energy shortages caused either by the monopoly power of cartels like the OPEC or the visions of resource depletion by the Club of Rome. The Brundtland Report *Our Common Future* of the World Commission for Economic Development (WCED 1987) formulated *sustainable economic development* as the long-term goal for economic policy. This aim is closely linked with the use of energy and the related problems of exhaustible resources and environmental problems, including global warming. These problems suggest a fundamental redesign of the global energy system.

The chapter starts with some empirical evidence about energy elasticities and looks into the emerging new paradigms for analysing energy systems. It continues by confronting conventional energy demand models with the more structurally oriented approaches in order to identify the limits of elasticity-based energy demand analysis. Finally suggestions are presented for improving the energy–economy link in macroeconomic models and some simulation results are provided for high energy price policies.

## 11.1 SOME EMPIRICAL EVIDENCE ABOUT ENERGY ELASTICITIES

Spurred by the oil price shocks in late 1973 and during the period 1979–80 a lot of attention was devoted to the analysis of energy demand. Numerous attempts were made to estimate price and income elasticities from time-series and cross-section samples. As a representative example of the problems encountered when microeconomic demand analysis is applied to energy data we present some results for Austria (Wohlgemuth 1992).

Figure 11.1 shows the final consumption of energy for Austria. Figure 11.2 contains for the same sample range real GDP and real energy price data. Visual comparison of these graphs suggests a pronounced impact of the energy price hikes on energy demand and a substantial decoupling of energy demand from real economic activity.

Specifying a log-linear demand model with partial adjustment we obtain the short-run and long-run income and price elasticites reported in Figures 11.3 and 11.4. The estimated coefficients represent moving window regressions over eleven years. Thus the estimates for 1977 are based on a sample ranging from 1967 to 1977 and the estimates for 1989 use data from 1979 to 1989.

As expected the long-run elasticities are larger than the short-run values. Striking, however, is the high sensitivity of the estimates with respect to variations of the sample period. A lot of experiments with other functional forms and improved dynamic specifications could not improve these obvious deficiencies of the estimated elasticities.

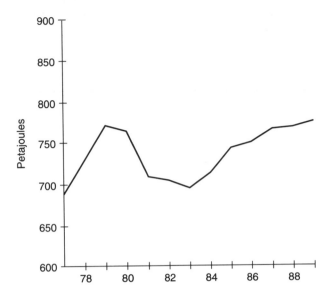

*Figure 11.1* Final energy consumption

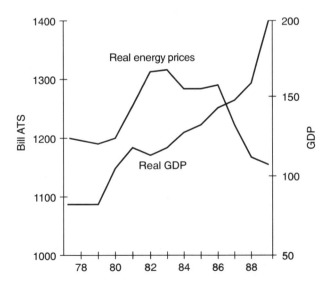

*Figure 11.2* Real GDP and real energy prices

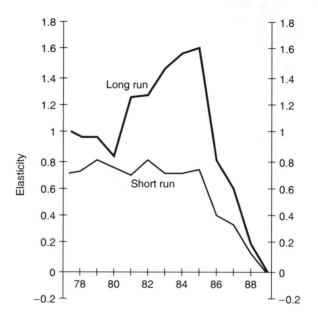

*Figure 11.3* Estimated income elasticities

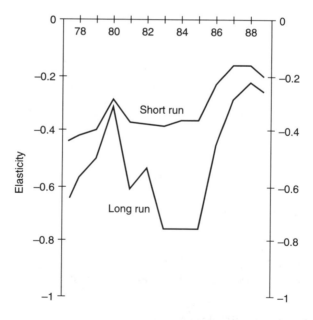

*Figure 11.4* Estimated price elasticities

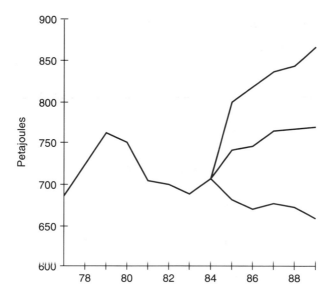

*Figure 11.5* Prediction bounds (two standard deviations) of one to five year *ex ante* forecasts

The time paths of the estimated elasticities suggest that, during the period of high energy prices, the absolute value of both price and income elasticities increased, but they sharply declined as real energy prices fell to pre-OPEC levels. Although these results question the assumption of structural stability of the postulated data-generating process we gain at least some insight into the kind of parameter variation that occurred within the sample period.

More disturbing are the results reported in Figure 11.5 which show the simulated forecasting bounds for an *ex ante* forecast of one to five years from 1984. The forecasting range is calculated for twice the simulated standard deviation of the prediction error. The empirical evidence of this experiment suggests that the forecasting power of this type of energy demand model is very limited.

## 11.2  EVOLUTION OF PARADIGMS FOR ANALYSING ENERGY SYSTEMS

There has been an evolution of the theoretical concepts used for analysing the energy sector of an economy over the last two decades. We put forward the hypothesis that the emerging new understanding of the structure of our energy systems requires a modification of our conception of causal relationships and an adjustment of methodologies.

### 11.2.1  The paradigm of abundant energy

Up to the first oil price shock cheap and abundant energy flows were widely considered as a prerequisite for economic development. The current energy structures in most industrialized countries, notably the United States, Canada and Eastern Europe, reflect this paradigm of abundant energy. International comparisons in addition reveal that energy intensities correlate highly negatively with energy prices.

### 11.2.2  The microeconomic energy paradigm

The first oil price shock in 1973–4 and the second oil price shock in 1979–80 introduced, at least into the Western industrial countries, least-cost concepts for finding the optimal mix of energy with other factors of production. One result of this microeconomic paradigm of energy use is the mounting evidence that current energy systems do not meet the criteria of cost-effectiveness. Another result is the policy recommendation that, even at current energy prices, marginal investment efforts concentrate on improving the end-use delivery of services rather than investing in new generation technologies. This concept of integrated resource planning (IRP) has been gaining increased attention in efforts to restructure the current energy systems.

### 11.2.3  The high energy efficiency paradigm

The 1980s saw the emergence of a new energy perspective, which may be termed a paradigm of high energy efficiency, as part of the process of sustainable economic development recommended by the report *Our Common Future* of the World Commission for Environment and Development (1987). This innovative concept of economic development requires that current economic actions must not impair the economic options of future generations, and therefore energy systems must be redesigned to reduce the use of exhaustible energy resources and limit emissions. An obvious consequence for energy policy is the need to move towards high energy efficiency. This in turn requires changes in economic incentives, particularly in the price system.

### 11.2.4  Investigating the technical structure of an energy system

A focus on the technical efficiency of energy systems leads to a more careful analysis of the structure of the energy sector of an economy which devotes more attention to the complex conversion processes of energy flows and distinguishes between *energy services* and *energy flows*.

Energy enters an economy as primary energy $E$ in the form of coal, crude oil, natural gas, uranium, hydropower, biomass and other energy resources.

The transformation system converts primary energy to energy for final consumption or end-use energy $F$ in the form of coal products, gas, oil products, electricity and heat. Conversion and distribution losses are an indicator of the efficiency of the transformation system. The application system in households (appliances, cars) and industries (motors, heaters) converts end-use energy to useful energy $U$. Application losses are an indicator of the efficiency of the application system. Primary energy, end-use energy and useful energy are energy flows usually measured in thermal equivalents like joules, oil equivalents or coal equivalents. In Austria, for example, out of 100 units of primary energy only 72 are available as end-use energy and only about 40 serve as useful energy. The missing 60 energy units indicate the technical potential for improving the efficiency of the energy system. The ultimate aim of an energy system is to provide energy services $S$. These may be thermal services, such as providing a certain amount of heated space for residential use, mechanical services, like mobility of persons or commodities in a transport system, or chemical services in the production process of a chemical fibre.

Energy services cannot be measured as energy flows. Distinguishing between energy flows and energy services leads to a number of important conclusions.

• The relevant indicators to measure the contribution of the energy sector to economic wealth are energy services rather than energy flows. Energy flows are at best a proxy indicator of economic development.
• There is in most cases a wide range of possible substitutions between energy flows, capital and labour to provide the amount of energy services needed.
• Measures to promote energy efficiency should as far as possible be directed towards energy services rather than energy flows.
• The mix of energy flows and other factors of production to provide energy services depends in a market economy on the relative prices of energy flows and the other factors.
• Energy statistics, unfortunately, do not yet reflect this distinction between energy flows and energy services. It is rather difficult to obtain data on useful energy and even more difficult to obtain information about energy services.

## 11.3 ANALYTICAL STRUCTURE OF AN ENERGY SYSTEM

### 11.3.1 Basic variables

We introduce an analytical framework for the specification of the fundamental relationships between energy flows and energy services. The following variables are used: $S$, energy services; $U$, useful energy; $F$, final consumption (end-use) energy; $E$, primary energy; $K$, capital; $N$, labour.

## 11.3.2  Energy services

Energy services are composed of various types, e.g. $S_t$, thermal energy services; $S_m$, mechanical energy services; $S_c$, chemical energy services; $S_o$, other energy services. Accordingly the index set $i$ of types of energy services is described by

$$i \in \{t, m, c, o\}$$

## 11.3.3  Energy flows

Primary energy flows typically comprise $E_c$, coal; $E_o$, crude oil; $E_g$, natural gas; $E_w$, hydropower; $E_n$, nuclear power; $E_r$, renewable energy (e.g. biomass, geothermal, solar). The index set $l$ of primary energy flows is given by

$$l \in \{c, o, g, w, n, r\}$$

Final consumption or end-use energy may be distinguished by $F_c$, coal products; $F_o$, oil products; $F_g$, gas; $F_e$, electricity; $F_h$, heat. Thus the index set $k$ of end-use energy flows is determined by

$$k \in \{c, o, g, e, h\}$$

Useful energy may be partitioned into $U_l$, low temperature useful energy; $U_h$, high temperature useful energy; $U_m$, mechanical useful energy; $U_o$, other useful energy. The corresponding index set $j$ is

$$j \in \{l, h, m, o\}$$

## 11.3.4  Energy conversion technologies

Every energy system converts primary energy to end-use energy, useful energy and finally energy services. Three crucial technologies determine the amount of energy services obtained from a unit of primary energy:

$T^f$  technologies for transforming primary energy to end-use energy, i.e. technologies of the transformation system;

$T^u$  technologies for transforming end-use energy to useful energy, i.e. technologies of the application system;

$T^s$  technologies for transforming useful energy to energy services, i.e. technologies of the service system.

## 11.3.5  Fundamental technological relationships

The output of these technologies is determined mainly by the inputs of energy flows and capital. In a few cases the amount of labour used may be relevant too.

Thus energy services $S$ obtained from useful energy $U$ depend on the selected technology $T^s$ of the service system and the amount of capital $K^s$ and labour $N^s$ provided for these services:

$$S = T^s(U, K^s, N^s) \qquad (11.1)$$

Similarly the technological relation for the application system $T^u$ describing the conversion of end-use energy $F$ to useful energy $U$ can be represented by

$$U = T^u(F, K^u, N^u) \qquad (11.2)$$

Finally the transformation system technology $T^f$ determines the conversion of primary energy $E$ to end-use energy $F$:

$$F = T^f(E, K^f, N^f) \qquad (11.3)$$

### 11.3.6 Some useful technological measures

These technological relations serve to develop some technological measures which characterize the technology of an energy system.

A first group of measures is based on the concept of *mass efficiency*. Omitting indices for types of energy flows and services we define mass efficiency for the transformation system by

$$e^F = F / E \qquad (11.4a)$$

for the application system by

$$e^U = U / F \qquad (11.4b)$$

and for the service system by

$$e^S = S / U \qquad (11.4c)$$

Overall mass efficiency may be defined both for useful energy

$$e^{UE} = U / E \qquad (11.5a)$$

and for energy services

$$e^{SE} = S / E \qquad (11.5b)$$

Substituting the fundamental technological equations (11.1)–(11.3) into (11.5) we obtain

$$e^{UE} = e^{SE}(T^f, T^u, K^f, K^u, N^f, N^u) \qquad (11.6a)$$

and

$$e^{SE} = e^{SE}(T^f, T^u, T^s, K^f, K^u, K^s, N^f, N^u, N^s) \qquad (11.6b)$$

These measures of overall energy mass efficiency (11.6) reveal the influence of capital and labour and the corresponding technologies in all stages of energy conversion.

A second group of efficiency measures is of special relevance for thermal conversion processes and is based on either the concept of *exergy* or the related concept of *entropy*. Two energy flows (e.g. low temperature heat and electricity) with the same energy content (e.g. measured in joules) may nevertheless have a different quality (e.g. measured by their ability to provide mechanical work).

A third group of measures may describe the *environmental impact* of the energy system by evaluating the content of renewable energy in the primary energy mix and the intensity of emissions (e.g. $CO_2$) with respect to a unit of energy services or a unit of energy flows.

## 11.4  CONVENTIONAL ENERGY DEMAND MODELS RECONSIDERED

The analytical framework of an energy system outlined in the previous section is a very useful tool in order to obtain a better understanding of many difficulties related to conventional energy demand models.

### 11.4.1  Implicit assumptions about time invariance

A first remark concerns the inherent reduced form structure of simple demand specifications since the complex conversion from primary energy to energy services is just lumped into the assumption of a given and time-invariant technology. If energy is demanded by a consumer then the implicit assumption of invariant preferences with respect to energy services and other items in the bundle of consumer goods has to be made. These assumptions of time-invariant technologies and preferences can only marginally be relaxed by introducing time-dependent variables.

### 11.4.2  Limited empirical evidence of optimizing behaviour

A second remark concerns the postulated optimizing behaviour of neoclassical microeconomic analysis. Energy costs in industrialized economies on the aggregate level comprise only 2–4 per cent of production costs. The share of energy costs is considerably higher in the basic industries which typically contribute less than 20 per cent to industrial GDP but require about three-quarters of industrial energy consumption. For households, expenses for energy are typically less than 10 per cent of their consumer budget. These comparatively low shares of energy costs can be traced as a main reason why we observe a large potential for energy savings which would even reduce energy costs for the individual decision-maker. In many cases, however, optimizing behaviour faces institutional barriers. Electric utilities prevent companies from applying cogeneration technologies by offering unattractive rates for surplus electricity. Households may want to reduce their heating bills by improving the thermal quality of an apartment but face problems if the tenant is different from the owner.

### 11.4.3  Relevance of the time horizon for decision-making

This leads to a third remark which emphasizes the important role of the time horizon in energy decisions. In the very short run, e.g. in the case of predicting electricity demand in a grid for the next hour, prices and income will hardly be important. Cross-section studies which investigate the reactions of a specific phenomenon, e.g. a change in energy prices, seem to be appropriate for conventional demand analysis if an appropriate reaction time is allowed for.

### 11.4.4  Rethinking causalities

The fourth remark challenges the causality structure of conventional energy demand models. Rather than looking at the effect of prices and income on a given structure of energy supply and demand, the new approach seeks to devise a system of economic incentives which would lead to a desired structure of the energy system. Although it is in striking contrast to conventional analytical methods, this new approach is gaining increasing attention for long-run decisions.

This line of argumentation stresses the wide range of technical substitution opportunities of energy by capital. In energy-intensive countries, as the United States and Eastern Europe, the same energy services can be provided with available technologies by reducing primary energy flows by a factor of 10. In Western Europe this reduction factor is approximately 5. Aspects of sustainability which impose limits to the use of exhaustible resources and to the emissions into the natural resources air, water and soil define the set of feasible energy structures.

The validity of this argumentation rests on the proposition that it is much easier in the long run to predict required energy services, the corresponding technologies and as a consequence the resulting energy flows which together meet certain sustainability constraints than to speculate about required energy flows without explicitly considering the complex structure of an energy system.

In a second step this approach requires the adjustment of the economic incentive system in order to induce decisions which meet the desired energy structures. The level of energy prices in general will have to be raised to provide incentives for switching to energy-efficient technologies. Prices for renewable energy sources will have to be lower than for exhaustible resources. Prices for final energy consumption will also have to reflect the impact on the environment and their exergy content. If markets are not able to process this information adjustments by selective taxes will have to be made.

A wide range of other policy instruments is available to provide incentives for restructuring an energy system towards the desired paths. Permits for emissions, e.g. $CO_2$, can be issued and traded at regional, national and international levels. Funds can be created which recycle the revenues of energy taxes by supporting the propagation of efficient energy technologies. Technical standards, e.g. for the average fleet fuel consumption of cars, may be considered.

## 11.5 LINKING THE ENERGY SECTOR TO A MACROECONOMIC MODEL

The structural approach in the analysis of an energy system proposed in Section 11.4 also reveals additional links between the energy sector and other sectors in an economy which have been rather neglected in conventional energy demand analysis.

There are a number of transmission channels for the interaction between energy and the other components of a macroeconomic model. We start from the basic aggregate supply–demand relationship relating imports $M$, gross domestic product $Q$, private consumption $C$, public consumption $G$, investment $I$ and exports $X$:

$$M + Q = C + G + I + X \tag{11.7}$$

We split this relationship into its energy and non-energy components:

$$M^n + M^e + Q^n + Q^e = C^n + C^e + G + I + X^n + X^e \tag{11.8}$$

We observe that (11.8) holds both for current values and volumes. Current values and volumes of these variables determine the implicit price index of the items which is denoted by a leading letter P (for price) in the variable name.

The following balance equation for energy states that supply has a domestic gross output $\bar{Q}^e$ component (note that $Q^e$ in equation (11.8) above is net output) and import $M^e$ component which is matched by demand of consumers $C^e$, demand by the domestic production sector $D^e$ and exports of energy $X^e$:

$$M^e + \bar{Q}^e = C^e + D^e + X^e \tag{11.9}$$

The demand components for private non-energy consumption $C^n$, public consumption $G$, fixed investment and non-energy imports $M^n$ are determined by the usual specifications at constant prices. Both the specification for fixed investment, labour employed and the price index of net national non-energy income follow from a postulated Cobb–Douglas production function with constant returns to scale.

The energy components are linked with the non-energy components via both flow and price relationships. Following the arguments outlined in Section 11.4 we postulate for both energy demand for private consumption $C^e$

and energy demand for production $D^e$ that the corresponding not directly observable services $S^c$ and $S^q$ are determined by energy flows and non-energy capital stock $K^c$ and $K^q$, respectively:

$$S^c = S^c(C^e, K^c) \qquad\qquad (11.10a)$$

$$S^q = S^q(Q^e, K^q) \qquad\qquad (11.10b)$$

In addition we assume that there is a range of substitution between energy flows and capital stock which depends mainly on the time span allowed for substitution.

A number of important substitution relationships can be observed.

- In the production sector capital and labour can be substituted at least to some extent depending on relative factor prices.
- Energy flows for consumption $C^e$ can be substituted by increasing the corresponding capital stock of the energy application system of the households (e.g. the efficiency appliances).
- Energy flows for production $D^e$ can also be substituted by changing the capital stock of production equipment (e.g. by using more energy-efficient technologies).

Finally we specify the price linkages between energy and non-energy sectors. Import prices of energy $PM^e$ and non-energy $PM^n$ determine together with the domestic prices $PQ^e$ and $PQ^n$ the aggregate price levels of energy products $PV^e$ and non-energy products $PV^n$, which again affect the various demand components.

## 11.6 AN APPLICATION: SIMULATION OF HIGH ENERGY PRICE POLICIES

### 11.6.1 Linking the energy sector to a macroeconometric model for Austria

We apply the concept for the energy–economy linkage outlined in the previous section to a macro model for Austria. The basic idea of this linkage is to apply the energy model outlined in Section 11.4 to evaluate the technical potential for substituting energy flows by capital. Thus, for example, it is estimated what amount of capital would be needed to substitute a certain amount of energy for space heating in households or how much additional capital would be required to switch from the technology of a conventional thermal plant for electricity generation to a unit for combined heat and power generation. Both examples demonstrate that the energy model implicitly reveals information about the marginal elasticity of substitution between energy and capital for various energy services. This energy model is complemented with a fairly standard macro model with econometrically estimated parameters in order to evaluate the macroeconomic effects of some emission reduction policies. Detailed information about these models is contained in Glueck and Schleicher (1994).

These simulations, in addition to empirical findings, revealed a remarkable result: at the margin there is a considerable amount of investment opportunity both for generating and applying energy, indicating that the savings in energy or the gain in energy efficiency would provide the same services by the new technology for no higher costs than by the old technology. This means, however, that the elasticity for substitution of energy by capital is at least one. As a conservative estimate we used this estimate for our simulations with the macro model.

The macro model contains econometrically estimated relationships only for non-energy flows. However, a number of important transmission links between the energy and non-energy sectors are included. Households are assumed to substitute energy through an improved thermal quality of the buildings. Assumptions are made concerning what amount of investment will be devoted to improvement in the thermal quality of buildings. The energy model then estimates the amount of energy saved and the amount of capital needed to implement such an investment. The same linkage is used in the production sector to evaluate, for example, the effects of cogeneration technologies both on the reduction of primary energy flows and on the demand for additional capital in order to implement such a technical change. It is further assumed that the incentives for these new technologies stem from two sources: either higher relative energy prices caused by a hike of energy taxes or the availability of an energy efficiency fund or both.

We want to demonstrate by these specifications of the transmission mechanism of higher energy prices that instead of an explicit price elasticity for energy we need to collect information about the rate of substitution between energy and capital in the provision of energy services. In addition we have to check the potential for institutional barriers if an incentive is given for a change of technologies either by a price signal or the availability of subsidies. As a consequence we obtain reactions both for the demand for energy and the demand for additional capital. These numbers reflect implicit elasticities and are based on sound technological and institutional information.

In a number of simulation experiments we want to check the operational aspects of the proposed theoretical concepts. In particular we went to investigate the macroeconomic effects of high energy price policies and alternative recycling schemes for energy taxes.

### 11.6.2 Maintained high price policy of OPEC

Energy prices peaked in 1985 and dropped about 50 per cent afterwards because of the loss of power of the OPEC cartel. We assume in our first simulation that OPEC was able to maintain the oil price level at 1985 values for five more years. As a consequence all other energy sources would adjust to a generally higher energy price level. This OPEC tax scenario would lead to an increase in the general price level of about 5 per cent accompanied by a slight decline of GDP and a loss of about 6,000 jobs in five years.

### 11.6.3 Domestic energy import tax with income tax compensation

The next scenario maintains the same high energy prices for imported energy with a special energy import tax. The annual yield of this tax at current low international energy prices is about 30 billion Austrian schillings per year. We use these revenues from the energy tax to reduce income-based taxes which are paid by employers, e.g. social security contributions. Thus the basic idea of this tax shift scenario is a shift in the tax base from income to resource use. This shift results in a change in relative factor prices which makes labour cheaper in relation to capital. The result of this scenario is disappointing at least in the framework of the model used since the factor substitution effects expected are almost negligible.

### 11.6.4 Energy efficiency fund for energy demand management

Given the unsatisfactory results of the income tax compensation approach, in the next scenario the revenues of the energy import tax are used to stimulate energy conservation both in households and in companies. We propose that the additional tax revenues are used in a fund for improving energy efficiency. Thus special programmes to improve the energy quality of buildings and equipment could be launched. Our simulations assume that the energy tax revenues are split between households and companies. Estimates have to be made about the potential-energy saving effect and the impact on investment and non-energy consumption.

A conservative estimate drawn from various pilot projects leads to the conclusion that the energy conservation investments would lead to an annual reduction in energy flows of 15 per cent. There is also plenty of evidence that at least at the margin an energy unit saved is not more expensive than an energy unit consumed. We therefore assume that the amount of energy costs saved is used for investments in buildings and equipment with households and with companies. Thus the revenues of the energy fund are sufficient to maintain a 15 per cent reduction in energy flows without reducing the related energy services.

This demand management scenario will generate over the first five years between 10,000 and 26,000 additional jobs and will have a strong-short term impact on real GDP.

### 11.6.5 Energy fund for integrated energy resource management

We modify the previous scenario of an energy fund by spending the revenues not only on energy efficiency projects on the demand side but also on supply-side measures. These activities would propagate the utilization of renewable energy resources. A typical example would be the use of biomass in high efficiency technologies, e.g. by converting biomass to gas which is used in cogeneration technologies together with heat pumps. These policies would save imported fossil fuels and would increase the efficiency of energy supply.

Our simulations indicate that this integrated resource management scenario will generate between 20,000 and 40,000 new jobs over the first five years. The impact of the policy is mainly the substitution of imported energy by domestic renewable resources. Thus the substitution of energy flows is smaller than in the previous scenario.

### 11.7 SOME TENTATIVE CONCLUSIONS

Given the fundamental changes in energy markets over the last two decades, from the oil price shocks to deregulation activities, it is not surprising that conventional energy demand models are of very limited use.

For long-run analyses the use of models which emphasize the technological structure of the energy system is highly desirable. The choice of technologies which meet specified sustainability goals and provide the desired energy services seems to be the first step necessary for long-run energy projection. In a second step an adjustment of the economic incentive systems is made to promote the desired technological restructuring process.

This perspective on the energy system also reveals new links to the other sectors of an economy by emphasizing the demand effects caused by substituting energy flows by capital without reducing energy services and without increasing at least at the margin energy costs of consumers and firms.

In addition our simulations emphasize the need to use other instruments as well as energy prices to induce technological adjustments. The results suggest that raising energy prices by energy taxes is not sufficient to yield the desired restructuring of our energy systems because of low reaction speeds and institutional barriers. In production, for example, energy costs are on average less than 3 per cent of the value of gross production. Therefore reducing the use of labour and capital has in most production sectors a higher priority than reducing the use of energy.

Nevertheless high energy prices are important to signal the implementation of energy-efficient technologies. The main reason for raising energy prices, however, seems to be to obtain the funding for an active technology policy for promoting energy technologies via an energy efficiency fund which is financed by the revenues of a moderate energy tax. With a proper design such a policy could very well prove to be an all-winner strategy.

# Chapter 12

# Revisiting the costs of $CO_2$ abatement

*Paul Ekins*

## ABSTRACT

The economic analysis of global warming seeks to balance the costs of damage from or adaptation to it with the costs of preventing it. The costs of adaptation and damage have been estimated using techniques of environmental evaluation but are subject to a wide margin of uncertainty. The costs of prevention, principally by reducing the emissions of $CO_2$, have been estimated using different kinds of economic models, some of the results of which have suggested that very little abatement of carbon emissions is justified before the costs of abatement exceed the benefits of it in terms of forgone damage and adaptation costs. The chapter analyses the extent to which this conclusion is a function of the modelling assumptions and techniques used, rather than a likely practical outcome, with regard to the models' treatment of unemployed resources, revenue recycling, prior distortions in the economy due to the tax system and possible dynamic effects from the introduction of a carbon energy tax. It concludes that, with different and arguably more appropriate treatment of the above issues, especially when the secondary benefits of reducing $CO_2$ emissions are also taken into account, it is not clear that even substantial reductions in the use of fossil fuels will incur net costs if there is the prospect of even only moderate costs from global warming.

## INTRODUCTION

The economic approach to analysing global warming attempts to equate the marginal damage of greenhouse gas (GG) emissions to the marginal cost of reducing them, and so preventing the damage (Nordhaus 1991a; Cline 1992). Estimates of the costs of reducing GG emissions, in so far as they rely on increasing the price of fossil energy (use of which is the greatest cause of such emissions), are influenced by implicit or explicit elasticities of demand for energy. However, the way that reductions in energy demand are shown to affect output depends on a number of assumptions of the modelling process and the nature of the model used.

Chapter 1 gives a brief review of the nature and possible impacts of global warming; this chapter describes the costs associated with it and their relation to each other. The chapter continues with a discussion of how the costs of preventing global warming have been modelled, and gives some estimates of those costs from the literature. It then identifies several factors that may have exaggerated the costs in many of the studies and presents alternative estimates, also from the literature. Finally, the chapter draws some conclusions.

## 12.1  THE COSTS OF GLOBAL WARMING

The review of the science and possible impacts of global warming indicates the formidable difficulty of assessing the costs of the damage that will be associated with it. Yet, in order to arrive at an economic evaluation which can inform policy-making, two further categories of cost need to be assessed, corresponding to the two broad possible responses to the phenomenon: adaptation, and attempts at prevention.

### 12.1.1  Damage and adaptation

As stated above, it is unlikely that global warming resulting from a doubling of $CO_2$ equivalents can or will be prevented. The IPCC's central estimate of this warming is 2.5°C, and it is likely to be realized by 2050 under business-as-usual or 70–80 years later under IPCC's scenario of 'accelerated policies' to mitigate it (Cline 1992: 36). Nordhaus (1991a: 933), Cline (1992: 132) and Fankhauser (1992: 43, Table 15) estimate the 'damage' caused by this level of warming at 1–2 per cent of world GDP, but it is clear from their detailed figures that these costs might better be termed 'damage and adaptation' costs. Thus Table 12.1 reproduces Fankhauser's and Cline's 'damage' costs for doubling $CO_2$ equivalents and Cline's estimates for (much higher) long-term warming, from which it is clear that several entries (e.g. construction of dykes, electricity requirements and migration) actually represent the costs of adapting to climate change rather than the costs of damage associated with it.

This distinction is important because the costs of damage and adaptation are not independent. In particular, incurring costs of adaptation may reduce the costs of damage. Indeed it should do so by more than the cost of adaptation if adaptation is economically rational. Dykes are built to protect land from sea-level rise. Air-conditioning in hot climates may reduce death and morbidity from heat stress (a significant item in Cline's damage costs). With the exception of the figures on sea-level rise, it is not clear in any of the estimates how far it has been possible to take these trade-offs into account.

*Table 12.1* Estimates of annual damage and adaptation costs from global warming incurred by the US economy at 1990 scale (billions of 1990 dollars)

| | Fankhauser[a] (2 × CO$_2$ warming) | Cline | Cline (long term) |
|---|---|---|---|
| Agriculture | 8.4 | 17.5 | 95.0 |
| Forest loss | −2.0 | 3.3 | 7.0 |
| Species loss | 7.3 | 4.0+[b] | 16.0+ |
| Sea-level rise | | | 35.0 |
| Coastal defences | 0.2 | 1.2 | |
| Wetlands loss | 9.5 | 4.1 | |
| Drylands loss | 2.4 | 1.7 | |
| Electricity requirements | | 11.2 | 64.1 |
| Non-electric heating | | −1.3 | −4.0 |
| Human amenity[c] | 7.7 | + | + |
| Human life | 18.9 | 5.8 | 33.0 |
| Human morbidity | + | + | + |
| Migration | 0.6 | 0.5 | 2.8 |
| Hurricanes | 0.2 | 0.8 | 6.4 |
| Tourism | | 1.7 | 4.0 |
| Water supply | 15.6 | 7.0 | 56.0 |
| Urban infrastructure | | 0.1 | 0.6 |
| Air pollution | 7.3 | | |
| Tropospheric ozone | | 3.5 | 19.8 |
| Other | | + | + |
| Total (billion 1990 $) | 76.1 | 61.6 | 335.7 |
| Total (% GNP) | 1.3 | 1.1 | 6.0 |

*Sources*: Cline 1992: 131, Table 3.4; Fankhauser 1992: 44, Table 16
*Notes*: [a]In the source the figures given are in 1988 $. They have been scaled up in the column below by the ratio of 1990 to 1988 GDP.
[b]Source indicates (further) unquantified costs of the sign shown.
[c]This entry in Fankhauser corresponds to the previous two rows in Cline. Cline indicates further unquantified costs under this heading as shown.

## 12.1.2 Prevention

Global warming beyond present commitments can be prevented or mitigated by deflecting incoming solar radiation, increasing the earth's absorption of CO$_2$ from the atmosphere or reducing the emission of greenhouse gases. These actions may incur costs, the extent and techniques for the calculation of which will be explored in the next section. By mitigating global warming, these costs, like the costs of adaptation, will reduce the damage caused by it. They will also reduce the need for adaptation and its associated costs.

There are therefore three interdependent kinds of costs associated with global warming: damage costs ($C_D$), adaptation costs ($C_A$) and prevention costs ($C_P$). The total cost can therefore be written

$$C_T = C_D + C_A + C_P$$

It is the purpose of optimal policy to reduce this total cost to a minimum.

Each of these individual components of the total cost needs to be calculated net of all benefits other than their reduction of other components in the equation, which will be taken into account directly. Thus $C_P$ will be the cost of reducing $CO_2$ emissions *net* of any secondary benefits this reduction may bring about. Its benefit in reducing global warming, in contrast, will be reflected in reductions in $C_D$ and $C_A$.

Because many of the costs will be in the future, the choice of discount rate will make a great difference to the optimal policy indicated. This complex issue can only be briefly discussed here. It is a source of considerable controversy and a wide range of discount rates has been advocated and used in global warming calculations. After a lengthy review, Broome concludes that only 'pure discounting' (as opposed to using the consumer or producer interest rates) is appropriate theoretically for the global warming issue, and further finds no reason to adopt a discount rate different from zero (Broome 1992: 108). Cline notes that Mishan, too, advocated a zero discount rate for intergenerational comparisons (Cline 1992: 239). Cline, however, advocates the conversion of quantities to 'consumption equivalents', which are then discounted at the social rate of time preference (SRTP). Setting the 'pure impatience' component of SRTP equal to zero, Cline arrives at his preferred SRTP, related to the diminishing marginal utility of income, of 1.5 per cent.

Cline also performs benefit–cost analyses with SRTPs of 3 per cent and 5 per cent. The effect of varying this parameter is shown by the different benefit–cost ratios obtained for Cline's programme of 'aggressive abatement action'. With high damage assumptions, this ratio is 2.60 for an SRTP of 1.5 per cent, 1.09 for an SRTP of 3 per cent and 0.56 for an SRTP of 5 per cent. The central estimate of Nordhaus (1991a: 934) uses a discount rate that is 1 per cent higher than the rate of growth. Nordhaus (1992: 15, 18) uses a discount rate that is 3 per cent higher than the growth rate, which falls from a mean of 2.3 per cent before 2000 to 1.0 per cent after 2025. These examples show the kind of variations in discount rate that arise and the difference they make to assessments of optimal policy.

The choice of optimum can be illustrated in a two-stage diagrammatic process as follows. At any level of emissions that causes accumulation of greenhouse gases in the atmosphere, there will be an optimum (least cost) mix of adaptation and damage at the point where, for any given adaptation, the marginal $C_A$ ($MC_A$) equals the marginal $C_D$ ($MC_D$). A number of adaptation measures will need to be considered (e.g. dyke-building, more air-conditioning, migration). Not all of them will have the increasing marginal and total costs shown in Figure 12.1 which gives an optimal combination of adaptation and damage at point A*, where $MC_A$ equals $MC_D$. But it seems reasonable to assume that their total cost curves will be monotonically increasing and, assuming that the damage function has the total and marginal profiles shown (i.e. marginal damage falls to zero at a certain level of adaptation), which seems reasonable, then for any particular adaptation level and level of emission, there will always be an optimal combination of damage and adaptation. If these optimal combinations for

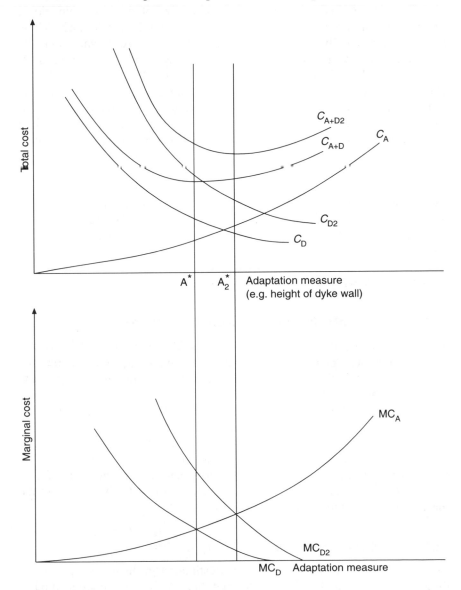

*Figure 12.1* Costs of adaptation and damage at a given (net accumulating) level of greenhouse gas emissions

different measures are aggregated, then an overall optimal combination of damage and adaptation, at a given level of emissions, can be obtained.

As the level of emission increases, the $C_D$ curve may be expected to shift upward, and so will $C_{A+D}$, to $C_{D2}$ and $C_{A+D2}$. The slope of the $C_D$ curve ($MC_D$) will also tend to increase with the emission level. This is because, as Cline says, 'one would expect the economic size of damage from global warming to rise more than linearly with the magnitude of warming' (Cline 1992: 72). He actually uses the damage function $D = k(\Delta t)^a$, where $D$ is the economic damage, $\Delta t$ is the temperature change and $a$ is a non-linear exponent, to which Cline gives the value of 1.25 or 1.5 (Cline 1992:131–2). The non-linearity of the damage function with respect to warming (and therefore to accumulating emissions) means that any given measure of adaptation at a higher level of warming will prevent more damage than at a lower level.The $C_A$ curve will not change because the cost of a given adaptation measure (e.g. raising a dyke to a certain height, cooling air temperature by a certain amount) will not depend on the emission level.

As accumulating emissions (and associated warming) increase, therefore, more adaptation measures will become economically rational and a set of optimal minimum values of $C_{A+D}$ will be generated. These are shown as $C^*_{A+D}$ in Figure 12.2, which also shows total and marginal cost curves for preventing emissions ($C_P$ and $MC_P$) and the total cost curve $C_T$ (= $C_P$ + $C^*_{A+D}$). The optimum level of emissions is then where $C_T$ is a minimum, at $E^*$, where $MC_P = MC^*_{A+D}$.

## 12.2  COSTS OF MITIGATING GLOBAL WARMING

As already noted, global warming can be reduced by reducing GG emissions, by increasing GG global sinks or by deflecting solar radiation away from the earth. NAS (1991) lists some 'geoengineering' possibilities of large-scale deflection or sink-creation, but no detailed costings are available and they will not be further explored here. The increase in carbon sink capacity through reforestation has been investigated in detail, as has the reduction of GG emissions. Because $CO_2$ has contributed about 60 per cent of the 'radiative forcing' from the increase in the greenhouse effect over the past 200 years, and is expected to continue to provide approximately this share in the future (Cline 1991: 906), among the GGs the abatement of $CO_2$ has attracted the most attention and will be the focus of discussion here.

### 12.2.1  Modelling $CO_2$ abatement

The costs of $CO_2$ abatement have been estimated in three principal ways: through the use of global models; through the use of single-country models (the results of which may or may not then be generalized to the world level); and through detailed calculations of the cost and environmental performance

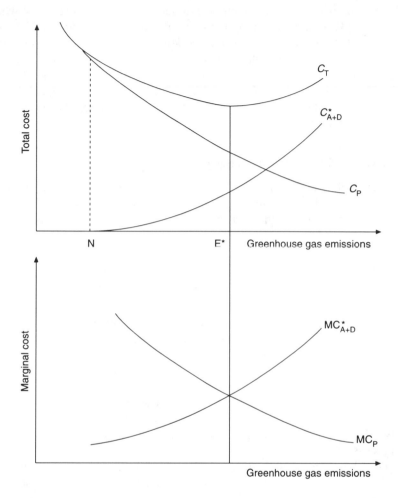

*Figure 12.2* Calculation of the optimum greenhouse gas emission level. Point N is the highest emission level at which net greenhouse gas accumulation in the atmosphere is zero

of different carbon-saving technologies. The models may be either general equilibrium models, macro models or technology-based models. Whole economy modelling is sometimes referred to as a 'top-down' approach; modelling based on detailed technological analysis is sometimes called 'bottom-up'.

There have been several reviews in varying amounts of detail of the studies reporting results of various CO$_2$-abatement modelling exercises: Boero *et al.* (1991), Hoeller *et al.* (1991), Nordhaus (1991b), Cline (1992: ch. 4), Dean and Hoeller (1992).

Boero *et al.* divide the $CO_2$-abatement models into two broad classes, while emphasizing that many of the models contain characteristics from each class. There are the general equilibrium models, concentrating on long-term equilibrium resource allocations and relative prices; and there are the macroeconomic models focusing more on short-term adjustments and disequilibrium. It is not the purpose of this chapter to repeat or extend Boero *et al.*'s analysis, but rather to concentrate on a few issues that have been important in influencing the results obtained.

### 12.2.2  Increasing the price of energy

For energy-related $CO_2$ emissions to be reduced, so must the consumption of fossil fuels, and this is typically achieved in models by raising the price of such fuels, often through the imposition of a carbon tax – a tax related to the carbon content of the fuel in question (coal, oil, gas have different carbon contents per unit of energy, in descending order of magnitude).

Increasing the price of energy according to its carbon content can be expected to result in the following effects (over different timescales):

- a reduction in demand for carbon-based fuels;
- substitution between more and less carbon-intensive fuels;
- substitution between carbon-based and non-carbon fuels;
- substitution between energy and other factors of production;
- substitution between more and less carbon-intensive products and processes;
- improvements in the efficiency of fuel use in delivering a particular energy service;
- development of new, less carbon-intensive technologies, products and processes;
- general energy saving by means of more investment in the heat-retention qualities of buildings and in less carbon-intensive forms of transport.

Whether the reduction in demand for carbon-based fuels induced by energy price increases results in reduced output (GDP) depends in the first instance on possibilities for substitution, efficiency improvements and technological development, so that the 'costs' of $CO_2$ abatement will depend very largely on how these factors are modelled.

### 12.2.3  Prices and substitution

Much general equilibrium greenhouse modelling is based on a production function approach (including Nordhaus and Yohe 1983; Manne and Richels 1991; Whalley and Wigle 1991; Burniaux *et al.* 1992; Nordhaus 1992) such that

$$X = F(C, E)$$

where $X$ is output, $E$ is energy, $C$ is all other factors and $F(.)$ is the production function.

The model first establishes a 'base run', incorporating assumptions about future supplies, demands and prices of all production factors and such parameters as 'autonomous energy efficiency improvement' (to be discussed later). This base run proceeds on the assumption that there are no unemployed resources. When a carbon tax is introduced, this raises the price of energy and, through the model's demand system, inevitably reduces the demand for it. Because the other factors are in unchanged supply, a lower demand for energy will convert, through the production function, into a lower output. If the base run is considered non-distortionary, i.e. is itself an optimum path, then inevitably output will fall. As Boero *et al.* note, the assumption in the general equilibrium models of full equilibrium means that 'any deviation from a "no distortions" base run necessarily involves economic costs' (Boero *et al.* 1991: 34). Several of the models in Boero *et al.*'s survey report GDP losses from the imposition of a carbon tax as a result of this modelling procedure, as shown in Figure 12.3, taken from Boero *et al.* (1991).

In Figure 12.3 models MR, N, WW and B take the production function approach. C, EB, ER and M use the IEA–ORAU model, which does not use a production function but links energy prices directly to GDP in a manner that ensures an inverse relationship (AB is not discussed here).

The question which will be examined here is whether the assumptions and modelling procedures which have led to this fall in output as a carbon tax is introduced are valid. The following issues will be addressed in turn.

1   *Revenue recycling*    The revenues raised from a carbon tax could be considerable. The macroeconomic effect of the tax can be expected to vary depending on whether the tax is retained or recycled through the economy, and how such recycling is effected.

2   *Unemployed resources*    It seems unrealistic to assume no unemployed resources at the present time, when most OECD countries have a registered unemployment rate of around 10 per cent. The existence of this unemployed pool of labour must change the energy/labour substitution possibilities and the costs associated with them. Macro models which incorporate unemployment indicate that this is indeed the case.

3   *Distortions*    No economy is at a point of non-distortionary equilibrium. There are distortions due to current taxation patterns, which bear most heavily on labour; and there are distortions due to market failure, such as, perhaps, in the market for energy efficiency, and, of course, the negative externality exhibited by the phenomenon of global warming itself. The macroeconomic effect of a carbon tax will depend on whether the mode of recycling its revenues, or other associated policy, affects the distortions.

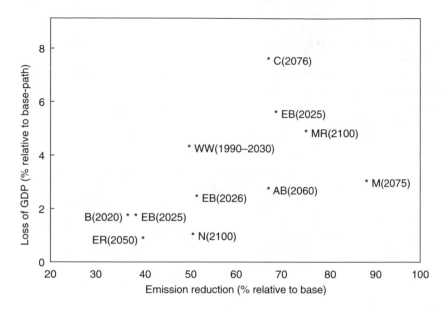

*Figure 12.3* GDP losses associated with reductions in global $CO_2$ emissions relative to base projections (various studies and years)

Key to models shown:

AB    Anderson, D. and Bird, C.D. (1990) 'The carbon accumulations problem and technical progress', University College London and Balliol College, Oxford, November

B    Burniaux, J.-M., Martin, J.-P., Nicoletti, G. and Martins, J.-O. (1991a) 'The costs of policies to reduce global emissions of $CO_2$: initial simulation resultus with GREEN', Working Paper 103, OCDE/GD(91)115, June, Resource Allocation Division, Paris: OECD

C    Cline, W. (1989) 'Political economy of the greenhouse effect', Institute for International Economics, Washington, DC, April

EB    Edmonds, J. and Barnes, D.W. (1990a) 'Estimating the marginal cost of reducing global fossil fuel $CO_2$ emissions', Global Environmental Change Programme, PNL-SA-18361, Pacific Northwest Laboratory, Washington, DC

ER    Edmonds, J. and Reilly, J.M. (1985) *Global Energy: Assessing the Future*, Oxford: Oxford University Press

MR    Manne, A.S. and Richels, G. (1991) 'Global $CO_2$ emission reductions – the impacts of rising energy costs', *The Energy Journal*, 12(1): 87–107

M    Mintzer, I.M. (1987) 'A matter of degrees: the potential for controlling the greenhouse effect', Research Report 5, Washington, DC: World Resources Institute

N    Nordhaus, W. (1990) 'An intertemporal general equilibrium model of economic growth and climate change', Mimeo, Yale University

WW    Whalley, J. and Wigle, R. (1990) 'The international incidence of carbon taxes', Mimeo, National Bureau of Economic Research, Cambridge, MA, and Wilfrid Laurier University, Waterloo

*Source:* Boero *et al.* 1991: 2

4   *Investment and technical change*    One would expect changes in relative prices, implying changes in both production costs and patterns of demand, to change the relative attractiveness of investment options. They might also be expected to affect the rate and direction of technical change and, through the technical bias of energy use, perhaps also the rate of productivity growth.

## 12.3 REVENUES FROM THE CARBON TAX

The levels of the carbon taxes proposed in the various models as necessary to make substantial reductions in carbon emissions are between $100 and $400 per ton of carbon (see Boero *et al.* 1991: 87–9, Table 5). A $250 tax is equivalent to $0.75 per gallon on petrol or $30 per barrel on oil (Cline 1992: 147). Taxes at these levels would raise large sums of revenue. A $100 per ton global tax rate would raise of the order of $500 billion annually, and about $130 billion from the USA alone (Cline 1992: 151). Schelling considers that 'a carbon tax sufficient to make a big dent in the greenhouse problem would have to be roughly equivalent to a dollar per gallon on motor fuel ... (which) would currently yield close to half a trillion dollars a year in revenue' (Schelling 1992: 11).

Of the global studies only Whalley and Wigle (1990, as reviewed in Boero *et al.* 1991) vary the international distribution of the carbon revenues, considering a producer tax (revenues retained by energy producers), consumer tax and a distribution to countries on an equal per capita basis. Not surprisingly they find that changing the distribution makes a large difference to different regions' GDP losses.

GDP losses are not only affected by who gets the revenues. They also crucially depend on what is done with them. If they are simply saved, then the short-term effect of the carbon tax is one of contractionary pressure, with reductions in GDP as a result. The long-run effect depends on the way the extra government saving influences the evolution of the economy.

However, evaluating the tax on the basis of these effects is to confuse the issue. In reality, carbon tax revenues will accrue to national governments, which will have the option of saving them or cutting other taxes. For the effects of the carbon taxes alone to be assessed, independently of such issues as the overall level of aggregate demand or the public-sector borrowing requirement, it is highly desirable that they are offset by the reduction of other taxes. This is the clear view of both Boero *et al.* and Cline:

> We suggest that, in order to keep the debate clear, GHG exercises should always be conducted in a revenue-neutral fashion.
>
> (Boero *et al.* 1991: 93)

> In most cases it would be desirable to recycle these tax revenues, to avoid contractionary pressure on aggregate demand and thus recession .... This

contractionary pressure is the chief reason the Congressional Budget
Office (1990) estimated that a phase-in of a $100 carbon tax over 10 years
for the United States would cause a loss of 2% of GDP annually by the
second five years. Such estimates reflect primarily the demand-depressing
effects of any tax, rather than the production-possibility effects of
curtailing energy .... However, for long-term analysis it seems preferable
to exclude short-term macroeconomic effects. Keynesian demand-reduc-
tion overstates the damage, because collected revenue can be returned to
the economy.

(Cline 1992: 151; and note 15, p. 151)

Pearce (1991: 940, note 6) expresses surprise 'that most of the simulations of
hypothetical carbon taxes do not consider revenue neutrality. This may reflect
limitations of some of the models, e.g. computable general equilibrium
models .... In this case macroeconomic models are also needed.'

Using such macromodels, the effects on national economies of recycling
the tax revenues are clearly shown in several country studies, most
consistently in the HERMES modelling of the effects of an energy tax on the
economies of different member states of the European Union (Table 12.2).

The three revenue use variants in Table 12.2 were simple retention by the
government (Tax retained) and complete revenue-recycling, through either
the reduction of employers' social security taxes (Social security) or reduction
in direct taxation (Direct taxes). In every case it can be seen that, as expected,

*Table 12.2* GDP and employment effects in 2005 of constant real $10 per barrel
energy tax imposed in 1990 with different revenue use, four countries
separately and together

| | Direct taxes[a] | Social security[a] | Tax retained[b] | Direct taxes[b] |
|---|---|---|---|---|
| GDP effects (% difference from baseline) | | | | |
| West Germany | −0.6 | −0.2 | −1.37 | 0.51 |
| France | −0.7 | −0.3 | −0.92 | −0.13 |
| Italy | −0.0 | 0.2 | −2.19 | 0.45 |
| United Kingdom | −0.7 | −0.2 | −2.05 | 2.69 |
| Europe-4 | −0.53 | −0.12 | | |
| Employment effects (unemployment rate, % difference from baseline) | | | | |
| West Germany | −0.3 | −0.7 | −0.7 | −0.83 |
| France | −0.0 | −0.2 | 0.03 | −0.54 |
| Italy | −0.0 | −0.2 | 0.43 | −0.13 |
| United Kingdom | 0.4 | −0.1 | 0.78 | −1.20 |
| Europe-4 | 0.01 | −0.37 | | |

*Sources*: [a]Standaert 1992: pp. 9, 14, Tables 3/1, 4/1; pp. 22–36, Tables A1a–A8a
[b]Karadeloglou 1992: pp. 182, 195, Tables 3/2, 7/2

*Table 12.3* Effects on GDP and employment in four EU countries in 2000 after introduction of $10 energy tax in 1991

|  | (A) | (B) | (C) | (D) |
|---|---|---|---|---|
| **GDP effects (% difference from baseline)** | | | | |
| (1) Belgium[a] | −0.69 | −0.09 | 0.52 | 0.34 |
| (2) Denmark[b] | −1.07 | −0.25 | −0.17 | −0.12 |
| (3) Portugal[a] | −2.62 | −1.6 | −1.83 | −2.14 |
| (4) Ireland[b] | −0.8 | 0.3 | 0.5 | 0.2 |
| **Employment effects (employment, % difference from base)** | | | | |
| (1) Belgium[a] | −0.35 | 0.15 | 1.33 | 1.12 |
| (2) Denmark[b] | −0.57 | −0.04 | −0.24 | −0.22 |
| (3) Portugal[a] | −2.55 | −2.13 | −0.59 | −1.65 |
| (4) Ireland[b] | −0.8 | 0.6 | 0.9 | 0.3 |

*Sources:* (1) Bossier 1992: p. 46, Table 3/1
(2) Andersen 1992: pp. 88, 90–2, Tables 3/1, 4/1, 4/2, 4/3
(3) Modesto 1992: pp. 123, 125, 126, 128, Tables 2/1, 3/1, 4/1, 5/1
(4) Fitzgerald and McCoy 1992: p. 156, Table 7/1
*Notes:* [a]Common EU tax.
[b]Tax imposed unilaterally.

the effects on both GDP and employment are markedly less negative under the tax recycling variants: with regard to employment the unemployment rate falls absolutely in all four countries under consideration.

These results are broadly consistent with HERMES modelling results for other countries. Table 12.3 shows HERMES results for the year 2000 for four small EU countries of the introduction in 1990 of a $10 per barrel energy tax, maintained in real terms. The four columns show simulations in which the tax is retained by the government (A) and three different methods of recycling it through the economy: by reducing direct taxes on households (B), by reducing payroll taxes on employers (C) and by reducing VAT (D). As with Table 12.2, the macroeconomic effects of recycling the revenue are significantly more positive than in the tax retention case.

The positive employment effect of a carbon tax is not only due to the lower relative price of labour compared with energy. It also derives from the relative labour intensity of non-carbon-intensive sectors, which can expect to experience increased demand due to the relative price shift. The effect is brought out clearly in the detailed study by Proops *et al.* (1993). In order to provide insights into the implications of a changed structure of final demand due to measures to limit CO$_2$ emissions, they used input–output techniques to calculate the embodied energy and CO$_2$ emissions of different industrial sectors. In one of their simulations they impose, on an underlying growth rate of 2 per cent, an extra 8 per cent per annum increase in the demand for commodities in the tertiary sectors (e.g. telecommunications, financial and other services) and cut demand in energy-intensive sectors proportionally to maintain the overall 2 per cent growth rate. They find that, in the UK, $CO_2$ emissions fall by 3.45 per cent per annum and employment rises by 4.60 per cent per annum, reflecting the tertiary sector's higher labour intensity (Proops *et al.* 1993: 206–7).

Another country model that has been used to analyse the macroeconomic effects of carbon abatement is the MDM model of the UK economy. Barker and Lewney (1991) offset the tax by reducing VAT and find that the GDP effects of reaching the Toronto target (20 per cent cut in $CO_2$ emissions from 1988 base by 2005) 'are so small that they can be ignored' (Barker and Lewney 1991: 22). Sondheimer (1991) modelled the introduction of a tax of £30 per ton in 1991, reducing direct and indirect taxes equally in compensation. By the year 2000, GDP was up by 0.52 per cent and unemployment down 0.07 per cent, both from base.

These results relied on a fairly simplistic treatment of energy demand and the possibility of interfuel substitution, which was substantially improved by the introduction of a linked energy sub-model for the study, reported by Barker *et al.* (1992), of the effects on the UK economy of the proposed EU carbon/energy tax. Their scenarios were tax retention by the government, what Barker *et al.* call the 'depression scenario', EU tax with VAT offset and EU tax with income tax offset. The percentage differences of GDP from base by 2005 were –0.37, 0.17 and 0.09. Once again, the recycling of the tax converted a cost into a benefit.

The issue of how carbon tax receipts should be recycled through the economy leads to consideration of distortions in the economy and how the carbon tax affects them.

## 12.4   ECONOMIC DISTORTIONS AND CARBON TAX RECEIPTS

An explicit assumption of the general equilibrium models is that deviations from the base run entail 'distortions' which incur costs. Thus Gaskins and Weyant write of 'the distortions to the economy caused by the imposition of the carbon tax' (Gaskins and Weyant 1993: 320). Jorgenson and Wilcoxen write of the 'introduction of distortions resulting from fossil-fuel taxes' (Jorgenson and Wilcoxen 1993: 518).

On the revenue side, a common procedure is to recycle the revenues by means of lump sum rebates to households. This is the procedure followed by Jorgenson and Wilcoxen (1992: 88; 1993) and in the models participating in the comparative study co-ordinated by the Energy Modelling Forum at Stanford University. Gaskins and Weyant, reporting on the study, say that under this procedure the GDP losses caused by the carbon tax can be calculated 'without adding a credit or subtracting a penalty for the way the revenues are used' (Gaskins and Weyant 1993: 320). Jorgenson and Wilcoxen note that this procedure 'is essentially the replacement of a lump-sum tax (the rebated labor tax) by a distorting one (the carbon tax)' (Jorgenson and Wilcoxen 1992: 96, note 53).

This way of proceeding can therefore be summarised as follows:

- The economy is presumed to start from and finish in a position of equilibrium with no unemployed resources.
- The carbon tax introduces distortions while raising revenue.
- The revenue is recycled through the economy by reducing non-distortionary taxes (even where it could replace distortionary taxes).

Such a procedure would not appear to accord with economic reality or optimal policy-making possibilities. For example, it is clear that there are considerable unemployed resources in the economy (i.e. labour) and substantial distortions are likely to be present in the base run from the existing tax regime, which bears heavily on labour and capital. Moreover, the phenomenon of global warming itself is a classic example of a negative distorting externality. Ballard *et al.* calculate the marginal excess burden (MEB) of taxation in the United States to be in the range 17–56 cents per dollar of extra revenue (Ballard *et al.* 1985: 128). Jorgenson and Yun (1990) find that the MEB of the US tax system as a whole, even after the tax reform of 1986 which was widely held to have reduced the excess burden, is 38 cents per dollar of revenue raised. Some components of the tax system had far higher costs, e.g. the MEB for individual capital taxes was 95 cents per dollar (Jorgenson and Yun 1990: 20). Jorgenson and Yun acknowledge that their MEB estimates 'are considerably higher than previous estimates. This can be attributed primarily to the greater precision we employ in representing the US tax structure' (Jorgenson and Yun 1990: 6). Nordhaus notes that 'some have estimated [the marginal deadweight loss of taxes in the United States] as high as \$0.50 per \$1.00 of revenue' (Nordhaus 1993: 316). However, in his simulation using carbon tax revenues to replace burdensome taxes, he uses the value \$0.30. Cline uses the value \$0.33 (Cline 1992: 294).

Jorgenson and Wilcoxen argue against their own earlier practice of lump-sum recycling of revenues thus: 'This is probably not the most likely use of the revenue. ... Using the revenue to reduce a distortionary tax would lower the net cost of a carbon tax by removing inefficiency elsewhere in the economy' (Jorgenson and Wilcoxen 1993: 20).

This is precisely the effect that is obtained in all models that do in fact reduce distortionary taxes to offset a carbon tax. Jorgenson and Wilcoxen (1993: 22, Table 5) themselves find that a 1.7 per cent GDP loss under lump-sum redistribution is converted to a 0.69 per cent loss and a 1.1 per cent gain by reducing labour and capital taxes respectively.

This effect has also been shown in the work of Nordhaus. Nordhaus (1991a), on the basis of an abatement-cost curve derived from his survey of extant models in Nordhaus (1991b) and his own calculation of a global warming damage function, arrived at an efficient level of a carbon tax of $7.33 per ton $CO_2$ equivalent (Nordhaus 1991a: 934). By 1993, using his own DICE model, the optimum carbon tax had fallen to $5.24 per ton $CO_2$ equivalent. Using a carbon tax of $56 per ton to cut emissions in 1995 by 20 per cent from 1990 levels caused an annualized global GDP loss of $762 billion (Nordhaus 1993: 315). However, these DICE results came from recycling the carbon tax revenues through lump-sum rebates. When instead carbon taxes are used to reduce other burdensome taxes, then the optimal tax rate becomes $59 per ton, emissions go below the 20 per cent cut and annualized GDP *rises* by $206 billion. Nordhaus notes: 'The importance of revenue recycling is surprising and striking. These findings emphasize the critical nature of designing the instruments and use of revenues in a careful manner. The tail of revenue recycling would seem to wag the dog of climate-change policy' (Nordhaus 1993: 317).

Barker has consistently argued against lump-sum rebates to offset revenues: 'An alternative treatment would be to find which existing tax creates the largest distortions in the economy and the highest loss of welfare and then to use the carbon tax revenues ... to reduce the marginal rates of this tax' (Barker 1992: 9). Boero *et al*. agree: 'Economically we should seek to reduce the most distortionary (tax)' (Boero *et al*. 1991: 93). On Jorgenson and Yun's figures this would mean initially offsetting taxes with an MEB of 95 cents per dollar. Because of interaction effects between the taxes, it is not possible to argue that, for this tranche of offset, each dollar of carbon tax revenue raised would generate a 95 cent increase in welfare because of distortionary reductions elsewhere; but it may be noted that this rate of offset is more than three times that used by Nordhaus in his 'tail-wagging' calculation discussed earlier, and could thus be expected to yield a substantially higher optimal tax rate than his $59 per ton $CO_2$ equivalent.

While they do not report the MEB figure they used, Gaskins and Weyant confirm the importance of this approach to revenue recycling: 'Simulation with four models of the US economy indicate that from 35 per cent to more than 100 per cent of the GDP losses could ultimately be offset by recycling revenues through cuts in existing taxes' (Gaskins and Weyant 1993: 320). This means that the figures of GDP loss as surveyed by Boero *et al*. (reproduced here as Figure 12.3) and Gaskins and Weyant (1993: 321) indicate possibly excessive costs, because they are based on suboptimal policy-making.

With regard to the supposed 'distortions' introduced by the carbon tax, this too would appear to be a mis-statement of the situation. Global warming is likely to entail substantial external costs imposed by high emitters of greenhouse gases on low emitters of greenhouse gases and future generations. It is an economic distortion caused by the use of the atmosphere as a free good for the disposal of greenhouse gases. The carbon tax is intended to rectify this distortion by bringing the marginal costs and benefits of GG emissions back

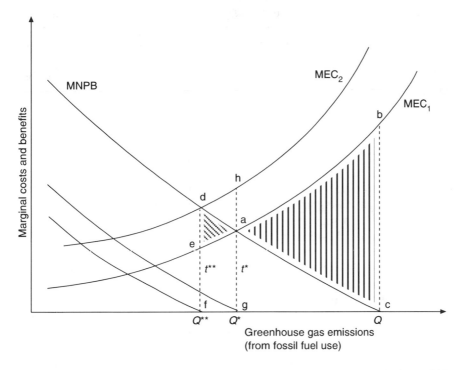

*Figure 12.4* Marginal costs and benefits of greenhouse gas emissions: MC, marginal cost curve of damages from global warming; MNPB, marginal net private benefit of emitting greenhouse gases

into balance, thereby internalizing some of the costs of global warming into the activities which cause it. As Pearce says: 'While most taxes distort incentives, an environmental tax corrects a distortion, namely the externalities arising from the excessive use of environmental services' (Pearce 1991: 940).

The situation is as set out in Figure 12.4. With no carbon tax, GGs will be emitted at a level $Q$. With the imposition of an optimal carbon tax $t^*$, emissions will fall to $Q^*$, which must be regarded as the *undistorted* position of economic activity. The imposition of the tax has removed the distortionary loss equivalent to the area abc.

It should be noted that, even at the optimal position $Q^*$, society is subject to an external cost burden equal to the area under the MEC$_1$ curve between the origin and $Q^*$. This cost is borne because, below $Q^*$, the marginal private benefits are greater than the marginal external costs, and the private benefits are assumed to add to the social benefit overall. However, it is clear that there are many people in the world (low GG emitters) who may be expected to incur damage from global warming but who derive practically no benefits from GG emissions, because, perhaps, they and the societies in which they live use little fossil fuel. To be fully inclusive, the MEC curve must include, in addition to a comprehensive and correct valuation of the damage costs, appropriate weightings that take account of both distributional issues and uncertainty.

The intergenerational issues will be dealt with directly through the discount rate that is chosen. The intragenerational distributional issue is normally ignored in damage cost calculations, i.e. no extra weight is given to damage suffered by low GG emitters than to that suffered by high GG emitters. In fact, a negative weight is often implicitly implied, because high GG emitters, being richer, have a higher willingness to pay to avoid damage, so the damage incident on them is valued more highly than that incident on poorer low GG emitters. If the damages facing low GG emitters were given higher weight, this would have the effect of shifting the MEC curve to the left, perhaps to $MEC_2$, yielding a new optimum tax rate $t^{**}$ ($> t^*$) and lower GG emissions $Q^{**}$. In effect, the external cost aefg would have been revalued at hdfg.

A similar result would occur if a weight was given to risk aversion by policy-makers against the possibility of higher than expected damage. $Q^{**}$ could again become the optimal position, with the excess lost private benefit over external cost saved, aed, being regarded as an insurance payment in case the expected damage given by $MEC_1$ is underestimated. The incorporation of risk aversion into a benefit–cost analysis in this way can make a substantial difference to its outcome. In Cline's study, the application of risk-aversion weights of 0.125 to his low damage estimate, 0.5 to his central estimate and 0.375 to his high damage estimate converts the central estimate's benefit–cost ratio of 0.74, with no adjustment for risk, to a ratio of 1.26, thus justifying a programme of 'aggressive abatement action' (Cline 1992: 300).

The conclusion of this analysis is that, where external costs are important and their valuation is complex, the incorporation of considerations of distribution, equity, uncertainty and risk can make a significant difference to where the 'undistorted' position of economic activity is taken to be.

## 12.5  INVESTMENT, EFFICIENCY AND TECHNOLOGICAL CHANGE

Implementing a carbon tax will increase the relative price of fossil energy compared with other inputs, an effect which may be enhanced by reducing taxes on these other inputs (e.g. labour, capital). As has been seen, choosing the offsetting taxes carefully can cause both employment and GDP to rise in an inflation-neutral way. But the change in relative prices could affect economic development in a number of other ways.

### 12.5.1 Increased scrapping

A change in relative prices caused by the imposition of a carbon tax might affect economic development by making existing capital equipment uneconomic, thereby bringing forward its scrapping date. This could be a major potential source of adjustment costs related to the tax.

One would expect that the least disruptive imposition of a carbon tax would be one introduced initially at a low level, with modest annual increases over a substantial, pre-announced period of time. This would allow responses to the tax to be synchronized with normal investment schedules. If a carbon tax were introduced in this gradual, expected way, it is doubtful whether experience gained in response to the energy price shocks of the 1970s would provide a reliable guide to the economy's response. As explained in Chapter 1, elasticities derived from these responses should therefore be treated with caution when applied to this different situation.

Ingham *et al.* (1992) have developed a vintage model of the UK manufacturing sector which allows firms to change their machines' energy–output ratio according to relative factor prices, both between different machine vintages and with existing machines. Technical change is thus at least partly endogenized. The model further allows the energy–output ratio to depend on the rate of growth of output.

Ingham *et al.* (1992: 128–9) then identify, for UK manufacturing, the separate contribution to the decline in the energy–output ratio of relative factor prices, output and an exogenous component of technical progress. They conclude that in the period 1971–80 energy prices, which increased markedly, played the dominant role in reducing the energy–output ratio. Although they stress the tentative nature of their result, at the least it suggests what might have been expected from theory, namely that investment and innovation in the achievement of energy efficiency would increase with the price of fossil energy. This casts doubt on other models' treatment of energy efficiency as autonomous and unaffected by the imposition of the carbon tax.

### 12.5.2 Improvements in energy efficiency

Several of the global models (see the review in Dean and Hoeller 1992: 26–7) employ a parameter called AEEI (autonomous energy efficiency improvement) to capture a perceived economic tendency to move towards greater energy efficiency independently of relative price changes (i.e. of substitution effects, which Manne and Richels (1991), for example, model through a separate parameter, ESUB, the elasticity of price-induced substitution).

The values of AEEI vary in the models between 0.25 per cent and 1.0 per cent. Even this range does not encompass the uncertainty associated with AEEI. Williams (1990), for example, considers that a 1 per cent value is too low, on the basis of historical decreases in energy intensity from 1973 to 1986.

Hogan and Jorgenson (1991), on the other hand, find on the basis of econometric estimates using US data that AEEI is effectively negative, in other words that, without substitutions between factors induced by relative price changes, the energy–GDP ratio would increase. This is because their results indicate a positive technical bias for energy. Their analysis further suggests that increasing the price of energy, for example through a carbon tax, could reduce the growth of total factor productivity and thereby bring about a reduction in the growth rate. Their initial calculations suggest that the effect of this on output could be of the same order of magnitude as the reduction in output due directly to energy's higher price.

The value chosen for AEEI makes a substantial difference to the baseline $CO_2$ generated, as Dean and Hoeller report: 'A difference of 0.5 per cent in this parameter [AEEI], given compounding, can lead to an outcome in 2100 which is as much as 20 billion tons [of carbon emissions] different. . . . Uncertainty about the size of this parameter is likely to remain large as it depends on future technical progress' (Dean and Hoeller 1992: 19; and p. 28, Table 4). Obviously differences in baseline emissions of this magnitude would greatly affect the cost of reducing these emissions to any particular level.

Whether or not investment and improvements in energy efficiency will accelerate with a carbon tax, many analysts have argued that market failures are preventing the implementation of some cost-efficient energy conservation measures now (e.g. Jackson and Jacobs 1991, Lovins and Lovins 1991; Chapter 10 in this volume). After reviewing this issue, Cline (1992: 227) decides that a reasonable estimate is that the first 22 per cent of carbon emissions from base can be cut back at zero cost. The incorporation of such costless cuts in the cost-generating models would obviously reduce their negative outcomes from a carbon tax.

### 12.5.3 Changed investment opportunities

The changing relative price of energy would change patterns of investment and demand. There are opposite tendencies at work here. One tendency is the possible complementarity between energy and capital, a still unresolved issue (Solow 1987). If energy and capital are complements, then increasing the price of energy will reduce the demand in production for both energy and capital, thereby reducing both investment and growth. Another tendency working in the same direction is the possible energy-using bias of technical change, already mentioned in the context of energy efficiency (Hogan and Jorgenson 1991). The results of Jorgenson's empirical work in this area have shown that, in thirty-two out of thirty-five sectors studied, productivity growth had an energy-using bias (Jorgenson 1990: 83), which would mean that, in these sectors, increasing the price of energy would reduce productivity growth. A third negative effect on investment of an energy price increase is the obvious one that certain investments involving energy-intensive capital goods or processes would become uneconomic and therefore would not be made.

Working in the opposite direction to these growth-reducing tendencies is the stimulus that the relative price change would give to energy-saving investment. If it is true that at present many economic opportunities for energy saving remain unimplemented because of market failures, as suggested in Chapter 10, then it might be expected that a continuously increasing energy price, by providing a continuously increasing incentive to correct such failures, would result in substantial investments in energy efficiency and further innovation in this area. If energy efficiency could be increased at the same rate as the price of energy, then the negative effect of the rising price on investment plans would be completely cancelled out but the positive stimulus with regard to energy-saving innovations and non-fossil energy technologies would remain.

As for the issues of energy–capital complementarity and technical bias, in addition to the uncertainties involved in the empirical estimates, the whole methodology by which the estimates are derived has been called into question by Scott, using reasoning which 'effectively knocks out the production function and the measurement of total factor productivity as they are currently used' (Scott 1992: 622). Scott's basic argument is that, in contrast to conventional growth theory, it is gross investment rather than changes in the gross or net capital stock which plays the dominant role in the growth process. Defining investment as 'the cost (in terms of consumption forgone) of changing, hopefully, of improving, economic arrangements' (Scott 1992: 625), he writes:

> Investment is a much more important proximate cause of growth than conventional theory, backed up by many growth-accounting studies, would have us believe. Furthermore, raising the investment ratio raises the rate of growth indefinitely, and not by an amount which diminishes asymptotically to zero. Finally, there is a large externality of investment, due mainly to the learning effect whereby investment by one firm creates and reveals investment opportunities for other firms. These are all conclusions from my study which, if accepted, point to the need for policies to promote investment. There is, on these grounds, a rather strong case for reducing taxes on savings and replacing them by other taxes, for example on consumers' expenditures, or, better still, taxes designed to protect the environment and reduce traffic congestion.

(Scott 1992: 629)

Scott's views cannot be explored in detail here, but if they are correct and if the stimulus to energy efficiency and innovation from a rising energy price is greater than its dampening effect, then this conclusion is a striking echo of the earlier one which advocated the substitution of environmental taxes for those on capital and labour in order to reduce economic distortions. In that case, a carbon tax was perceived as yielding a double dividend by internalizing an externality *and* reducing other distortionary taxes. A conclusion of Scott's view of the relation between investment and growth would seem to be that a carbon tax can yield a double dividend here too, both by creating investment opportunities directly related to the changes in energy's relative price (always assuming that these are greater than the investment opportunities lost) *and* by removing taxation disincentives to investment elsewhere. On this view, a carbon tax could act as a spur to growth.

## 12.6  CONCLUSIONS

Many of the models seeking to elucidate the economic implications of abating $CO_2$ emissions show that such abatement will incur costs in terms of lost output of the order of several per cent.

The issues raised in this chapter suggest at the least that this conclusion should not be accepted without close examination of the modelling structures and assumptions which have generated the perceived costs, and an investigation as to whether different, perhaps equally plausible, assumptions would generate different results. Questions to be investigated include whether the revenue from a carbon tax has been recycled in a way calculated to remove prior distortions in the economy; whether currently unemployed resources in the economy may permit emissions to be reduced at lower net cost; whether positive economic effects connected with a boost to investment in energy efficiency and other relevant technologies that could derive from continuous change in the relative price of energy would outweigh negative effects from the same change; and finally whether the secondary benefits of abatement, which have been estimated to be several times some estimates of the primary benefits (Pearce 1992), have been taken into account.

The chapter has shown that there are good theoretical reasons to expect that implementing a carbon tax sensitively with regard to issues such as these could partially or totally offset the negative economic effects deriving from increasing the price of energy. The chapter has also quoted a number of model simulations that indicate the practical plausibility of these theoretical expectations.

While it is too early to be certain that the appropriate imposition of a sizeable carbon tax would not be costly, the considerations set out in this chapter certainly suggest that an *a priori* conclusion that it will be costly is unwarranted. More modelling of the critical issues could undoubtedly help to throw more light on this matter, but a justifiable conclusion at present would appear to be that, even if only moderate costs from unchecked global warming are in prospect, a carbon tax rising gradually but steadily over a number of years to a level that would achieve considerable abatement of $CO_2$ emissions would not only not impose an excessive net burden, but would probably yield net benefits.

# Chapter 13

# Asymmetrical price elasticities of energy demand

## Michael Grubb

**ABSTRACT**

This chapter discusses some of the reasons for prices elasticities of energy demand being asymmetric in the sense that the fall in energy demand following a price rise can be substantially greater than the subsequent rise in demand if prices revert towards former levels. Thus history matters in energy demand forecasting. The chapter reviews the evidence for asymmetrical responses, the explanations for them and the implications for studies of GG abatement.

## INTRODUCTION

This chapter takes the form of a brief note to highlight a specific issue of direct and central relevance to studies of energy elasticities, and the use of elasticity estimates for demand projections and policy analysis. The chapter[1] does not seek to develop estimates of elasticities or to review in detail methodological issues. Rather it addresses an underlying issue in the estimation and use of elasticities, one which in the author's view is of primary importance and which will come to be seen as such in future developments in the field.

This issue concerns asymmetries in response to price changes – asymmetric elasticities – and the directly associated issue of induced technology development.[2] It is important because allowing for this possibility can greatly alter econometric estimates of elasticities, and hence alter energy demand projections and our overall understanding of responses to energy price changes. Indeed, the issue carries deeper implications of relevance to energy and environmental policy. In economic terms the proposition is extremely simple, namely that the response to price rises is not matched by an equal response to equivalent price falls. More specifically, it is that the reduction in energy demand following a price rise can be substantially greater than the subsequent rise in demand if and when prices revert towards former levels. Thus, not only are current and recent prices important, but the history of prices is important. This simple proposition is one which many non-economists might take as inherently plausible. Nevertheless, in economic terms it is a departure from the norm, and challenges the assumption that the *magnitude* of demand responses to a price change is independent of the *direction* of the price change.

## 13.1 THE EVIDENCE

Before discussing the notion and implications more fully, what is the evidence? The evidence is both direct and indirect. The direct evidence concerns the history of bulk energy price and energy demand over the past twenty years. Econometric analysis indicates that the energy price shocks of the 1970s had a large impact on energy demand. Previous trends of rapidly rising demand were broken, and demand was persistently far lower than projections.

But as prices of all fossil fuels began to decline in the 1980s – and oil prices in particular collapsed in 1986 – energy demand did not leap upwards. It did start to increase in most areas, but not to anything like an extent equal and opposite to the preceding demand suppression. In real terms, energy prices in some sectors and countries in the early 1990s were lower than they were in 1972. Traditional econometric models based on price elasticities suggest that response to the price rise, marking a sharp decline in the trend of energy consumption, especially outside the heavy industrial sector, should have been mirrored by an equivalent rise after the price fall (after allowing for autonomous trends). In fact, as one recent detailed econometric study (Walker and Wirl 1993) observes:

> Energy demand since 1986 seems inconsistent with the notion of constant income and price elasticities reported in the literature. Energy demand growth remained sluggish despite the simultaneous substantial reduction in real fuel costs and increases in real income.

This chapter does not attempt to examine the data critically, because a burgeoning literature of such studies is beginning to emerge. Dargay (1993: note 2) cites no less than nine studies which address the issues of irreversibility and asymmetry in energy demand[3] – in addition to his own empirical studies which encompass France, Germany and the UK. In addition, the Autumn/Winter 1993 edition of *The Energy Journal* carries four articles on the subject of asymmetric price responses. Two focus on the macro-economic asymmetries, arguing that the energy price falls have not benefited economies in a way that parallels the negative impacts of the 1970s' price rises. The other two focus on energy demand responses. One (Walker and Wirl 1993) carried the general conclusion cited above. The other (Gately 1993) sought to quantify the price irreversibility of world oil demand, concluding that:

> The response to price cuts in the 1980s is perhaps only one-fifth of that for

price increases in the 1970s. This has dramatic implications for projections of oil demand, especially under low-price assumptions.

Such quantitative results should be interpreted with some caution. Price changes and demand responses differ between fuels, sectors and countries. Prices to consumers are affected also by a multitude of taxes, many of which are higher than in the early 1970s. There are many other complicating factors, including various autonomous trends, saturation effects and widely differing economic growth rates. There was also a difference in government responses in the two periods: in the 1970s the oil price increases were seen as an important contributor to inflation in consuming countries, and often an important cost to the national economy, and regulations and institutions (energy efficiency offices and the like) were introduced to encourage energy saving; when oil prices fell in 1985, these regulations and institutions were not automatically removed, although there has been some relaxation of regulations and reductions in subsidies for energy efficiency. It is also quite possible that some of the observed asymmetry is not absolute but reflects different timescales – responses to price falls may be slower than equivalent responses to price rises. Related to this point is the important position of price expectations: if in the 1970s it was believed that the price increases were unlikely to be reversed, then responses might have been greater than if they were expected to be temporary; and in the late 1980s, the response to the price falls might have been lower, if it was expected that the falls in prices would eventually be reversed. Nevertheless, the various studies carried out seek to correct for some of these factors, and it seems clear that substantially asymmetric price responses persist.

## 13.2 EXPLANATIONS

Why is the response asymmetric? Many factors may be involved, but a central role is probably that of induced technical change, in a very broad sense. The issues can be illustrated in terms of an orthodox production function. In the simplest economic model, the function shows the combinations of energy and other inputs required to produce a given output and is assumed to be fixed when relative prices change: the effect of a change in energy prices is to change the mix of energy and other factors employed in production, and it is initially assumed that the response to price changes is symmetric. Autonomous technology development would be reflected in a reduction of inputs required to produce a given level of output. In most economic models, however, after allowing for this autonomous trend, responses are still symmetric.

Induced technical change, however, also changes production possibilities according to changes in relative prices. An energy price rise stimulates more rapid development of energy-saving technologies, or alternative fuel technologies, in the direction of saving even more energy. Upon a price reversal, these technical changes will not be reversed or forgotten, leaving the outcome very different from what it might otherwise have been. The effect of changes in government regulations affecting energy efficiency and energy use in general is similar: when prices rise, especially when this takes the form of a strong signal to governments affecting national interests, new laws are enacted and new institutions created, but on price reversal the laws are not revoked or the institutions disbanded. For example, the United States introduced regulations for fuel efficiency in light vehicles in 1978 (the CAFE standards); after the 1985 oil price falls, these standards were relaxed for some manufacturers but were not removed and more recently they have been tightened again.

In fact, at least three factors may be involved in such an induced shift and consequent irreversibilities: infrastructural investments, behavioural change, and induced technological development. Infrastructural investments are easy to comprehend: cavity wall insulation installed in the 1970s is not going to be removed during the 1990s just because of low energy prices. More subtly, cavity wall insulation may have become a standard part of building practice and codes, so that even new investments will sustain the change. Similarly, it is not hard to grasp the possibilities that people may get used to switching off lights in response to an energy price rise, and continue to do so when prices fall.

Induced technical development is a more complex issue. The process of innovation is not understood – given the high level of failure of innovation it has been characterized as 'the triumph of action over analysis' (Ausubel 1991). Various technology diffusion studies emphasize the complexity of factors which determine whether or not technological ideas are developed and adopted, but it is clear that development does depend heavily upon conditions external to the firm (Freeman 1986).

In the energy sector, many examples can be given. The cost of offshore oil rigs declined sharply as companies struggled to keep North Sea operations viable in the face of falling oil prices during the 1980s. Wind energy costs fell dramatically in response to Californian tax incentives for development. The author's own study of 'Emerging energy technologies' – those which seem likely to have significant market impact over the next decade or two – also concluded that 'most of technologies considered reflect primarily a process of "demand pull" rather than "supply push"' (Grubb and Walker 1992: ch. 14). All this points to the importance of induced technology development, and its direct corollary – asymmetric price responses.

Dargay (1993) clarifies his study of asymmetric responses in these terms when he describes and justifies his analysis as

> challenging two of the common assumptions made ... that a return to low
> energy prices ... would eventually restore demand to what it would have

been had prices never risen . . . not only does this not seem to be happening, but it also appears highly unrealistic. It is obvious that high energy prices induced the development and application of considerably more energy-efficient technologies in all sectors of the economy, many of which will remain economically optimal despite falling prices.

## 13.3 IMPLICATIONS

The issue of asymmetric price responses matters for several reasons. At the technical level, estimates of elasticities derived from periods with both rising and declining prices will clearly be skewed if they try to impose an assumption of symmetry which does not exist. Gately (1993) also notes that such an assumption may lead to an underestimate of income elasticities from econometric data.

Second, as noted in the quote by Gately above, the issue can profoundly affect projections of energy demand. Companies and governments increasingly believe that energy prices may remain low over the next decade or two. If their models assume a response which is inverse to that of the price rise of the 1970s, demand estimates will be far too high.

Third, exploring the causes and components of asymmetric price responses opens up a rich field of research which may greatly enhance our understanding of energy economics and market behaviour as well as of the phenomenon itself. Some first steps in this direction are illustrated for example in the study by Walker and Wirl (1993) which seeks to divide responses into those due to technical efficiency and those due to consumer behaviour, and explores the implications.

Fourth, the indication from asymmetric price responses that energy price rises may induce technological development has important policy implications, e.g. with respect to global warming, because this technological development may have profound long-term impacts. If it is assumed that technology development is exogenous – the classical assumption – then prices have to rise substantially to hold down emissions in the face of continuing economic growth. This perspective has led some economists to conclude that stabilizing atmospheric concentrations would incur large costs. Near-term abatement may also have rather small benefits since it is such a long-term problem.

Conversely, if price rises stimulate technical development and in addition governments take further associated action to encourage energy saving, long-term solutions may emerge at relatively lower cost as a result of the accumulation of technical change in the direction of lower $CO_2$-emitting technologies, infrastructure and behaviour. Furthermore, because short-term responses may have very long-term consequences, the benefits of near-term action may be much greater.

Possible implications of these different perspectives are illustrated in a study by the author (Grubb 1993) which developed a simplified dynamic optimizing model of abatement responses. The model allows abatement costs to be a function of both the *extent* of abatement in physical terms and the *rate* at which it is achieved in temporal terms. If it is assumed that most of the costs are associated with the extent of abatement and that price responses are reversible, the costs of deviating from the rising baseline emissions increase quadratically, and the standard – and pessimistic – result is obtained. But if many of the costs are associated with the rate of abatement rather than the degree, then there is no continuing cost pressure to reverse the initial abatement efforts. On the contrary, a continuing moderate cost pressure – seeking the benefits of reduced atmospheric change – results in emissions diverging steadily from the baseline, to the point ultimately at which first emissions and later concentrations, are stabilized. Furthermore, stronger initial abatement efforts may be justified because of their continuing long-term benefits. It should be noted that this result stems from an assumption of continuing induced technical development and is *not* a direct corollary of irreversible price responses. However, the existence of irreversible price responses suggests that the assumption may be plausible.

Currently, not enough is known about either the phenomenon of asymmetric price responses or the related determinants of induced technology development to reach clear quantitative conclusions. However, this chapter illustrates a new recognition of the phenomenon and demonstrates the importance of incorporating these issues and researching them further.

## NOTES

1    The chapter was prepared at the request of the editors and differs from many of the others in this volume in that it was not presented at the Cambridge workshop and as a result has not benefited from discussion at that meeting.
2    Note that this is not the same issue as that of 'embodied' technical change discussed for example in Berndt *et al.* (1993), which refers to the persistence of technological change as embodied in the unmalleable capital stock.
3    The two concepts, although closely related, should be carefully distinguished. Whereas irreversibility is related to responses across time, asymmetry is concerned with responses at a point in time. In the discussion which follows the two will be treated simultaneously since the discussion is neither purely theoretical nor purely ahistorical.

# Chapter 14

# Conclusions

*Terry Barker, Paul Ekins and Nick Johnstone*

This book has shown that there are particular econometric problems associated with the estimation of energy elasticities. On the one hand, in the analysis of global warming, the unit of interest (carbon) is not energy itself but is instead merely embodied in energy carriers; hence the substitution of low-carbon fuels for high-carbon fuels may be more important than the conservation of energy. This implies that the relationship between energy consumption and $CO_2$ emissions must be analysed in terms of individual fuels and not energy *per se*. Moreover, energy services are characterized by very high capital intensities. Oil, coal and gas supply industries are amongst the most capital-intensive industries; energy consumption nearly always involves capital equipment and often long-lasting infrastructure (e.g. dwellings and roads). And finally, the length of the planning horizon which is of relevance to such an analysis is a century or more, whereas much of the energy elasticities literature is concerned with a 'long term' of perhaps twenty years at most. For these reasons the structural/technological characteristics of production involving the use of energy need to be addressed.

On the other hand, the revenue accruing from carbon or energy taxes of the magnitude likely to be required to reduce emissions significantly are huge, certainly large enough to change the structure of the overall tax system, and thus the economy. Thus macroeconomic modelling of the fiscal system, and of institutional change more generally, is also required. For instance, some of the revenue generated by the tax will in all likelihood be used to address some of the imperfections and rigidities which exist in sectoral energy markets (e.g. the domestic sector, the transport sector and the electricity supply industry). In this sense reduced $CO_2$ emissions will be a reflection not only of behavioural demand responses but also of institutional, structural and technological supply responses, encouraged by the government itself and made possible by the revenue generated from the tax.

Numerous models have been developed to forecast both $CO_2$ emissions and the economic consequences of policies designed to reduce such emissions. However, since orthodox macroeconomic and general equilibrium models use monetary values as the basic unit of analysis, and since they are not designed to deal specifically with the kinds of fundamental changes implied by such a tax, they are ill-equipped to deal with some of the characteristics discussed above. As if these problems are not enough, there are a number of related difficulties involved in applying estimated energy elasticities to the analysis of the economic implications of seeking to abate carbon emissions by raising the price of energy. Some of these can be listed.

1    The elasticities derive from a history of price movements (the OPEC oil shocks and subsequent price decline) which bears little relation to the likely price path associated with the introduction of a carbon tax. Given differences in perceived permanence, rate of introduction and degree of forewarning related to the two cases, it is not clear that demand responses will be the same in this very different situation.

2    Even the 'long-term' elasticities estimated are for a much smaller time period than the period of interest related to global warming. This is related to the problem of the treatment of capital in such models. On the one hand, adjustments in the capital stock in the face of such price changes may be more a reflection of qualitative change than quantitative change, indicating that the notion of 'homogeneous' capital inputs is inappropriate. On the other hand, changes in the capital stock which are beyond the consumer's control (i.e. transport infrastructure) may be more important than those which are under their control (i.e. vehicles).

3    The elasticities of demand for carbon fuels reflect the elasticities of demand for energy services as well as the possibilities of substitution between fuels and between energy service supply paths. The latter substitution possibilities, in particular, can easily be affected by government policy. This takes the elasticities of demand for fuels out of the realm of pure market response. Models that are based on pure market responses will find it very difficult to capture this effect, yet it may be very significant in an aggressive abatement policy that goes beyond energy price increases.

4    Continuing increases in income may result in market saturation of energy services or energy-intensive consumption goods or capital equipment. This would undermine the appropriateness of using constant long-term elasticities to estimate consumption patterns over the course of many years, irrespective of their ability to treat changes in the capital stock satisfactorily.

5    In the long term, continuously rising energy prices will be likely to bring about changes in the structure of production and consumption, and possibly completely different development paths, to which energy elasticities from an earlier period might bear little relevance. This is at odds with the basic assumption of most models that the future is nothing more than a continuation of the past.

All these points do not mean that energy elasticities have no role to play in the analysis of the economic implications of using energy price rises to abate carbon emissions over the long term. But they do suggest that these elasticities should not simply be taken as given, that the methods and time periods relating to their derivation should be scrutinized and other factors relevant to the above issues should also be taken into account in the analysis. To some extent, the integration of bottom-up engineering-based energy models with top-down macroeconometric economic models has the potential to do this. However, this points to a complex and painstaking research agenda for the future.

# Bibliography

Andersen, F.M. (1992) 'The macroeconomic effects of an energy tax: an analysis using the Danish HERMES model', in Laroui, F. and Velthuijsen, J. (eds) *The Economic Consequences of an Energy Tax in Europe: an Application with HERMES*, SEO Foundation for Economic Research, Amsterdam: University of Amsterdam, 85–93.

Angelier, J.P. and Sterner, T. (1990) 'Tax harmonization for petroleum products in the EC', *Energy Policy*, December, 18 (3): 500–5.

Apostolakis, B.E. (1987) 'The role of energy in production functions for Southern European economies', *Energy Economics*, 12 (7): 531–41.

Asian Development Bank (1992) *Energy Indicators of Developing Member Countries*, Manila: Asian Development Bank, July.

Ausubel, Jesse H. (1991) 'Rat race dynamics and crazy companies: the diffusion of technologies and social behaviour', in Nakicenovic, Nebojsa and Grubler, Arnulf (eds) *Diffusion of Technologies and Social Behaviour*, Berlin/Heidelberg: Springer.

Ayres, R.U. (1989) *Energy Inefficiency in the US Economy: A New Case for Conservation*, Laxenburg: IIASA, RR-89-12.

Ballard, C.L., Shoven, J.-B. and Whalley, J. (1985) 'General equilibrium computations of the marginal welfare costs of taxes in the United States', *American Economic Review*, 75 (1): 128–38.

Baltagi, Badi H. and Griffin, James M. (1983) 'Gasoline demand in the OECD: an application of pooling and testing procedures', *European Economic Review*, 22 (2): 117–37.

—— and —— (1984) 'Short and long run effects in pooled models', *International Economic Review*, 25: 631–45.

Bardsen, G. (1989) 'Estimation of long run coefficients in error correction models', *Oxford Bulletin of Economics and Statistics*, 51 (3): 345–50.

Barker, T. (ed.) (1991) *Green Futures for Economic Growth – Britain in 2010*, Cambridge: Cambridge Econometrics.

—— (1992a) 'UK energy price elasticities and their implications for long-term analysis', paper presented to a workshop on Estimating Long-Run Energy Elasticities, Robinson College, Cambridge, September.

—— (1992b) 'The carbon tax: economic and policy issues', Energy–Environment–Economy Modelling Discussion Paper 3, Department of Applied Economics, University of Cambridge.

—— (1993a) 'The carbon tax: economic and policy issues', in Carraro, C. and Siniscalco, D. (eds) *The European Carbon Tax: An Economic Assessment*, London: Kluwer, 239–54.

—— (1993b) 'The economic feasibility of achieving a 60 per cent reduction in UK

$CO_2$ emissions by 2040', paper presented at a symposium on The Environment and British Energy Policy, Green College, Oxford, April.

—— (1993c) 'Secondary benefits of greenhouse gas abatement: the effects of a UK carbon-energy tax: the effects of a UK carbon/energy tax on air pollution', Energy–Environment–Economy Modelling Discussion Paper 4, Department of Applied Economics, University of Cambridge.

Barker, Terry and Lewney, Richard (1991) 'A green scenario for the UK economy', in Barker, Terry (ed.) *Green Futures for Economic Growth*, Cambridge: Cambridge Econometrics, 11–38.

Barker, T., Baylis, S. and Madsen, P. (1992) 'A UK carbon/energy tax: the macroeconomic effects', Energy–Environment–Economy Modelling Discussion Paper 3, Department of Applied Economics, University of Cambridge; also published in *Energy Policy*, March 1993, 21 (3): 296–308.

Beckerman, W. (1991) 'Global warming: a sceptical economic assessment', in Helm, D. (ed.) *Economic Policy Towards the Environment*, Oxford: Blackwell, 52–85.

Beenstock, M. and Dalziel, A. (1986) 'The demand for energy in the UK: a general equilibrium analysis', *Energy Economics*, 8: 90–8.

Beenstock, M. and Willcocks, P. (1981) 'Energy consumption and economic activity in industrialized countries', *Energy Economics*, 3 (4): 225–32.

—— and —— (1983) 'Energy and economic activity: a reply to Kouris', *Energy Economics*, 5(3): 212.

Bentzen, J. and Engsted, T. (1993) 'Short- and long-run elasticities in energy demand', *Energy Economics*, 15 (1): 9–16.

Berndt, E.R. (1991) *The Practice of Econometrics: Classic and Contemporary*, New York: Addison-Wesley.

Berndt, E.R. and Wood, D.O. (1975) 'Technology, prices and the derived demand for energy', *Review of Economics and Statistics*, 57 (3): 259–68.

—— and —— (1979) 'Engineering and econometric interpretations of energy–capital complementarity', *American Economic Review*, 69 (3): 342–54.

Berndt, E.R., Morrison, C.J. and Watkins, G.C. (1981) 'Dynamic models of energy demand: an assessment and comparison', in Berndt, E.R. and Field, B.C. (eds) *Modelling and Measuring Natural Resource Substitution*, Cambridge, MA: MIT Press, 259–89.

Berndt, E., Kolstad, C. and Lee, J.K. (1993) 'Measuring the energy efficiency and productivity impacts of embodied technical change', *The Energy Journal*, 14 (1): 33–56.

Boero, G., Clarke, R. and Winters, L. (1991) *The Macroeconomic Consequences of Controlling Greenhouse Gases: A Survey*, Department of the Environment, London: HMSO.

Bohi, Douglas R. (1981) *Analyzing Demand Behaviour: A Study of Energy Elasticities*, Baltimore, MD: Johns Hopkins University Press, for Resources for the Future.

Boone, B., Hall, S. and Kemball-Cook, D. (1992) 'Fossil fuel demand for nine OECD countries', Discussion Paper DP 21-92, Centre for Economic Forecasting.

Bossier, F. (1992) 'Consequences pour l'économie belge de l'introduction d'une taxe sur l'énergie', in Laroui, F. and Velthuijsen, J.(eds) *The Economic Consequences of an Energy Tax in Europe: an Application with HERMES*, SEO Foundation for Economic Research, Amsterdam: University of Amsterdam, 39–65.

Brookes, L. (1990) 'The greenhouse effect: the fallacies in the energy efficiency solution', *Energy Policy*, 18 (2): 199–201.

—— (1992) 'Energy efficiency and economic fallacies: a reply', *Energy Policy*, 20 (5): 390–2.

Broome, J. (1992) *Counting the Cost of Global Warming*, Cambridge: White Horse Press.

Building Research Establishment (1992) 'A reference scenario for energy use and $CO_2$ emissions by the residential sector in the UK', *Proceedings of the American Council for an Energy Efficient Economy*, Summer Study on Energy Efficiency in Buildings.

Building Research Establishment *Domestic Sector Factfile*, Shorrock, L.D., Henderson, G. and Bown, J.H.F.

Burniaux, J.-M., Martin, J.P., Nicoletti, G. and Martins, J.O. (1991a) 'The costs of policies to reduce global emissions of $CO_2$: initial simulation results with GREEN', Working Paper 103, OCDE/GD(91)115, June, Resource Allocation Division, Paris: OECD.

——, ——, —— and —— (1991b) 'GREEN – A multi-region dynamic general equilibrium model for quantifying the costs of curbing $CO_2$ emissions: a technical manual', Working Paper 104, Paris: OECD.

Burniaux, J.-M., Nicoletti, G. and Oliveira-Martins, J. (1992) 'GREEN: a global model for quantifying the costs of policies to curb $CO_2$ emissions', *OECD Economic Studies*, Winter (19): 49–92.

Capros, P., Karadeloglou, P. and Mentzas, G. (1990) 'Carbon tax policy and its impacts on $CO_2$ emissions', National Technical Union of Athens, paper presented at a meeting organized by the Commission of the European Communities DGXII/E5, Brussels, 26 April.

Chernoff, H. (1983) 'Individual purchase criteria for energy-related durables: the misuse of lifecycle cost', *The Energy Journal*, 4 (4): 81–6.

Christensen, L.R. and Greene, W.H. (1976) 'Economies of scale in U.S. electric power generation', *Journal of Political Economy*, 84 (4): 655–76.

Christensen, L.R., Jorgenson, D.W. and Lau, L.J. (1971) 'Conjugate duality and the transcendental logarithmic production function', *Econometrica*, 39: 255–6.

Cline, W.R. (1991) 'The scientific basis of the greenhouse effect', *Economic Journal*, July (101): 904–19.

—— (1992a) *The Economics of Global Warming*, Washington, DC: Institute for International Economics.

—— (1992b) *The Greenhouse Effect: Global Economic Consequences*, Washington, DC: Institute of International Economics.

Common, M.S. (1981) 'Implied elasticities in some UK energy projections', *Energy Economics*, 3: 153–8.

Cuthbertson, K., Hall, S.G. and Taylor, M.P.T. (1992) *Applied Econometric Techniques*, London: Phillip Allen.

Dahl, C. and Sterner, T. (1991a) 'A survey of econometric gasoline demand elasticities', *International Journal of Energy Systems*, Spring: 53–76.

—— and —— (1991b) 'Analysing gasoline demand elasticities: a survey', *Energy Economics*, 13 (3): 203–10.

Dargay, J.M. (1992) 'Are price and income elasticities of demand constant?', Working Paper EE16, Oxford Institute for Energy Studies.

—— (1993) 'Are price and income elasticities of demand constant? The UK experience', Oxford: Oxford Institute for Energy Studies.

Darmstadter, J. and Edmonds, J. (1988) 'Human development and $CO_2$ emissions: the current picture and long-term prospects', in Rosenberg, N.J., Easterling, W.E. III, Crosson, P.R. and Darmstadter, J. (eds) *Greenhouse Warming: Abatement and Adaptation*, Washington, DC: Resources for the Future.

Dean, A. and Hoeller, P. (1992) 'Costs of reducing $CO_2$ emissions: evidence from six global models', *OECD Economic Studies*, Winter (19): 16–47.

DEn (1984) *Energy Use and Energy Efficiency in UK Manufacturing Industry up to the year 2000*, Energy Efficiency Series 3, Energy Efficiency Office, Department of Energy, London: HMSO.

—— (1988) *Energy Use and Energy Efficiency in UK Commercial and Public Buildings up to the year 2000*, Energy Efficiency Series 6, Energy Efficiency Office, Department of Energy, London: HMSO.

—— (1989a) 'The demand for energy', in Helm, D., Kay, J. and Thompson, D. (eds) *The Market for Energy*, Oxford: Clarendon Press.

—— (1989b) *Industrial Energy Markets*, Energy Efficiency Series 9, Energy Efficiency Office, Department of Energy, London: HMSO.

—— (1990a) *Energy Use and Energy Efficiency in the UK Domestic Sector up to the year 2010*, Energy Efficiency Series 11, Energy Efficiency Office, Department of Energy, London: HMSO.

—— (1990b) *Energy Efficiency in Domestic Sector Appliances*, Energy Efficiency Series 13, Energy Efficiency Office, Department of Energy, London: HMSO.

Denison, E. (1957) 'Theoretical aspects of quality change, capital consumption and net capital formation', *Problems of Capital Formation*, Studies in Income and Wealth 19, New York: NBER.

Denny, M. and Fuss, M.A. (1977) 'The use of approximation analysis to test for separability and the existence of consistent aggregates', *American Economic Review*, 67: 404–18.

Diewert, E. and Wales, T. (1987) 'Flexible functional forms and global curvature conditions', *Econometrica*, 55: 43–68.

*Digest of United Kingdom Energy Statistics* (various issues), Department of Energy/ DTI, London: HMSO.

Dolado, J.J., Jenkinson, T. and Sosvilla-Rivero, S. (1991) 'Cointegration and unit roots', *Journal of Economic Surveys*, 4 (3): 249–73.

Dornbusch, R. and Poterba, J. (eds) (1991) *Global Warming: Economic Policy Responses*, Cambridge, MA: MIT Press.

Drummond, D.J. and Gallant, A.R. (1979) 'TSCSREG: a SAS procedure for the analysis of time-series cross-section data', *SAS Technical Report S-106*, Raleigh, NC: SAS Institute.

Edmonds, J. and Barnes, D.W. (1990a) 'Estimating the marginal cost of reducing global fossil fuel $CO_2$ emissions', Global Environmental Change Programme, Washington, DC: Pacific Northwest Laboratory.

—— and —— (1990b) 'Factors affecting the long-term cost of global fossil fuel $CO_2$ emissions', Global Environmental Change Programme, PNL-SA-18361, Pacific Northwest Laboratory, Washington, DC.

Edmonds, J. and Reilly, D.W. (1983a) 'Global energy and $CO_2$ to the year 2050', *The Energy Journal*, 4 (3): 21–47.

—— and —— (1983b) 'A long-term global energy-economic model of $CO_2$ release from fossil fuel use', *Energy Economics*, 5 (2): 74–88.

*Energy Paper 58* (1989) 'An evaluation of energy related greenhouse gas emissions and measures to ameliorate them', London: HMSO, October.

*Energy Paper 59* (1991) Department of Trade and Industry, London: HMSO.

Engle, R.F. and Granger, C.W.J. (1987) 'Co-integration and error correction: representation, estimation, and testing', *Econometrica*, 55 (2): 251–76.

—— and —— (eds) (1991) *Long Run Economic Relationships: Readings in Cointegration*, Oxford: Oxford University Press.

Engle, R.F. and Yoo, B.S. (1987) 'Forecasting and testing in cointegrated systems', *Journal of Econometrics*, 35: 143–59.

Fankhauser, S. (1992) 'Global warming damage costs: some monetary estimates', Working Paper GEC 92-29, CSERGE, London: University College London.

Fiebig, D.G., Seale, J. and Theil, H. (1987) 'The demand for energy: evidence from a cross-country demand system', *Energy Economics*, 9 (3): 149–53.

Field, B.C. and Grebenstein, C. (1980) 'Capital-energy substitution in US manufacturing', *Review of Economics and Statistics*, 61 (2): 207–12.

Fitzgerald, J. and McCoy, D. (1992) 'The impact of an energy tax on the Irish economy', in Laroui, F. and Velthuijsen, J. (eds) *The Economic Consequences of an Energy Tax in Europe: an Application with HERMES*, SEO Foundation for Economic Research, Amsterdam: University of Amsterdam, 131–57.

Freeman, Chris (1986) 'The diffusion of innovations – microelectronic technology', in Roy, Robin and Wield, David (eds) *Product Design and Technical Innovation*, Milton Keynes: Open University Press.

Fuller, W.A. (1976) *Introduction to Statistical Time Series*, New York: Wiley.

Fuller, W.A. and Battese, G.E. (1974) 'Estimation of linear models with crossed-error structure', *Journal of Econometrics*, 25 (2): 67–78.

Fuss, M.A. (1977a) 'The structure of technology over time', *Econometrica*, 45: 1797–821.

—— (1977b) 'The demand for energy in Canadian manufacturing: an example of the estimation of production structures with many inputs', *Journal of Econometrics*, 5 (1): 89–116.

Fuss, M.A. and McFadden, D. (1976) *Production Economics: A Dual Approach to Theory and Applications 1 and 2*, Amsterdam: North-Holland.

Fuss, M.A. and Waverman, L. (1975) 'The demand for energy in Canada', Working Paper, Institute for Policy Analysis, University of Toronto.

Fuss, M.A., Hyndman, R. and Waverman, L. (1977) 'Residential, commercial and industrial demand for energy in Canada: projections to 1985 with three alternative models', in Nordhaus, W.D. (ed.) *International Studies of the Demand for Energy*, Amsterdam: North-Holland.

Fuss, M.A., McFadden, D. and Mundlak, Y. (1978) 'A survey of functional forms in the economic analysis of production', in Fuss, M.A. and McFadden, D. (eds) *Production Economics: A Dual Approach to Theory and Applications 1*, Amsterdam: North-Holland.

Gallant, A.R. and Goebel, J.J. (1976) 'Nonlinear regression with autoregressive errors', *Journal of the American Statistical Association*, 71 (356): 961–7.

Gaskins, D.W. and Weyant, J.P. (1993) 'Model comparisons of the costs of reducing $CO_2$ emissions', *American Economic Review Papers and Proceedings*, 83 (2): 318–23.

Gately, Dermot (1993) 'The imperfect price-reversibility of world oil demand', *The Energy Journal*, 14 (4): 163–82.

Glueck, Heinz and Stefan P. Schleicher (1994) 'Endogenous technical progress induced by $CO_2$ reduction policies: simulation results for Austria', paper presented at the International Conference on Economic Instruments for Air Pollution Control, International Institute for Applied Systems Analysis, Laxenberg, October 1993.

Goldemberg, J. *et al.* (1988) *Energy for a Sustainable World*, New Delhi: Wiley Eastern.

Greene, D.L. (1990) 'CAFE OR PRICE?: An analysis of the effects of federal fuel economy regulations and gasoline price on new car mg, 1978–1989', *The Energy Journal*, 13 (3): 37–57.

—— (1992) 'Vehicle use and fuel economy: how big is the rebound effect?', *The Energy Journal*, 13 (1): 117–43.

Greene, W.H. (1990) *Econometric Analysis*, New York: Macmillan.

Greenhalgh, G. (1990) 'Energy conservation policies', *Energy Policy*, 18 (3): 293–8.

Gregory, K., Matthews, A., Newton, A. and Nind, A. (Operational Research Executive of British Coal) (1991) 'The potential impact of a $10/barrel energy/carbon tax on UK carbon dioxide emissions', paper presented to the OECD Workshop on Carbon Taxes, Paris, 5–6 November.

Griffin, J.M. (1979) *Energy Conservation in the OECD: 1980 to 2000*, Cambridge, MA: Ballinger.

—— (1981a) 'Engineering and econometric interpretations of energy–capital complementarity: comment', *American Economic Review*, 71 (5): 1100–4.

—— (1981b) 'The energy–capital complementarity controversy: a progress report on reconciliation attempts', in Berndt, E. and Fields, B. (eds) *Modelling and Measuring Natural Resource Substitution*, Cambridge, MA: MIT Press.

Griffin, J. and Gregory, P. (1976) 'An inter-country translog model of energy substitution responses', *American Economic Review*, 66 (5): 845–57.

Griliches, Z. and Mairesse, J. (1990) 'Heterogeneity in panel data: are there stable production functions?', in Champsaur *et.al.* (eds) *Essays in Honour of Edmund Malinvaud*, Cambridge, MA: MIT Press.

Grubb, M. (1990) 'Energy efficiency and economic fallacies', *Energy Policy*, 18 (8): 783–5.

—— (1992) 'Reply to Brookes', *Energy Policy*, 20 (5): 392–3.

—— (1993) 'Optimising climate change abatement responses: on inertia and responsive technology development', IIASA International Workshop on Integrated Assessment of Climate Change, IIASA, Laxenberg, October.

Grubb, Michael and Walker, John (eds) (1992) *Emerging Energy Technologies: Impacts and Policy Implications*, Aldershot, Brookfield, VT: Dartmouth.

Haavelmo, T. (1947) 'Family expenditures and the marginal propensity to consume', *Econometrica*, 15: 335–41.

Hall, S.G. (1986) 'An application of the Granger and Engle two-step estimation procedure to UK aggregate wage data', *Oxford Bulletin of Economics and Statistics*, Special Issue, 48 (3): 229–41.

—— (1989) 'Maximum likelihood estimation of cointegrating vectors: an example of the Johansen procedure', *Oxford Bulletin of Economics and Statistics*, 51 (2): 213–18.

—— (1991) 'The effect of varying length VAR models on the maximum likelihood estimates of cointegrating vectors', *Scottish Journal of Political Economy*, 38 (4): 317–23.

Hall, V.B. (1986) 'Major OECD country industrial sector interfuel substitution estimates, 1960–79', *Energy Economics*, 8 (2): 74–89.

Harvey, A.C. (1987) 'Applications of the Kalman filter in econometrics', in Bewley, T.F. (ed.) *Advances in Econometrics: Fifth World Congress*, Econometric Society Monograph 13, Cambridge: Cambridge University Press.

Hawdon, D. (ed.) (1992) *Energy Demand: Evidence and Expectations*, Guildford: Surrey University Press.

Helm, Dieter, Kay, John and Thompson, David (eds) (1989) *The Market for Energy*, Oxford: Clarendon Press.

Hesse, D.M. and Tarkka, H. (1986) 'The demand for capital, labor and energy in European manufacturing industry before and after the oil price shocks', *Scandinavian Journal of Econometrics*, 88 (3): 529–46.

Hodgson, D.J. (1992) 'The EC carbon tax and energy demand in the United Kingdom', paper presented to the Energy Taxation and $CO_2$ Emissions Workshop held in Milan, 19 March; to appear in Carraro, Carlo and Siniscalco, Domenico (eds) *The European Carbon Tax: An Economic Assessment*, London: Kluwer.

Hodgson, D.J. and Miller, K. (1992) 'Modelling UK energy demand', paper presented to a Workshop on Estimating Long-Run Energy Elasticities, Robinson College, Cambridge, September.

Hoeller, P., Dean, A. and Nicolaisen, J. (1991) 'Macroeconomic implications of reducing greenhouse gas emissions: a survey of empirical studies', *OECD Economic Studies*, Spring (16): 46–78.

Hogan, W.W. and Jorgenson, D.W. (1990) 'Productivity trends and the cost of reducing $CO_2$ emissions', Global Environmental Policy Project, Cambridge, MA: Harvard University.

—— and —— (1991) 'Productivity trends and the cost of reducing $CO_2$ emissions, *Energy Journal*, 12 (1): 67–86.

Horton, G.R., Rollo, J.M.C. and Ulph, A. (1992) 'The implications for trade of greenhouse gas emission control policies', Department of Trade and Industry and Department of the Environment, Environmental Economics Series, London: HMSO.

Hsiao, C. (1986) *Analysis of Panel Data*, Cambridge: Cambridge University Press.

—— (1992) 'Random coefficients models', in Matyas, L. and Sevestre, P. (eds) *The Econometrics of Panel Data*, London: Kluwer, ch. 5, 71–93.

Hudson, E.A. and Jorgenson, D.W. (1974) 'US energy policy and economic growth, 1975–2000', *Bell Journal of Economics and Management Science*, 5: 461–514.

Hunt, L.C. and Lynk, E.L. (1992) 'Industrial energy demand in the UK: a co-integration approach', in Hawdon, D. (ed.) *Energy Demand: Evidence and Expectations*, Guildford: Surrey University Press.

Hunt, L.C., and Manning, N. (1989) 'Energy price- and income-elasticities of demand: some estimates for the UK using the co-integration procedure', *Scottish Journal of Political Economy*, 36 (2): 183–93.

Ingham, A. and Ulph, A. (1990) 'Carbon taxes and the UK manufacturing sector', Discussion Paper 9004, Department of Economics, Southampton University; in Dietz, T., van der Ploeg, R. and van der Straten, J. (eds) *Environmental Policy and the Economy*, Amsterdam: North-Holland.

—— and —— (1991a) 'Carbon taxes and the UK manufacturing sector', in Dietz, F., van der Ploeg, F. and van Straaten, J. (eds) *Contributions to Economic Analysis*, Amsterdam: North-Holland.

—— and —— (1991b) 'Market based instruments for reducing $CO_2$ emissions: the case of UK manufacturing', *Energy Policy*, 19: 138–48.

Ingham, A., Ulph, A. and Toker, M. (1988) 'A vintage model of scrapping and investment', *Recherches Economiques de Louvain*, 54: 169–90.

Ingham, A., Maw, J. and Ulph, A. (1991a) 'Testing for barriers to energy conservation – an application of a vintage model', *The Energy Journal*, 12: 41–64.

——, —— and —— (1991b) 'Empirical measures of carbon taxes', *Oxford Review of Economic Literature*, 7 (2): 99–122.

——, —— and —— (1992) 'Energy conservation in UK manufacturing: a vintage model approach', in Hawdon, D. (ed.) *Energy Demand: Evidence and Expectations*, Guildford: Surrey University Press, 115–41.

Intergovernmental Panel on Climate Change (1992)*IPCC Supplement: Scientific Assessment of Climate Change* (Summary), Geneva/Nairobi: World Meteorological Organization/United Nations Environment Programme.

International Energy Agency (1991a) *Energy Prices and Taxes*, Paris: OECD.

—— (1991b) *World Energy Statistics and Balances*, Paris: OECD.

—— (1993) *World Energy Outlook*, Paris: OECD.

Jackson, T. (1989) 'The role of nuclear power in global warming abatement strategies', Proof of Evidence FOE 10 submitted to the Hinkley Point Inquiry, July.

—— (1991) 'Least-cost greenhouse planning – supply curves for global warming abatement', *Energy Policy*, 19 (1): 35–46.

—— (1992) *Efficiency Without Tears: No Regrets Energy Policy to Combat Climate Change*, London: Friends of the Earth.

Jackson, T. and Jacobs, M. (1991) 'Carbon taxes and the assumptions of environmental economics', Barker, T. (ed.) *Green Futures for Economic Growth – Britain in 2010*, Cambridge: Cambridge Econometrics, ch. 4.

Jackson, T. and Roberts, S. (1989) *Getting out of the Greenhouse*, London: Friends of the Earth.

Jochem, E. and Gruber, E. (1990) 'Obstacles to rational electricity use and measures to alleviate them', *Energy Policy*, 18 (4): 340–50.

Johansen, S. (1988) 'Statistical analysis of cointegration vectors', *Journal of Economic Dynamics and Control*, 12: 231–54.

—— (1991) 'Estimation and hypothesis testing of cointegration vectors in Gaussian vector autoregressive models', *Econometrica*, 59 (6): 1551–80.

Johansen, S. and Juselius, K. (1990) 'Maximum likelihood estimation and inference on cointegration – with applications to the demand for money', *Oxford Bulletin of Economics and Statistics*, 52 (2): 169–210.

Johansson, T., Bodlund, B. and Williams, R. (eds) (1989) *Electricity: Efficient and New Generation Technologies and their Planning Implications*, Lund: Lund University Press.

Jorgenson, D.W. (1977) 'Consumer demand for energy', in Nordhaus, W.D. (ed.) *International Studies of the Demand for Energy*, Amsterdam: North-Holland.

—— (1990) 'Productivity and economic growth', in Berndt, E. and Triplett, J. (eds) *Fifty Years of Economic Measurement: the Jubilee of the Conference on Research in Income and Wealth*, Chicago, IL: University of Chicago Press, 90–118.

Jorgenson, D.W. and Lau, L.J. (1975) 'The structure of consumer preferences', *Annals of Social and Economic Measurement*, 4: 49–101.

Jorgenson, D.W. and Wilcoxen, P. (1992) 'Energy, the environment and economic growth', Harvard Institute for Economic Research Discussion Paper 1604; in Kneese, A.V. and Sweeney, J.L. (eds) *Handbook of Natural Resource and Energy Economics 3*, Amsterdam: North-Holland, 1993.

—— and —— (1993) 'Reducing US carbon emissions: an econometric general equilibrium assessment', *Resource and Energy Economics*, 15 (1): 7–25.

Jorgenson, D.W. and Yun, K.-Y. (1990) 'The excess burden of taxation in the US', Harvard Institute of Economic Research Discussion Paper 1528, November.

Kang, H. and Brown, G.M. (1981) 'Partial and full elasticities of substitution and the energy–capital complementarity controversy', in Berndt, E. and Fields, B. (eds) *Modelling and Measuring Natural Resource Substitution*, Cambridge, MA: MIT Press.

Karadeloglou, P. (1992) 'Carbon tax vs. energy tax: a quantitative analysis', in Laroui, F. and Velthuijsen, J. (eds) *The Economic Consequences of an Energy Tax in Europe: an Application with HERMES*, SEO Foundation for Economic Research, Amsterdam: University of Amsterdam, 177–201.

Kmenta, J. (1986) *Elements of Econometrics*, New York: Macmillan.

Kopp, R.J. and Smith, V.K. (1978) 'Capital–energy complementarity: further evidence', Mimeo, Washington, DC: Resources for the Future.

Kouris, G. (1976) 'The determinants of energy demand in the EEC area', *Energy Policy*, 6 (4): 343–55.

—— (1983) 'Energy consumption and economic activity in industrialised economies – a note', *Energy Economics*, 5 (3): 207–12.

Lau, L. (1986) 'Functional forms in econometric model building', in Griliches, Zvi and D. Intriligator, Michael (eds) *Handbook of Econometrics*, Amsterdam: North-Holland.

Lazarus, M. *et al.* (1992) 'Towards global energy security: the next energy transition', Draft Report for Greenpeace International, Boston Centre, MA: Stockholm Environment Institute.

Lee, K.C., Pesaran, M.H. and Pierse, R.G. (1990) 'Testing for aggregation bias in linear models', *Economic Journal*, 100: 137–50.

Lovins, A.B. and Lovins, H.L. (1991) 'Least cost climatic stabilization', *Annual Review of Energy and Environment*, 16: 433–531.

Lynk, E.L. (1989) 'The demand for energy by UK manufacturing industry', *The Manchester School*, 57 (1): 1–16.

Maddala, G.S. (1992) *Introduction to Econometrics*, 2nd edn, New York: Macmillan.

Malcomson, J. and Prior, M. (1979) 'The estimation of a vintage model of production for UK manufacturing', *Review of Economic Studies*, 46: 719–36.

Manne, A.S. and Richels, R.G. (1989) $CO_2$ *Emission Limits – an Economic Cost Analysis for the USA*, Palo Alto, CA: EPRI.

—— and —— (1990) *Global $CO_2$ Emission Reductions – the Impacts of Rising Energy Costs*, Palo Alto, CA: EPRI.

—— and —— (1991) 'Global $CO_2$ emission reductions – the impacts of rising energy costs', *The Energy Journal*, 12 (1): 87–107.

—— and —— (1992) *Buying Greenhouse Insurance: The Economic Costs of $CO_2$ Emission Limits*, Cambridge, MA: MIT Press.

Manning, D.N. (1988) 'Household demand for energy in the UK', *Energy Economics*, 10: 59–78.

Matyas, L. and Sevestre, P. (eds) (1992) *The Econometrics of Panel Data*, London: Kluwer.

McElroy, M.B. (1987) 'Additive general error models for production, cost and derived demand or share equations', *Journal of Political Economy*, 95 (4): 737–57.

McFadden, D. (1978) 'Estimation techniques for the elasticity of substitution and other production parameters', in Fuss, M.A. and McFadden, D. (eds) *Production Economics: A Dual Approach to Theory and Applications*, vol. 2, Amsterdam: North-Holland.

Meier, A. and Whittier, J. (1983) 'Consumer discount rates implied by purchases of energy efficient refrigerators', *Energy, The International Journal*, 8 (12): 957–62.

Mills, E., Wilson, D. and Johansson, B. (1991) 'Getting started: no-regrets strategies for reducing greenhouse gas emissions', *Energy Policy*, 19 (6): 526–42.

Mintzer, I.M. (1987) 'A matter of degrees: the potential for controlling the greenhouse effect', Research Report 5, Washington, DC: World Resources Institute.

Modesto, L. (1992) 'Macroeconomic effects of an energy tax in Portugal: simulation results for 1991–2000', in Laroui, F. and Velthuijsen, J. (eds) *The Economic Consequences of an Energy Tax in Europe: an Application with HERMES*, SEO Foundation for Economic Research, Amsterdam: University of Amsterdam, 121–9.

Nachane, D., Nadkarni, R. and Karnik, A. (1988) 'Co-integration and causality testing of the energy–GDP relationship: a cross-country study', *Applied Economics*, 20: 1511–31.

NAS (National Academy of Sciences) (1991) *Policy Implications of Greenhouse Warming*, Washington, DC: NAS.

Nordhaus, W.D. (1977) 'The demand for energy: an international perspective', in

Nordhaus, W.D. (ed) *International Studies of the Demand for Energy*, Amsterdam: North-Holland.

—— (1990a), 'An intertemporal general equilibrium model of economic growth and climate change', paper presented at Workshop on Economic/Energy/Environmental Modelling for Climate Policy Analysis, October, Washington DC, Yale University.

—— (1990b) 'Greenhouse economics - look before you leap', *The Economist*, 7 July.

—— (1991a) 'To slow or not to slow: the economics of the greenhouse effect', *Economic Journal*, July (101): 920–37.

—— (1991b) 'The cost of slowing climate change: a survey', *The Energy Journal*, 12 (1): 37–65.

—— (1991c) 'Economic approaches to greenhouse warming', in Dornbusch, R. and Poterba, J. (eds) *Global Warming: Economic Policy Responses*, Cambridge, MA: MIT Press.

—— (1992) 'The "DICE" model: background and structure of a *D*ynamic *I*ntegrated *C*limate–*E*nergy model of the economics of global warming', Cowles Foundation Discussion Paper 1009, February.

—— (1993) 'Optimal greenhouse gas reductions and tax policy in the "DICE" model', *American Economic Review, Papers and Proceedings*, 83 (2): 313–17.

Nordhaus, W.D. and Yohe, G. (1983) 'Future carbon dioxide emissions from fossil fuels', in National Research Council/National Academy of Sciences, *Changing Climate*, Washington, DC: National Academy Press, 87–153.

Özatalay, S., Grubaugh, S. and Long, T.V. (1979) 'Energy substitution and national energy policy', *American Economic Review*, 69 (2): 369–71.

Patry, M., Nappi, C. and Taghvai, H. (1990) 'Energy demand in seven OECD countries: a comparison of the impact of the oil price shocks', *Conference Proceedings, Energy Supply/Demand Balances: Options and Costs*, Ottawa: International Association of Energy Economists, 131–42.

Pearce, D. (1991) 'The role of carbon taxes in adjusting to global warming', *Economic Journal*, July (101): 938–48.

—— (1992) 'The secondary benefits of greenhouse gas control', CSERGE Working Paper 92-12, April, University of East Anglia, Norwich, University College London.

Perron, P. (1988) 'Trends and random walks in macroeconomic time series', *Journal of Economic Dynamics and Control*, 12: 297–332.

Pesaran, M. Hashem and Pesaran, Bahram (1991) *Microfit 3.0 An Interactive Econometric Software Package*, Oxford: Oxford University Press.

Pesaran, M.H. and Smith, R.P. (1995) 'Estimating long-run relationships from dynamic heterogenous panels', *Journal of Econometrics* (forthcoming).

Pesaran, M.H., Pierce, R.G. and Kumar, M.S. (1989) 'Econometric analysis of aggregation in the context of linear prediction models', *Econometrica*, 57: 861–88.

Peterson, A.W.A. (1987) 'The demand for energy', in Barker, T.S. and Peterson, A.W.A. (eds) *The Cambridge Multisectoral Dynamic Model of the British Economy*, Cambridge: Cambridge University Press, 275–91.

—— (1992) *MREG A Matrix-Oriented Regression Package - Users' Manual*, Faculty of Economics and Politics, University of Cambridge.

Phillips, P.C.B. (1987) 'Time-series regression with a unit root', *Econometrica*, 55: 277–301.

Phillips, P.C.B. and Ouliaris, S. (1990) 'Asymptotic properties of residual based tests for cointegration', *Econometrica*, 58 (1): 165–93.

Phillips, P.C.B. and Perron, P. (1988) 'Testing for a unit root in time series regression', *Biometrika*, 71: 335–46.

Pindyck, R.S. (1979a) 'Interfuel substitution and the industrial demand for energy: an international comparison', *Review of Economics and Statistics*, 61 (2): 169–79.

—— (1979b) *The Structure of World Energy Demand*, Cambridge, MA: MIT Press.

Pindyck, R.S. and Rotemberg, J.J. (1983) 'Dynamic factor demands and the effects of energy price shocks', *American Economic Review*, 73 (5): 1066–79.

Poterba, J. (1991) 'Tax policy to combat global warming: on designing a carbon tax', in Dornbusch, R. and Poterba, J.M. (eds) *Global Warming: Economic Policy Responses*, Cambridge, MA: MIT Press, 71–98.

Price, E.H.M. (1991) 'The use of official long-term energy projections in the United Kingdom', International Energy Market Modelling, XXXIInd International Conference of Applied Econometrics Association, Montpellier, October.

Proops, J., Faber, M. and Wagenhals, G. (1993) *Reducing $CO_2$ Emissions: a Comparative Input–Output Study for Germany and the UK*, Berlin: Springer.

Prosser, R.D. (1985) 'Demand elasticities in OECD countries: dynamic aspects', *Energy Economics*, 7 (1): 9–12.

Prywes, M. (1986) 'A nested CES approach to capital–energy substitution', *Energy Economics*, 8 (1): 22–8.

Quah, D. (1990) 'International patterns of growth: I. Persistence in cross-country disparities', Mimeo, Economics Department, Massachusetts Institute of Technology, Cambridge, MA.

Reilly, J.M., Edmonds, J.A., Gardner, R.H. and Brenkert, A.L. (1987) 'Uncertainty analysis of the IEA/ORAU $CO_2$ emissions model', *The Energy Journal*, 8 (3): 1–29.

Robertson, D. and Symons, J. (1992) 'Some strange properties of panel data estimators', *Journal of Applied Econometrics*, 7: 175–89.

Saicheua, S. (1987) 'Input substitution in Thailand's manufacturing sector', *Energy Economics*, 9 (1): 55–63.

Salter, W. (1966) *Productivity and Technical Change*, Cambridge: Cambridge University Press.

Sargan, J.D. and Bhargava, A. (1983) 'Testing residuals from least squares regression for being generated by the Gaussian random walk', *Econometrica*, 51 (1): 153–74.

Schelling, T. (1992) 'Some economics of global warming', *American Economic Review*, 82 (1): 1–14.

Schipper, Lee and Meyers, Stephen (1992) *Energy Efficiency and Human Activity: Past Trends and Future Prospects*, Cambridge: Cambridge University Press.

Scott, M. (1992) 'Policy implications of "A New View of Economic Growth"', *Economic Journal*, May (102): 622–32.

Semple, M. (1989) 'Energy consumption in the United Kingdom', *Economic Trends*, London: CSO.

Sevestre, P. and Trognon, A. (1992) 'Linear dynamic models', in Matyas, L. and Sevestre, P. (eds) *The Econometrics of Panel Data*, London: Kluwer, ch. 6, 94–116.

Siddayao, C.M., Khaled, J., Ranada, J.G. and Saicheua, S. (1987) 'Estimates of energy and non-energy elasticities in selected Asian manufacturing sectors', *Energy Economics*, 9 (2): 115–27.

Sims, C.A. (1980) 'Macroeconomics and reality', *Econometrica*, 48 (1): 1–48.

Smil, V. and Kuz, T. (1976) 'European energy elasticities', *Energy Policy*, 14 (2): 171–5.

Smith-Gavine, A. and Bennett, A. (1993) 'Index of percentage utilisation of labour', Mimeo, De Montfort University, Leicester.

Solow, A. (1991) 'Is there a global warming problem?', in Dornbusch, R. and Poterba, J., (eds) *Global Warming: Economic Policy Responses*, Cambridge, MA: MIT Press, 7–28.

Solow, John L. (1987) 'The capital–energy complementarity debate revisited', *American Economic Review*, 77 (4): 605–14.

Sondheimer, J. (1991) 'Macroeconomic effects of a carbon tax', in Barker, T. (ed.) *Green Futures for Economic Growth*, Cambridge: Cambridge Econometrics, 39–47.

Standaert, S. (1992) 'Simulating an energy tax (with HERMES-Link)', in Laroui, F. and Velthuijsen, J. (eds) *The Economic Consequences of an Energy Tax in Europe: an Application with HERMES*, SEO Foundation for Economic Research, Amsterdam: University of Amsterdam, 1–37.

Sterner, T.M. (1989a) 'Oil products in Latin America: the politics of energy pricing', *Energy Journal*, 10 (2): 25–45.

—— (1989b) 'Les Prix de l'energie en Afrique', *Revue de l'Energie*, (415).

—— (1990) *The Pricing of and Demand for Gasoline*, Stockholm: Swedish Transport Research Board.

—— (1991) 'Gasoline demand in the OECD: choice of model and data set in pooled estimations', *Opec Review*, 15 (2): 91–101.

Sterner, T. and Dahl, C. (1991) 'Modelling the demand for highway transport fuels', in Sterner, T. (ed) *International Energy Modelling*, London: Chapman and Hall.

Summer, R. and Heston, A. (1988) 'A new set of international comparisons of real product and price levels estimates for 130 countries, 1950–1985', *Review of Income and Wealth*, 34 (1): 1–25.

Swamy, P.A.V.B. (1971) *Statistical Inference in Random Coefficient Regression Models*, Lecture Notes in Operations Research and Mathematical Systems 55, Berlin: Springer.

Taylor, L.D. (1977) 'Decreasing block pricing and the residential demand for electricity', in Nordhaus, W.D. (ed) *International Studies of the Demand for Energy*, Amsterdam: North-Holland.

Turnovsky, M., Folie, M. and Ulph, A. (1982) 'Factor substitutability in Australian manufacturing with emphasis on energy inputs', *Economic Record*, 58 (160): 61–72.

UK Department of Energy (1977) *Report of the Working Group on Energy Elasticities*, London: HMSO.

—— (1982) 'Proof of evidence for the Sizewell B Public Inquiry', Unpublished mimeo.

—— (1983) 'Energy projections methodology', Unpublished mimeo.

—— (1987) *Sizewell B Public Inquiry: Report by Sir Frank Layfield*, London: HMSO.

—— (1989) 'The demand for energy', in Helm, D., Kay, J. and Thompson, D. (eds) *The Market for Energy*, Oxford: Clarendon Press, ch. 4, 77–91.

United Nations (1992) *The United Nations Energy Database*, UN Statistical Division, New York, June.

Waide, P. (1992) 'Towards global energy security: the next energy transition', Technical Report for Greenpeace International (draft).

Walker, I.O. and Wirl, Franz (1993) 'Irreversible price-induced efficiency improvements: theory and empirical application to road transportation', *The Energy Journal*, 14 (4): 183–205.

Watkins, G.C. (1991) 'Short- and long-term equilibria', *Energy Economics*, 13 (1): 1–9.

Waverman L. (1992) 'Econometric modelling of energy demand: when are substitutes good substitutes?', in Hawdon, D. (ed.) *Energy Demand: Evidence and Expectations*, Guildford: University of Surrey Press.

World Commission for Economic Development (1987) *Our Common Future*, Oxford: Oxford University Press.

Welsch, H. (1989) 'The reliability of aggregate energy demand functions', *Energy Economics*, 11 (4): 285–92.

Westoby, R. and Pearce, D. (1984) 'Single equation models for the projection of energy demand in the UK, 1954–80', *Scottish Journal of Political Economy*, 31: 229–54.

Whalley, J. and Wigle, R. (1990) 'The international incidence of carbon taxes', paper presented at the conference on Economic Policy Responses to Global Warming, Rome, National Bureau of Economic Research, Cambridge, MA, and Wilfrid Laurier University, Waterloo.

—— and —— (1991) 'Cutting $CO_2$ emissions: the effects of alternative policy approaches', *The Energy Journal*, 12 (1): 109–24.

White, H. (1980) 'A heteroskedasticity-consistent covariance matrix estimator and a direct test for heteroskedasticity', *Econometrica*, 48: 817–38.

Wigley, K.J. (1983) 'United Kingdom energy projections 1982', paper presented to the Workshop on Methods of Formulating Energy Policy, Paris, November.

Wigley, K.J. and Vernon, K. (1982) 'Methods for projecting UK energy demands used in the Department of Energy', Mimeo, UK Department of Energy, London.

Williams, J. (1990) 'Will constraining fossil fuel carbon dioxide emissions cost so much?', Mimeo, Center for Energy and Environmental Studies, Princeton University, April.

Williams, R.H. (1990) 'Low-cost strategy for coping with $CO_2$ emission limits (A critique of "$CO_2$ emission limits: an economic cost analysis for the USA" by Manne and Richels)', *The Energy Journal*, 11 (4): 35–59.

Williams, M. and Laumas, P. (1981) 'The relation between energy and non-energy inputs in India's manufacturing industries', *Journal of Industrial Economics*, 30 (2): 113–22.

Wilson, D. and Swisher, J. (1993) 'Exploring the gap: top-down versus bottom-up analyses of the cost of mitigating global warming', *Energy Policy*, Special Issue, 21 (3): 249–63.

Wohlgemuth, N. (1992) *Strukturen und Perspektiven des oesterreichischen Energiesystems*, Frankfurt: Lang.

Wood, D.O. and Hirsch, R.B. (1981) 'Reconciling econometric studies of factor demand: data and measurement issues', Energy Laboratory Working Paper MIT-EL 81-011WP, Massachusetts Institute of Technology.

Zellner, A. (1969) 'On the aggregation problem: a new approach to a troublesome problem', in Fox, K.A. *et al.* (eds) *Economic Models, Estimation and Risk Programming: Essays in Honor of Gerhard Tintner*, Berlin: Springer, 365–78.

# Index